THE LOST FORTUNE

OF THE TSARS

By the same author

Planning for Europe: 1992
The Secret Life of Wilkie Collins
How the City of London Works
Inside the City
The World's Money
Britain's Invisible Earnings
Private Enterprise in Developing Countries
The City in the World Economy
The City's Invisible Earnings

THE
LOST
FORTUNE
OF THE
TSARS

WILLIAM
CLARKE

St. Martin's Press
New York

Library of Congress Cataloging-in-Publication Data

Clarke, W. (William)
The lost fortune of the tsars / William Clarke.
p.   cm.
ISBN 0-312-13118-6
1. Nicholas II, Emperor of Russia, 1868–1918—Estate.
2. Nicholas II, Emperor of Russia, 1868–1918—
Assassination.   3. Russia—Kings and rulers—
Biography.   4. Russia—History—Nicholas II,
1894–1917.   I. Title.
DK258.C58   1995
947.08′3′092—dc20   95-15465   CIP

First published in Great Britain by
Weidenfeld & Nicolson

First U.S. Edition: July 1995
10 9 8 7 6 5 4 3 2 1

To Faith

Contents

APPENDICES

Illustrations

The illustrations come between pages 138 and 139

Nicholas and Alexandra[1]
The five children of Nicholas and Alexandra in about 1910
King George V with Nicholas II in 1913[2]
Fabergé's Tercentenary Egg, 1913
Tobolsk. Grand Duchess Tatiana, Countess Hendrikoff, and Nicholas[1].
    Olga and Alexis[3]. Nicholas with Pierre Gilliard[3]
Four Brothers mine[3]
The box containing the remains and relics of the Imperial family[3]
Alexandra's personal jewel book[4]
Cataloguing and packing the contents of the Catherine Palace, Tsarskoe
    Selo, October 1917[4]
Christie's catalogue, 1927[5]
Cataloguing the Russian Imperial regalia in the 1920s[6]
The tiara of Grand Duchess Vladimir
Queen Mary[7]
Queen Elizabeth[8]
Imperial Easter Eggs[9]
Mrs Anna Anderson[7]
Michael Goleniewski
The Russian gold reserve, 1905[10]
Nicholas II account at the Bank of England[11]
Peter Bark[10]
Restricted Cabinet paper on Tsarist funds, 1927[12]
A gathering of Romanoffs in Paris, 1992
'Grand Duke' Vladimir's widow, grandson, and daughter, 1993[13]

Illustration credits
[1] Mansell Collection
[2] The Wernher Collection, Luton Hoo
[3] Gibbes Collection, Luton Hoo
[4] The State Archive of the Russian Federation, Moscow

5 Christie's Images, London
6 Sotheby's, London
7 Hulton–Deutsch
8 Camera Press
9 The Royal Collection © 1994 Her Majesty The Queen
10 Illustrated London News
11 Bank of England
12 Public Record Office
13 Frank Spooner

Acknowledgements

I first became intrigued by Tsarist money in the mid-1950s when I was Financial Editor of *The Times*. I received a call from the Chairman of Baring's, Sir Edward Reid, asking for help. He was worried at exaggerated newspaper reports of Tsarist funds (even the Tsar's family money) in the merchant bank, partly encouraged by the Soviet authorities who were engaged in yet another round of debt talks with the British authorities. They were preparing for the visit of Khrushchev and Bulganin. I saw him at his office in Bishopsgate and promised to help if he would tell me the facts. He did – up to a point.

Then came several books exploring the possibility that not all the Tsar's family had been massacred at Ekaterinburg – Guy Richards' *The Hunt for the Tsar*, Gary Null's *The Conspirator Who Saved The Romanovs*, Anthony Summers' and Tom Mangold's *The File on the Tsar*, and, finally, Peter Kurth's *Anastasia*. All seemed to confirm the allegations of Mrs Anna Anderson that not everyone had perished and most of the books, in their different ways, seemed to lend indirect support to her own claim to be the youngest daughter of the Tsar, Anastasia.

The real fate of the Romanoffs continued to attract major attention, but I was also inclined to wonder what had happened to their wealth and to make the occasional inquiry on my travels. The research that followed covered several continents and several years. In that time I received help from countless people, all of whom deserve acknowledgement. First the helpful enthusiasts. These have ranged from Gretchen Haskin in San Francisco (whose husband, David, was the first to decipher the mirror writing on the wall of the Ipatiev House in Ekaterinburg) to Prince Michel Romanoff in Paris, from Makgorzata Stapinska in Krakow, Poland to Dr Idris Traylor Jnr. in Texas, and Edward Kasinac and Norman Ross in New York, and from Anya Urnova in Moscow to Prince Rostislav Romanoff, Arthur Addington and Kyril Fitzlyon in this country.

More formal, though no less grateful, thanks are due to Dr Hugh Richards in London; Richard Davies at Leeds University; Professors Alexander Fursenko and Boris Anan'ich in St Petersburg; Mrs Barbara

Peters, the archivist at Coutts & Co.; Nicholas Bark in London and Pierre Semenoff-Tian-Chansky in Paris, grandsons of Sir Peter Bark; Prince David Chavchavadze in Washington; the late Robert Roosa and his wife Ruth in New York; Pierre de Villemarest and Jacques Ferrand in Paris; Mrs Molly Chalk at Broadlands; and Olga Kulikovsky-Romanoff in Toronto.

The use of archive material is acknowledged, where appropriate, in the notes to individual chapters. But I must particularly thank the following institutions for their help: Archivio Segreto Vaticano, Vatican City, Rome; Bank of England Archives; Bodleian Library, Oxford; Broadlands Archives; Brotherton Collection, University of Leeds; Butler Library, Columbia University, New York; Cambridge University Library; Central Intelligence Agency; Danish National Archives; Forensic Science Service of the Home Office, London; Hoover Institution Archives, Palo Alto, California; Houghton Library, Harvard University; House of Lords Library; Library of Congress, Washington; National Archives, Washington; Nottingham University Library; Public Records Office, London and Kew; Rhodes House Library, Oxford; Rothschild Archives, London and Paris; Southampton University Library; the State Archives of the Russian Federation, Moscow; and the Wernher and Gibbes Collections, Luton Hoo.

Her Majesty the Queen has graciously permitted the publication of extracts from George V's diaries in the Royal Archives at Windsor.

Of the members of the Romanoff family outside London and Paris, I particularly have to thank Prince Nicholas in Rome, and Prince Dimitri in Copenhagen, along with the late Tihon Kulikovsky, the son of the Tsar's younger sister Olga, in Toronto, a true Romanoff in everything but name, for their helpful responses to my enquiries. Like their other cousins, they clearly had an interest in the outcome. But it hardly showed. And the acknowledged current leader of the family, Prince Nicholas Romanoff, has signalled his own wider disinterest by proclaiming himself a 'republican' on St Petersburg television, or at least willing to be a democratically elected monarch, should the occasion arise.

My own family has helped too. My younger daughter, Pamela, in Copenhagen, opened essential doors at the Danish Foreign Office and the Court, translated Danish texts relating to Empress Marie and other Romanoffs and kept in close touch with the local Russian community. My elder daughter, Deborah, coped with the majority of French and European research, translations and banking contacts whether she was living in Switzerland, Portugal or France. Faith, my wife, has once again provided continuous support and detailed research help, at home and abroad, including the brief, though brutal, shock of a St Petersburg winter.

William Clarke

Note

Russian calendar
In February 1918 Russia changed from the old Julian Calendar to the Gregorian Calendar already used in the rest of Europe. The gap between the two had widened from ten days (in the seventeenth century) to twelve (in the nineteenth) and thirteen (in the twentieth). Thus February 1, 1918 (Old Style) became February 14 (New Style). As a result the Bolshevik Revolution was from then on celebrated on November 7 (New Style) instead of October 25 (Old Style) when under the Julian Calendar it actually took place. In this book dates are given in the New Style (Gregorian) from February 1, 1918.

Currencies
The rate of exchange was 10 roubles to the pound (£) sterling in 1897, when the rouble joined the gold standard. This rate was roughly maintained until the 1914–18 war. For the purposes of this book the rate of 10 to £1 is used until 1917, when a figure of 15 roubles to £1 is used. Thereafter, because of the onset of hyper-inflation, individual years are treated separately.

Inflation
In efforts to relate historical monetary values to current ones it has been necessary to allow for inflation (occasionally deflation) between then and now. The book uses the money values of the time, and where there is a need to express this in present-day values the following yardstick, allowing for changes in values, is used:

£1 in 1914 would be worth £39·17 in 1993

1918	18·80
1920	15·62
1929	23·90
1939	24·74
1946	19·05

Note

Russian calendar

In February 1918 Russia changed from the old Julian Calendar to the Gregorian Calendar already used in the rest of Europe. The gap between the two had widened from ten days (in the seventèenth century) to twelve (in the nineteenth) and thirteen (in the twentieth). Thus February 1, 1918 (Old Style) became February 14 (New Style). As a result the Bolshevik Revolution was from then on celebrated on November 7 (New Style) instead of October 25 (Old Style) when under the Julian Calendar it actually took place. In this book dates are given in the New Style (Gregorian) from February 1, 1918.

Currencies

The rate of exchange was 10 roubles to the pound (£) sterling in 1897, when the rouble joined the gold standard. This rate was roughly maintained until the 1914–18 war. For the purposes of this book the rate of 10 to £1 is used until 1917, when a figure of 15 roubles to £1 is used. Thereafter, because of the onset of hyper-inflation, individual years are treated separately.

Inflation

In efforts to relate historical monetary values to current ones it has been necessary to allow for inflation (occasionally deflation) between then and now. The book uses the money values of the time, and where there is a need to express this in present-day values the following yardstick, allowing for changes in values, is used:

£1 in 1914 would be worth £39·17 in 1993

1918	18·80
1920	15·62
1929	23·90
1939	24·74
1946	19·05

Preface

The Romanoff massacre at Ekaterinburg has shocked and intrigued the world as no other tragedy this century. It involved not simply a revolution and abdication but enough bloodshed, brutality, secrecy and mystery to spawn a new industry: shoals of articles, books and films have attempted to unravel what happened to the tsar and his family and a succession of claimants have sought the fabulous wealth said to be locked away in western banks. Only now in the age of *glasnost* and a new Russia is it possible to get near the truth.

The full circumstances of the massacre have still not been entirely resolved. Following Nicholas II's abdication in the wake of the Revolution, the Russian royal family, along with a dwindling number of courtiers, were moved from their home in the Alexander Palace at Tsarskoe Selo to Siberia, first to Tobolsk, finally to Ekaterinburg. And it was there in July 1918, amid the swirling civil war between Whites and Reds, that they were last seen.

The White Russian, Nicholas Sokolov, whose investigation took place in a period of White supremacy, stated that all members of the royal family had been massacred on the instructions of the local Soviet. He concluded that the bodies of the royal family had been brought to the seclusion of a pine forest, had been stripped of their clothing, burnt and hurriedly thrown down the old Four Brothers Mine. It is now known that the remaining bones of the victims were subsequently buried elsewhere, but the mine gave adequate evidence of the remains of human bodies and of burnt clothing and other charred belongings of the royal family.

Some, but by no means all, of the basic mystery has been cleared away by the recent discovery of most of the missing bodies on the outskirts of Ekaterinburg. The subsequent efforts of modern science at Aldermaston in determining, through DNA analysis, whether the bodies belonged to the tsar, tsarina and members of the royal family demonstrated once again the pulling power of the Romanoff story. The results of the British Home Office Forensic Service not only confirmed that five of the bodies were

Romanoffs but, three-quarters of a century after the massacre, still dominated the front pages of the western press. At present the bodies of two members of the family – presumed to be those of either Alexis and Anastasia or Alexis and Maria – are still missing, and, until they have been satisfactorily accounted for, the reports of individual escapes from the massacre at Ekaterinburg will flourish.

The ashes and relics from Ekaterinburg subsequently found their way to the West. The main items of value were quickly identified. Two small diamond-studded shoe buckles belonged to two of the grand duchesses. Brass buttons with coats of arms from military overcoats and two belt buckles belonged to Nicholas and his son Alexis. A brilliant weighing 12 carats, mounted in green gold and platinum, had belonged to Empress Alexandra and had been valued at 20,000 roubles before the Revolution. An emerald cross of Kulm with pearl pendants had belonged to one of the girls.

Right to the end, therefore, the Russian royal family was surrounded by what remained of its once fabulous wealth. The remainder of the Romanoff wealth, over which legal battles have been waged and on which fanciful visions have been based, was either left behind in their last home in the Alexander Palace or their other palaces, invested at home or abroad, or simply stolen immediately after the Revolution. Only days after the Revolution the family's total wealth was put at $9,000 million, the present-day equivalent in pounds sterling of no less than £30 billion. Though the figures are not directly comparable, this estimate of Nicholas's fortune compares with a peak estimate for Queen Elizabeth II of £7 billion in 1991 and £5 billion in 1994.

Whatever the truth, such estimates have been readily believed, if only to explain the Russian upheavals to a startled world. Stories of a Romanoff private fortune secretly tucked away in London, Paris, Berlin and New York were neatly 'confirmed' by reports of huge gold shipments from St Petersburg to London in the last days of the tsarist regime. Difficult to refute, these reports acted as a natural bait for the scores of pretenders who quickly claimed 'their' inheritance. Thus a jackpot of gold, jewels and cash awaiting the right claimant at the right place at the right time has been the last ingredient in prolonging one of the century's more brutal mysteries.

Both puzzles – who died at Ekaterinburg and what happened to their wealth – have thus been inextricably linked by the number of claimants coming forward. Most of them claimed to be one of the tsar's children. The first, an alleged Grand Duchess Tatiana, even appeared while the family was still captive in Siberia. She was reported to have arrived in America in the summer of 1917. Sydney Gibbes, English tutor to the tsarevich, read the report of the claimant published in the *Daily Graphic*

to Tatiana while they were all sitting in the drawing-room of the
Governor's House in Tobolsk.

Other claimants followed, especially those purporting to be Anastasia.
Anna Anderson, whom DNA tests have now proved to be false, was only
the most notable of those who subsequently kept the mystery alive. Nor
was the truth helped by the court battles which followed, some in the
United States, some in Germany, Britain and France.

The trail blazed by these claimants simply deepened the mystery and
added to the confusion of anyone attempting to discover the lost fortune
of the Romanoffs. My own investigative efforts have encompassed the
big and the small, the glittering and the dull, the obvious and the elusive:
the books the family read, the stamps Nicholas collected, the jewels they
wore, the gold they thought they owned, the land they inherited, the
palaces they lived in, the money they rarely used, and the foreign deposits
they are thought to have possessed.

I have uncovered new monetary evidence in the main financial centres
of London, Paris and New York. Former tsarist accounts, and their partial
ownership, have been confirmed at two European central banks, a London
merchant bank and two New York banks. Most, though not all, of the
tsarist gold mystery has been resolved from private papers originally
gathered by the American Embassy in Paris, with the secret help of the
last White Russian financial attaché in Omsk. I turned up details of Soviet
sales of Romanoff jewels in London's diamond district, Hatton Garden,
in secret attempts to subsidise the London *Daily Herald* in the early 1920s,
in a secret intelligence report among a former Prime Minister's papers in
the House of Lords, as well as in a US military intelligence report in
Washington. And the truth about how Queen Mary acquired several
Romanoff jewels now worn by the Queen and other members of the
British royal family I finally tracked down in New Bond Street.

New York newspaper reports of an enormous Russian munitions
explosion in New York harbour at the end of the First World War, and
consequent insurance claims pursued through the courts, led directly to
details of tsarist funds in New York banks. And enquiries at Coutts, the
British royal family's private bankers, produced not monetary evidence
but yet another manuscript describing the last hours of the Romanoffs in
a tin box in one of their vaults. It had been left there by Lord Northcliffe's
secretary, following his death in 1922, and left unopened for seventy
years. He had received it from New York, ostensibly from a Russian
princess, by way of Japan, in 1920.

All these clues left in different parts of the world were the only evidence
available to investigators or claimants for close on seventy-five years.
They proved to be a rich seam, the basis of some semblance of the truth,
as well as of untold rumours and fantasies. The sifting of one from the

other created a new thriving industry. The heart of the Romanoff story, however, lay untouched where it had been filed and largely forgotten – in the Central State Archives of the October Revolution of the USSR in Moscow. And it was to this essential source, at last opened to foreign researchers, that my own investigations eventually led in the spring of 1994. The final confirmation of what private wealth remained in the hands of the Romanoff family was at last fully revealed.

Such a world-wide search could hardly ignore the Romanoff descendants. In 1917, at the outbreak of the February Revolution, there were fifteen grand dukes and ten grand duchesses still living. One grand duke was living permanently in England; seven escaped, and seven were murdered during the course of the Revolution and its aftermath. In spite of the claims of Grand Duke Kyril, who proclaimed himself the tsar's successor in 1924, and especially of his son, the late self-styled Grand Duke Vladimir, no grand dukes have existed for some time, simply princes. Alexander III had decreed in 1886 that the title of Grand Duke would be restricted to the sons and grandsons of the tsar.

The remaining twenty-nine Romanoff princes are widely scattered round the world and can be found in Melbourne, New York, San Francisco, Rome, Biarritz, London, Madrid and Copenhagen. In exile they have taken on a variety of different nationalities, but all seem to carry with them some of the original Romanoff characteristics. Not all of them are 'as tall as a birch tree or as round as a bear', as is often claimed; but they have style and presence; they are still aware of who they are; and most of them remain romantics at heart. One of them made films in Hollywood; two have been bankers (one even operating a secret dollar account for the close aide to a Communist leader); one has written an expert's book on Montenegrin medals; another a book on Ivan the Terrible; yet another is regarded as the family historian and can still tell you which grand duke stayed incognito with which mistress in what room at a Geneva hotel in the early 1900s (I checked one story and found it was borne out by the hotel register); and one worked for British Intelligence during the Second World War and later met the Russian spy Donald Maclean in Cairo in the late 1940s during one of his drinking bouts.

These scattered Romanoff grandchildren are now all that are left of what was once regarded as 'the richest family in the world'. How the panoply of wealth that once surrounded that family – the fabulous state jewels, the exquisite Fabergé eggs, the palaces in and around St Petersburg and in the Crimea, the royal yachts and trains, and the glittering state balls at the Winter Palace before the First World War – was lost and subsequently claimed, and where it may now be, is the substance of this book.

'L'Etat c'est Moi'

Louis XIV, Parlement de Paris, April 13, 1665

'It shall need that the king have such treasure as he may make new buildings when he will for his pleasure and magnificence; and as he may buy him rich clothes, rich furs, rich stones and other jewels and ornaments convenient to his estate royal . . . for if a king did not so, nor might do, he lived then not like his estate, but rather in misery, and in more subjection than doth a private person'

Sir John Fortescue, The Governance of England, *1471, citing magnificence as the first rule of kingship*

THE FAMILIES OF TSAR NICHOLAS II AND HIS WIFE ALEXANDRA

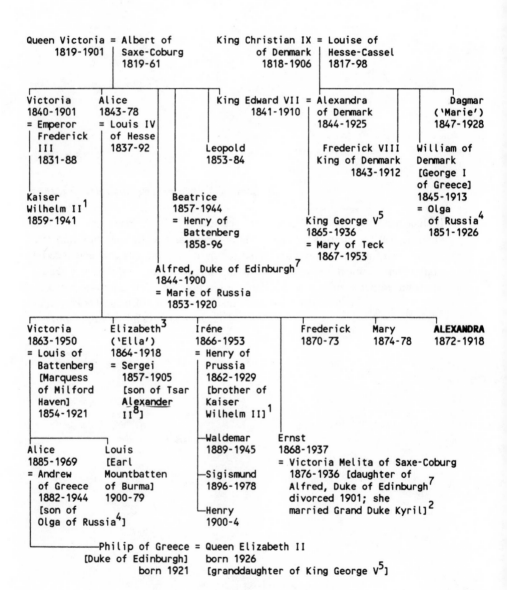

Queen Victoria = Albert of
1819-1901 | Saxe-Coburg
1819-61

King Christian IX = Louise of
of Denmark | Hesse-Cassel
1818-1906 | 1817-98

Victoria
1840-1901
= Emperor
Frederick
III
1831-88

Alice
1843-78
= Louis IV
of Hesse
1837-92

King Edward VII =
1841-1910 |

Alexandra
of Denmark
1844-1925

Dagmar
('Marie')
1847-1928

Kaiser
Wilhelm II[1]
1859-1941

Leopold
1853-84

Frederick VIII
King of Denmark
1843-1912

William of
Denmark
[George I
of Greece]
1845-1913
= Olga
of Russia[4]
1851-1926

Beatrice
1857-1944
= Henry of
Battenberg
1858-96

King George V[5]
1865-1936
= Mary of Teck
1867-1953

Alfred, Duke of Edinburgh[7]
1844-1900
= Marie of Russia
1853-1920

Victoria
1863-1950
= Louis of
Battenberg
[Marquess
of Milford
Haven]
1854-1921

Elizabeth[3]
('Ella')
1864-1918
= Sergei
1857-1905
[son of Tsar
Alexander
II[8]]

Iréne
1866-1953
= Henry of
Prussia
1862-1929
[brother of
Kaiser
Wilhelm II][1]

Frederick
1870-73

Mary
1874-78

ALEXANDRA
1872-1918

Alice
1885-1969
= Andrew
of Greece
1882-1944
[son of
Olga of Russia[4]]

Louis
[Earl
Mountbatten
of Burma]
1900-79

—Waldemar
1889-1945

—Sigismund
1896-1978

—Henry
1900-4

Ernst
1868-1937
= Victoria Melita of Saxe-Coburg
1876-1936 [daughter of
Alfred, Duke of Edinburgh[7]
divorced 1901; she
married Grand Duke Kyril][2]

—Philip of Greece = Queen Elizabeth II
[Duke of Edinburgh] born 1926
born 1921 [granddaughter of King George V[5]]

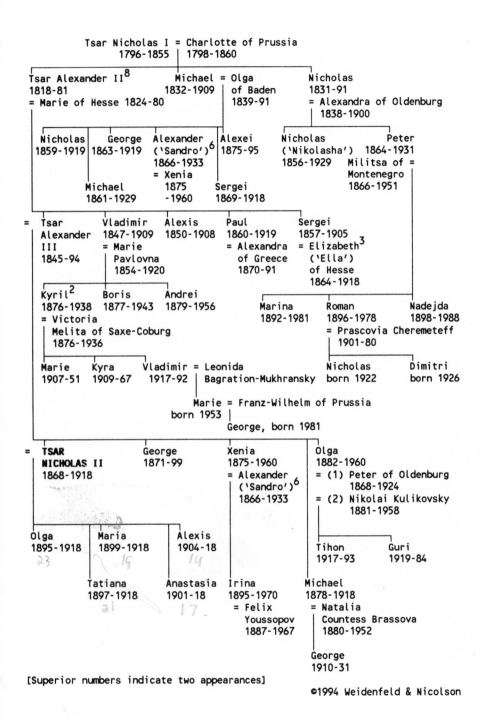

Tsar Nicholas I = Charlotte of Prussia
1796-1855 | 1798-1860

Tsar Alexander II[8]
1818-81
= Marie of Hesse 1824-80

Michael = Olga
1832-1909 | of Baden
1839-91

Nicholas
1831-91
= Alexandra of Oldenburg
1838-1900

Nicholas
1859-1919

George
1863-1919

Alexander
('Sandro')[6]
1866-1933
= Xenia
1875
-1960

Alexei
1875-95

Nicholas
('Nikolasha')
1856-1929

Peter
1864-1931
Militsa of =
Montenegro
1866-1951

Michael
1861-1929

Sergei
1869-1918

= Tsar
Alexander
III
1845-94

Vladimir
1847-1909
= Marie
Pavlovna
1854-1920

Alexis
1850-1908

Paul
1860-1919
= Alexandra
of Greece
1870-91

Sergei
1857-1905
= Elizabeth[3]
('Ella')
of Hesse
1864-1918

Kyril[2]
1876-1938
= Victoria
Melita of Saxe-Coburg
1876-1936

Boris
1877-1943

Andrei
1879-1956

Marina
1892-1981

Roman
1896-1978
= Prascovia Cheremeteff
1901-80

Nadejda
1898-1988

Marie
1907-51

Kyra
1909-67

Vladimir = Leonida
1917-92 | Bagration-Mukhransky

Nicholas
born 1922

Dimitri
born 1926

Marie = Franz-Wilhelm of Prussia
born 1953 |
George, born 1981

= TSAR
NICHOLAS II
1868-1918

George
1871-99

Xenia
1875-1960
= Alexander
('Sandro')[6]
1866-1933

Olga
1882-1960
= (1) Peter of Oldenburg
1868-1924
= (2) Nikolai Kulikovsky
1881-1958

Olga
1895-1918

Maria
1899-1918

Alexis
1904-18

Tihon
1917-93

Guri
1919-84

Tatiana
1897-1918

Anastasia
1901-18

Irina
1895-1970
= Felix
Youssopov
1887-1967

Michael
1878-1918
= Natalia
Countess Brassova
1880-1952

George
1910-31

[Superior numbers indicate two appearances]

Part 1

LOSS

1

St Petersburg

The crystal and bronze of the massive chandeliers sparkled in the reflected light, magnified many times in the wall-length mirrors of the Winter Palace. The strains of the court orchestra greeted the guests as they walked up the deeply carpeted steps of the Jordan staircase, banked with fresh flowers from the Crimea and the French Riviera. The opulence of the Romanoffs was once more on display.

Outside the palace the desolate St Petersburg winter had been transformed. The river Neva was frozen solid to the opposite bank, as far as the Peter-Paul Fortress; the cold intense. But the three blocks of the Winter Palace and its snow-covered entrances glowed with light from open braziers round the Alexander Column.

The carriages, even the open sledges carrying the hardier officers, were still arriving in an endless line, couples slowly ascending the stairs: ladies in elegant ball gowns, cut very low, their bare shoulders and necks adorned with lavish jewels; court dignitaries in black uniforms embroidered in gold, with white trousers; officers in their colourful parade dress and occasional gold aiguilettes.

All knew their place, the grand dukes moving to the Saltykov entrance, courtiers to Their Majesties' entrance, civil officials to the Jordan entrance and officers to the Commanders' entrance. Even after arrival the imperial formalities continued, the ladies being forbidden to bring their own footmen into the palace. Their cloaks, with visiting cards sewn neatly inside, had to be given to the palace attendants who discreetly whispered where they would be found after the ball.

It was 1913. The Romanoffs had ruled Russia for three hundred years and Tsar Nicholas II and his German-born tsarina, Alexandra, were celebrating the occasion with appropriate pomp, though hardly full of enthusiasm. Even after nineteen years as tsar he was still painfully shy and she, in spite of her pale beauty, remained awkward in St Petersburg society, being neither fully accepted nor apparently willing to meet her subjects halfway. Both seemed resigned to see the year through as best they could.[1]

The tercentenary celebrations had started the previous day with a *Te Deum* sung in Kazan Cathedral, followed later that evening with a gala performance at the Maryinska Theatre, at which the tsar's former mistress Mathilde Kschessinska danced the mazurka from the second act of Glinka's opera *La Vie pour le Tsar*. Nicholas and Alexandra had watched the performance from gold-backed armchairs in the big centre loge, the rest of their family filling the royal boxes nearer the stage.

It was the first time for years that Alexandra had visited the Maryinska. Obviously ill at ease, she seemed unable to relax, even to smile, and as the performance progressed the British Ambassador's daughter in the next box noticed that the fan of white eagle's feathers the empress held began trembling convulsively, and a flush spread across her face. She felt she could hear her laboured breathing as the diamonds on her bodice rose and fell spasmodically. With a quick word to her husband, Alexandra suddenly rose and withdrew to the back of the box. Nicholas saw the rest of the performance alone.

A sympathetic public would have sensed a deeply disturbed woman; St Petersburg society simply seethed with resentment. From the outset Alexandra had had difficulty in matching the warmth and style of her mother-in-law, the Dowager Empress Marie. Unlike Marie, Alexandra had found it hard to accept Russian habits and was unable to lead society in a relaxed way. Her apparent coldness, even shyness, were increasingly taken as implied criticism. As her own family burdens, and anxiety over her son's haemophilia, increased, she and Nicholas instinctively cut down public engagements and the active social life that went with them. So when it was needed most Alexandra was unable to attract public support, even sympathy.

The next night, at the Winter Palace, Alexandra faced another test. Grand balls, attended by the royal family with close on three thousand guests, had become no more than annual events. Alexandra preferred them to be even less frequent, but the tercentenary year could not be avoided. Nor could the first polonaise with which the emperor and empress led the opening of the ball. Protocol stood before the evening's enjoyment. And once again we have an eye-witness from the British embassy.

Meriel Buchanan, Sir George Buchanan's daughter, had been some-what distracted for the past two or three seasons in St Petersburg. Her fair hair and good looks had not gone unnoticed by Alexander, Duke of Leuchtenberg. She too had hardly been unmoved by the handsome young Russian in his blue and gold tunic, with a crimson fur-trimmed dolman, and the golden epaulettes of an ADC to the tsar on each shoulder. St

Petersburg balls to her had become evenings of enchantment.

This particular evening she was awaiting the appearance of the tsar and tsarina, with both anticipation and, with memories of the Maryinska the previous evening, not a little anxiety. Her fears were not misplaced. 'Heading the long procession of Grand Dukes and Nobles,' she remembered later:

the Emperor and his wife went slowly round the great hall, keeping step to the wonderful measure of Chopin's music and changing partners at the end of each round. The Empress was a beautiful and stately figure in a sweeping dress of white and silver, a magnificent diamond tiara crowning her fair hair, and cascades of diamonds rippling over her shoulders, but here again her face remained grave and unsmiling and here again she retired before the end of the evening, leaving the Emperor behind with the Grand Duchess Olga, who on this occasion made her first public appearance in [St Petersburg] society. Dressed in a simple pale-pink chiffon frock, her fair hair shining like burnished gold, her blue eyes very bright, her cheeks softly flushed, she danced every dance enjoying herself as simply and wholeheartedly as any girl at her first ball.[2]

The royal couple were nearing a turning point, both in their own relations and with the society they represented. Their personal dilemma, as they tried to come to terms with the tragic illness of their son and with the empress's growing dependence on Gregory Rasputin, the holy man whose unique healing powers had already saved Alexis from much suffering, was slowly putting a strain on their own genuine affection for each other. And it was beginning to merge into the wider tragedy facing the Russian people.

Alexis Nicholaievich, the Sovereign Heir Tsarevich, was born in 1904 following the birth of four daughters and was thus a double cause for celebration for Nicholas and, particularly, Alexandra. Yet within weeks of his birth the first signs of haemophilia were seen, first small haemorrhages, then the more familiar bruising and swellings under the skin. His parents kept the knowledge to themselves and to a few members of the court for several years, at least until Alexis began to need a tutor and Pierre Gilliard was appointed to coach him in French. In efforts to release Alexis from over-protection, even pampering, Gilliard persuaded Alexandra to allow him to be treated like any normal child. It was a sensible move but, on one occasion when Alexis fell off a chair in the classroom the consequent swelling and prolonged agony endured by the boy over several days put such strain on the tsarina that Gilliard later wrote, 'Now I understood the secret tragedy of her life.'[3]

It was a tragedy that took its inevitable next step. Not long afterwards, when the family were holidaying at their hunting lodge at Spala in Poland, Alexis fell while jumping into a boat. Severe haemorrhages followed and, with doctors in attendance and his mother constantly at his side, he lay semi-conscious for days. National prayers and special services were held throughout the land. Just as the last sacrament had been administered and the nation had been prepared for the worst, Alexandra sought help from Rasputin. His response was immediate. He cabled from Siberia: 'God has seen your tears and heard your prayers. Do not grieve. The Little One will not die. Do not allow the doctors to bother him too much.' The haemorrhage stopped two days later. Whatever the reasons for the tsarevich's recovery (and they can extend from the medical to the mystical) this was the episode, above all others, that from then on ensured Rasputin's influence over the empress, and indirectly over the tsar. Alexis's haemophilia was not public knowledge and the empress's need to share her despair, and to relieve it, pushed her inexorably in the direction of the one man who seemed to have the power to assuage her young son's agony: the somewhat mystical *staretz* from Siberia. And from this growing interdependence between Rasputin and the empress rose yet another threat to the whole regime.

On the eve of catastrophe Nicholas, an ill-equipped though well-intentioned tsar, was already finding himself torn by the conflicting advice of his ministers and the magnitude of the pressures, from home and abroad, on his country and its rickety institutions. Presiding over an opulent court, he may have had doubts about what lay ahead, even a strange premonition. But he did not show it. And, as 1914 approached, his more well-to-do subjects in St Petersburg seemed determined to forget the upheavals of the recent past, the disastrous and humiliating naval defeat by the Japanese and the even more disturbing revolutionary clashes between workers and troops in 1905, almost as if to convince themselves of their own prosperity. The tercentenary celebrations spilled over into what, in retrospect, was to be the last peacetime social season of the imperial court.

The years before 1914 for the privileged few of western Europe were a golden era. Travel was leisurely, grand hotels at last beginning to offer an acceptable alternative to country houses, even palaces. The south of France, Switzerland and Italy were becoming the annual goals of the aristocratic and moneyed classes. Russian society was already sharing in this growing western prosperity. The life of a grand duke was a simple mirror of such habits. 'Our travels continued, taking us all over Europe,' Grand Duke Alexander was later to reminisce about his pre-1914 lifestyle, 'the traditional spring reunion with Queen Alexandra of England in Denmark; early summer season in London; Xenia's cure in Kissingen or Vittel and after-cure in Biarritz; children's excursions to Switzerland; late winter season in Cannes ... We covered plenty of ground.'[4]

It was not simply the St Petersburg season that vied with the rest of the Continent. The royal trappings of the Romanoffs were hardly hidden from view. As Alexander Mossolov, who was head of the Court Chancellery for most of Nicholas's reign, candidly remarked, it was the principal function of a sovereign's court to heighten his prestige; and the Russian court was 'certainly the most opulent' in Europe. 'Great wealth had been accumulating during three hundred years in the hands of those responsible for its safe keeping. In its splendour the Russian Court came nearest to those of Louis XIV and Louis XV. In its etiquette it resembled the Court of Austria.'[5] From the royal palaces in St Petersburg, Tsarskoe Selo, Peterhof and Livadia in the Crimea to the royal yacht *Standart*, the royal train and the royal jewels (some inherited, some fashioned by Fabergé), the Russian royal family could hold its own with any other crowned heads of Europe.

The Winter Palace, on the banks of the Neva, runs through Romanoff history like a recording angel and an avenger combined. It was the site of both triumphs and bloody disasters. It housed the country's prime art treasures (in l'Hermitage) and the crown jewels (in the White salon), and was the focal point for all state occasions and state balls. But it never appealed to Nicholas or Alexandra. Their inclination, throughout their reign, was to stay at Tsarskoe Selo (literally the tsar's own village), 15 miles south of St Petersburg. They were there for most of the year, preferring the smaller Alexander Palace to the grander, more ornate Catherine Palace. It was to them a peaceful oasis in its own parkland, and was the scene of the family's happiest and most tragic experiences. Nicholas took Alexandra there as a bride; their children were born there; and Alexandra greeted Nicholas there, tearfully, for their first meeting after his formal abdication, shorn of all his power.

In normal times, when the summer came, the royal family had the pleasant choice of either their Peterhof Palace on the shores of the Gulf of Finland, with its blend of waterfalls, fountains, canals and lakes, or the warm contrast of Livadia near Yalta on the Crimean, with its Greek marbles, Italianate style and views of both sea and mountains. For Nicholas and his family Livadia became a pleasant autumn alternative to the Alexander Palace, an escape from the worries of office in a warm climate, some 1,200 miles and a six-day journey from St Petersburg. They once spent Christmas there and, following its complete rebuilding in the autumn of 1911, this was where the tsar's eldest daughter, Olga, had her first full-dress ball.

Nor did Nicholas and his family lag behind other royals in the comfort and splendour of their travel. The imperial train (actually 'trains', for a duplicate, identical train was often used to ensure the tsar's security) glistened with a small gold monogram NII on its deep-blue doors. Inside its eight cars it carried a complement of Cossacks, for guard duty outside the tsar's quarters on each station platform, a kitchen and full kitchen staff, a bedroom, bathroom and boudoir in grey and lilac, a small drawing-room with a piano, the tsar's study, a dining-car for sixteen and sufficient room for their children, ladies-in-waiting, local visiting dignitaries, a doctor with his own dispensary and court officials. And at sea they had the royal yacht, the *Standart*, a 4,500 ton vessel, built in Denmark and sufficiently impressive to catch the practised eye of Edward VII on their visit to Cowes in 1909. He immediately asked for plans of the yacht, in case he needed a new one himself.

Behind these day-to-day trappings of royalty lay the Romanoffs' array of state jewels, a collection rivalled only perhaps by the present British royal family and the former Persian royal family. Nicholas had inherited (not personally, but as head of state, a distinction originally underlined by Peter the Great) three fabulous symbols of power: the Grand Imperial Crown of Catherine the Great, the Imperial Sceptre and the Imperial Orb. The crown alone was encrusted with 4,936 diamonds weighing 2,858 carats, and was made for Catherine's coronation. The sceptre contained the famous Orlov diamond, said to have been prised from the eye of a Hindu idol in southern India. And the Imperial Orb was made of gold, with a wreath of diamonds and surmounted by a particularly large diamond-trimmed sapphire.[6] Nicholas had worn the crown and been presented with the sceptre and orb at his coronation in May 1896.[7]

The rest of the imperial collection comprised the rarest of diamonds, pearls, emeralds, rubies and other jewels accumulated over three hundred years of Romanoff rule. And quite apart from earlier acquisitions, both Nicholas and his father, Alexander III, encouraged Peter Carl Fabergé, as court jeweller to the tsar, to turn his genius to the production of further exquisite items for their family and friends – brooches, cigarette cases, necklaces, miniatures of all kinds and, of course, to the creation of the famous Fabergé Easter eggs. These were begun in 1884, originally as a special gift from Alexander III to his wife, and later continued by Nicholas as annual gifts to his wife and mother. Fifty-six were completed by Fabergé for the two tsars, but the last two in 1917 were never delivered.

Nicholas may have had modest tastes in his living habits, but in an era when many monarchs in Europe had become constitutional figure-heads of democratic governments he remained a strictly autocratic ruler. In spite of the concessions he had been forced to make in 1905 he, more than most, could still say '*L'etat c'est moi*'. And, as we shall see, Louis XIV's apocryphal remark holds the key to the real scale of monarchist wealth, and its ownership, almost everywhere and nowhere to quite the same extent as in pre-1914 Russia.

In the week before New Year's Day 1914 the normal start to the 'season', St Petersburg seemed as prosperous as anywhere in western Europe. Money flowed freely as crowds filled the fashionable shops in Morskaya and along the Nevski: 'Conradi's, which sold superb confectionery; Denisor-Uralski's, specialising in jewels and carved animals of jade, amethyst, chalcedony and topaz; and Fabergé's, home of some of the most expensive and exquisite jewellery in the world and with an atmosphere of breathless opulence'[8] – these and other establishments were crowded with the aristocratic, merchanting and moneyed classes of the city.

As one contemporary observer put it, any stranger in St Petersburg at that time

felt an irrepressible desire to settle down permanently in the brilliant capital which combined the classical beauty of arrow-like avenues with a passionate undertone of life, cosmopolitan in its leanings but thoroughly Russian in its recklessness. The coloured barman of Hôtel d'Europe hailed from Kentucky; the actresses of the Theatre Michel rattled off their lines in French; the majestic columns of the imperial palaces bore witness to the genius of Italian architects.[9]

The shops too reflected this cosmopolitan tone, from Watkins, the English bookshop, and Druce's selling Harris tweeds and English soap, to Cabassue's selling French gloves.

In the empress's continued absence in that last winter of peace, other hostesses led the season's festivities: Grand Duchess Marie Pavlovna, the widow of the tsar's uncle, and as President of the Academy of Fine Arts a natural focal point for leading artists and society; the cosmopolitan and much-travelled Countess Kleinmichael; and, above all, the tsar's mother, Dowager Empress Marie Feodorovna. It was in fact the Dowager Empress who took it on herself to plan the introduction of her granddaughters, the four grand duchesses, to the society she had once led with such enthusiasm and style.

They were visibly growing up and one by one would be throwing off their childish habits. Olga, at eighteen, had already been introduced to her first season during the previous year's celebrations. Tatiana, now sixteen, was eager to join her sister in the round of St Petersburg parties. At fourteen and twelve, Maria's and Anastasia's time would come. So as an introduction their grandmother decided to act as chaperon to the two elder sisters at a small dance given by Grand Duchess Marie Pavlovna.

This was a huge success, but little more than an *hors d'oeuvre* to a much grander ball she herself gave for the two girls at her own Anichkov Palace on the fashionable Nevski Prospect. Both girls were highly attractive in their different ways, Olga fair-haired and blue-eyed, perhaps the more poised, Tatiana darker with remarkably shaped, light-brown eyes and probably the more striking, even self-assured. They were determined to make the most of their new-found freedom, teasing the two 'stay at homes' (Maria, who at fourteen had already declared her admiration for one of the evening's partners, and Anastasia the young, well-loved tomboy of the family) and dancing every dance until well into the night. Their father finally took them home at 4.30 in the morning.

Sadly, it was to be the sisters' first and last society ball together. Within six months Russia would be at war. Within three years their father would have been forced to abdicate. Within little more than four and a half years they and their father, mother, sisters and brother would have been killed in Ekaterinburg or have vanished, never to be seen again. And the fate of the 'richest family in the world' and its wealth would become the centre of speculation and intrigue for more than three-quarters of a century.

Yet it is still the small things that stick in the mind. The contrast between the tsar's young daughters' spontaneous enjoyment of their first and last peacetime season, as they each slowly reached maturity; and the evidence of the jewels still sewn in their underclothes amid the ashes and debris of the mine shaft outside Ekaterinburg only four years later brings home, as nothing else can, the appalling chasm that had opened up in such a short time. In four years the Romanoffs had vanished and only memories of their wealth and of prewar St Petersburg remained. Yet those memories have stirred untold reminiscences as well as the natural urge to trace and claim what wealth remains.

2

Revolution

For Nicholas and his family it took fewer than four fateful years to go from the peak of St Petersburg's last glittering season to the bleakness of abdication and revolution. In that short time Europe's most autocratic monarch moved from having more wealth at his command than any other contemporary leader to a state of abject humility, spending the first weeks of his reduced status caring for five children with measles, shovelling snow, cutting logs and awaiting his fate. How far such a loss of power was reflected in a corresponding loss of ultimate wealth is a question that has continued to intrigue claimants and observers alike.

The answers lie largely in what such a deposed autocrat might have done while in power, why he did it and under what circumstances he lost control. Nicholas II's 'lost' wealth was only different in kind, say, from that of Haile Selassie, the last Shah of Iran, or President Marcos of the Philippines. Like Elizabeth II, they all had personal wealth and they could all draw on state wealth; but the stronger the autocrat, the more the distinction between the two sources was likely to become blurred. Not until one was divorced from the other by the loss of political power did the puzzles begin. Nicholas's situation was little different. The clues to his bequeathed wealth lie deep in his tsarist past and it is there that our investigative trail must begin.

Nicholas was never in doubt about the dangers facing him. His main anxieties were about his own ability to cope with them. Of one thing he was clear: that Russia must avoid war at almost all costs, until she was ready for it, and even then must weigh in the balance what this would do to her prosperity and stability. In 1911 he told one of his ambassadors:

It would be out of the question for us to face a war for five or six years – in fact until 1917 – although if the most vital interests and the honour of Russia were at stake we might, if it were absolutely necessary, accept a challenge in 1915; but not a moment sooner in any circumstances or under any pretext whatsoever.[1]

On Sunday, June 28, 1914 the first of the catastrophes that Nicholas had been dreading occurred at Sarajevo, the capital of Bosnia. Archduke Ferdinand, nephew of Austrian Emperor Franz Joseph and heir to the throne, was assassinated with his wife by a Bosnian Serb. It was enough to bring to a head the simmering rivalries and enmities of western Europe. Within a week Austria had threatened Serbia; Germany had supported Austria, and Russia was considering mobilisation. And within five weeks Austria had issued an unacceptable ultimatum to Serbia, followed by a declaration of war; Russia had mobilised; Germany had issued an ultimatum to Russia and a neutrality warning to France, and had followed this up by a declaration of war against both; and Britain, having sought and been refused a German promise not to violate Belgian neutrality, declared war on Germany.

The pattern for the ultimate destruction of Europe's main autocratic monarchies – the German Kaiser, the Austro-Hungarian Emperor and the Russian Tsar – was complete. Each had played a prime role in this final débâcle. So far as Nicholas was concerned, he did his best to restrain the Kaiser personally, even excusing his own partial mobilisation: 'I hope with all my heart that these measures won't interfere with your part as mediator which I greatly value. We need your strong pressure on Austria to come to an understanding with us.' But his older cousin, the Kaiser, mistook reasonableness for weakness and was unwilling to change course. He demanded the cancellation of Russian mobilisation.

Discussing this final threat from the Kaiser with his Foreign Minister, Serge Sazanov, in Tsarskoe Selo, Nicholas wrestled with his conscience. 'You know I have already suppressed one mobilisation decree and then consented only to a partial one,' he told Sazanov. 'If I agreed to Germany's demands now, we should find ourselves unarmed against the Austrian army, which is mobilised already. It would be madness.' Sitting opposite Nicholas, Sazanov watched him intently. The tsar was pale and his expression betrayed an inner struggle. After some hesitation, Nicholas spoke, 'You are right. There is nothing left us but to get ready for an attack upon us. Give then the Chief of the General Staff my order for mobilisation.'

Faced with Russia's decision, from which she did not waver, the Kaiser instructed his ambassador to hand over Germany's declaration of war. Next day Nicholas issued a manifesto to his people in St George's gallery in the Winter Palace, in the presence of the whole court. In front of an altar, on which was placed the miraculous ikon of the Virgin of Kazan, Nicholas, with Alexandra by his side, presided over a religious service and made this pledge to his people: 'I solemnly swear that I will never make peace so long as one of the enemy is on the soil of the fatherland.' It was the same oath given to the Russian people by Alexander I at the time of Napoleon's threat to Russia in 1812.

The Russia Nicholas committed to war on August 2, 1914 was a country poised on a knife-edge between progress and disaster. Seeds of both were already present. Like other parts of western Europe, Russia was on the threshold of industrialisation and had been the recipient of extensive railway loans from the capital markets of Paris and London. The rouble was stable and her internal currency was backed up to 98 per cent by gold. Her budgets had been in balance for some years. And she was sitting on the largest gold reserve in the world.

Since the turn of the century she had conformed to the pattern of modern economic growth shown by other leading countries of western Europe, her growth rate reaching an annual average of $3\frac{1}{4}$ per cent, her exports and imports doubling over that period. By 1914 her economy was the world's fourth largest, almost equal in total output to that of the United Kingdom. One leading French economist forecast in a book published in 1914 that if Russia maintained this pace to mid-century she would dominate Europe politically, economically and financially.

It was not to be. The war gradually exposed the precarious basis of the country's rigid administration. Her manner of financing the war, by a combination of foreign borrowing and the excessive issue of domestic banknotes, slowly weakened her currency. The war effort was also undermined by the absence of a coherent command structure, glaring transport deficiencies and, above all, the absence of firm political decisions to cope not only with the normal tensions of wartime but the growing social unrest on the home front. As one parliamentary clash followed another after 1905, Nicholas's continuing inability to come to terms with the political aspirations of successive Dumas brought decision-making to a dangerous impasse. Essential war needs were eventually frustrated by uncertainty, rumour-mongering and unhealthy court intrigue. In such an atmosphere Gregory Rasputin was bound to flourish.

Rasputin's role at court and his part in the downfall of the Romanoffs has attracted almost as much attention as the family itself. His origins were simple. He came from peasant stock in the village of Pokrovskoe, not far from Tobolsk in Siberia, a place the royal family were later to be sent to in exile. The story goes that after a youth spent in drunkenness, dishonesty and licentious habits, a chance meeting with the Bishop of Kazan reawakened a latent religious faith and turned him into a religious pilgrim, touring the countryside, visiting shrines, worshipping as he went, dependent on the hospitality of the local peasants and tradespeople: in short he became a *staretz*, a holy man, widely recognised in the pre-revolutionary villages of Russia.

It was apparently a short step for Rasputin from the introductions of the Bishop of Kazan to the religious community in St Petersburg, especially the Theological Academy, and from there to a wider circle of religious students. He was soon at the head of one of the many Orthodox sects then flourishing in the capital, the *Khlysty*, stressing the sins of the flesh and religious rites designed to assuage them. Bishop Theophanus supported the movement and was clearly the channel between Rasputin and the leading members of St Petersburg society. Anna Vyrubova, for long Alexandra's only close confidante, was among those impressed and influenced by the *staretz* and was instrumental in introducing him to the empress. And it was not long, in such a closed community, before scandal and rumour followed. Rasputin's mystical powers became common currency, as did the accompanying tales of debauchery, and after some six years in the capital Bishop Theophanus had Rasputin sent back to Siberia.

His exile, arranged in 1911, did not last. His connections at court, and particularly his close relationship with Alexandra, tightened even further by his undoubted ability to treat her son's tragic illness, were instrumental in his return to the capital before the onset of the war. It was not long before officers, courtiers, even ministers, became aware of his influence over Alexandra and thus, indirectly, over the tsar. His help began to be sought in almost every doubtful intrigue. While Nicholas remained reluctant to hear the worst, Rasputin maintained the ear of the empress. He was both despised and feared. As the war progressed and Russia's fate was ultimately decided first at the front, later at home, Rasputin's shadow widened and deepened.

Initially Russian troops made significant headway against the Austrians and even, for a few weeks, against the German armies in East Prussia. But by the end of 1914 the Russian Second Army had surrendered to the Germans and total Russian losses (killed, wounded, missing or prisoner) exceeded a million. The following year brought further disasters with the loss of the whole of Russian-held Poland and most of Lithuania and Latvia. Germany's enormous effort on the eastern front may well have undermined the Kaiser's long-term strategy, especially on the western front, but the impact of such defeats on the Russian people and the possibility that Kiev, Riga and even Petrograd (St Petersburg's new wartime name) might have to be evacuated were devastating.

The tsar's autocratic rule was a natural target for the discontent. Over the coming months he provided several scapegoats: the Minister of War, the Minister of the Interior and the Minister of Justice were all replaced. But pressure to recall the Duma could not be resisted and the full force of liberal outrage was reflected in its tense deliberations throughout the months of June and July 1915.

Something had to be done to reassure the country. Nicholas's twin decisions in August and early September were taken more by instinct than design, but both in their different ways ultimately led to further disaster. First he decided to take over full personal command of the army from his uncle, Grand Duke Nikolai Nikolaevich, as commander-in-chief; and secondly he suspended the Duma.

From that moment all reverses at the front or social unrest at home were inevitably blamed on the tsar himself. At the same time, by setting up his personal headquarters with his troops, he absented himself from his capital for months at a time, allowing the void to be filled by others when circumstances and opportunities permitted. The upshot was that Alexandra was encouraged to be his eyes and ears in the capital; and any distortion in her appraisal of affairs was instantly reflected in her almost daily letters to Nicholas, ranging as they did from the most warm-hearted sentiments to the almost strident pleas for the dismissal or appointment of this minister or that. Rasputin could hardly have wished for a readier or more influential listener.

For a time, under Nicholas's personal command, Russian troops regained some of their poise, shielded by the Allies' preparations on the western front and ultimately, by the severity of the Somme offensive, which persuaded the Germans to switch several divisions from the East. Russian divisions even advanced against the Austrians, gaining hundreds of thousands of prisoners, forcing a significant reappraisal of Austrian capabilities, and providing a respite from the initial disasters. But as 1916 progressed a greater malaise began to spread from the home front until it affected even those in the front line. It all stemmed from the impact of government policies on social conditions. The war effort was being financed by the continuous issue of domestic notes, thus stimulating inflation and pushing prices well ahead of wages. At the same time shortages of essential supplies of food and fuel aggravated the situation.

Discontent swiftly followed, particularly in the urban areas. One historian has painted this depressing picture of the prospects facing Petrograd that winter:

In late 1916 the food and fuel situation in the major cities became critical. By then, Petrograd and Moscow were getting only one-third of their food requirements and faced hunger: the reserves covered at best a few days' consumption. Fuel shortages compounded the difficulties: Petrograd could obtain only half of the fuel it needed, which meant that even when bakeries got flour they could not bake ... Petrograd, which by virtue of its remoteness from the food-producing areas suffered the most, entered the winter of 1916–17 in desperate straits. Factories had to be repeatedly shut either for lack of fuel or in order to enable their workers to scour the countryside for food.[2]

As conditions deteriorated a political paralysis seemed to grip the capital in Nicholas's absence. Spasmodic strikes, aimed at minor grievances, had begun in the autumn. Some workers simply took time off to search for food and provisions. Clashes between urban workers and the peasantry became more frequent. And, hardly surprisingly, the discontent slowly infiltrated the trenches, where rising casualties and growing shortages of ammunition were beginning to undermine morale among the younger troops. The absence of any coherent administrative response to the social difficulties was, with hindsight, one of the most crucial elements in the tragedy that was to follow.

From the autumn of 1916 onwards the political turmoil caused by the regime's inability to respond to the growing social crisis grew in intensity, highlighted by the haphazard changes in government posts, nationally and regionally. By the time the Duma was recalled in early November, ostensibly to approve the budget, political emotions were already reflecting widespread opposition to the regime, even to the tsar himself. Not only were liberal politicians speaking out against Nicholas; so were members of his own family. Sturmer, the Prime Minister, who took the brunt of the political storm in the Duma, immediately sought its dismissal once more. But by this time Nicholas's resolution was wavering. Instead he dismissed Sturmer.

It was a signal that few of those with a political sense could ignore. Move and counter-move followed swiftly, culminating in intense struggles round the future of the Minister of the Interior and even of the new Prime Minister, with the inevitable appeals to Alexandra and, naturally, Rasputin. Political turmoil had now joined serious social unrest in a potentially explosive mixture. To some the instant removal of Rasputin became the obvious and logical solution, if the regime was to be saved. His malign influence on the country's destiny in the absence of Nicholas, whether real or imagined, was becoming the accepted obstacle to progress. That assassination should be the method preferred in tackling it was a reflection of the crisis now facing the whole country.

The plot to kill Rasputin seems to have matured throughout November. Inspired by a fiery speech in the Duma in early December, Prince Youssopov, the son of one of Russia's richest families, and four other conspirators, including a grand duke cousin of the Tsar, began to work out the details. The date, place and method were quickly agreed. They decided to entice Rasputin to Youssopov's house by an invitation to meet Princess Irina, his wife, on the night of December 16. This proved to be the easiest part of the plot. Rasputin's subsequent resilience under attack from poisoning, shooting and drowning still remains a mystery and has added to the legend.

Having failed to poison him with pastries and Madeira, said to be doctored with potassium cyanide, Youssopov shot Rasputin in the back and left him for dead. A little time later the 'body' staggered to its feet, seized Youssopov by the throat and then rushed out of the house. As he was leaving the gate Rasputin was shot three times by another of the conspirators (and presumably killed), beaten by a truncheon, tied up with chains and dumped in the Malaia Neva. This somewhat over-dramatic end to a turbulent year was, in retrospect, simply the *hors d'oeuvre* to the even more dramatic weeks just ahead.

Nicholas spent that Christmas quietly at Tsarskoe Selo with his family, deliberately shielded from the stirrings of discontent outside, aggravated as they were by one of the coldest winters Petrograd had experienced. He stayed in the capital long enough to make his last change of Prime Minister and to approve the arrest of the leadership of the Workers' Group, following its call for the removal of the regime. But it was all too late. Spurred by the rapidly deteriorating living conditions and shortages, what was to prove to be the last wave of dangerous unrest broke out in the middle of February, almost immediately after Nicholas's return to his army headquarters at Mogilev.

Fears of bread rationing added to the gloom as workers were laid off by fuel shortages and bakeries were unable to bake what flour they had. The streets of the capital were filled with idle, sometimes hungry workers. Some were on strike; others simply expressing their frustration at the authorities. International Women's Day, with its organised dem-onstrations, added to the turmoil in the streets, while the political voices in the Duma became ever more strident. Skirmishes followed the growing protests. In some areas police came under attack.

Misjudging both the severity of the situation and the mood of the protesters, Nicholas sent a telegram demanding military suppression to restore order. A curfew was immediately imposed in Petrograd. But as the crowds began to assemble again all over the capital sporadic clashes took place between workers and troops. In one square a Guards regiment, attempting to disperse the crowd, opened fire, killing forty protesters. Similar attacks on workers were reported from other parts of the capital. Although calm seemed to have been restored for a time, the impact of the killings on the troops was to prove decisive. Within twenty-four hours mutiny broke out in several barracks and soon troops and workers were out on the streets together. Violence grew. Officers came under attack. Shops and private houses were looted and government buildings broken into and set on fire.

Law and order had now collapsed. Three quite different eye-witness accounts of that particular week paint a vivid picture of the mounting chaos. First the impressions of the British Ambassador's wife, Lady (Georgina) Buchanan, in a private letter to her sister-in-law in England:

We have been living through an awful time ... We arrived here knowing nothing on Sunday. On the way we heard rumours of tram strikes, etc., but we did not take it seriously, but when we arrived we found it all in a state of revolution.

Monday and Tuesday were terrible, shooting going on all round and one wondered how it would all turn out. The army went over almost at once to the people
but the police had machine-guns and shot down on the soldiers and the people.
It seems that on Sunday the soldiers were ordered to shoot on the people who
were quite quietly walking about. This was the last straw and they refused to go
on and went over to the people one regiment after the other.[3]

Next a rather laconic description from a Yorkshireman working in a textile
firm with his father to his brother in Leeds, from the vantage point of a
window on Nevsky Prospect:

We have been living through very, very interesting times this last week, for there
has been a revolution in Petrograd! By now it is more or less over and we are
working in the office again ... Munition workers had to wait in long queues for
their bread for hours before going to work ... They went on strike ... The street
was crowded with people, cossacks riding in and out of them armed with spears,
rifles and loaded whips ... On Monday a terrific change took place: 25,000
soldiers went on the side of the people. During the week trams have not been
running, telephones disrupted, etc. Nobody seems to know anything about the
Tsar or where he is but that does not matter for he will have to agree with the
people.[4]

Now a more detailed description from a fourteen-year-old to his uncle
living in the country:

Terrible things are happening in Petrograd. It has become a real battlefield. Five
regiments have joined the revolt. Gunfire never ceases in our part of the City –
Liteiny. The officers cannot go out into the streets, because the crowd disarms
them, molests them and even kills them. There is no police. Two prefects of
police were killed. Worst of all, the soldiers have got hold of the vodka and are
drunk. There is bound to be terrible looting of shops, banks, and private apartments ... We, the students of the Lyceum, are on leave till the time when order
can be restored; but when will this be?[5]

Against this turbulent background and in the tsar's absence the Cabinet,
far from insisting on the suspension of the Duma, as Nicholas had
intended, adjourned their own meetings and allowed the Duma to take
responsibility for security. Out of this administrative chaos grew two
centres of future power and influence. The Duma set up a Provisional
Committee, out of which emerged the Provisional governments of Prince
Lvov and, later, Alexander Kerensky; and the Petrograd Soviet, while
initially representing workers and soldiers, was soon the creature of the
main Socialist parties. Both bodies continued to clash and co-operate
over the next nine months until Lenin's final *coup d'état* established
Bolshevik control in November.

The tsar's power had thus been usurped. His continued absence had also proved fatal to his own future. His constitutional position was still being fought over, even as he planned his return to Petrograd, and his journey was symptomatic of the deteriorating conditions throughout the country. He should have been back in Petrograd within a day and a half from headquarters; instead he deliberately took a circuitous route to avoid blocking essential military traffic and thereby ran into an area under the control of mutinous troops. His path was deliberately blocked, he was forced to make a detour and ended up overnight at Pskov, the head-quarters of the northern front. It was to prove to be a fateful halt and the scene of his final humiliation.

Even as he travelled events had moved swiftly in Petrograd. Violence had flared, decisions had been forced on his Cabinet and power had already passed to the Duma and the Petrograd Soviet. It was no longer a question whether Nicholas should, or even could, give concessions to the Duma; what was now at issue was whether the concessions already taken should be accompanied by the continuation of the tsarist regime itself, or at least with Nicholas as its head, a choice that the Duma leaders in Petrograd and the army leaders jointly agreed should now be put to the tsar.

At Pskov Nicholas was forced to face this stark reality alone, accompanied as it was with the candid views of the army commanders which had been sought overnight. As he read their responses stressing the need for him to abdicate and heard those present in the railway car, people who had given him, as their commander-in-chief, an oath of loyalty, reaffirming the same views, Nicholas knew he had no option. In the words of one of those present, he

walked over to the table and absently peeped several times through the drawn blind; his face, normally inexpressive, was twisted to one side by some curious movement of the lips, which I had never before observed. It was clear that he was wrestling in his heart with a painful decision. Not a sound came in to relieve the silence ... Suddenly with a sharp jerk Emperor Nicholas II turned towards us and pronounced in a firm voice, 'I have decided ... I shall give up the throne in favour of my son Alexis.' With this he made the sign of the cross and we did the same.[6]

This was his first instinct. Later, following advice from the court physician about the unlikelihood of any cure for his son's haemophilia, he decided to abdicate in favour of his younger brother, Grand Duke Michael.

Nicholas was thus left alone to brood over what might have been, to wonder what had happened to personal loyalty ('Around me,' he wrote that night, 'I see treason, cowardice and deceit'), to draft his notice of abdication and to prepare himself for his sorrowful return to his family

at Tsarskoe Selo. His successor, Michael, whom Nicholas had plunged
into a crisis not of his own making and without adequate warning, quickly
felt the brunt of his brother's decision.

In Nicholas's absence Michael had personally witnessed some of the
violence on the streets of Petrograd. On the day of the first troop mutinies,
according to his diary, he had encountered 'heavy machine-gun fire' and
had seen 'hand grenades ... exploding' not far from the War Ministry.
His car and escort had run into revolutionary detachments and patrols
close to the Nicholas Bridge on the Embankment and had been called to
a halt. They decided to risk it and drive on and quickly found sanctuary
in the Winter Palace, which was still being held with a thousand troops
under two loyal generals. 'I managed to persuade the generals not to
defend the palace,' Michael recalled in his diary, 'as they had intended to,
and to lead their men before dawn out of the Winter Palace and thereby
prevent the inevitable destruction of the palace by the revolutionary
forces.'[7]

This experience was fresh in Michael's mind when he met members of
the Provisional Committee immediately following Nicholas's abdication.
There was little doubt what most of them wanted him to do. He was told
by several members that if he succeeded Nicholas there would be a violent
outcry against him, even civil war. Although others disagreed, one hinting
that he might consider becoming regent, the pressure on him was intense.
Michael insisted on a final, private talk with the leader of the Duma, if
only to clarify what support he could really rely on. With thoughts of his
own recent street experience in mind and in full knowledge of the violent
passions his family had already aroused, Michael had by this time only
one major anxiety on his mind: could the Duma really guarantee his
safety. When such an assurance was clearly impossible he made it plain
that he could not accept the throne unless and until the Constituent
Assembly offered it to him. In short he would only accede to the throne
as a constitutional monarch, and with the support of a national ref-
erendum. Later that evening he signed his own abdication. Both his and
Nicholas's formal abdications were published simultaneously the next
morning.

Over three hundred years of Romanoff rule had thus come to an
end. For Nicholas, however, the misery and humiliations were only just
beginning. He had his sad goodbyes to make to his former troops and to
his immediate colleagues at the main army headquarters at Mogilev,
before undertaking the long journey back to his family. Even before that
he had a poignant, tearful meeting with his mother, the Dowager Empress
Marie, who had travelled up to Mogilev from Kiev in her private train.

Who knows what was said between them at that first meeting after his
momentous decision. When they were seen immediately afterwards she

was 'sobbing bitterly' and Nicholas was 'silent, smoked and stolidly kept his eyes fixed to the ground – as he always did on disturbing occasions'. Four days later, the day of their joint departure, she to Kiev, he to Tsarskoe Selo, they had a last leisurely lunch together in her dining-car. Then at about four o'clock two representatives of the Duma and his top general arrived to escort him back to Petrograd, basically under arrest:

There came the moment of separation – for ever, as it turned out, though they hoped to meet again soon, be it in Crimea or in England. The last seconds sped by. For a moment the Emperor lost his self-control, could not break away from his mother, wept ... Then his face became mask-like again and with his usual measured step, not glancing back, he walked over to his own train. There he came to the window. On the other side of the platform his mother also stood by the window and made signs of the cross as though to bless him.[8]

Nicholas's abdication proclamation had been precisely timed and dated: 3.05 p.m. on March 2, 1917. But only gradually between his departure from Pskov, his short stay in Mogilev and his final arrival back with his family in Tsarskoe Selo did the full implications of his decision become abundantly clear. He was returning in his private car, in his own train, surrounded by familiar courtiers and attendants. The usual courtesies were still being offered. But even then there were already subtle differences. Kerensky later reported the impressions of one of Nicholas's generals who accompanied him on that return journey: 'There were still the old bows, smiles and words, but the words held other meanings, the eyes looked aside while the lips smiled, and the heads bowed less easily and less eagerly.' Actions, most in self-protection, soon followed. The tsar's initials were removed from courtier's epaulettes, and their golden shoulder knots, once an emblem of pride, were now hidden from view.

Worse was to follow. His Duma escorts back to the capital were demonstrably in charge of the whole return journey, censoring all messages to the train, controlling communications and arranging station contacts at all points en route. On arrival at Tsarskoe Selo station the tsar is said to have 'walked very rapidly, without a glance at anyone' into a waiting car. But those accompanying him were already bent on distancing themselves from the deposed monarch. 'There were many other people on the Emperor's train,' a loyal officer claimed later, 'but as soon as he left the carriage, these people swarmed out on the platform and scuttled rapidly in all directions, casting back furtive glances – for fear, apparently, that they might be recognised.'

Ahead of him Nicholas had a tearful reunion with Alexandra, but even as he arrived at the gates of the palace the guards were determined to show their contempt. They were in no hurry to unlock the gates. He and

Alexandra finally met in the children's quarters, and were still not alone. 'They embraced each other and kissed with a smile,' according to their personal attendant, 'and went to see the children. Not until later, when they were left alone, did they give way to their feelings, and wept quietly for a long time.'

Nicholas had left as tsar and Commander-in-Chief; now he and Alexandra were both under arrest, ostensibly (and probably truly) for their own safety. He found on his return that his wife, still in hospital uniform, was caring for the five children, all of whom had contracted measles. Anastasia was the last to be affected, the two elder daughters, Olga and Tatiana, were now convalescent, Alexis and Maria were still very ill, the latter also having gone down with pneumonia.

The deposed tsar was soon reminded of his new status in every direction. The desertions within the court continued. They had started, of course, on Nicholas's arrival at Tsarskoe Selo station, where a major-general and several army commanders took the opportunity to make themselves scarce. And as conditions deteriorated further, in and around the palace, several familiar faces were soon noted as missing: the Head of Chancery Naryshkin, Count Grabbe, the Duke of Leuchtenburg, Count Apraxine, General Racine, as well as ADCs Sablin and Colonel Mordinov.

The exodus went on until the household was reduced to a handful of devoted courtiers, officials, doctors, tutors and servants. And even this loyal core was given precise instructions about how the royal family was now to be treated. It was symptomatic of the changes that Kerensky, the Minister of Justice in the new Provisional government, soon to be its leader, arrived at the palace in one of the tsar's private cars driven by a chauffeur from the imperial garage. Meanwhile the family was restricted to certain rooms within the palace and, as a gesture, allowed to walk within a fenced-off section of the grounds. Everywhere Nicholas found deliberate insolence from the guards and indifference to his plight. Some called him 'Colonel'; others ignored him. On his first stroll outside he had to wait twenty minutes for the key leading out of the drawing-room. He and one of his aides began to clear away the snow and break the ice in one of the ponds for exercise.

Although a routine of sorts was shortly established within the palace – the reduced staff even sharing the chore of giving lessons to the younger children, with Nicholas, for example, taking over arithmetic, Russian language and history, and Alexandra undertaking religious instruction – the sharp changes in the running of it reflected a major shift in Nicholas's personal fortune. Not only had power shifted; but the source of the funds to implement that power had also moved significantly. And although Nicholas was protected for a time by the devotion, even ingenuity, of his courtiers, particularly the Grand Marshal of the Court, Count Paul Benckendorff, the stark reality was revealed day by day.

The former royal family remained in the Alexander Palace at Tsarskoe Selo from March until the end of July 1917. By his abdication and subsequent arrest Nicholas's relations with the government had been transformed. No longer was he head of state. No longer therefore was he in charge of his own financial destiny. The accoutrements of state had vanished overnight. The crown lands, the imperial palaces themselves, the royal trains and the royal yacht were no longer his to use without permission. The state jewels were no longer at his disposal. He no longer controlled the palace budget. And it was in this narrow area of day-to-day living, and wondering who should pay for the rising cost of the captive royal family and its entourage, that Nicholas's changed financial circumstances first came to a head.

By the middle of May, after two months in captivity, the cost of feeding the royal family had risen by 50 per cent and of other items by as much as 75 per cent, even 100 per cent. The Provisional government's commissioner in charge of the court, Golovin, who well understood the reasons for the inflationary increases, was fearful that the news of such large increases would become known more widely and inflame feelings even further among the revolutionary troops and workers. He naturally turned for help to the courtier who, as the former empress's private secretary (Nicholas himself deliberately had no secretary of his own), looked after the private fortunes of the royal family – Count Rostovtsev.

In spite of strong resistance from both Count Rostovtsev and Count Benckendorff, a compromise was quickly reached under which Nicholas and his wife and children all agreed to share the costs with the Provisional government, 'each paying a share out of his or her personal fortune'. And, according to Benckendorff's later reminiscences, for the first time the ex-tsar's own capital in Russia was revealed as just below 1 million roubles (£66,000 at the 1917 rate of exchange); the ex-tsarina's fortune as 1,500,000 roubles (£100,000); and that of the five children, at home and abroad, as varying between 2 million and 3 million roubles each (between £133,000 and £200,000).[9] So their joint accounts at the State Bank began to be drawn upon to pay for part of the cost of their captivity.

3

Abdication

Within days of the tsar's return to the Alexander Palace, under arrest, reports of his immense wealth were already circulating at home and abroad. In Petrograd the imperial family came under constant attack in the press from the Soviet of Workers' and Soldiers' Deputies and the Provisional Committee, the new twin sources of power.

Gossip and rumour soon concentrated on the royal family's German connections, and the possibility of the empress's treason by communications with her relations in Germany. Such accusations were quickly given great prominence in the newspapers and formed a major part of the questions Kerensky, as Minister of Justice, felt obliged to clarify officially at the outset. But behind these doubts lurked the far more human suspicion that all the recent food shortages, deprivations and poverty on the home front had a simple explanation: the excessive indulgence of the tsar and the vast numbers of Romanoff dependants. The imperial family's lifestyle, and its outward manifestations, suddenly became the source of all ills and the target of every enemy.

The foreign press was not slow to reflect Petrograd sentiment. A couple of days after Nicholas's abdication the *New York Times* had a report stressing that the tsar derived an enormous income from the 70 per cent of Russian land which he owned personally and which the paper quickly calculated amounted to one-tenth of the earth's surface. His annual income alone was put at $42 million. The source of the story was a Russian author and former editor of an Anglo-Russian magazine in London. Though it was denied next day by the Legal Department of the Russian Zemstvo and Citizens' Union, quoting official figures which suggested that the original report represented only a small part of the truth, the tone had been set. The imperial family, it was widely assumed, was enormously wealthy.

Soon there were reports from Russian language newspapers of the tsar's wealth abroad, *Russki Colos* claiming that Nicholas had substantial investments, running into several millions, in US railroad stock such as

New York Central and Pennsylvania Railroad. And within weeks the *New York Times* was again reporting on the tsar's wealth, this time putting it at no less than $9,000 million. The paper reported that it was such revelations in Petrograd that had persuaded the Soviet of Workers' and Soldiers' Deputies to prevent the royal family from seeking asylum abroad, especially in England.[1] It was not the only reason for their retention.

Kerensky was torn between his obligation to protect the royal family, until he had more solid evidence against them, and his need to deal with the emotional demands of the Workers' Soviet. In those early days he seemed far from persuaded that Nicholas and Alexandra were entirely innocent of communicating with their German cousins. So his first steps seemed to be a combination of clearing up such treasonable accusations through a personal examination, even a trial; of planning their possible exile to the Crimea or abroad; and, in the short term, of sorting out the royal court's financial obligations. It was against this complex and explosive situation in Petrograd that Britain's own muddled efforts to get a coherent rescue plan for King George V's Russian cousins finally foundered. Little wonder that the recriminations are still reverberating to this day.

Kerensky was later to say that the original intention was to retain the imperial family for a short spell only, while clearing up the initial accusations against them. The outbreak of measles among the children was bound to delay the departure for some weeks. And it was in that time that the Workers' Soviet, sensing the escape of its prime target, made it clear to Kerensky that his original plan, to allow the exile of the imperial family once they had been cleared of treasonable or other offences against the state, was simply not possible. Revenge was in the air.

The first intimations of an overseas exile came even before Nicholas's return to Tsarskoe Selo. General Kornilov, the Commander-in-Chief, in explaining to Count Benckendorff the reasons for the 'arrest' of Nicholas and Alexandra told him that it was simply a precautionary measure. As soon as the health of the children allowed it, the emperor's family would be sent to Murmansk, where a British cruiser would await them and take them to England. In retailing this news later that day to the empress herself the general hardened up the intentions, indicating that the cruiser was 'already waiting' at Murmansk. Benckendorff knew this was not true, but still advised the empress to make preparations for the journey, and, as he later reported, 'packing was begun'. It was clearly on this basis that Nicholas was to write the following entry in his diary a few weeks later:

After two o'clock it cleared and thawed. Walked for a short time in the morning. Sorted my belongings and books, and sorted the things I want to take with me in case I go to England. After lunch I took a walk with Olga and Tatiana, and worked in the garden.

These hopes were to be shattered within a matter of weeks but it has taken close on seventy years to clarify exactly what prevented their exile to England. And even now it is a matter of conjecture which change of heart came first: that of Kerensky, prompted by the Workers' Soviet, or that of the British government, prompted by George V.

Until Kenneth Rose's biography of George V a decade ago the role of the main players in this country seemed clear enough. The British government, under the liberal influence of Lloyd George and the Foreign Office, it was assumed, had managed to undermine the natural concern of George V for his Russian cousins. Meriel Buchanan, the British Ambassador's daughter, had provided a filial warning that her father had been prevented from telling the full truth by the Foreign Office, by a threat to his pension. But the main assumption remained undisturbed: the basic opposition to any British rescue of the tsar had rested with the elected government and Whitehall.

As files have become available, memories stirred and reminiscences published, however, the sequence of events has taken on a different flavour. The story really began in the British Embassy a few days after Nicholas's abdication. As she was sorting out clothes in the Embassy ballroom for the British Colony Hospital, Meriel Buchanan had an unexpected call from her erstwhile suitor, the handsome Alexander, Duke of Leuchtenberg. She noticed that he seemed both distracted and somehow different. 'I looked at him curiously, wondering what it was that I missed, and realised suddenly that he had discarded all his decorations, and no longer wore the golden aiguilettes. Russia had no Emperor now, I remembered.'[2]

He quickly explained his purpose. He said he had come to implore her father, Sir George, to take immediate action to get the emperor and his wife and children out of Russia. They stood in the gravest danger and if they were not removed soon to England it would be too late to get them away, too late to save them from possible disaster. She called her father at once to her sitting-room, watched the two of them meet and thought how much they had all changed over the past three years.

My father's hair was almost white now, his face was tired, his former upright bearing had gone, and his shoulders drooped wearily. And Alexander was no longer the light-hearted, perhaps rather volatile young man I had met on that lovely spring day in the forest, the man who had lived for pleasure, who had made love to so many women and spent money with lavish extravagance. The world we had known, where we had danced and been happy and made so many mistakes, was changing too, and disintegrating around us, being swept away by violence and hatred.

She heard her father promise to do all he could and explain that he had already sent several messages to London warning of the dangers. He would, he told Alexander, write again and go to see Miliukoff, the new Minister of Foreign Affairs, and urge him to make arrangements for the journey of the imperial family. An immediate meeting with Miliukoff and a flurry of telegrams, to and from Whitehall, followed.

The ambassador was told by Miliukoff that as extremists were already agitating against the emperor he was anxious for him to leave Russia. The Foreign Office, when told of this on March 22, replied immediately to Buchanan:

The King and His Majesty's Government readily offer asylum to the Emperor and Empress in England which, it is hoped, they will take advantage of during the war. You should, at the same time, impress upon the Russian Government the necessity for making suitable provision for their maintenance in this country.

This was unequivocal and, for the first time, raised the question of finance: that is, who would pay and what resources could the tsar command. Next day the ambassador received a more urgent telegram from the Foreign Office: 'You should,' he was told cryptically, 'immediately and urgently press Russian Government to give absolute safe conduct to whole Imperial family to Port Romanoff and England as soon as possible.'

The king had been kept informed of these exchanges through his secretary, Lord Stamfordham, and had even sent a personal telegram to Nicholas a few days earlier. 'Events of the last week,' he cabled his cousin, 'have deeply distressed me. My thoughts are constantly with you and I shall always remain your true and devoted friend as you know I have been in the past.' A sympathetic enough message and yet, such were the tensions of the time in Petrograd that it was never delivered.

The cable had been sent by Lord Stamfordham, by way of the Foreign Office, to General Hanbury Williams, who was assumed to be with the emperor at headquarters. The general was unable to deliver the telegram, since Nicholas had already left for Tsarskoe Selo under arrest, and he gave it to the ambassador, who in turn took it round to Miliukoff for delivery direct to Nicholas. The Foreign Minister was full of promises but, in the event, was so fearful of the extremists misinterpreting such a message from one monarch to another (even though deposed) that he failed to do so.

George V was initially irritated that such a simple family gesture should have caused so much discussion in diplomatic circles in London and Petrograd. But, as we now know,[3] as the days passed his anxieties about the wider implications of the presence of the tsar, and especially his German wife, in London during wartime began to grow. Within ten days of the official offer of asylum the king was expressing serious doubts to the Foreign Office, even wondering through Lord Stamfordham whether the invitation might be withdrawn. The Foreign Office, sensing the embarrassments ahead, initially resisted.

Within a matter of weeks, however, not only had the government changed its mind about the desirability of the tsar coming to England but it had finally confirmed to Buchanan the reasons for this, including the king's anxieties, and the need for the original offer to be withdrawn. Lord Hardinge, the head of the Foreign Office and a former Viceroy of India, spelt out the volte-face personally to Buchanan:

Although the King is devoted to the Emperor he is most anxious that he should not come here, for it would make his position extremely difficult. The Radicals and Socialists in the country are hot against the Imperial family coming to England, and although the King has been opposed to the proposal from the very outset it will undoubtedly be attributed to him if they should come here, especially as owing to his relationship and affection for the Emperor he will, as the King told me himself, go out of his way to be civil to him. I cannot blame the King for this but it is very desirable that the Imperial family should not come to England.

He was, he added, sounding out the French government about their attitude but held out few hopes.

By the middle of May Buchanan was able to report to Hardinge what was later described as a tearful meeting with the new Minister for Foreign Affairs, at which he finally brought himself to explain the British government's change of heart.[4] He had clearly been encouraged to do so by the corresponding confession from the Foreign Minister that the Provisional government, in its turn, had no intention at present of allowing the royal family to leave Russia. So both governments had now turned against any plans for immediate asylum in England, one by the pressures of the reigning monarch, the other by the pressure of left-wing extremists. The irony would hardly have been appreciated by the royal family still retained at Tsarskoe Selo.

While this tangled web had been closing in on Nicholas and his family, their financial position had, of necessity, been raised in the discussions both in London and Petrograd. The British government had touched delicately on the question of the cost of their upkeep should they escape to this country early on in the preliminary talks. Prompted by the Foreign Office, Buchanan had asked whether the Provisional government would make 'suitable provision' for the royal family in England. He had been assured that the Provisional government would certainly do so, but had been asked to keep such an assurance confidential in case extremists in Petrograd heard of it.

Buchanan had even gone further and asked about the tsar's own resources. The Foreign Minister, having made immediate inquiries, later told the ambassador[5] that the money question would be 'treated in a liberal spirit' and that, in any case, he believed that His Majesty 'had a large private fortune of his own'. No details were given. But it is clear from evidence given much later, and published in the French report of the Sokolov inquiry into the death of the imperial family, that both Prince Lvov, the first Prime Minister of the Provisional government and Alexander Kerensky, his immediate successor, had also looked into the tsar's resources. They put his personal balances in England and Germany at about 14 million roubles (some £1,400,000).[6] We shall be looking much more closely at these figures later, for they have been used, in part, as the basis for one claim after another.

In the middle of this stalemate, with both London and Petrograd moving away from their original liberal intentions, with both sides discussing financial costs, with the Russian royal family itself grappling with convalescent invalids at Tsarskoe Selo, and with the world still in turmoil, the tsar's brother, Grand Duke Michael, decided to take a personal initiative about himself and Grand Duke George. He called on Sir George Buchanan at the British Embassy and asked whether, if the Russian government would give its consent, they could come to England. Could he also transfer money to London?

Once again the safety of part of the Russian royal family was linked to corresponding financial issues, a theme that was to recur time and again over the next two years. And, not surprisingly, it was the start of a detailed, if at times somewhat unreal, financial correspondence between the Foreign Office and palace officials in London and the Embassy staff in Petrograd. It was symptomatic of the way in which big issues spawned trivial details even in wartime.

The request from Grand Duke Michael to come to England naturally dragged its way slowly through Whitehall, as the fate of the tsar and his immediate family still remained unresolved in Tsarskoe Selo. Several months later Grand Duke George again applied to visit relations in this country, even suggesting that he might travel incognito under the name of 'Mikaeloff'. He also asked whether the Dowager Empress Marie – sister of Queen Alexandra, the queen mother – might be allowed to visit her sister in London. Buchanan naturally felt obliged to approach both London and the Provisional government in Petrograd. London quickly indicated that Grand Duke George was to be discouraged, but that there was no reason why Empress Marie should not come to England.

In Petrograd Buchanan was finally told early in September that the Russian Cabinet had met secretly and had decided that 'certain members' of the Russian royal family were to be allowed to go abroad.[7] The Dowager Empress Marie was to be the first and would be free to go wherever she pleased. Grand Duke Michael would be next and, thereafter, Grand Duke George would probably be allowed to see his family in Sweden or Norway. The Russian Foreign Minister, in informing Buchanan, asked for this decision to be kept secret. He also asked whether Grand Duchess Xenia, the tsar's eldest sister, might accompany her mother. The Foreign Office quickly assented.

Meanwhile the financial hare started by Grand Duke Michael was already beginning to move and leave its mark in Whitehall. He had asked for permission to transfer funds to London: a simple request which quickly embroiled not only the Foreign Office and the British Embassy in Petrograd, but also the equerry to Queen Alexandra, and even the coachman looking after the grand duke's horses.

Michael had told Buchanan that he had been in the habit since 1914 of sending Princess Victoria of Battenberg (sister of tsarina and mother of the future Earl Mountbatten) certain sums of money from time to time for the payment of rent on his country house in England and other expenses. He now wanted to transfer a lump sum, but did not specify how much. After some discussion in Whitehall, and clearly a natural referral to Queen Alexandra's adviser at Marlborough House, Sir Arthur Davidson, Buchanan finally pinned Michael down about the sum involved. It was 100,000 roubles (about £10,000).

Grand Duke Michael's country house had been acquired in rather special circumstances before the war. 'Misha', as Michael was known, had met, fallen in love with and eventually married Natasha Wulfert, a beautiful, twice-married wife of one of Michael's officers in the Blue Cuirassiers. It was a tempestuous affair, played out in Russia and the various capitals of prewar Europe. On one occasion Michael arrived at the Amalienburg Palace in Copenhagen and was greeted by a telegram from Natasha staying at a hotel within walking distance of the palace: 'Arrived Hôtel d'Angleterre. Room 102. Will await you all day impatiently.'

Even when they were apart, travelling separately through Europe, they kept in touch by telegram. In one such spell of frustrated passion, while in Switzerland and Austria, she sent 377 telegrams to Michael.[8] It ended eventually in Natasha having Michael's baby, getting a divorce from her husband, marrying Michael and attracting the natural anger of Michael's brother, the tsar. The upshot was that Natasha was allowed the title of Countess Brassova and both were banished abroad. That was in 1912.

They ended their European journeying in Britain, initially taking a lease of Knebworth House in Hertfordshire from Lord Lytton and eventually settling down in 1914 on Lord Cowdray's estate at Paddockhurst in Sussex. Hardly had they done so than war broke out. In fact Michael's tenancy agreement with Lord Cowdray was dated August 4 and was to run from September 1, 1914 to September 1, 1916. The estate accounts[9] reveal that the lease was not cheap. The estate extended to some three thousand acres close to the South Downs, and Michael was to be charged not far from £3,400 for the first year's tenancy (rental plus running expenses). He was however allowed to deduct any produce, such as eggs, sold to the public. Otherwise he also had to pay for the upkeep of the mansion, the gardens and woodland, including all the staff wages.

Michael had installed his own horses in the grounds, before the outbreak of war and his brother the tsar recalled him to Russia. Memories of those horses are still vivid in the mind of at least one member of the staff, who remembers seeing Russian captions on what were clearly the horses' gravestones in the grounds. The whole estate was eventually sold to Benedictine monks and, during the consequent rebuilding, the gravestones were buried. Insisting that it was consecrated ground, the abbot would not allow the gravestones to be retrieved. So only personal memories now remain. Those of Michael's horses which survived until 1916 – and transferred to another estate, at Ely Grange in Sussex – were to become of sufficient interest to the Foreign Office to warrant secret telegrams to and from Petrograd that year.

The outbreak of war brought Michael not only a pardon from his brother but a last-minute, discreet rebuke from King George V, clearly egged on by the Foreign Office.[10] Lord Stamfordham, his private secretary, was asked to write to the Russian Ambassador, Count Benckendorff, about Michael's German butler. The point was made, in a letter appropriately marked 'secret', that the butler was 'always present at meals where much conversation takes place as to the military situation, position and movement of troops, etc.' The king, through Stamfordham, asked Benckendorff whether he could give a hint to Grand Duke Michael that caution ought to be exercised as to what was said before his butler. The letter also stressed the butler's 'capacity for acquiring news' and hinted at various sources confirming this. The letter was sent on August 8, four days after Britain's entry into the war, and was possibly among the last communications Michael received from his cousin at Buckingham Palace before his departure.

Michael's request to transfer money in 1917 quickly revived many of these memories of his prewar stay in England and soon revealed the complicated way in which royalty was able to maintain overseas property even in wartime. He was clearly reluctant to involve the Russian Ministry of Finance in transferring his money direct and wanted to continue using the method he had been using since 1914. This needed an explanation and Whitehall soon found part of the answer at Marlborough House and the rest from Princess Victoria of Battenberg.

On the outbreak of war, what had clearly happened was that Michael and Natasha had been granted an immediate pardon by Nicholas and left Paddockhurst to return to Russia just after agreeing the cost of its upkeep. On arrival Michael telephoned Princess Victoria asking if he could transfer money, through her, for the rent and other expenses. The arrangements had started on September 22, 1914. Sir Arthur Davidson explained the system to the Foreign Office:

Barings write to Princess Victoria saying they have received instructions from the Ministère des Finance, Section Etrangère, Petrograd, to pay the sum of so many £s to Her Royal Highness and they enclose a cheque for the amount. The cheque is signed by Princess Victoria and is sent to the Comptoir National d'Escomte de Paris, 52 Threadneedle Street, EC to be placed to the credit of Madame Johnson-Missievitch. I hold all Messrs Barings' letters and the receipts for the corresponding amounts mentioned from the Comptoir National. The whole procedure is both clumsy and senseless as obviously the proper course would be for the Ministère des Finance to instruct Barings to pay the amount sent to Madame Johnson-Missievitch direct – the channel of Princess Victoria being wholly unnecessary.[11]

Not surprisingly the Foreign Office wondered about these complications and made further inquiries of Marlborough House. The reasons for them – again, not surprisingly – turned out to be straightforward. Whether by chance or original design, the complex method of payment had one clear advantage to Grand Duke Michael. It enabled him to transfer his roubles in Petrograd to London at par, whereas, as the war progressed, the rouble had gradually lost 15 per cent of its value. But, once questions were asked, the routing of payments through Princess Victoria were immediately stopped.

It was not the last of Whitehall's preoccupations with Grand Duke Michael that spring and summer. Not only did they still have to decide whether his presence would be acceptable in the country; the revolution in Petrograd had also plainly alerted Michael's last landlord in England about Michael's credit-worthiness. And again Sir Arthur Davidson's advice was sought by the Foreign Office.

He felt it only right to mention, in Michael's favour, what he had done before leaving for Russia in 1914. As he explained, Michael's enthusiasms ran to expensive sports cars. Before departure he presented his brand new 80 mph Opel touring car to the War Office, who were then seeking cars for the war effort. He had also, Sir Arthur stressed, placed the house and park of Paddockhurst at the disposal of the War Office for training, billeting or any other purpose they required. As it happened Sir Arthur had advised against full acceptance, because of damage clauses in the lease, and only the stables and outhouses were eventually used by the War Office. But at least a generous offer had been made.

Although Michael continued to pay the rent on Paddockhurst for the first two years of the war, estimated at between £7,000 and £8,000 for the two years, even he found the cost somewhat excessive and had eventually taken Ely Grange, a smaller property at Frant in Sussex, where Madame Johnson-Missievitch (the Russian mother of his private secretary) had been instructed to offer hospitality to the wounded soldiers of the local hospital. This reduced his annual rental to something like £900 a year. But even these smaller payments were soon interrupted by the Revolution and understandably raised questions about his ability to pay.

By mid-June the owner of Ely Grange, a Mr Waddington of Brighton, was beginning to press Whitehall for financial reassurances; otherwise he would be forced to give Grand Duke Michael a legal warning about non-payment. Sir Arthur was anxious to avoid any embarrassment to the royal family, and especially Queen Alexandra, and said as much to the Foreign Office:

There is so much obscurity about the position of the Russian Imperial family – especially in regard to finance – that I should be grateful if you could ascertain, either from Sir George direct or if you could ask him to find out from the Grand Duke Michael as delicately as he can what is his financial position ... If Sir George could telegraph in general terms the Grand Duke's financial situation it could be explained to Mr Waddington.

Sir Arthur also attempted to steer the Foreign Office away from one obvious solution.

It would not do for any members of the English royal family to guarantee payment or to bear responsibility as this would naturally be seized as a pretext by the Provisional government for either reducing or cancelling whatever provision was intended for the Grand Duke so as to throw the onus of any responsibility for English expenses on his English relations.

The upshot was that Michael told Sir George Buchanan that the landlord should not be anxious about the rent and he in turn told Sir Arthur that Michael was trying to get permission unofficially to transfer enough money to pay the current rent. At the same time Sir Arthur reported, from Madame Johnson, that Michael's imperial coachman had become 'insubordinate and insolent' and wanted to know what should she do. This at least was something Michael could cope with. He telegraphed precise instructions through Sir George Buchanan and the Foreign Office: 'The coachman is to be dismissed and the horses left at grass.'[12]

It is still a little difficult to believe that all this took place in the middle of a world war, three months after the March 1917 revolution and while his brother, the tsar, and his family were under arrest. But it is not the only puzzling aspect of the period between the start of the February Revolution and the final Bolshevik *coup d'état* in November. In this same period, while the Provisional government was pursuing revolutionary aims, urged on by the Soviet of Workers' and Soldiers' Deputies, it was also desperately trying to maintain some semblance of normality, both in its conduct of the war and in its own finances.

The Allies were naturally keen to come to terms with the new regime, if only to keep open the eastern front. At the same time western business interests wished to maintain relationships with Russian financial partners. So it seemed only natural in New York and London for discussions to continue on the basis of further loans to their Russian 'ally', whatever its new complexion. An American loan of $75 million was quickly followed by a further loan of $100 million. And the Russians' own internal Liberty Loan was treated with understanding in western capitals. What was somewhat puzzling, looking back on this interim revolutionary period in the light of contemporary State Department documents, was the fact that members of the Romanoff royal family actually subscribed to the internal Liberty Loan. Grand Duke Serge Michaelovitch, for example, subscribed as much as 514,650 roubles (roughly £50,000) to the loan. More surprisingly Nicholas himself was reported in the middle of July, five months after his abdication, to have offered to subscribe to the loan. No doubt pressures of all kinds played their part, especially among the minor Romanoffs, but the ex-emperor's own offer can only have been part of the deals he was being forced to make to pay for his own upkeep in captivity.

While these somewhat unreal financial issues were being faced, the inquiries into the Romanoffs' alleged treason were being undertaken, almost single-handedly, by Kerensky. This was the initial period of his ascendancy, during which he managed to hold the various Soviets at bay and at the same time indulge his new-found power. He spent over three weeks in and out of the Alexander Palace, going through papers, talking to individual courtiers, interviewing both Nicholas and Alexandra and, for a time, keeping them deliberately apart from each other most of the day.

By the late spring he seems to have at last satisfied himself that, whatever their other faults, Nicholas and Alexandra had remained patriotic. It was a short step from that to a reconsideration of their immediate destiny for the rest of the war. Though an overseas destination was now out of the question, the possibility of the Crimea was again mooted. Nicholas too began to talk of their former palace in Livadia, as an alternative to the other possibility of his brother's country estate at Gatchina.

What finally tipped the scales in a completely different direction was the renewal of internal violence and an attempted Bolshevik coup, with all its dangers for the Romanoffs, in early July. Leon Trotsky, who had been prominent in the 1905 revolution, rather than Lenin, who had temporarily fled to Finland, personally stirred up the soldiers and led to the outbreak of severe and extensive rioting on July 4 at the Taurida Palace. Strategic spots all over Petrograd were quickly occupied by troops sympathetic to the Bolsheviks and even the garrison at the Peter and Paul fortress went over to them. The coup seemed almost complete, when the Bolsheviks, and especially Lenin, who was at this precise moment accused of dealing with the German enemy, hesitated, still hardly believing in their ultimate success. It proved to be fatal to their plans, and within twenty-four hours loyal troops of the Provisional government put down the revolt. The episode gave Kerensky a considerable fright and was enough to persuade him to provide a safer refuge for the royal family.

Six days later Kerensky became President of the Provisional government, moved into the Winter Palace (taking over the late Emperor Alexander III's rooms) and, the next day, immediately visited Nicholas to tell him, quite bluntly, that the Bolsheviks were now after him as President 'and then will be after you'. He asked the family to start packing and to be ready for departure in a few days. And on July 25 Colonel Kobylinski, who had become the new Commandant, arrived to inform Nicholas that their departure would take place on the night of July 31 and that the journey would take three or four days.

From various hints over the next few days, what was left of the court quickly guessed their destination was to be Siberia, not the Crimea. Three days before departure Count Benckendorff realised it was to be Tobolsk. He also realised that a major turning point was facing the royal family: in deciding what to pack and what to leave behind in Tsarskoe Selo, they were in essence at last being forced to decide what possessions were really personal to the royal family and what belonged to the state.

The first practical question was the length of their possible stay in Tobolsk: should they simply take sufficient clothes and other personal things for a few weeks or a few months or even longer? When approached on this Kerensky left a strong impression that the royal family would be away for only 'a few months' and even told Benckendorff that in the month of November, little more than four months away, once the Constituent Assembly was closed, there was nothing to prevent them returning to Tsarskoe Selo, or going elsewhere should they wish.

Whether Kerensky himself really believed this or not is difficult to assess. Benckendorff certainly did not, but was still determined to arrange the royal packing on the basis of such a return. So by the eve of departure he had already persuaded the family to divide what they regarded as their possessions into two distinct groups: things to be packed into their luggage and things to be locked up in the private apartments for their later return. The luggage was hardly inconsiderable for in addition to the clothes, jewels, books and other personal effects of the seven members of the family, including the tsar's stamp collection, there was the luggage of their companions, advisers and servants, quite apart from kitchen utensils, cutlery and even several cases of wine from the palace's cellar, which Benckendorff had insisted on including not only to liven up the journey but for any possible cellar at Tobolsk. It eventually took fifty men over three hours to have it all moved from individual rooms to the waiting cars en route for the two trains awaiting them at the Alexandrovskaya station.

Both the departure from the palace and the accompanying 'goodbyes' in the antechamber, stretched out interminably from the original expected departure time of 1 a.m. to the actual time of 7.30 a.m. In that time Kerensky visited them twice, on the first occasion bringing Grand Duke Michael for a poignant and embarrassing final farewell, played out semi-publicly before Kerensky and the officer on duty, Michael eventually emerging in tears, having hardly noticed, as he later said, whether his brother was looking well or not. They were never to meet again. Other embarrassments followed. Despairing of sleep or even rest while they awaited the absent cars, Benckendorff's wife tried to arrange tea for everyone, and the former emperor asked if he could join in. Immediately several officers got up and refused to sit at the same table. Benckendorff himself, having said his formal farewells to the former emperor and empress the previous day, took leave of him again around 4 a.m. and finally, once more, at 6.30 a.m.

Even when they reached the station to board one of the two trains, the *wagons-lits* of the International Sleeping Car Company, Nicholas and Alexandra had to walk for about 50 yards because the train was in a siding; and since no steps were available the empress had to be hoisted on to the train and even the grand duchesses had difficulty in getting aboard. Thus a combination of avoidable inefficiencies and deliberate, provocative actions marked their last sad hours in what had always been their favourite home.

4

Captive

By all accounts the family's three-day rail journey to Tyumen, where they had to transfer for a further two days by boat to Tobolsk, was not too uncomfortable. They were in the first of the two trains, with sleeper accommodation and a restaurant car for themselves and their immediate suite. The second train carried their remaining servants and the military escort which was also to guard them on arrival in Tobolsk. Although they largely travelled with the curtains drawn, arrangements had been made for regular stops of an hour or so in the open country, so that they could stretch their legs.

Apart from the former empress, who remained somewhat aloof, everyone took a walk along the railway line. There was the inevitable intermingling of passengers at these stops and a feeling of a 'shared adventure'. One of the escorts later remarked how delightful and cheerful the royal children were, though he was surprised at their lack of knowledge of Shakespeare. They and Nicholas entered into the spirit of their simple daily exercise; even played games. Alexis survived the journey well, but fell over on arrival at Tyumen and had to be carried on board the awaiting steamer. From there on the weather deteriorated, and their final day on what was a somewhat overcrowded boat was both rainy and melancholy.

At Tobolsk little or nothing had been prepared. Benckendorff's stepson, Prince Basil Dolgorukov, who accompanied the family and throughout these early hardships kept in touch with Benckendorff in Petrograd, described the scene graphically:

What we found made a terrible impression on us and completely contradicted Kerensky's wonderful promises. He had talked of a chic place with a bakery, confectionery, wine cellar, etc. Nothing of the sort. We found a dirty, smelly house closed for a long time containing thirteen rooms with a few bits of furniture and disgusting baths and toilets. Also there were five attic rooms for the servants ... I am outraged by the criminal negligence of the authorities.[1]

The Governor's House in Tobolsk had until recently been used by troops as a barracks and had plainly not been cleaned since. Eight days were spent acquiring furniture, cleaning, painting and putting the house back into some sort of order, while the family remained on the boat in very small cabins, taking it all rather calmly. Food at least seemed plentiful with adequate supplies of eggs, butter, milk and fish. There were no shops to speak of in town, but a good chemist.

The choice of Tobolsk was ostensibly a matter of choosing a spot where the Provisional government could be assured of the family's safety. Siberia was said to be safer to reach than the Crimea because of the fewer Soviet-dominated regions en route; and Tobolsk, a former capital of Siberia with a population of only twenty thousand, was 200 miles from the nearest railway and very much a backwater. As one of those accompanying the family put it, 'Had it not been for several large whitewashed churches and a few government buildings, it would have been impossible to guess that Tobolsk was not a plain village of wooden shacks, with dirt roads for streets, a few wooden planks thrown carelessly here and there substituting for sidewalks.'

The move to Siberia had inevitably reduced the accompanying court staff even further. Immediately after the abdication courtiers and servants had been faced with whether or not to continue in Nicholas's service. Count Benckendorff, as Grand Marshal of the Court, had been advised to cut down the number of court staff in the interests of economy and, no doubt, revolutionary fervour. That was in early March. Three months later, as catering costs continued to rise, further belt-tightening had been imposed. And on the transfer to Siberia the same combination of loyalty and economy left its toll on numbers.

The inner suite accompanying the family to Tobolsk was thus reduced to Countess Anastasia Hendrikoff, the former empress's lady-in-waiting; Catherine Schneider and Pierre Gilliard, two tutors to the children (Sydney Gibbes, Alexis's English tutor, arrived later); Eugene Botkin, the doctor; Prince Dolgorukov; and General Tatischev, who had taken Benckendorff's place as head of the household. The commandant in charge of the troops and all financial arrangements was Colonel Koby-linski. Although Baroness Sophie Buxhoeveden, Alexandra's lady-in-waiting, was invited to join the family, illness and a subsequent oper-ation prevented her and she eventually reached Tobolsk three months later.

Count Benckendorff was thus deliberately left behind in Tsarskoe Selo to clear up outstanding questions and, initially, to look after his wife who had bronchitis. But it is now clear that the problems that needed sorting out were crucial ones for Nicholas, particularly if, as he still seems to have hoped, he might eventually be allowed to return to the Alexander Palace. Before departure from the palace he had in fact given Benckendorff 'several commissions with regard to his private interests'. It is not hard to guess what they were.

The dilemma faced by the royal family in having to decide what to pack for their journey and what to leave behind was only the preliminary step in a far wider decision now facing both them and the Provisional government. Benckendorff had already broached the problem with Fedor Golovin, the man appointed as Commissioner for the Ministry of the Court, when they had had to cope with the rising costs of the imperial household. In short how were they going to work out Nicholas's personal resources?

In the middle of August, once he knew of the imperial family's safe arrival in Tobolsk, Benckendorff called on Golovin in the Winter Palace, where he, like so many other functionaries in the Provisional government, had established their offices. Golovin's rooms were on the ground floor overlooking the river Neva. Above him on the second floor, in Alexander III's apartment, was Kerensky's new suite of offices.

Golovin was a reasonably balanced individual. He had gained rec-ognition from his work in the Zemstvo, the system of provincial and local self-government, and as a former President of the Second Duma. In the eyes of one of his appointees he was 'kindly, highly cultured, perfect in manners and an enlightened public man'. Not only was he now in direct charge of the finances of the court in these new circumstances; he was also responsible for the new art committees set up to monitor, catalogue and, indirectly, protect all the works of art in the royal palaces.[2] Paul Benckendorff eventually found him to be someone he could do business with; and he had much to do.

On arrival Benckendorff was shocked at what he found in the Winter Palace. Kerensky, in his fear for his own safety, had plainly surrounded himself with scores of troops, who were stationed in all the corridors and rooms of what had once been a show-piece of tsarist Russia. 'The dirt,' according to Benckendorff, 'was appalling.' His assessment is not the only one we have. One of Golovin's own staff has left us with a further description:

When Kerensky stayed in the Palace, it was like an armed and watchful camp in battle order. Military units of every kind – infantry, artillerymen, sailors – periodically [replaced] each other and filled the better half of the passages and some of the ball rooms, i.e. the Nicholas and White Halls, the Portrait Gallery and others. There were always several hundred men there, with rifles on stands and revolvers in their pockets. A good half of them would snore all day long, unconcernedly stretched out all over the floors, blocking doors and entrances with their prostrate bodies ... vulgar harmoniums resounded through the old Palace for the first time ... The Palace became unrecognisable ... Floors and walls were covered with filth of all descriptions, statues in the White Hall festooned with wet towels, caps, tunics, jackets, sword-belts, coats ... So began the gradual destruction of Rastrelli's inspired work.[3]

Benckendorff was thus surrounded, on his visit to Golovin at the Winter Palace, with ample evidence that the Provisional government had not only decided that the palaces were now the property of the state, and not of the former tsar, but had occupied them as such. His main purpose, of course, was to clarify on Nicholas's behalf exactly what he could now regard as his own property. Even though he must have known what the answer would be he still reminded Golovin that the Romanoff family regarded the estates of Livadia in the Crimea and Alexandria at Peterhof as their own private property, since they had bought them themselves. Livadia had been acquired by Alexander II from Count Potocki in the 1860s and furnished from private funds; Alexandria had been passed down within the Romanoff family until Alexander III had bequeathed it to his widow, the Empress Marie, Nicholas's mother. But all to no avail. As Golovin now explained, the Provisional government simply regarded all the palaces and other 'royal' estates as state property.

When the contents of the palaces were raised, Golovin seemed willing to discuss individual items separately, without final commitment. He assured Benckendorff that personal manuscripts and documents, as well as other items such as those at present locked away separately in the family's private quarters at Tsarskoe Selo, would be safeguarded. As for the empress's jewellery, apart from individual items that she and her daughters had carefully packed in their luggage to Tobolsk, that had mainly been deposited in the storerooms of the Imperial Office. So had her furs, gowns and other clothing. Special gifts still regarded as their own, such as the large silver service given to Nicholas as a wedding present from his father, Alexander III, were also in store in one or other of the palaces. Although Golovin promised to support Benckendorff's claim that these should be restored to the former emperor, their subsequent fate after the Bolshevik take-over in October was quite different.

In prompting Benckendorff what issues to raise with Golovin, Nicholas had not forgotten other people, especially his mother and the royal servants. Empress Marie had no private fortune of her own to fall back on, and no regular income, simply her personal jewellery. Either Benckendorff was particularly persuasive or Golovin excessively sympathetic but it was quickly decided that Marie would be allowed to retain her marriage settlement income of 300,000 roubles and all her personal jewels, works of art and other possessions. As for the royal servants, Nicholas's earlier promises to them of adequate pensions and other family subsidies, which he felt strongly should be confirmed by the new regime, were not immediately ruled out by Golovin.

Benckendorff was also aware that Alexandra had been keeping the jewels of her eldest sister, Princess Victoria of Battenberg, in her personal keeping throughout the war. She and her daughter, Princess Louise, had been visiting St Petersburg when war broke out in 1914 and, in their haste to get back to London and fearful of the dangers en route through Finland and Sweden, had left them with Alexandra. They had not been forgotten in the imperial family's departure for Tobolsk and had been carefully packed in a special case and sent to the Imperial Office. As Benckendorff told Golovin, a receipt had been prepared and was now in the hands of a Mrs Geringer. Again Golovin promised to help.

All these were important matters, but they were no more than a preliminary to the meaty question of Nicholas's private fortune and the income he had previously relied upon from the state budget and the crown lands (the so-called 'udely' or 'appanage' income) from which he had financed not only the rest of the Romanoff family but the running costs of the palaces, the royal yacht, the trains, theatres, ballet schools and hospitals and so on. Golovin had a quick answer. Not only did the crown lands, and therefore the income arising from them, now belong to the state, but the royal family could no longer expect to receive money from either the crown lands or the Civil List. The state would simply look after the cost of their welfare, that is, their day-to-day expenses. No more, no less. Golovin did, however, give Benckendorff one major assurance: the former tsar's private fortune, specifically defined as 'those sums which he actually held and which were administered by Count Rostovtsev, the Empress's secretary' would be formally recognised as his.

As Benckendorff must have instinctively realised, this was a mixture of good and bad news for the former tsar. Nicholas had already, in effect, lost personal control of state expenditure and to that extent could no longer influence either the state budget or other affairs relating to the Romanoff family. At the same time the burden of having to distribute such money as he felt able to squeeze out of state coffers, and all the pain and anguish that such family financial affairs inevitably brought with them, would now be lifted from his shoulders.

In short, though Benckendorff must have found it hard to accept, Nicholas had been given something of a financial breathing space. Whether in the shock and turmoil arising from abdication, arrest and the consequent fears for the future he and Alexandra could be persuaded to regard Golovin's decisions in that light was another matter. Their life, their beliefs and their expectations had been shattered. The assumptions on which all their financial decisions had previously been made had been destroyed. But at least while the Provisional government remained in office, and provided they could rely upon Golovin's financial assurances, the family had been allowed the remnants of their private funds and, where these could be defined, their private possessions. Yet even that narrow cushion was soon to be squeezed further.

The break with the past, now spelt out by Golovin, was fundamental. At a stroke the three-hundred-year encroachment of the Romanoffs on the state finances had come to an end. In spite of the 1905 revolution, in spite of democratic promises to successive Dumas, and in spite of the extension of crown lands to some of the peasants, the money the reigning tsar could extract from the State Budget (the equivalent of the British Civil List distribution to members of the royal family) and from the crown lands (that is, the 'udely' or 'appanage' income, the equivalent of the income from the Duchies of Lancaster and Cornwall for the British royal family) had been virtually at his command alone. Even in the last peacetime budget of 1913, the basic money allotted to the Ministry of the Imperial Household was made up of 'grants not to be debated on by the legislative institutions and grants not subject to reduction': the twin hallmarks of an autocratic ruler.[4] Now all that was gone.

What is of continuing interest, particularly in any attempt to assess Nicholas's real wealth, is what the last tsar had felt obliged to do with the money he was able to allocate annually to himself. The gap between the money paid to him by the state and that spent by him as head of state and as head of the Romanoff family was not always as great as is generally assumed. His obligations were not inconsiderable. Take his close relatives alone. Each grand duke was entitled to 280,000 roubles (roughly £28,000) a year and each grand duchess received an individual dowry of 1 million roubles (£100,000) on her marriage. Such titles were given to the children and grandchildren of emperors. Generations beyond these were given the title of prince or princess and received 1 million roubles at their birth as a final settlement.[5] The number of grand dukes varied considerably over the century before the Revolution. There were twenty-three at the turn of the century and fifteen in 1917. So, by simple arithmetic, it can be calculated that it was costing Nicholas between, say, 6,440,000 roubles (£644,000) a year and 4,200,000 roubles (£420,000) a year to maintain the grand dukes in that period.

It was not his only expenditure on the upkeep of his close relations and their royal way of life. The budget funds provided annually to the so-called Ministry of the Imperial Household were expected to cover the expenditure of the individual palaces, the grand ducal households and other similar institutions, as well as the cost of the imperial theatres (three in St Petersburg and two in Moscow) and the ballet schools attached to them, the Imperial Academy of Arts, the Archaeological Commission and the Museum of Alexander III. The expenditure went on people as well as buildings. The Winter Palace alone employed some twelve hundred servants, all with wages and pensions, and the Alexander Palace another six hundred. Beyond all that, grants were provided to run the tsar's own administrative office and to foot the bill to meet individual petitions presented to him, whether for the completion of a church roof or an individual in need.

Three separate sources fed this continuing tsarist appetite.[6] Romanoff inheritance from the land, the capital value of which was worth some 100 million roubles (£10 million), produced 'udely' income of around 2,500,000 roubles (£250,000) annually, not perhaps as good a return as might have been expected. In addition some 6,500,000 roubles (£650,000) came from the interest on foreign bank deposits, though this was a variable amount. But the bulk of Nicholas's annual income was provided from the State Budget, the amount averaging some 11 million roubles (£1 million) in the prewar years. In total, from these three sources he could expect up to 20 million roubles (£2 million) a year to cover his imperial outgoings.

All this had now been cut off at source. Paul Benckendorff thus left the Winter Palace, following his meeting with Golovin, appalled at what he had seen, but with a realistic assessment of what the royal family could now expect from the state. He knew the worst, or thought he did, and provided he could rely on individual assurances – Kerensky's about the future home of the royal family and Golovin's concerning Nicholas's private funds and possessions – his main concern now was to ensure that he could keep sufficiently in touch with Dolgorukov, his stepson, and the royal entourage in Siberia, and advise them accordingly.

Apart from the shambles on arrival in Tobolsk, he knew that Colonel Kobylinski, the appointed commandant, was not only a conscientious officer but had been provided with 50,000 roubles to cover the costs of travel and settling in. He also knew that the government had agreed to pay for the servants and the royal suite and that Nicholas himself would simply be asked to pay 140 roubles a day for himself, his wife and children. This was to cover 'full pension' – breakfast, lunch and dinner – at 20 roubles a head for the seven members of the royal family. One of the first letters received from his stepson in Tobolsk, in the second half of August, had other reassuring news.

Prince Dolgorukov had discussed further details of the Provisional government's intentions towards the royal family with Makarov, the commissioner who had escorted them to Tobolsk and who, basically, was Golovin's assistant. He was known to be a good friend of Kerensky and in tune with the new leader's thoughts. In deliberately talking about the royal family's money problems, Makarov said that the Minister of the Court was preparing a draft law to present to the Constitutional Assembly 'to allocate funds to the Emperor and all his family to enable them to live with dignity and comfort abroad'. Makarov also indicated that the Gatchina Palace might eventually be regarded as Nicholas's private property and that several million works of art and jewels had already been sent from the Winter Palace and elsewhere for safe-keeping to Moscow. 'All of this and other wealth which still belongs to Him is perfectly safe.'[7] Whether true or not, a good deal of this, especially the reference to the provision of state funds to enable the family to live abroad, was more than Golovin had vouchsafed a few weeks earlier. But it had the ring of good intentions that the Provisional government was still proclaiming privately in the late summer of 1917.

In the early days in Tobolsk the imperial family found that the atmosphere, both inside and outside the house, was much more relaxed. Political agitation had hardly penetrated the region. The soldiers guarding them, though hardly over-sympathetic, were less aggressive and volatile than in the Alexander Palace. And many of the locals, while prompted to gather outside the house out of curiosity, remained friendly enough.

The family, however, still had to get used to living in a much more restricted space than at Tsarskoe Selo, occupying no more than the first floor of the house. Their movements were similarly restricted. During the whole of their stay in Tobolsk, from the beginning of August to the following May, no member of the family was allowed to take a walk outside the house, apart from a small period in the early winter months, when they were taken once a week under escort to a church service. Otherwise they were confined to their rooms or to a small courtyard at the side of the house, fashioned out of part of an unpaved street surrounded by a wooden fence some 8 to 10 feet high. This space was 'dusty when dry, a quagmire in spring and summer and a deep snow plain in winter', according to one of the royal suite. 'Beyond that the house had no garden, unless a tiny cabbage patch could be called by that name. It was pitiful for the children.' In contrast the courtiers, who were lodged in a house immediately opposite the Governor's House, were able to go into town unescorted, at least for the first few months.

Nicholas and Alexandra not only had to come to terms with their new surroundings but also with their prospects. They did it in different ways. Nicholas bore the burden stoically, keeping in touch as best he could with outside events and occupying his hours with a mixture of exercise, reading and a deliberate routine. Alexandra hardly ventured outside, and concentrated on a variety of occupations from embroidery to painting and from letter-writing to playing the piano. The children, grown up though some of them were, still had regular lessons from 9 to 11 every morning. Only Olga was excused. Lessons in Russian, mathematics and English were given by the tutors. As in Tsarskoe Selo, Alexandra gave lessons in theology, history and German. Nicholas also helped Alexis with his history.

But it was not all work. During the day, before the onset of winter, most of them took what exercise and distractions they could. 'We continue to saw and cut logs and it is nice to go out,' Olga wrote to a friend from Tobolsk. 'We mended our swing and now we can once again start to use it. But probably the ropes will get torn as they are badly made.' (Alas, it wasn't the rope which eventually stopped them using the swing, but indecent words written on it by their guards.) After dinner in the evenings, everyone assembled upstairs, some to play patience, some bridge, some bezique. Occasionally Nicholas would read aloud to everyone. Plays too were put on by the children, from Russian classics to Edwardian comedies, under the gentle guidance of the tutors Gilliard and Gibbes. One in particular became memorable, a farce by Edward Grattan, in which sixteen-year-old Anastasia played the main male part. At the end of the play she had to turn her back to the audience, adjust her dressing-gown and say her final line. On one occasion her hand caught the side of her gown and, without realising what she had done, she pulled it all the way up her back, exposing to the audience her chubby legs and bottom packed into her father's Jaeger underwear. The audience collapsed and she remained blithely unaware of what had provoked it.

'I shall always remember that night,' said Gibbes many years later. 'It was the last hearty, unrestrained laughter the Empress ever enjoyed.'[8] He was probably right, for it was at Tobolsk that their situation deteriorated, initially out of neglect, ultimately because of the Bolshevik take-over in October and the subsequent decisions made in Petrograd and elsewhere. The winter brought their first real challenge. The Siberian winter, they discovered, is like no other. 'There is no escape from a temperature of forty below zero,' one of their companions later wrote:

Neither walls nor stoves can keep such cold out. One shivers at the moment of awakening, one shivers throughout the day, one shivers going to bed, one keeps on shivering in one's sleep ... One can't work, one can't even think, one can only sit in despair and shiver, certain that never again will one be able to breathe freely. In short, one no longer lives during the Siberian winter but merely vegetates in a sort of frozen stupor.

And to this was added a growing anxiety about food, or at least its cost.

In the early weeks in Tobolsk the family ate simply but well. Lunch consisted of soup, fish, meat and dessert, with coffee being served separately upstairs. Dinner was similar with rather more fruit included. At first Kobylinski had little difficulty in providing such meals: he had an initial money reserve to call on and local shopkeepers and farms to provide what he needed. Even after several weeks, during which he submitted accounts to Petrograd for payment, he still continued to assume that money would be transferred on a regular basis. He was slowly proved wrong, however, and in spite of persistent requests to Golovin and others in the Winter Palace, he received no reply. By the end of October he was facing a financial crisis. He had virtually run out of ready cash, he already owed shopkeepers money and the servants had had no wages since the beginning of August. He calculated that he needed 100,000 roubles (about £70,000) immediately.

He quickly persuaded Dolgorukov to send a *cri de coeur* to his stepfather, Benckendorff, in Petrograd, seeking either a credit through the State Bank or a messenger with cash. He reported that bills already submitted to, but still unpaid by, the Provisional government totalled 85,000 roubles. Dolgorukov added a forlorn postscript to his letter: 'They have forgotten us in Petrograd.' And they continued to do so. The upshot was that servants and others remained unpaid and Kobylinski, Tatischev and Dolgorukov were forced to sign a bill of exchange under their own names to raise 20,000 roubles at the State Bank.[9] It was the start of essential fund-raising, the scraping together of money from a variety of sources, including Nicholas's own private accounts.

Apart from elements of deliberate neglect, the Provisional government had much else on its mind: the conduct of the war; the social problems it had both exploited and inherited; and, above all, its continuing skirmishes with the Bolsheviks. The former imperial family hardly merited a side glance from such pressing issues. Kerensky in particular had been grappling first with the dangers of a counter-revolution, whether real or imagined, from General Kornilov; then with the not unexpected boost which such a right-wing effort was bound to have on the Soviets; and finally with the German encroachment on Petrograd itself.

Not unnaturally Kerensky began to see enemies on all sides, even among the military command whose basic aim was a patriotic defence of the country but whose efforts to restore discipline among the troops inevitably seemed otherwise. And, hardly surprisingly, the Bolsheviks under Lenin's leadership chose such an atmosphere to convene a crucial Congress of Soviets, under their own domination. Given their determination, it was a brief step from all this to the formation of a 'Soviet' specifically designed to defend the capital, not only from the German enemy, but from domestic enemies too.

The details of Lenin's return to Petrograd and of the day-by-day plotting that led to the Bolshevik coup on October 25, to the downfall of Kerensky's Provisional government, and to the noisy intervention of the cruiser *Aurora*, have been recounted many times. That it brought about a dramatic change in the potential fortunes, both general and financial, of the former tsar and his family is our sole concern.

Such a development now seems to have been inevitable. But the final Bolshevik coup was by no means regarded as such by many informed contemporaries. Nowhere were such blinkers kept in place so long as in the financial world; and nowhere were the first impacts seen so quickly. Consider the views and actions of National City Bank, New York's leading overseas bank, during that fateful year. Having had a representative in Russia for some years, the bank chose mid-January, 1917 to open its first branch in Petrograd. A month later its American manager was reporting positively back to head office: 'We are working hard and I think the position of our Petrograd branch at the end of this year will be a most pleasant surprise, even to you.' He was 'anxious to start another branch in Moscow as soon as possible'.[10] Even when disturbances broke out a few weeks later, he continued to maintain a more than brave face: 'The Russian Revolution, no inkling of which reached us until yesterday afternoon, seems to be received with apathy by people whose appetites are jaded by sensation. The stock market remains firm in the face of it all.' Throughout that summer and autumn both the American government and National City Bank continued to provide extensive dollar loans to the Provisional government.

This was not an isolated aberration on the part of American bankers alone. Their actions in opening branches in Russia had not gone unnoticed in London, whose bankers were still relying on individual representatives and on what are known as correspondent banks in Petrograd. (Correspondent banking is basically where, say, a London-based bank will undertake business for a Russian bank in London as a quid pro quo for the Russian bank doing similar business on its behalf in Russia.) London and New York banks were watching each other warily throughout the war, partly because the centre of international finance had switched temporarily to New York during hostilities, but mainly because both centres had their eyes on areas formerly dominated or influenced by Berlin. Russia was a prime example and it continued to fascinate British and American bankers as a future potential market long after the danger signals were there for all to see.

London banks began to put pressure on the British government to help them follow the National City Bank's example, in spite of the political turmoil still unfolding in Petrograd. The Foreign Office was approached early in July by the British Bank for Foreign Trade seeking its help in opening a Russian branch. They made the point that Russian banks were free to operate in London and that four were already well established there. Moreover not only was the National City Bank operating in Petrograd, but the Paris-based Credit Lyonnais had been operating there for some time. Why not a British bank? A few weeks later the London City and Midland Bank made similar approaches both to the Foreign Office and to the Ministry of Finance in Petrograd. The British Trade Corporation also applied to open a subsidiary in Russia. All received strong support from Sir George Buchanan in Petrograd and the Foreign Office in London.

The London City and Midland Bank eventually received the State Bank's approval to open a branch within days of the October coup. National City Bank actually opened its Moscow branch *after* the coup and, according to a Foreign Office telegram from Petrograd,[11] was offering depositors guarantees of repayment in roubles in New York 'even if they should be confiscated by the Bolshevik authorities'. They reportedly received deposits of 300 million roubles on this basis in the month of December. All this is hard to believe. But such blindness was hardly confined to New York. On the telegram reporting these American moves to the Foreign Office in Whitehall, dated December 29, 1917, are written two approving, hardly tongue-in-cheek, comments: 'This is evidently the way to do business'; and, 'A very smart stroke.'

How smart was quickly revealed by the brutal actions of the Bolshevik authorities. The first warning had come in *Pravda* on November 23, when an article on page 1 reported that it had become 'necessary to annul all war loans either granted to, or guaranteed by, previous Russian governments'. The paper gave details of the first draft decrees. A few weeks later the banking system felt the first impact. On December 14 banking was declared to have become a state monopoly. And on December 27, without prior notice, all private banks in Petrograd were closed and a decree nationalising them announced. That same day a squad of Red guards marched into the National City Bank and demanded the keys. The manager refused. He was immediately placed under arrest and marched to the headquarters of the revolutionary government at the Smolny Institute. Two days later deposits belonging to 'wealthy' depositors were declared to belong to the state. 'Small' depositors and 'small' investments in securities were assured for the time being. By mid-January the Bolsheviks were even insisting on opening all safety deposits. Bolshevik harassing of the 'wealthy' had begun.

The financial repercussions were felt at once. Before the end of 1917 the head of international banking in National City Bank had resigned and, once the true damage to the bank became known, other resignations followed, including that of the President of the bank itself, Frank Vanderlip, who had been personally responsible for its overseas expansion. The Russian venture left the bank with $5 million of virtually worthless Russian securities, a further $2 million lent to Russian creditors and some $26 million worth of deposits in its newly opened Russian branches.[12] On the other hand, a point which was overlooked at the time though has loomed much larger since, National City Bank happened to have tsarist deposits in New York. The true ownership and size of those deposits will be occupying our attention in due course.

The imperial family had hardly been cut off from news of the momentous events as they unfolded in Petrograd. They were simply delayed. As late as November 24 Nicholas was writing in his diary: 'No newspapers or telegrams have come from Petrograd for some time. At such a grave time this is serious.' Three days later he knew the worst: 'Heartbreaking to learn from the papers descriptions of what happened two weeks ago at Petrograd and Moscow. It is much worse and more dishonourable than before.' And as the winter went on changes in their treatment and in the people put in charge of them began to reflect the spread of Bolshevik influence throughout Siberia.

The first change came from the replacement of the older guard by younger troops fresh from the turmoil in Petrograd and imbued with hatred for all tsarist affairs. They were quick to resent what they saw as privileges. They objected to members of the imperial suite being able to go into town unescorted. So sentry escorts were imposed and visits were restricted to two hours twice a week. When a consignment of non-vintage wine arrived from Petrograd (a small glass had been prescribed by the doctors for the children at lunchtime), the soldiers took hold of the cases, broke all the bottles and poured all the contents into the Irtych river.

Nicholas did not escape these acts of pique. On one occasion he had dressed himself in a Caucasian tribal dress complete with dagger. It led to an immediate search for weapons. Then they noticed that he was occasionally reading *The Times* when copies arrived from London. They were immediately suspicious of a foreign paper and the local Soviet insisted that it should be translated into Russian and submitted to their censorship daily. Later, as earlier in Petrograd, the soldiers insisted that all officers would no longer wear shoulder straps indicating their rank. Even the commandant Kobylinski was forced to comply. Worse was to follow. They then insisted that the former emperor's shoulder straps too should be removed in their presence. Kobylinski did his best to persuade them otherwise, but was eventually obliged to advise Nicholas to put on a black sheepskin coat to avoid any future aggravation.

In their way these were no more than irritants. But official acts, reflecting the same revolutionary sentiments, soon followed. Not only had the Bolsheviks taken over all the banks and requisitioned the deposits of all wealthy citizens, they were now to impose maximum allowances on the former imperial family. On February 20 Kobylinski received a telegram from Petrograd stating quite bluntly: 'Nicholas Romanoff and his family must be put on soldiers' rations and each member of the family will receive 600 roubles per month drawn from the interest of their personal estate.' The minimum of 600 roubles a month was the guaranteed wage established by the new Bolshevik government not only for all servants in private houses, but also for everyone employed by the state. For the seven members of the royal family it implied a total allowance of no more than 4,200 roubles a month; they would also be expected to find the money from their own resources at the State Bank. Heating and lighting was to be paid separately by the government.

The new regime was due to start on March 1. It meant that the amount available for food was to be severely reduced and that the wages of a number of the servants could no longer be met. A completely new budget was needed. Pierre Gilliard, the French tutor, later reported that Nicholas came to see him and jokingly announced that, since everyone seemed to be appointing committees, or Soviets, he was going to do the same and appoint one to look after the welfare of his own community. Gilliard, Dolgorukov and Tatischev were immediately given the task of working out what could be afforded.

'The imperial table', as it was still called, was cut down to 5 roubles per person a day, from which two courses at lunch and dinner, soup included, could be paid for. Sweet courses and coffee were cut out immediately. Sugar and butter too were regarded as luxuries. The few remaining courtiers and tutors were forced to pay for their own food. But the main blow fell on the servants. It was clear that at least nine could no longer be afforded from the new budget. These were people who out of loyalty had deliberately decided to follow the royal family to Siberia and were now to be deprived of any means of support. It was a personal grief to Nicholas that he was incapable of helping them all. But he did what he could from spare cash he had been able to put aside. While several servants persisted in staying without pay, three were given enough money to get back to Petrograd.

Although delays continued in the reimbursement of funds to maintain the family and their guards in Tobolsk, leading to housekeeping crises, the plight of the family eventually led to money emerging from various supportive quarters. Nicholas, Alexandra and the children were all in correspondence with friends by letter, and other means of communication grew up during that winter. Count Benckendorff in Petrograd and his stepson Prince Dolgorukov in Tobolsk also kept in touch regularly, and arrangements for the transfer of lump sums gradually emerged. All kinds of well-wishers came forward: friends and former courtiers in Petrograd, a millionaire in Moscow, a foreign ambassador, local monasteries, and even shopkeepers in Tobolsk offering eggs, fish, or meat whenever urgently needed. Anna Vyrubova, for so long Alexandra's almost sole confidante in Tsarskoe Selo, then living in lodgings in Petrograd, acted as a 'go-between' for some of them. 'Poor as were the small group of

friends who worked with me to communicate with the Imperial family,'
she wrote some years later:

we managed to get to them the necessities they lacked. Dangerous and difficult
as travel was in those days, every traveller being almost certain to be searched
several times along the way, there were three, two officers and a young girl, who
at the risk of imprisonment and death by the most unspeakable tortures, calmly
and fearlessly acted as emissaries back and forth between Petrograd and remote
Tobolsk.

At first the traffic was not all one way. Alexandra sent coffee, flour, tea
and lapscha (a sort of macaroni) and even Christmas presents made by
her and her daughters. In return over those early months Alexandra was
brought a dressing-gown, red slippers, a little perfume, brooches for
the girls, books for them all, and of course news, which she discreetly
reciprocated. Nicholas also kept in touch with his mother and sisters.

As conditions deteriorated, small sums of money replaced gifts.
Although Alexandra asked Anna personally not to send any further
money, in a letter as late as January, both Kobylinski and Dolgorukov in
Tobolsk and Benckendorff in Petrograd had for some time been deliberately seeking funds to pay for the upkeep of the family and their entire
suite. They had not been disappointed.

One of the largest individual sums was donated by Carol Yaroshinsky,
a wealthy financier and industrialist, who provided 175,000 roubles over
a period of close on six months. Yaroshinsky had previously organised
and financed a hospital at Tsarskoe Selo. He later approached the British
government and tried to involve them in a scheme to gain control of
several Russian banks. British officials thought well of him.[13] Beyond that
a foreign ambassador (whose name Benckendorff does not reveal either
in his book or in his private papers) gave him 'a very large sum, sufficient
to cover costs for several months'. The Danish minister, hearing that
former Empress Marie was also running short of money in the Crimea,
where she had fled from Kiev, gave Benckendorff 25,000 roubles. It took
a French governess all of four weeks to travel the 1,200 miles to the
Crimea with the cash.

As the news of money difficulties spread to the public, more offers
came in. Friends in Moscow joined together and with the help of one
particular family, who contributed half the total, produced 200,000
roubles. The sum was sent direct to Dolgorukov in Tobolsk and, according
to Benckendorff, was one of the reasons why the Bolsheviks finally decided
to move the family from Tobolsk.

It was not the only reason. 'Unfortunately the comings and goings and
probably also the money, which was in the hands of the suite, raised
suspicions and around the month of April the letters from my stepson

Dolgorukov,' Benckendorff wrote later, 'talked of the appearance of new commissioners, of new upsets and eventually of rumours which were going round on the subject of a probable change of residence.'[14] The rumours were forerunners of the last fateful stage of the royal family's journey to Ekaterinburg.

5

Massacre

Nicholas had stoically accepted all the humiliations heaped on him from the beginning of the Revolution. Individual insults – and there had been many at Tsarskoe Selo in the early days of his arrest – had been absorbed without emotion. Deprivations, even attempts to personalise insults through deliberate hardships, seemed to be taken in their stride.

His basic concerns throughout these early months of captivity were for his wife, his son and daughters, their close friends at court and the welfare of their loyal servants. He passed his time in physical pursuits, sawing logs, mending fences, shovelling snow, almost as if deliberately to clear his mind of any disturbing thoughts. Even the depressing news that filtered through to them from Petrograd, especially after their move to Tobolsk, did not appear to cause any ruffling of the outward calm. Yet at some point in the early spring of 1918 he plainly began to show the first signs of agitation.

Several developments combined to produce the change in his composure. It was in this period that the true colours of the Bolshevik coup became manifest. There was further talk of a trial of Nicholas and Alexandra, under pressure from individual Soviets outside Petrograd. Rule by Soviet diktat became widespread, even in the Governor's House at Tobolsk. No longer was the Petrograd government simply anti-tsarist: it was increasingly anti-capitalist and anti-democratic. It was also, in Nicholas's view, anti-patriotic.

From the early part of December onwards Lenin's government had been negotiating for a peaceful end to the war with Germany on almost any terms. Although Trotsky, who had taken over foreign affairs, had walked out of the post-armistice talks in February, ostensibly in protest at the humiliating terms then on offer, Lenin accepted almost all the same terms only weeks later at Brest-Litovsk. Not only did he lose over a quarter of former Russian territory, giving up Poland, Finland, Estonia, Latvia and Lithuania and seeing the Ukraine gain its independence, but he was forced to exempt Germany and German nationals from his recent nationalisation decrees, hand over gold to Germany, resume interest payments on German debts and demobilise the Russian army.

The humiliation, in Nicholas's eyes, was complete. As Pierre Gilliard later recalled:

All the efforts made by the Emperor to conceal his feelings could not hide his real sufferings from any observant person, and especially after the Brest-Litovsk Treaty a marked change was noticed in him that indicated his condition of mental depression. I can honestly say that His Majesty was overwhelmed with grief at the news of this Treaty.

What struck him forcibly was that his own act of abdication, taken entirely alone, under pressure from his generals, and in full consciousness of the solemn oaths to his people (not only on becoming tsar but at the outbreak of war), had all been in vain. His self-sacrifice, taken in what he regarded as the interests of the Russian people, in order to enable others to pursue the war with more vigour and determination, had come to nothing. And, as he was to discover, defeat on the battlefield was soon to be accompanied by a veiled rescue offer from his cousin, the Kaiser, if only he would agree to certain conditions.

The unravelling of what exactly happened between the signing of the Brest-Litovsk Treaty with Germany and the departure of Nicholas from Tobolsk some six weeks later has been going on for the best part of seventy-five years. On top of the aims and different motives of the two signatories to the treaty, one has to take into account the actions of the central authorities in Petrograd, the powerful local Soviets in both Omsk and Ekaterinburg and the real allegiances of the individuals destined to play major roles in the ultimate fate of the royal family.[1]

Cleared of the major anxiety of fighting on two fronts simultaneously, against the German enemy and the Russian bourgeoisie, Lenin and his comrades were able to turn their main attention to the domestic front early in March. While the previous Provisional government stood accused of neglecting, even forgetting the existence of the royal family in Tobolsk, the Bolshevik government was soon reflecting an obsession with them at all levels.

During the months of the Provisional government Nicholas's relatives had reacted in different ways to the new regime. Though many of them had been highly critical of Nicholas and his handling of state affairs in the final months before the February Revolution, only a few such as his cousin, Grand Duke Kyril, had openly demonstrated their quick allegiance to the new Red flag. The majority had maintained low profiles, rescuing what they could from the débâcle, some in prison for a time, some under house arrest, all under close scrutiny and surveillance.

Who can blame them for trying to retrieve and hold on to some of the wealth they had acquired or inherited? But, as in all families, there were some who did not hesitate to overdo their acceptance of the new regime to save their own skin, or possessions. Grand Duke Nicholas Michaelovitch, the historian of the family, was certainly one of Nicholas's fiercest critics and openly espoused liberal sentiments. But in a letter said to have been found in Kerensky's files the grand duke openly abdicated his share of his 'appanage' property 'in favour of the people' and undertook, in somewhat obsequious terms, to persuade his brothers to do likewise. And in the same period Grand Duke Michael was seen waiting patiently in Kerensky's office, among other supplicants, to seek a favour. He waited two hours and was eventually summoned as 'M. Romanoff'.[2]

It is easy to understand, even to sympathise with the sad plight of the Romanoffs. Some had seen the deluge approaching and given what warnings they could. Their treatment by the Provisional government reflected the double, unstable, character of the regime, part liberal, part Bolshevik. The new Bolshevik government thought, and acted, differently from the outset. Against growing fears that the remaining Romanoff relatives still in Petrograd, especially the former tsar's brother, Grand Duke Michael, might quickly become the focal point for opposition to the new regime, they were rounded up, forced to register, and eventually removed to Perm, some 700 miles south-east of Moscow. At the same time tentative preparations were begun for a possible trial of Nicholas before a Revolutionary Tribunal and rumours and counter-rumours began to appear in the press. Hardly surprisingly, the most revolutionary Soviets, particularly those nearest to Tobolsk in Omsk and Ekaterinburg, began to show growing interest in claiming the family for their own. Both towns sent missions to Tobolsk in efforts to promote their claims.

Not only were cries of revenge in the air once more, but genuine fears were roused that, as the spring weather led to the reopening of the rivers north of Tobolsk, so the opportunities for rescuing the family, and transporting them either northwards or eastwards, would increase. These were hardly idle fears. Throughout the winter Tobolsk itself and, more important Tyumen, the nearest railway junction, had become a magnet for monarchist sympathisers intent on providing help, food and even cash for the upkeep of the royal family. Some had been foolish. Some extremely careless. Several had been more intent on idle chatter than action.

An early visitor to Tobolsk was Rita Khitrovo, a former lady-in-waiting, who acted as a courier with letters and who knows what else between Anna Vyrubova, still in Petrograd, and the former empress. She spoke to too many locals and was quickly arrested and interrogated. Others too spoke out of turn, some even boasting of their intentions. There was also money to be made. Some of the cash pouring in to help feed the royal suite was easily diverted into private pockets. And so it went on throughout that winter and early spring.

It was against this background of local intrigue in and around Tobolsk that efforts such as those of Boris Soloviev have to be judged. He had been befriended by Rasputin and Anna Vyrubova during the war and, through them, had been drawn into the orbit of the Romanoffs. This had not prevented him from sympathising, even supporting, the Provisional government for a while after the Revolution broke out. None the less his friendship with Anna continued and, once the royal family had been exiled to Tobolsk his energies were increasingly channelled towards supporting them in whatever way was possible. Why is another matter.

How far his sudden decision to marry Rasputin's daughter, Maria, was geared to their joint decision to move to Siberia to be close to the royal family and to act as a focal point for monarchist support there is difficult to discern. It certainly helped in convincing Alexandra that Soloviev was their main potential saviour and in convincing others that he was the man to liaise with in Tyumen. Whatever his deeper motives, he quickly established contact with one of the empress's maids and was soon passing on both news and money to the family. Some of the large sums of money raised by Benckendorff, which we examined in the last chapter, were ultimately channelled through Soloviev. And the reports that so buoyed up Alexandra in Tobolsk, for example, that three hundred loyal officers were simply awaiting the signal to rescue them, can only have come from Soloviev. Even other monarchist plotters, such as Sergei Markov, a former officer in the Empress's Own Crimean Cavalry, who had earlier gathered thirty officers near Tsarskoe Selo in an abortive attempt at a rescue, felt obliged to approach Soloviev and Maria before making separate plans. Most were quickly rebuffed. For whatever reason, either monarchist loyalties or his alleged work as a secret informer for the Bolsheviks, or simply money, Soloviev had become the main cog in what was being plotted in and around Tobolsk.

Official reports and personal reminiscences have since thrown serious doubts over the real role played by Soloviev and other so-called monarchist rescue teams in Tobolsk and the neighbouring town of Tyumen. Exaggerations and empty boasts seemed to abound. Evidence gathered by Sokolov in Paris for the official White Russian inquiry into the murder of the royal family opened up the serious possibility that large sums of money meant for the royal family had been siphoned off elsewhere. Soloviev, for example, forwarded some 35,000 roubles to the royal family from the banker Yaroshinsky. Yet in testimony gathered in Paris in 1920 Yaroshinsky told Sokolov that he had in fact provided 175,000 roubles, as Benckendorff also reported. The missing 140,000 roubles remain unaccounted for.[3]

At one stage even Colonel Kobylinski, the commandant at Tobolsk, was said to have nurtured plans for the rescue of his charges. In the early part of the winter there, he considered fleeing with them with an escort of some thirty loyal soldiers northwards towards the Arctic ocean, where he hoped they might quickly escape on one of the regular Norwegian schooners at Obdorsk. Hundreds of German and Austrian prisoners had escaped that way in earlier months. What Kobylinski needed, of course, was money but none was forthcoming from any of the monarchist groups in Tobolsk or Tyumen. Whether this was a reflection of doubts about Kobylinski's loyalties or, more likely, the general malaise, even cupidity, that had spread through the tsarist supporters is difficult to say. Gleb Botkin, the son of the tsar's doctor, who was there at the time and subsequently escaped to the West, was convinced that the monarchists had simply 'resolved to squander the money in their possession for their own personal benefit'.[4]

While Russian monarchist groups were thus preoccupied in Tobolsk, German interest in the royal family had hardly waned. Kaiser Wilhelm found it difficult to ignore the close family ties with Nicholas and the German ancestry of Alexandra, quite apart from the mixed feelings he must have had in having to deal, even as a victor, with the Bolsheviks. Contacts between those loyal to the royal family and German representatives were also maintained, following the treaty signed in March. Benckendorff, for one, is believed to have written to Count Mirbach, the German Ambassador, in his continuing efforts to secure the safety of the royal family, once conditions began to deteriorate in Tobolsk. The Germans for their part could also see merit in ensuring that the royal family remained within their own orbit as their forces continued to encroach on Russian territory. What was not spelt out were the terms on which a real rescue of the family might be undertaken by the Germans; and it was precisely this that so agitated Nicholas.

As with so many of these participants, it is far easier to establish motives than to unravel the detailed actions taken or even contemplated by them. Double agents and double-crosses emerged on all sides. As a result, within a matter of months, far from being neglected, the royal family had become the centre of interest for a variety of disparate groups: monarchist loyalists, the central authorities in Moscow, two separate Soviets in Omsk and Ekaterinburg, and even representatives of the German government in Petrograd and Moscow. All, for different reasons, were being tempted to play the royal card. And all, in their different ways, succeeded in muddying the historical waters for at least three-quarters of a century.

Little wonder that news of an impending move from Tobolsk raised more questions than answers. One fact stands out. Vasily Yakovlov arrived from Moscow on April 22 with credentials from the Central Executive

Committee, which by then had moved for security reasons from Petrograd to Moscow, and with a hundred and fifty soldiers at his command. He quickly presented himself to Kobylinski and is said to have explained that he was under instruction to take at least the ex-tsar back to Moscow for trial. He is also thought to have hinted that the ultimate destination of the whole family would be somewhere abroad, by way of Finland, Sweden and Norway. Yet why he had really come; what his real motives were; and whose side he was really on have remained a mystery ever since.

Nicholas and Alexandra, when faced a few days after Yakovlov's arrival with his request that Nicholas should accompany him to an unknown destination, seemed in no doubt what the ultimate object was, immediately suspecting the Kaiser's hand behind it all. 'They want me to sign the Treaty of Brest-Litovsk. But I'll see my right hand cut off before I do it,' Nicholas declared. But Yakovlov was adamant, and faced with his insistence, even perhaps his slight deference, which has puzzled many people ever since, the only question to be resolved was who would accompany Nicholas. Alexis had recently bruised himself badly again and, the doctors insisted, was unfit to be moved. Alexandra was once more torn between the emotional pull of her son and the crucial needs of her husband. But after much agonising she decided to go with Nicholas, along with their daughter Maria, leaving Alexis in the care of his sisters Olga, Tatiana and Anastasia and the doctors.

So began one of the more puzzling episodes of this whole period. They left Tobolsk in the early morning of April 26, four days after Yakovlov's arrival, Nicholas and Yakovlov in one tarantassy (a long cart pulled by two or three horses), Alexandra and Maria in another, the entourage accompanied by a bodyguard of thirty-five soldiers. It was a tearful departure. The family were being split up for the first time since the Revolution and none of them knew where they would meet again. One also gets the feeling that some of the escorts did not know either. The train they transferred to in Tyumen, a coach and four passenger cars, first went westwards towards Ekaterinburg, then after only one station stopped, took on another engine and reversed direction, moving once again through Tyumen towards Omsk in the east.

The sudden change in direction did not go unnoticed either by the passengers or by interested parties watching the royal family's movements in Tyumen. The first morning Nicholas recorded in his diary that they were travelling eastwards, and wondered whether they might be going to Vladivostock or even Moscow by a roundabout route; the following morning he noticed that they were now going westwards, which seemed to him to confirm Moscow as their destination. What he did not know was that other observers had noticed too and were already taking action to prevent any such move. What action and conversations then took place is still debated, but the telegraph wires to Moscow, Omsk and Ekaterinburg were particularly active that night. Claimants for final custody of the royal family were still in competition.

As a result Yakovlov was alerted that his manoeuvre had not gone unreported and that he would probably be stopped before he could branch off towards Moscow. He pulled up short of Omsk, and went into the city on his own to communicate directly with Moscow. What advice he gave or what instructions he received, or even what prompted the next steps, remains conjectural, but quite soon thereafter the train proceeded towards Ekaterinburg. Perhaps he hoped to persuade the local Soviet to allow him to go on to Moscow; perhaps Moscow had already given instructions for him to hand over his charges to the local Soviet. Whatever the intentions, the reception in Ekaterinburg was particularly noisy and hostile. Yakovlov still seemed determined to keep custody of his charges, but after hours of argument and, no doubt, further communication with Moscow, he had to concede defeat. He handed over his charges to the regional Soviet. Later that afternoon Nicholas, Alexandra and Maria were escorted in an open car to a largish two-storey house, owned by Nicholas Ipatiev, a rich businessman, which seemed significantly to have been prepared for their arrival.

While Yakovlov's task was thus finished, the real purpose behind his mysterious efforts has remained unresolved. Was he always intent on delivering the family to the Ekaterinburg Soviet on subtle instructions from Moscow (basically from Iakov Sverdlov, chairman of the Central Executive Committee, after whom Ekaterinburg was subsequently renamed)? Or was his first, and basic, intention to take Nicholas back to Moscow, which his overnight switch of direction certainly suggests, to stand trial at a Bolshevik inquiry? Yakovlov could also have been part of a Moscow-inspired attempt to deliver Nicholas safely to the Kaiser in some effort to get his signature on the Brest-Litovsk Treaty, a ploy that Nicholas himself both feared and resisted. Or was Yakovlov even bent on rescuing the ex-tsar for delivery to the Whites, a possibility that is not as far-fetched as it may seem when one remembers his slight deference to Nicholas, extending to the occasional salute and several courtesies, and the fact that later in the year in his home town of Ufa he actually joined the White army.

For a time Yakovlov's career seemed to have ended in a White guard counter-intelligence cellar where he was shot by the Whites shortly afterwards. That at least was the assumption for many years. But evidence which has since surfaced, both from old comrades and subsequent inquiries, confirms that he was not shot as originally reported and actually survived by fleeing to China. He eventually returned to the Soviet Union in 1927, was initially convicted of treason, sent to a labour camp but quickly released. Then ten years later, during one of Stalin's frequent purges, the same fate overtook him again, he was banished to another labour camp but this time he vanished for ever. Edvard Radzinsky, who has examined all the new Russian evidence, has persuaded himself that Yakovlov was sympathetic to the tsar; but Richard Pipes, who has also been over the new material, remains convinced that his aim was to take Nicholas for trial to Moscow. That is my view, but we shall probably never know for certain.[5]

Those left behind in Tobolsk after the departure of Nicholas, Alexandra and Maria were already reflecting the change in the atmosphere. Baroness Sophie Buxhoeveden, who joined the remaining grand duchesses and their brother Alexis, was horrified to see how ill he looked and how greatly the eldest, Olga, had changed. 'The suspense and anxiety of her parents' absence, and the responsibility she bore when left as head of the house with her sick brother to look after, had changed the lovely, bright girl of twenty-two into a faded and middle-aged woman.' Even before Alexis was fully fit to travel, they were all instructed to pack to follow their parents to Ekaterinburg.

The journey which followed was a foretaste of the harsh and uncaring regime they were all to encounter in Ekaterinburg. On the boat no one was allowed to keep their cabin doors closed; sentries were placed outside the lavatories; and the escorts, with little regard for others, let loose at ducks with their machine-guns whenever an opportunity occurred. On the train journey which followed, the grand duchesses and their brother were put in an 'indescribably dirty' second and third class carriage, with the tutors and servants in an equally filthy cattle truck, with sentries at every door. On arrival late at night in Ekaterinburg they were prevented from leaving the train until the next morning and had to sleep fully clothed in their compartments.

Next day was a grey, drizzly affair. While Alexis was carried to the horse-drawn cabs awaiting them, the three grand duchesses, loaded with valises and small personal belongings, had to look after themselves. Pierre Gilliard, the French tutor, who had been prevented from trying to help them, watched the scene from his carriage window:

Tatiana came last, carrying her little dog and struggling to drag a heavy brown valise. It was raining, and I saw her feet sink into the mud at every step. Nagorny [the sailor looking after Alexis] tried to come to her assistance; he was roughly pushed back by one of the commissaries.[6]

It was the last that Gilliard and several of the accompanying suite saw of any of the family. The thinning out of the ranks of courtiers supporting the royal family, which had begun at Tsarskoe Selo from a combination of disloyal desertion and budget necessity, was now being imposed by

Soviet diktat. The twin moves from Tobolsk to Ekaterinburg – first Nicholas, Alexandra and Maria; then Alexis, Olga, Tatiana and Anastasia – had been accompanied by decisions to send General Tatischev, Countess Hendrikoff and Mademoiselle Schneider to prison. Prince Dolgorukov soon joined them. When the final party, including the young Alexis and his sisters, reached Ekaterinburg, it was decided that while Dr Botkin would join the whole royal family in the Ipatiev House four others would simply be set free. So Dr Derevenko, Baroness Bux-hoeveden (whose illness had delayed her arrival in Tobolsk), and the tutors Gibbes and Gilliard spent the next couple of weeks in their railway compartment, before returning to Tyumen, where they were eventually freed by the White Russian advance. Most of those sent to prison were never seen again.

The arrival in Ekaterinburg of their parents four weeks earlier had hardly been more welcoming than that suffered by Alexis and the girls. Nicholas, Alexandra and Maria had been stopped in a siding and had had to make their way to an open-top car, accompanied by three soldiers with rifles, through an extremely hostile and noisy crowd. Nicholas, like his daughters later, had had to carry his own luggage. They were taken to the local committee, where Nicholas was made to wait for two hours in a corridor, before they all joined each other in the Ipatiev House.

To judge by their individual diaries[7] they adapted themselves to their new, far more restricted, conditions in different ways. Nicholas wrote:

The house is fine, clean. We have been assigned 4 rooms: a corner bedroom, a lavatory, next door a dining-room with windows on to a little garden and a view of a low-lying part of town, and finally a spacious hall with arches in place of doors. We have arranged ourselves in the following manner: Alix, Maria and I together in the bedroom. A shared lavatory. Demidova [the maid who stayed with them to the end] in the dining-room, and in the hall – Botkin, Chemodurov and Sednev ... A very high wooden fence has been built around the house 2 sazhens [4.5 metres] from the windows; a chain of sentries has been posted there and in the little garden too.

Nicholas himself took all these restrictions with equanimity; Alexandra with increasing frustration, almost constant migraine and indigestion. He went outside in the small garden for their allotted two hours, pacing up and down; she refused, reclining on her couch, 'her head bound with a compress'.[8] Before Alexis and the girls finally joined them another irritant was introduced: the windows of their room were painted over with lime, restricting their view.

Nicholas's diary entry for May 23, recording the arrival of his children, says it all: 'Great joy to see them again and embrace them after four weeks of separation and uncertainty. No end of mutual questions and answers, the poor things endured much moral suffering in Tobolsk and during their three-day journey.' The four grand duchesses, together again, were put into one of the four rooms together, sleeping on folding camp beds, along with Alexis until he moved in with his parents the following month.

Their life was, to say the least, monotonous and fearful. They were cramped together, with limited outside opportunities, lacking outside news and real contacts, and surrounded by coarse guards and unsympathetic protectors. They read books to themselves and, occasionally, aloud to each other. *War and Peace* was one of them. Sewing, embroidery and a little painting occupied some of them. Diaries too. They played bezique and a form of backgammon. Time went slowly, and there was little if any privacy. Mealtimes were constantly interrupted by the coarse, perhaps deliberately intrusive, habits of their guards. So was the use of the lavatory, where guards were constantly on duty. In spite of all this they all had their different inner strengths and beliefs, supported once a week by the visit of a priest and an improvised chapel in the hall.

Events outside, however, were beginning to move rapidly and in a way that might have encouraged them had they known, but which ultimately was to lead to their deaths. The Whites were not only resisting the advance of the Bolsheviks in the area of the Urals but were now pushing them back westwards. A combination of foreign intervention and Russian resistance, from Murmansk to the Ukraine and from the Pacific to the Urals, was beginning to have an impact, and nowhere with greater effect than between Omsk and Ekaterinburg. The Czech Legion, formerly prisoners of war who, on attempting to escape through Siberia, had met Bolshevik resistance and fought back, and who were now allied to Admiral Kolchak's White Russian Siberian forces, was already advancing on Omsk.

In Moscow the news had a double implication; not only was the civil war becoming a confirmed reality, but the fate of the former royal family now needed the authorities' urgent attention. In the middle of June Omsk fell to the Czechs and the advance on Ekaterinburg had clearly begun. Moscow had to move quickly and a series of anti-Romanoff decisions and actions can be almost dated accordingly. On June 12 five armed men arrived at the hotel in Perm where Grand Duke Michael, the tsar's brother and successor for a day, was staying under house arrest with his secretary, Nicholas Johnson. They were both taken into the woods out of town and shot. A rumour was spread by the Bolsheviks that they had been killed escaping.

Just over a week later other Romanoffs, who had also been under house arrest in Alapaevsk, about 100 miles north-east of Ekaterinburg, were suddenly put on a much more rigid regime and deprived of their staff. Grand Duchess Elizabeth, Alexandra's elder sister and known in the family as Ella, had been held there, along with Grand Duke Sergei Mikhailovitch, Prince Vladimir Paley and three sons of Grand Duke Constantine – Igor, Constantine and Ivan – since the previous May. Within a month they too were attacked and thrown down a mine shaft, several of them apparently still alive. One version told of their then being pelted with stones; but Prince Philip, Duke of Edinburgh, has recently added to the horror by reporting that in fact a hand grenade was thrown on them.[9] Their lingering death, and the compassion and bravery of Grand Duchess Elizabeth, who had devoted much of her life to her religious order, has haunted the civilised world ever since. Once again a rumour was encouraged that they had been killed by an unknown White guard.

Nor, of course, had Moscow overlooked the former royal family. It was from the middle of June that one particular supposed 'escape' move, which for some days must have given Nicholas and his family an enormous surge of hope, can now be seen to have been contrived by the Bolsheviks themselves. To their relief the family were suddenly allowed eggs, butter, milk and other local produce from the nuns of the local convent and, one day in the course of receiving a bottle of milk, they found a letter in French from an apparently loyal officer, promising help and asking for a sketch of the house. Nicholas responded as requested, received further instructions about a possible escape plan, and he and the family stayed awake all night, fully dressed, on June 26 in anticipation. 'The waiting and uncertainty,' he confided to his diary, 'were most excruciating.' Then they overheard a sentry talking about possible escapes and about tightened security. Nicholas passed back a final note stressing that they could not run the risk of an attempted escape, but would willingly be abducted.

For many years this whole episode was regarded as evidence of yet another monarchist plot that failed. But first Richard Pipes threw cold water on the authenticity of the original letter to Nicholas and, by cross-checking with later evidence from contemporary participants convinced himself that the letter had been fabricated by the Cheka, the newly formed Bolshevik security police. Then Edvard Radzinsky lent powerful support by identifying the composer of the letter in the milk bottle as Peter Voikov, one of the Bolshevik leaders in Ekaterinburg, a former graduate of Geneva University and later Soviet Ambassador to Poland.

It all strongly suggests that the original plan was for the family to be shot trying to escape, and that the chance gossip overheard from a guard persuaded Nicholas how dangerous such an attempt would be. But the intention was there and so clearly was the original Moscow-based decision, encouraged by the Ekaterinburg Soviet, about the fate of all the Romanoffs. It was only a matter of time, therefore – and the encroachment of the Whites – before an alternative plot was devised. And on July 4, when the commandant of the guard was changed at the Ipatiev House, the final phase began.

On that day Alexander Avdeyev was replaced by Jacob Yurovsky from the Cheka. There were other changes too noticed by the family. Almost all the guards inside the house were replaced. A railing was put up for no apparent reason outside their window. And Yurovsky began his short spell of duty on July 4 by insisting on the family bringing out all their jewels. Later on they heard military activity, artillery, infantry and cavalry passing by; and, on one occasion, troops marching with music. Then a few days later the young kitchen boy who helped the cook, Leonid Sednev (known as 'Leshka' to the family), was suddenly sent away. They were told he had gone to see his uncle, but they wondered whether they would ever see him again.

With hindsight, we can now see an ominous purpose behind these changes: a combination of White Russian military advances and the planned count-down to the inevitable end. It is tempting to see a similar awareness among some of the family and the suite too. After the let-down of the expected 'escape' and their all-night vigil, Nicholas and Alexandra seemed to lose heart and to fall back on minor discomforts and events in their diaries. Dr Botkin, in a letter he was still writing, was already reflecting the end:

My voluntary confinement here is restricted less by time than by my earthly existence. In essence I am dead – dead for my children, for my work ... I am dead but not yet buried, or buried alive – whichever: the consequences are nearly identical ... My children may hold out hope that we will see each other again in this life ... but I personally do not indulge that hope.

On Sunday, when they were allowed a church service in the house, even the priests noticed a profound change among the family, both in their reactions during the service and in their appearance. They looked exhausted. When the officiating priest came to the prayer 'Who resteth with the saints', they were surprised to notice the whole Romanoff family behind them suddenly fall to their knees. And, as the grand duchesses left after the service, one of them whispered a quiet 'Thank you'. As one priest said to the other afterwards: 'Something has happened to them; they are different.' Two months later one of the priests was still remarking on the fact that none of the family sang throughout that last service.[10]

Significantly, as we now know, the Ural Soviet Executive Committee had decided, two days before, with Moscow's prior approval and knowledge, to execute the whole family. There is now no doubt where the decision was made, for Boris Yeltsin confirmed it in his autobiography *Against the Grain*, published in 1990, after deliberate research ('I went to the provincial archives and read the documents of the time').[11] Just as significant, that Sunday was also the day on which Nicholas stopped writing his daily diary entries. The day before he had ended his comment with the words: 'Weather is warm and pleasant. We have no news from the outside.' While the diary's page numbers continued, he wrote no further entry. Alexandra continued hers to the end. Was Nicholas already despairing of rescue and had recognised, perhaps even learnt of, the inevitable?[12]

What was to prove their last full day, July 16, ended with the grand duchesses going to bed early. Alexandra played bezique with Nicholas and was in bed by 10.30. She probably remained restless. Dr Botkin was finishing his letter. At midnight they were all suddenly wakened by Yurovsky who, in his own later words,[13] explained that 'in view of the unrest in town', it was necessary to move the family downstairs. Botkin woke the others and advised them to get dressed. Just over half an hour later they were all led down to the cellar room. The guard commander, Pavel Medvedev, has described the scene:

The tsar carried the tsarevitch in his arms. The tsar and the tsarevitch were dressed in field shirts. They had service caps on their heads. The tsarina and her daughters wore dresses, without outer clothing. Their heads were uncovered. The tsar walked in front with the tsarevitch. Behind them were the tsarina, their daughters and others ... While I was present no member of the imperial family asked any questions of anyone. Also there were no tears, no sobbing. Having gone down the stairs leading from the second-floor ante-room to the lower floor, they went into the courtyard and from there through the second door to the inner rooms of the lower floor. Yurovsky indicated the way. They went into the corner of the lower room, adjacent to the sealed storeroom. Yurovsky ordered chairs to be brought. His assistant brought three chairs. One chair was given to the tsarina, another to the tsar, the third to the tsarevitch. The tsarina sat at the wall in which there is a window, nearer to the rear post of the arch. Behind her stood three of the daughters. The tsarevitch and the tsar sat next to each other, almost in the centre of the room. Doctor Botkin stood behind the chair of the tsarevitch. The maidservant [Demidova] ... stood at the left doorpost of the door leading into the sealed storeroom. With her stood one of the imperial daughters. The two men servants [the valet Trupp and the cook Kharitonov] stood in the left corner, against the wall adjacent to the storeroom. The maidservant had a pillow in her arms. The imperial daughters had also brought small pillows with them. They put one of the pillows on the seat of the tsarina's chair, another on the seat of the chair of the tsarevitch.[14]

What actually happened next has been pieced together by recent extensive detective work by Edvard Radzinsky. Following the discovery of the original 1920 report of Yurovsky, the commandant at the time of the massacre, and its publication by Radzinsky in 1989, during the blossoming of Gorbachev's *glasnost*, thousands of letters were received, lost archive reports were found and several new witnesses came forward. From all this response Radzinsky was left with six separate eye-witness accounts of the massacre. This is what, in total, they reported:

'With quick gestures Yurovsky directed who went where. In a calm, quiet voice he said: "Please, you stand here, and you here ... that's it, in a row." The prisoners stood in two rows: in the first, the tsar's family; in the second their people. The heir was sitting on a chair. The tsar was standing in the first row with one of his lackeys directly behind him.'

'When they were all standing, the detachment was called in.'

'When the detachment commandant [Yurovsky] walked in, he told the Romanoffs: "In view of the fact that your relatives are continuing their attack on Soviet Russia, the Ural Executive Committee has decided to execute you." Nicholas turned his back to the detachment, his face to the family, then sort of came to and turned around to face the commandment and asked, "What? What?"'

'The commandant quickly repeated it and ordered the detachment to get ready ... Nicholas did not say anything more, having turned back towards the family, the others uttered a few incoherent exclamations. It all lasted just a few seconds.'

'The detachment had been told beforehand who was to shoot whom, and they had been ordered to aim straight for the heart, to avoid excessive quantities of blood and get it over with quicker.'

'At his last word [Yurovsky] instantly pulled a revolver out of his pocket and shot the tsar. The tsaritsa and her daughter Olga tried to make the sign of the cross, but did not have enough time ... Nicholas was killed by the commandant, point blank. Then Alexandra died immediately ... Alexis, three of his sisters, the lady-in-waiting [actually Demidova] and Botkin were still alive. They had to be finished off.'

'I ran into the execution room and shouted to stop the firing and finish off those still alive with bayonets.'

'The smoke was blocking out the electric lamp. The shooting was halted. The doors of the room were opened for the smoke to disperse. They started picking up the bodies.'

'We took the bodies out on stretchers ... The tsar's body was carried out first. Then they brought out his daughters. When they laid one of the daughters on the stretcher, she cried out and covered her face with her arm. The others [the daughters] also turned out to be alive. We couldn't shoot any more – with the open doors the shots could be heard in the street ... Ermakov took my bayonet from me and started stabbing everyone dead who had turned out to be alive.'[15]

Only one poignant amendment has since been added to this composite account of the massacre. Nicholas did actually say something after Yurovsky had repeated his final message to them all. His last words to Yurovsky were remembered by Commissar Peter Ermakov and he in turn recalled them to several people, including Alexei Karelin, who wrote them down and finally sent them to Radzinsky. They were: 'You know not what you do.'

Eight days later, on July 25, Ekaterinburg fell to the Czech Legion and the White Russians, and the investigations into what the Soviets had done to the royal family began. When troops first entered the Ipatiev House they found traces of the occupation of the royal family in the upstairs rooms, and what was plainly a quickly cleaned up, though still blood-stained, room full of bullet holes below. A detailed investigation followed. In the midst of a swirling civil war it was far from easy to get the right man on the job; and after two early attempts to assess what had happened Admiral Kolchak, the White Russian leader in Siberia, put Nicholas Sokolov in complete charge and it was the results of his official inquiry which were ultimately published in the West, first in a Russian edition in 1924 and a year later in a French edition.

Sokolov's formal report was not the first to go into print. In fact Robert Wilton of *The Times*, who reached Ekaterinburg soon after the Soviets surrendered there and who eventually secured a complete record of Sokolov's findings, was the first to publish a detailed account of the massacre in 1920. Then came Pierre Gilliard's account published in Paris in 1921, followed a year later by a two-volume account by General Dieterichs, who was chief of staff to Admiral Kolchak and had himself been in charge of the initial inquiry.

The early questions being asked centred on the simple question of who was responsible for the apparent massacre. It was both a human tragedy and a political question. Both the original White investigators and the later Soviet apologists were highly conscious of the need to apportion blame. But, as time went on and claimants increasingly appeared on the scene, alleging to be a surviving member of the royal family, other questions began to creep in: was everyone actually killed at Ekaterinburg and, if so, what had happened to the Romanoffs' remaining wealth which they were now able to claim? More than seven decades later the answers are still being sought.

Individual reminiscences continued to emerge throughout the twenties and thirties. Some of the main personalities told what they knew or what they thought people ought to know: politicians such as Alexander

Kerensky, leader of the Provisional government; diplomats such as the British and French ambassadors in St Petersburg; members of the Romanoff Court – Baroness Buxhoeveden, Lili Dehn, Pierre Gilliard, Sydney Gibbes, Count Paul Benckendorff and Captain Paul Bulygin among them; some of the surviving Romanoffs and their relatives such as Grand Duchess Olga, the tsar's sister, Grand Duke Alexander and Prince Felix Youssopov, the killer of Rasputin; even Soviet leaders and officials such as Trotsky and Pavel Bykov added to the pile of Romanoff material.

A new industry had been born. From all this activity four basic sources of raw material now seem to have emerged: the Hoover Institute at Stanford University in Palo Alto, California; the Bakhmetev Archives at Columbia University in New York; the Houghton Library at Harvard University, outside Boston; and the State Archives of the Russian Federation in Moscow. It is among this material and the mass of earlier reminiscences that we shall now be seeking the answers to the two key questions: Who survived? Where is the wealth? First then a little essential ground-clearing. On their sad journey from Tsarskoe Selo to Ekaterinburg Nicholas and his family carried with them (on occasions literally) some of their most personal possessions. This needs tracing before we set our sights on higher and more expensive items.

Part 2
SEARCH

6

Plunder

One of the most moving impressions of the Nazis' infamous concentration camp at Auschwitz in southern Poland is of a display of personal possessions, preserved behind glass, left behind by the victims: piles of spectacles discarded for the last time; false teeth; hats and caps of all sizes; and battered suitcases, some still tied up with pieces of string, in which all their possessions had been quickly thrown together for their last journey. These are the remains of the most horrific European crime of the century. The sight haunts all those who see it.

Some of the same thoughts are prompted by the Sokolov inquiry's descriptions and photographs of the debris found in the Four Brothers Mine and other burial places near Ekaterinburg.[1] Again we are faced with the personal possessions of hapless victims: this time rich not poor. Here are false teeth; spectacle lenses; a lorgnette frame; a lady's shoe buckle; a suspender; a buckle from a boy's belt; scorched parts of burned corsets; pieces of burned cloth; a jewelled cross; an earring; splinters of sapphire and emerald; topazes; and broken parts of gold jewellery. There are also two pieces of human skin; a human finger; splintered bones of a mammal; and the corpse of a female dog. The poignancy is overwhelming.

What we are seeing in photographs is all that remained of the Russian royal family and of the personal possessions they had brought with them from Tsarskoe Selo. The Sokolov inquiry spent months sorting out what was left in the Ipatiev House; and even longer in clarifying what remains might have been hidden and buried outside Ekaterinburg. Their inquiries eventually led them close to a small village, Koptyaki, 13 miles away on the shores of Lake Isetsk, a community at that time of only half a dozen cottages, surrounded and almost hidden by pine forests.

The locals made a living out of fishing, hay-making and looking after local government officials who had modest country dachas close by. There had previously been a thriving iron-ore mining community nearby. Some of the old, derelict mine shafts were still open, though occasionally filled with water. And it was at one of these disused mines, identified as the

Four Brothers Mine because of its proximity to four legendary pine trees, that the investigators found their gruesome hoard. Apart from the human (and animal) remains, the relics were eventually identified as clothing and jewels belonging to the royal family. The two belt buckles belonged to Nicholas and Alexis. A spectacle case belonged to Alexandra. The false teeth and glasses were those of Dr Botkin. Two small diamond-studded shoe buckles belonged to two of the grand duchesses. Sydney Gibbes was convinced that the sapphire fragments were from Nicholas's ring, which he wore on his wedding finger and could not take off. Six charred corsets were those of the six women – Alexandra, her four daughters and the maid. The brass buttons with coats of arms were from the military overcoats of Nicholas and Alexis. A brilliant mounted in green gold and platinum had belonged to Alexandra. An emerald cross of Kulm, with pearl pendants, had been worn by one of the girls. The body of the dog was sadly identified by Sydney Gibbes as that of Jemmi which belonged to Anastasia. The experts concluded that the human finger was that of a middle-aged woman 'accustomed to manicuring' and 'with a well-groomed appearance', presumably Alexandra's.

These were all that remained of the cases of personal belongings packed at the outset of their journey from Tsarskoe Selo just under twelve months earlier. This, therefore, is where the search for tsarist wealth begins. Before chasing the millions we need to clarify exactly what the family took with them from Tsarskoe Selo and what happened to it. It was not inconsiderable. Their immediate possessions, which they had partly packed personally and even on occasions carried under duress, had been vulnerable throughout their journey from Tsarskoe Selo, and had not reached Ekaterinburg intact. Yet some of their favourite pieces of jewellery had been preserved until the end and were still found in what was left of their garments in and around the mine shaft outside Ekaterinburg.

We may recall that on departure from Tsarskoe Selo it took fifty men some three hours to pack the luggage needed by the royal family and their accompanying courtiers, advisers and servants. This was not just the personal luggage of Nicholas and his family. It included kitchen utensils, cutlery, provisions and wine for the whole entourage accompanying them. Before leaving Nicholas went through his personal papers and other valuables left in the private apartments at the Alexander Palace and locked and, where possible, sealed them. These were deliberately separated from the national works of art outside the private apartments and, after the royal family's departure, were gathered together on the second floor of the palace under the supervision of Count Benckendorff. He ensured they were put in eight packing cases and transferred, for safety, to Petrograd, where he signed a personal receipt for them in the Imperial Office. He assumed that, along with the works of art in the Hermitage, the crown plate and other valuables in the palace, they would thus be ready for transfer to Moscow, should Petrograd be in danger of occupation by the Germans.

As the family left for Tobolsk, Provisional government officials were already safeguarding what was left behind. Alexandra's maid was found upstairs still packing into drawers and boxes some of her personal things not needed on the journey. She was quickly reminded that it was now all national property. Even the calendar had to be left untouched, likewise flowers in their vases. Thereafter all the rooms were photographed and the rooms secured. As many as forty doors were sealed off in this way.

The royal family had gathered together not only sufficient possessions to act as distractions during their enforced absence, but had endeavoured to take what Nicholas, or more likely Alexandra, must have judged would tide them over any difficult periods ahead. So while their future cash needs had clearly been left to Benckendorff and his stepson to sort out with Colonel Kobylinski, Alexandra and her daughters had not overlooked their favourite jewels. Sydney Gibbes, who accompanied them, later estimated that they probably took with them jewels worth no less than a million roubles (about £100,000). Nicholas was far less interested in his own possessions and simply made sure that he and the tutors took sufficient books with them, not only for educational purposes, but for their daily enjoyment. Histories, biographies, the literary classics, especially English, predominated (Alexandra may have been German by birth, but she was Queen Victoria's granddaughter and her upbringing had been English and the language tended to predominate in their private conversations).

Nicholas did not overlook his stamp collection. At what point the pleasure from the stamps was replaced by their realisable value is not easy to pin-point, but the change probably took place in the early winter in Tobolsk, when a combination of cash shortages and the first impact of the Bolshevik coup penetrated that bleak landscape. Not only were the stamps vulnerable to the honesty of their entourage, but to their captors' envy. At the beginning of their stay in Tobolsk they were still exchanging letters and even small gifts with some of their closest friends in Petrograd. Money too was being received from Anna Vyrubova and put in their jewel box. But by early 1918, as their conditions deteriorated and their cash resources dwindled, the jewels they had brought with them took on a different meaning.

Trade-offs with local shopkeepers were an obvious first step, but as rumours of monarchist rescue plots proliferated, the temptation to make their own contribution must have been irresistible – especially to Alexandra, who continued to have implicit faith in Soloviev and his colleagues close by in Tyumen. Soloviev thus became part of the trade-off too and

the recipient of some of the jewels.² By April, when expectations of a
further move seemed imminent, the potential of the jewels in easing their
future plight became even more crucial. And the increasing vigilance of
their guards, including the occasional unexpected search of their possessions, ostensibly for weapons, but who knows what else, quickly persuaded the family to take a few self-protective measures.

So before Nicholas, Alexandra and Maria left Tobolsk the women
sewed choice jewels into their underclothes. Alexandra promised to let
her daughters know, once she had arrived at her destination, whether they
should sew even more of the jewels still stored in the jewel box into their
clothes before their own later departure. They agreed on an easy code:
'medicines' would mean 'jewels' in any future correspondence. But before
Nicholas and Alexandra departed they left further jewels for 'safe-keeping' in Soloviev's hands, which by all accounts led to a subsequent major
row between Soloviev and his so-called monarchist ally, Father Vasiliev.
Alexandra also gave a pearl necklace and diamonds to the deputy commandant at Tobolsk, Captain Aksyuta, and Nicholas gave him his sabre
as a gesture of thanks for preventing it being confiscated by the new
Bolshevik guards. Aksyuta later reported hiding the jewels and sabre on
the outskirts of Tobolsk. Since neither Aksyuta nor General Denikin, who
was also told of their whereabouts, ever returned to the district, they are
probably still there.

On arrival at Ekaterinburg Nicholas and Alexandra had to endure an
inspection of their luggage, almost as if they were crossing a national
frontier. Their guards confiscated a camera and a map of Ekaterinburg.
But they were clearly looking for more valuable things. Alexandra took
the point and, through her maid Demidova, quickly sent a letter to Mme
Tegleva in Tobolsk asking her and the grand duchesses to be 'careful how
you pack the medicines'. The message was instantly understood. In
evidence to the Sokolov inquiry, Alexandra Tegleva, the grand duchesses'
nurse who subsequently married Pierre Gilliard, described what was
done:

We took several brassières of heavy linen. We put the jewels in wadding, covered
the wadding with two brassières and then sewed the brassières together. In this
fashion the jewels were sewn between two brassières, which were then covered
with wadding on both sides. The jewels of the empress were sewn in two pairs of
brassières. In one of such double brassières the weight of the jewels together with
the brassière and wadding was 4½ pounds. The other was of the same weight.
Tatiana wore one of them, and Anastasia the other. In these were sewn brilliants,
emeralds, amethysts.

The jewels of the grand duchesses were sewn into a double brassière in the
same fashion and it was worn by Olga.

In addition they put many pearls on their bodies under their blouses.

We also sewed jewels into the hats of the grand duchesses, between the lining and the velvet. Among the jewels of this type I remember a large pearl necklace and a brooch with a large sapphire and brilliants.

We ripped off the buttons [of their blue outer garments] and in place of the buttons sewed jewels, brilliants I believe, wrapping them first in wadding and then with black silk.

We also ripped the buttons off [their autumn garments of English tricot with black stripes] and sewed on jewels, after wrapping them in wadding and black silk.[3]

In total, it was later reported, the grand duchesses managed to conceal in their clothing some 8 kilograms of jewels before they left Tobolsk. When they finally reached Ekaterinburg, they brought with them a good deal of the whole family's possessions too. As this began to be unloaded from the railway coach the day following their arrival it quickly attracted a hostile crowd and the first major pilfering. They mocked and jeered as individual items were brought out. One box was quickly opened up and several pairs of Nicholas's boots appeared. 'He has six pairs and I have none!' came the shout. 'All these boxes contain the gold dresses of these wanton women. Off with their heads!' Though the crowd was quickly dispersed by the soldiers, that hardly ensured the safety of the luggage. Baroness Buxhoeveden, who witnessed the whole unloading process from the railway compartment, was convinced that 'most of Their Majesties' belongings went to the Soviet or to the lodgings of the Commissars themselves and were never seen again by their lawful owners'.[4]

One pair of boots that escaped the wrath of the crowd can still be seen today. Because of their hasty departure Nicholas had given a special pair which he had used constantly throughout the previous winter in Tobolsk to Sydney Gibbes, the tutor, to bring with him later. Gibbes did so but, along with several other members of the entourage, was not allowed to join the family at the Ipatiev House. They had said goodbye to Nicholas and Alexandra in Tobolsk and were forced to do the same to the three grand duchesses and Alexis on arrival at Ekaterinburg. Gibbes and the others then spent nearly a fortnight virtually living in the train before being sent back to Tyumen.

The boots remained in his luggage and accompanied him across to Vladivostock and Harbin and eventually back to England. They were handed over to his adopted son, the late George Gibbes, who in turn before his death in 1991 bequeathed them to Luton Hoo, where they now remain. They are extremely large and have one unique quality: they are made entirely of felt. As Sydney Gibbes explained in his papers: the boots were 'made from one piece of felt on a mould and were widely worn in cold weather because the snow is so hard'. There was no danger, in the Siberian winter, of damp from melting snow penetrating the felt.

The royal family's luggage that was finally delivered to the Ipatiev House and put in a special storeroom was also soon at risk under the haphazard supervision of their first commandant, Alexander Avdeyev. Not only was he coarse and a heavy drinker, but he was lax in supervising the individual guards. When Nicholas and his family went to the store to examine any of their possessions they had to be accompanied by one or other of the guards. And it was not long before the guards were helping themselves to the contents of the trunks. Nicholas protested, but Avdeyev did nothing about it.

What worried Nicholas was not only the valuables, but their private correspondence and personal diaries also kept there. And by a cruel irony, it was the change-over in command from Avdeyev to Yurovsky, bringing with it the final stage of the family's eventual massacre, that brought short-term relief to Nicholas's anxieties. One of Yurovsky's first acts on taking over was to control the guards, and give Nicholas the impression that Avdeyev's laxness would not be tolerated. Yurovsky, Nicholas wrote in his diary,

explained that an unpleasant incident had occurred, referring to the dis-appearance of our things. Thus what I wrote on May 28 [he was using the old Julian calendar] is confirmed. I am sorry for Avdeyev but it was his own fault since he did not keep his people from stealing things out of the trunks in the shed.

Yurovsky even returned a stolen watch.[5]

Thus Nicholas took the subsequent stocktaking of their valuables as part of this welcome tightening up of discipline. Not so the more realistic Alexandra. She noted the incident quite differently in *her* diary:

The Commandant and his young assistant made us show all our jewels we had on and the younger one noted all down and then they were taken away from us. Why? For how long? Where? – I do not know – they left me only two bracelets from Uncle Leopold [the late Duke of Albany] which I cannot take off, and left each of the children the bracelets he gave them, and which cannot be slipped off, also N's engagement ring, which he could not take off. They took away all our keys from our boxes in the loft, which they had still left us – but promised to return them.[6]

Next day she reported that the commandant returned with their jewels, sealed them up in their presence and left them on the table. Yurovsky promised to come every day to see that the box had not been opened. And, according to Nicholas's diary, he did so.

As we now know, all the family's efforts to either conceal or conserve their valuables were to prove futile within a matter of days. Yurovsky, in charge of their planned execution, was also basically responsible for conserving what he could of their possessions. He was not always successful. Amidst the violence and chaos of the massacre itself and particularly the haste with which the Red guards had to conceal what they had done, opportunities for pilfering choice items were rarely ignored. On one occasion during the night of the murders Yurovsky insisted on the guards giving up gold items he knew they had taken. They immediately complied. But he did not prevent all forms of pilfering. Within days Alexis' rust-coloured spaniel Joy, which had survived the massacre, was found in the possession of one of the guards, along with Alexis' personal diary and an ikon from his bedside. Another guard had taken Alexandra's black silk parasol and the silver rings belonging to the grand duchesses. Other souvenirs, especially items of Nicholas's or Alexandra's clothing, were later handed out to loyal supporters.

The testimony of two of the guards eventually surfaced in a Moscow newspaper towards the end of 1991.[7] Before their death they had made written statements not only about the massacre but about the subsequent opening of the royal family's luggage that was left behind. They had had to use a jemmy to break open the inner locks of the suitcases. In the trunk belonging to Alexandra they found a suit of Rasputin's made up of long red silk with broadloom trousers and a belt. There were also portraits of the empress and her children. Others contained ikons and the four diaries of the grand duchesses. 'All the daughters kept careful day books,' one of the guards explained.

Yurovsky, however, at least ensured that the basic valuables, which he had deliberately itemised with Nicholas, were quickly accounted for. In fact the contents of the box of valuables were reported to be on his table in the Ipatiev House the day after the family were killed. The jewels were being examined and packed away by two of Yurovsky's deputies. One eye-witness reported: 'Piles of gold and silver objects were spread out . . . There were jewels lying there, taken from the imperial family prior to the shooting, and gold objects they had worn – bracelets, rings, watches.' In addition there were most of the valuables, necklaces and stones previously hidden in the underclothes of Alexandra and her daughters.

Eye-witness accounts of the massacre, brought together both by the original Sokolov inquiry and by the later efforts of Edvard Radzinsky, confirm that amid the first outburst of gunfire in the basement of the Ipatiev House two or three of the girls may have had bullets deflected from them by the jewels wrapped around them; even a bayonet attack was said to have been frustrated in one case. The result was that as the bodies were loaded on to the lorries outside the house some of the diamonds escaped through gashes in their outer clothing. The pearl belt containing jewel necklaces, sewn so carefully in Tobolsk, was thus found on Alexandra's body, and the girls' clothing was found to contain diamonds and other stones. Individual jewels were similarly strewn on the ground as the bodies were finally being undressed close to the mine shaft. While most of these were gathered up, several items of jewellery were trampled underfoot, only to be unearthed months later by the White investigators.

Two days after the murders, the main contents of the royal family's storeroom in the Ipatiev House, including all Nicholas's private papers and diaries, were put on a train in Ekaterinburg and departed for Moscow. At the same time the gold, silver and other jewellery brought together so assiduously by Yurovsky was handed over to one of his assistants to take north to Alapaevsk, where it was hidden from the Whites. That too arrived in Moscow a year later. In 1964 the assistant in question, Grigory Nikulin, described on the radio how he had carried the remaining Romanoff jewels out of Ekaterinburg in a dirty sack.[8]

So, as we saw earlier, all that was left for the White forces to record for posterity was the debris in the Ipatiev House, following the hasty departure of the Bolshevik guards, and the charred remains and personal items trampled into the ground close to the Four Brothers Mine. Although the basement had been cleared up of necessity, the upper rooms, where the royal family had spent their last days, still contained evidence of their day-to-day living: medicine bottles, toilet things, toothbrushes, hairpins, photograph frames and several books: among them *The Law of God, The Life of St Serafim of Sarov*, volumes of Tolstoy and Chekhov, the Bible and a book of prayer, as well as numerous personal ikons. When Pierre Gilliard visited the house some weeks later he found the end of a hairbrush, on the browned ivory of which he could still see Alexandra's initials: AF (Alexandra Feodorovna).

One item of some value, among all the personal possessions close to them to the last, was still conspicuous by its absence: Nicholas's stamp collection. It was hardly such a preoccupation or pleasure to him as was his cousin George V's whose diary is full of references to his turning for relief in the afternoons at Windsor from crucial affairs of state – on one occasion a political crisis – to his beloved stamps. But Nicholas was still an enthusiastic collector and the absence of his album, and any reference to it by the later evidence of eye-witnesses, suggests that it may have vanished en route to Ekaterinburg, most probably in Tobolsk, though just possibly in Ekaterinburg itself.

The stamps, however, had not been 'lost': examples from the collection began to appear on the western market in the early 1920s and have formed an intriguing puzzle for collectors ever since. One prominent collector, the Revd L. L. Tann, has done his best to piece together what exactly happened to the stamps since they were stolen some time in 1918. And I rely on his expert guidance in my attempt to trace just how one 'tsarist' collection suddenly reappeared and was put on sale by a Latvian collector at the International Stamp Exhibition of 1926 in New York, and how individual items from a similar 'tsarist' collection have also made their subsequent appearance.

The collection arose, not as in George V's case out of philatelic enthusiasm, but out of the Romanoff tercentenary celebrations in 1913. These naturally included the issue of a specially commissioned set of stamps, covering both Nicholas and his predecessors from Peter the Great onwards, as well as engravings of the Winter Palace and the Kremlin. Preparations began four years earlier and involved some of the finest Russian artists and engravers. All were under the control of the Director of the Imperial State Printing Office, Richards Zarrins. Before they were finally printed and issued, the stamps went through a long process of essays, trials, colour trials and specimens.

They were finally issued on January 2, 1913 and Zarrins had two separate sets produced, including essays and proofs, one for Nicholas and one for himself. Nicholas's set was in two handsome leather volumes and contained a total of 1,274 individual items. What has intrigued the experts ever since is which particular set (or extracts from such sets) has actually been offered on the market. But the first question is how Nicholas's set in particular managed to get from Tobolsk (or Ekaterinburg) to Latvia.

One version is that the twin albums of the tsar had been acquired from guards in the Ipatiev House by a local in Ekaterinburg and, when the Czech and anti-Bolshevik forces arrived at the end of July, they were sold to a White Russian officer for three loaves of bread and a packet of salt. He in turn, the story goes, sold them to a Swedish consular official who smuggled them to Riga. An alternative and more likely version, supported by the absence of any later references to the album by eye-witnesses in Ekaterinburg, strongly suggests that the tsar's two albums were pilfered in Tobolsk where, either together or separately, they were later acquired by a White Russian officer who flew them to Riga himself. Knowing what individual 'monarchists' were up to in Tobolsk, it is even conceivable that Nicholas offered the albums, as he did some of their jewellery, as his contribution to the financing of the expected 'rescue' efforts.

Whatever the source, the first substantive evidence of the collection's survival was the display and catalogue produced for the New York exhibition of 1926 by Mr Georg Jaeger of Lobau in Latvia. He claimed that what he was offering was the tsar's full collection and, as an added inducement to potential buyers, he quoted the then head of the Soviet

Printing Office as confirming that duplicates were now impossible as all the original matrices and patterns had been destroyed in 1918. The assumption at the time was that Mr Jaeger was offering the tsar's full two-volume collection and that the other collection was still in Mr Zarrins' possession. He stayed on after the Revolution, designing at least one further set of Soviet stamps, before moving to Latvia. The Revd Tann's present view is that only half of the tsar's collection was actually offered in New York in 1926 and that the other volume of Nicholas's collection came out separately and was broken up by dealers. He also believes that Zarrins' collection, which Zarrin, too, sold on the market, was maintained intact at least until the mid-1980s. After attracting a meagre £3,000 ($7,000) in 1967, it was sold for £30,000 ($65,000) twelve years later. Its present whereabouts is not known.

Even the tsar's single volume that first emerged in New York did not survive intact for very long. A London dealer broke it up into 'several substantial sections' in 1930. These were basically what are known as the 'proofs' from the original collection; the rarer rejected 'essays' from the total collection are thought to have been in the tsar's second volume, which was broken up earlier. The latter are on offer, from time to time, for prices upwards of £400 each, while 'proofs' attract around £100 each.[9] All these stamps may have given Nicholas a certain amount of distraction, even pleasure, during his extended exile in Siberia; yet they, like so many of the valuable possessions the family took with them from Tsarskoe Selo, proved worthless to him in the end.

The wealth they left behind in Tsarskoe Selo and Petrograd was also ultimately lost to the Romanoffs, either immediately in February 1917, when virtually all the palaces and most of the contents reverted to the Provisional government, or shortly after the Bolshevik coup in November, when Lenin simply took over the private possessions of the wealthy in a series of state diktats. The final tidying-up process the following summer even formed part of the planned massacre. It is now assumed[10] that the decree nationalising the Romanoff family's possessions was taken at the same meeting as that agreeing the details of their murder at the beginning of July.

The actual destruction of so many royal possessions occurred just before they left Tsarskoe Selo, when the Winter Palace was first taken over by hundreds of soldiers; and during their early months in Tobolsk, particularly on the night of the October Revolution when, following the dramatic intervention of the cruiser *Aurora*, mobs filled the palace looting and destroying as much as they could.

Nicholas and Alexandra were aware of some of this from letters they received from friends in Petrograd. 'What dreadful news about the robbing of the sacristy in the Winter Palace,' Alexandra wrote to Anna Vyrubova on one occasion from Tobolsk:

There were so many precious relics and many of our own ikons. They say it has been the same in the church of Gatchina. Did you know that the portraits of my parents and of father have been utterly destroyed? Also my Russian court dresses and all the others as well? But the destruction of the churches is the worst of all. They say it was the soldiers from the hospital in the Winter Palace who did it.

But they were spared the full horror of the looting and wanton destruction.

The irony of it all is that the Provisional government and even the Bolshevik government, in their different ways, took steps to monitor and to some extent conserve the treasures in the main royal palaces. Golovin, with whom Benckendorff had discussed the details of Nicholas's wealth, was directly responsible for the preservation of arts, museums and antiquities in general and the contents of the royal palaces in Petrograd, Tsarskoe Selo, Gatchina and Peterhof in particular. Special protective committees were set up, under his supervision, to undertake the task; and, to some extent, they did what they could to clarify exactly what of value remained in the various palaces and even set about packing up the most valuable items. The trouble was that carelessness, envy and outbreaks of sheer vandalism continued at the same time. While official posters were going up in Petrograd encouraging people to 'protect the records of bygone days', bronze ornaments were wrenched from palace railings as souvenirs, bonfires were made of old inlaid woodwork, noses deliberately knocked off statues and eighteenth-century pavilions broken up for matchwood.

Formal protection went hand in hand with the destruction of so much of the former royal possessions. The conservation efforts were quite considerable.[11] All the rooms used by the former royal family were photographed as quickly as possible, with the help of the remaining servants, to ensure that the rooms remained exactly as the family had left them. Some 225 photographs were taken. Thereafter began the slow process of identifying, cataloguing and packing up the contents, ready for urgent transfer to Moscow in the event of a continued German advance on Petrograd. In the first four months from the beginning of the Revolution, some three hundred major antiquities were catalogued and over a hundred boxes filled with precious items.

It was an uphill task, for the people busy cataloguing the treasures were surrounded in the Winter Palace by hundreds of soldiers, typists and other staff brought in to support Kerensky's new offices there, who were overwhelmed by their surroundings and filled with either apathy or a burning hatred of what they saw. The anonymous chairman of one of the main preservation committees has left a depressing account of this early period:

Bronze ornaments vanished from furniture and mantelpieces, costly coverings hung in tatters or were torn wholesale off sofas and couches, leaving them like bare skeletons and soldiers in dirty boots lounged on them. Some three dozen tables and chairs were crippled at once; several portraits in the gallery were instantly pricked with bayonets; abundant vermin appeared . . . We reasoned with the soldiers and tried to persuade them to spare the Palace; we complained to Makarov [who had accompanied the royal family to Tobolsk] and Golovin. The soldiers obtusely promised to conform to our solicitations, Makarov and Golovin shook their heads, but no changes ensued. Kerensky met our protests with complete indifference.

Far worse was to follow that October. The morning after the Bolshevik coup the preservation committee met to survey the further damage in the Winter Palace. Street fighting, ending with the shelling of the palace and its storming by the mob, had left rooms devastated, some walls smashed by shells, others riddled with bullet holes, windows shattered and glass everywhere. Looting had followed. As one eye-witness described the scene in the Winter Palace:

Apart from the rooms destroyed by the bombardment . . . the crowd had robbed whatever could be carried off, and demolished what it could not . . . oak chests . . . storing the crockery and china of the Winter Palace . . . had been either battered or pierced by the soldiers' bayonets. In the large oil-pictures . . . the eyes had been pierced through . . . In the private apartments of Alexander II and the last Tsar the devastation was indescribable . . . Under our feet lay valuable miniatures, picture frames, holy images [ikons], china, books and broken pieces of furniture.[12]

The uniforms of Nicholas I and Alexander II, including the one the latter had been murdered in, were in shreds on the floor. The grand duchesses' dresses and small bedroom items were scattered everywhere, along with the remains of the empress's dresses and ball gowns ('a fantastic medley of textures and colours from festival crimson to the palest greens and blues'). Alexander I's bureau had been pillaged and smashed into splinters. Six carefully prepared packing cases, ready for transport to Moscow, had been opened and ransacked, their contents (including a silver writing case presented to Alexander II) stolen. The safe room had been broken into and valuable plate worth some 2 million roubles (with the fall in the rouble, it was the equivalent of about £100,000) had vanished.

Even treasures that survived were hardly protected in the same way under the new regime. Nicholas's gifts from state and other visits overseas – an incredible mixture of carpets, sabres, Chinese jade, gold and silver objects, gifts studded with diamonds, rubies and sapphires – had been overlooked by the looters. The new Bolshevik overseer on the preservation committee quickly looked them over, took some items, including a gold Napoleon and some tea from China for his own use, and then ordered all the metal objects, including precious silver items, to be melted down and distributed to the people. The rest were placed in store.

The 'preservation' committee changed in other ways too. New members from the Boshevik party were quickly co-opted, some even who came 'fearlessly unasked to enquire into the state of the Palace'. The sacking of the palace and the pillaging of its contents had in any case undermined the protective purpose of the original committee set up by the Provisional government. Cataloguing of the remains was also inevitably postponed.

One complication which eventually defeated the committee was the tsar's incomparable wine cellar, begun under the Empress Elizabeth in the eighteenth century and built up over the years until it comprised a holding of tens of thousands of bottles. It quickly became a magnet to the soldiers who in any case had now taken much of the law into their own hands. The iron bars guarding the entrance to the cellars were persistently sawn through. The committee did what it could to provide extra pro-tection. 'We got a guard – the guard drank; we changed the men – the results were the same. They would at first fire at the invaders and after-wards drink all together.' Then the committee tried to sell the wine and got as far as receiving a Swedish offer of 'millions of roubles in gold'. But the stumbling block was the same: how could they get the cases of wine from the cellars to the boat without its being looted and drunk en route? The cellars remained a target for every marauding mob in Petrograd and a potential inflammatory element while they remained unprotected.

There remained one solution and eventually the decision was taken: an order was given to smash all the bottles and pour their contents in the Neva. 'The "noble" liquid began to flow into the Neva's cold waters,' an eye-witness later reported, 'lending them the tints of a rainbow ... and the grey wrathful river carried them away.' The operation took twenty-four hours. It was, in its way, the symbolic end to the Romanoff's private treasures remaining in Petrograd.

7

Bodies

Doubts about the fate of the Russian royal family and its wealth have thrived on the uncertainty surrounding the events at Ekaterinburg and the secrecy of the Bolshevik regime which succeeded it. Even now, after the DNA confirmation of the Romanoff remains, two bodies out of the eleven alleged to have been massacred are still said to be missing. And in the summer of 1993, only a few weeks before the final DNA announcement in London, a conference at the University of St Petersburg was solemnly told that the family was not executed. In such conditions conspiracy theories have continued to proliferate. And claimants for the remaining riches have been positively encouraged.

If such doubts still exist three-quarters of a century after the event, contemporary governments and claimants can perhaps be excused for behaving irrationally at the time. The rescue attempts said to have been made between the first arrest of the family at Tsarskoe Selo and the autumn of 1918 were all based on what was known or assumed at the time. Some, as we have seen, were either half-hearted or muddled or both. Others have alleged links to King George V or Kaiser Wilhelm, both of whom were close relatives of the Russian royal family – and the Kaiser had political ambitions and motives too. Whatever the source or motive of these efforts needs to be examined closely in any assessment of possible survivors and of what, subsequently, has been said about the lost wealth of the tsar.

One of the rescue attempts arose through the business connections of a Norwegian businessman, Jonas Lied, who had been closely involved with timber and mining concessions in Siberia, and had formed the Siberian Company and even taken on Russian nationality in 1914. While the royal family were in Tobolsk he had conceived the idea of rescuing them by one of his company's river steamers through the Arctic. He mentioned the idea to his friends in Vickers, the British armaments firm with connections in Russia, and in the spring of 1918 was encouraged to talk it over with appropriate people in London.[1] They included Sir Francis

Barker and Grand Duke Michael Michaelovitch, a cousin of the tsar, both Vickers directors, as well as top Foreign Office and Intelligence officials. Though he was offered 'a substantial sum' by a Norwegian business friend as backing, he was hardly encouraged by his reception in London and finally summed up the responses as simply: 'Please don't mention my name.' The removal of the family from Tobolsk in April of that year put an end to his plan and he returned to Norway.

Attempts have been made to link Lied's plans with George V, by implying that the top people seen by him in London were part of an establishment plot, naturally including the royal family. Much more likely is that the Foreign Office and intelligence people were simply checking out what Vickers had told them about Lied and assessing the possibilities. Evidence of any royal connection, as part of an intelligence plot going well beyond the normal obligation to keep Buckingham Palace informed about their cousins, remains tenuous.

Far more intriguing is the supposed plot to rescue the whole family and the apparent rescue of at least one of the grand duchesses by aeroplane from Ekaterinburg mentioned in the private diary of Colonel Richard Meinertzhagen, whose career in the Foreign Office and in the intelligence services is recorded in more than one biography. The basic evidence is still there for all to see in the Rhodes House Library at Oxford, on one page of a daily diary running to some 15,000 pages in seventy-six volumes.

Meinertzhagen kept a diary for many years of his career, as an ornithologist, intelligence officer, traveller and Middle East expert. It was in this latter capacity that he attended the Versailles Peace Conference in 1919 as a member of the British Military Mission and earlier had had to go regularly to Buckingham Palace to brief George V on the various Middle East campaigns. His last diary entry was on November 11, 1918, when he wrote:

For nineteen years I have kept up this diary without a break until February of this year when I entered the War Office. I then found that my work brought me in contact with so much very secret matter, and that whatever my opinions were they were based on essentially secret information.

This did not prevent him from including the occasional entry from February onwards. One of these, on March 17, 1918, referred to his latest chat with George V at Buckingham Palace. He reported laconically: 'From campaigns the conversation drifted on to stamps. Of course I had to go and see his stamp collection. I was there altogether over an hour.' But it was his entry for August 18, 1918 that has since riveted attention:

I have hesitated to record an exciting experience I had last month in connection with the murder of the Tsar and his family ... Even now I feel it a bit dangerous to disclose detail. Whilst at the War Office I had to visit the King at Buckingham Palace once a week to tell him about the campaigns in Iraq and German East Africa. On one occasion I found Hugh Trenchard [Chief of the Air Staff] there. Part of my work in the War Office was organising an intelligence service devoted to happenings in Russia. King George opened the conversation by saying he was devoted to the Tsar (his cousin) and could anything be done about rescuing them by air as he feared the whole family would be murdered. Hugh was very doubtful as the family must be closely guarded and there was no information regarding landing facilities for aircraft. I said I thought I could find out about that and perhaps arrange for a rescue party to bundle at least some of the royal prisoners into an aircraft. But it was taking a great risk as failure would entail the murder of the whole family. Hugh and I talked it over and after a few days I was able to try and get some of the children out, but the Tsar and his wife were too closely guarded. On July 1 everything was ready and the plane took off. Success was not complete and I find it too dangerous to give details. One child was literally thrown into the plane at Ekaterinburg, much bruised, and brought to Britain where she still is. But I am sure if her identity were known she would be tracked down and murdered as the heir to the Russian throne. What bestial swine the Russians are, murdering little girls because they are the daughters of the Tsar.[2]

While the first half of this entry has an authentic ring about it, doubts begin to creep in in assessing Meinertzhagen's diary note of his subsequent actions relating to the rescue attempt and the saving of one of the grand duchesses. If any of this were true, the evidence and memories of so many people about events in the first two weeks of July would have to be completely discounted or seriously amended. The references to a 'child' and 'little girls' also sit oddly with the fact that Anastasia, the youngest daughter, was seventeen at the time and her three elder sisters young women of nineteen to twenty-three. None the less one author, Michael Occleshaw, has diligently followed up almost every avenue in efforts not only to show that the entry may be true but that the single grand duchess rescued was Tatiana, that she was flown out of Ekaterinburg to Vladivostock, by stages, was accompanied by the then Prince Arthur of Connaught through Japan and Canada to Britain, and that she may be buried in a grave in Lydd in Kent.[3] In essence, however, the overriding question is whether Meinertzhagen can be believed; whether in fact he might have some tendency to fantasise. And on these grounds the doubts do crowd in.

Several authors have highlighted serious discrepancies in his diaries, extending from his references to Lawrence of Arabia to his contacts with political figures such as Chaim Weizman, Arthur Balfour, Lloyd George and even Nasser. The implication in some cases is that he wrote the daily entries later than indicated and in the knowledge of later events. His habit of typing the diaries on his italic typewriter – occasionally perhaps from notes written earlier – partly supports this possibility. One recent biographer summed it up this way: 'Clearly, Meinertzhagen could recreate events years later, but the carefully wrought realism could be ... largely the product of his imagination.'[4]

If Meinertzhagen's 'rescue' escapade still lacks positive support, no such doubts can now be entertained about the final initiative taken by the British royal family. George V in particular has been rightly criticised for the strenuous efforts to dissuade the British government from following through the original offer of asylum to Nicholas and his family in the spring of 1917. Evidence of a much more direct involvement of the British royal family in the summer of 1918, however, puts a different complexion on George V's behaviour and can now be set out in some detail. That it eventually proved to be too little and too late does not detract from its spontaneity. What is astonishing is that, throughout all the criticism of George V's cold-hearted response to his cousin Nicholas's plight in 1917, no effort was made by Buckingham Palace to highlight this evidence about a later initiative, which may be found in the Public Record Office at Kew and elsewhere. If the royal family behaved badly in 1917, they certainly did their best, somewhat belatedly, in 1918.

It all began in the May of that year when Princess Victoria of Battenberg, since June 1917, the Marchioness of Milford Haven, Lord Mountbatten's mother, wrote to the Foreign Secretary, Arthur Balfour, from Kent House in the Isle of Wight to express her anxieties about her sister, ex-Empress Alexandra, and the rest of the Russian royal family. The letter, in her own handwriting, explained that she had heard that while Nicholas, Alexandra and Maria had been taken to Ekaterinburg, Alexis and his three other sisters had been left on their own in Tobolsk. 'I dread to think,' she told Balfour, 'of the grief their separation must have been to them all and of the very great anxiety it must be to my sister, and which it also is to me, to think that her children are left without a single relation to take care of them.' She realised that Alexis might be 'a political asset', which might prevent him from being allowed out of the country, but she asked whether in some way the three girls, who could be of 'no value or importance as hostages to the Russian government' might be placed under her care in the Isle of Wight.

The Foreign Office file in the Public Records Office at Kew indicates that officials considered prevailing on Trotsky 'to give his secret consent' but felt that that would be only the first step in a hazardous exercise. To entrust the three girls to a Bolshevik escort would be unsafe and British officers might have to be sent to Tobolsk to escort them to Vladivostock, thus leaving the government open to accusations of a tsarist conspiracy and endangering many other lives. Balfour replied sympathetically at the end of May, explaining the difficulties and promising to look out for any other opportunities.

Princess Victoria was further alerted in July when all kinds of rumours began to circulate about events in Ekaterinburg. She once again wrote to the Foreign Office, no doubt keeping in close touch with Buckingham Palace. She asked quite simply whether some final effort could not be made to rescue her sister, Alexandra, and the rest of the Russian royal family. Perhaps help could be got from a neutral country, Sweden or Spain, or a royal court elsewhere? Or even from Lenin's wife, then living in Stockholm? The Foreign Office, through Lord Robert Cecil, was sympathetic but not immediately helpful, suggesting that Lenin's wife might cause 'more harm than good'; and suggested an approach to the Crown Princess of Sweden, the Swedish Ambassador in Moscow, or even the Danish Court. Robert Cecil added that he thought that there was still a Spanish representative in Moscow.

Presumably Princess Victoria felt that the Spanish approach might be best for she immediately wrote a letter to King Alfonso. She also clearly spoke to Buckingham Palace for the next step was a telegram from Queen Mary direct to Alfonso XIII in Madrid seeking his help. As the husband of a Battenberg princess who was a first cousin to ex-Empress Alexandra, Alfonso had already tried to do what he could for his Russian relatives a year earlier, without success. He was immediately responsive, but, showing a trace of male chauvinism, wanted to be quite sure that George V felt the same way. A telegram was sent from Madrid to King George at Windsor: 'May [that is, Queen Mary] wires me she would be grateful for any assistance I can give to save Russian Imperial Family. Can I count on your approval?' In King George's absence in France, Queen Mary consulted the Foreign Office and replied: 'George away. Telegram sent with knowledge of Foreign Office.'

Alfonso in any case had delayed no further and a flurry of telegrams had already been sent to Berlin, Vienna, Paris, Rome, Copenhagen and Moscow.[5] On August 6 King Alfonso sent this telegram to Princess Victoria in the Isle of Wight:

Letter received. I have started negotiations to save Empress and girls as Tsarevich think is dead. Proposition is to leave them to go to neutral country and on my word of honour they would remain here till the end of the war. Hope all the different sovereigns will assist me. Will let you know all news I get – Best love. Alfonso.

On August 15 George V returned from France and added his own backing to Queen Mary's earlier initiative in a telegram to Alfonso: 'Grateful if you will exert all your influence ... to rescue Imperial family of Russia.'

Two days after Alfonso's personal appeal to the Kaiser, he received a positive promise of help from Berlin. And within the week Berlin, Vienna and Moscow were receiving similar requests from the Pope, Benedict XV, and the King of Denmark backing up Alfonso. Encouraged by all this activity, the Director of Military Intelligence in London sent a cable to General Poole, then in charge of the British interventionist forces which had just landed in Archangel, telling him of King Alfonso's efforts on behalf of the Russian royal family. 'If you have a chance of helping and saving them,' the message concluded, 'Mr Balfour desires that you should do so.' He did not explain how. Meanwhile the Foreign Office sent copies of all these various moves to George V's mother, Queen Alexandra – who was also Nicholas's aunt – at Marlborough House.

The King of Spain made it clear that the royal family could stay in Spain at his expense until the end of the war and the Pope, through his Secretary of State, Cardinal Gaspari, promised that the Holy See was 'ready to provide, if needed, the finance for the ladies' maintenance in proper style'. He also offered the Dowager Empress Marie, then still living in the Crimea, where she had been persuaded to stay by the Provisional government, 'a life annuity to enable her to live in accordance with the dignity of her position'.

By mid-August, against the international uncertainty that still existed about the fate of the royal family, the assumption behind all these initiatives was that Nicholas had been killed, that there were still doubts about the fate of Alexis, but that Alexandra and her four daughters might still be alive. Fears were also growing about the four grand dukes still being held in the Peter and Paul Fortress in Petrograd.

Hard news about the royal family had emerged slowly and in a confusing way in western capitals. In Petrograd itself the Kremlin received a coded telegram from the Ural Regional Soviet at nine o'clock on the night of July 17, saying simply: 'Tell Sverdlov that the same fate has befallen the entire family as has its head. Officially the family will perish in the evacuation.' No doubt the message was understood, as it was intended to be. The following evening the Soviet of People's Commissars, with Lenin in the chair, was told of the message.[6] At the same time Karachan, one of Lenin's colleagues, reported the news to Robert Bruce Lockhart at the British Mission in Moscow. He was later to say: 'I believe that I was the first person to convey the news to the outside world.'[7] He immediately told the Foreign Office. Then on July 20, according to the memoirs of Sergei Markov, who had been involved with one of the monarchist rescue attempts with Soloviev, newsboys appeared on Nevsky Prospekt in the heart of Petrograd, shouting, 'Special edition. The ex-Tsar shot at Ekaterinburg. Death of Nicholai Romanoff.' The papers reported that his family had been 'transferred to a place of safety'.

Five days later the Danish royal family sent a message to King George, by way of the Foreign Office, indicating that in their opinion there was 'no longer any doubt about the death of the Tsar'. A month later Princess Victoria in the Isle of Wight received a message from the Crown Princess of Sweden reassuring her that she had heard from Ernst, Victoria's brother in Germany, that 'Alix [Alexandra] and the children are alive'. Then King George received a letter from a clergyman in Sidcup reporting that he had just escaped from Russia where he had been in gaol for some time. While in gaol he had met a Bolshevik general who had told him that the tsar and the tsarevich were dead but that the empress and her daughters were confined to a factory, he knew not where.

The royal grapevine was working overtime, even spanning belligerents in wartime through neutral relations. But it was shortly to be overwhelmed by conflicting news about Alexandra and the children. The British government received news at the beginning of September that all the family had been killed. This was reported to the War Cabinet on September 1 and King George sent the sad news to Princess Victoria in the Isle of Wight on September 4. Finally, to complete the confusion, came the report of Sir Charles Elliot, the British High Commissioner and Consul-General for Siberia, who travelled from Vladivostock to Ekaterinburg to undertake an on-the-spot investigation. His fifteen-page report for the Foreign Office was received in London on October 5. His conclusion was that 'the surviving members of the royal family', probably the empress and her son and daughters, had probably left Ekaterinburg by train to the north or west, though he remained apprehensive about their fate. The original report was immediately sent to Buckingham Palace.

These then were the conflicting reports being received in London, Madrid, Paris and Berlin throughout the period when talks about rescuing the empress and her daughters were at their peak. There is now strong reason to believe that hopes that some of the family had survived were deliberately encouraged by information fed from Moscow to Berlin. Thus the role of the Bolshevik government in the talks and negotiations that followed King Alfonso's and the Pope's initiative, especially in the light of Moscow's own knowledge of what had happened and what they had approved to be done in Ekaterinburg, is not only puzzling: it smacks of little more than double-dealing with a monetary purpose.

Even as late as the third week of September the Russian government was still informing the German government that a proposal had been made to the People's Commissaries to 'move the whole Imperial family to the Crimea' and that the grand dukes were simply being protected from the 'wrath of the people'. Inquiries made a few weeks later by the Vatican, through the Austro-Hungarian government, however, elicited the reply from Moscow that the authorities there 'did not know the whereabouts of the Tsarina and her daughters'. A request had been made for further inquiries to be made.[8] Cardinal Gaspari, the Secretary of State at the Vatican, reported this to the Archbishop of Westminster on October 28.

Thus two and a half months of talks, during which the survival and whereabouts of the family had been both assumed and discussed, had finally culminated in a dead-end. Perhaps the Bolshevik government had been genuinely negotiating from the outset and, in the turmoil of the White counter-attacks, had finally lost touch with any members of the royal family not killed in the Ipatiev House. Far more likely, in the light of Lenin's cynical view of any negotiations, is that the Bolsheviks kept the talks going as long as possible but, in the end, sensing that there was little more to be prised out of German and Austrian governments (tottering as they were to their inevitable defeat only a matter of weeks later) and knowing that the truth about the fate of the family was bound to emerge, simply decided that further negotiations were pointless.

What has to be realised is that complex manoeuvrings between the German and Bolshevik governments had been going on ever since the signing of the Brest-Litovsk Treaty, especially in relation to the royal family, and well before King Alfonso took his final initiative. A mixture of blood relations and political opportunities had naturally motivated the Kaiser. On the Bolshevik side, in spite of the humiliating financial terms imposed on them, and accepted by Lenin, the hostage value of Nicholas and his family could hardly have escaped their notice.

The Bolshevik government was also aware of the large deposits placed in Berlin by the imperial court before the war and so far left untouched because of hostilities. There is evidence that questions about these assets were raised by the Bolsheviks during the talks. It was known that close relations between the Mendelssohn Bank in Berlin and the Russian court and government had been maintained for years; and Peter Bark, the last tsarist Finance Minister, had worked at the bank in Berlin in his youth.

Rumours of an offer of asylum to the tsarina and the children from the Kaiser circulated round Tobolsk while the family were there in the winter and spring of 1917–18. The general assumption was that Alexandra's brother, the Grand Duke Ernst of Hesse, had taken the initiative at an opportune time. If true it could have been the reason for Nicholas's agitation when, against the background of the Brest-Litovsk Treaty, he and Alexandra were first asked to accompany Yakovlov away from Tobolsk to an unknown destination, possibly Moscow. To the Germans the royal family spelt political influence for the future; to the Russians a possible trade-off, with financial or political rewards.

It is now clear that the German government was not only negotiating with the Soviet government in Moscow but also with what were plainly monarchist elements in Petrograd. We know that Count Benckendorff and others had earlier made approaches to the German Ambassador on behalf of the tsar. Such contacts, with others now playing the lead role, were still going on as late as July 1918. The last such effort to be documented occurred in mid-July. Ironically, in a letter actually dated July 17, the date of the family's massacre, the Swiss Section of the League for the Restoration of the Russian Empire wrote to Arthur Balfour at the Foreign Office, explaining the latest German–Russian moves.

The letter[9] stated that the Duke of Leuchtenberg, Meriel Buchanan's old friend who had approached her father, the British Ambassador, fifteen months earlier in his first attempt to save the tsar, had recently been in Berlin on a similar mission and had eventually tried to get Nicholas to agree to a plan based on German help. The letter said that Nicholas had refused (hence no doubt his agitation at the time of his departure from Tobolsk) and that, as a result Berlin was 'considering kidnapping the Tsar and his family and bringing them to Germany'. The German government had asked the Swiss Section of the League for their agreement. They in turn wanted to know the views of the Allies and sent similar letters to Clemenceau in Paris and Orlando in Rome.

Nothing came of these monarchist plans largely because they could not agree either on whether to restore Nicholas or his son Alexis (some wanted one; some the other) with the Kaiser's help or not. And while they continued to dither among themselves and bombard European capitals with memoranda (the Quai d'Orsay received fourteen such missives in a matter of weeks) they were overtaken both by events and by the initiatives from London, Madrid and Rome.

The Germans were not the only players to realise the hostage value of the family. Thomas Preston, the British Consul in Ekaterinburg, reported to the Foreign Office in mid-September that the Bolsheviks in Ekaterinburg had had 'considerable friction with the Central Bolshevik Government on money matters' and in the final months before the murders they had begun to use the royal family 'as a means of extracting funds from the Central Government by means of threatening to kill them' at a time when the Central Government was anxious to hand over the family to the Germans in Moscow.

Ransom demands did not cease even with the disappearance or the death of most of the family. As late as December the King and Queen of Denmark, because of their close relationship with ex-Empress Marie, were also reported to have made an offer of 500,000 roubles for the release of four of the grand dukes still imprisoned in Petrograd and even to have provided the money to the Danish Minister in Moscow. The Danish

Minister had already sent 25,000 roubles to ex-Empress Marie in the Crimea eight months earlier.

All these efforts came to nothing, including a final plea to Lenin from Maxim Gorky for the life of Grand Duke Nicholas, well known as a historian. 'The Revolution does not need historians,' was the response. Grand Duke Nicholas, his brother Grand Duke George and their cousins Grand Dukes Paul and Dimitri were shot in the Fortress of Peter and Paul in Petrograd in January 1919.

Thus throughout this period and since, two issues have dominated any assessment of what happened in Ekaterinburg and its aftermath. Were all the royal family killed there? And who can be regarded as the legitimate inheritor of any wealth that remains? The first clearly has a direct bearing on the second. From the point of view of tracing the wealth, the clarification of who, if anyone, survived becomes a direct pointer to whose evidence about the wealth we need to take seriously and whose can be discounted.

All the evidence points to the fact that a massacre did take place and that the events leading up to it were basically as Edvard Radzinsky has outlined. The only real doubts left are whether all the family were killed.

Evidence given by individual witnesses to the original Sokolov inquiry in 1918–20, though ultimately dismissed by Sokolov himself in his conclusions, pointed to the possibility that the tsarina and one or more of her daughters might have escaped to Perm. Such thoughts were amplified in two subsequent books, first by John O'Conor in *The Sokolov Investigation* in 1971 and then a few years later by Anthony Summers and Tom Mangold in *The File on the Tsar* in 1976.

The absence of any bodies added spice to the idea that there might have been survivors and that any one of the claimants might be telling the truth. That is until 1989 when Geli Ryabov, amidst the *glasnost* beginning to sweep the Soviet Union, announced that he had found what he was convinced were the bodies of the Russian royal family outside Ekaterinburg. The story he had to tell was dramatic enough, but according to him he had in effect been sitting on his discovery for close on a decade. On Moscow television in the spring of 1989 he explained how, having become interested in what might have happened to the Romanoffs while working in Sverdlovsk (the Bolshevik name for Ekaterinburg), he had offered to share in the research of the area with the local site geologist.[10] Having gone through the Sokolov material, he went to Leningrad to search for the survivors of Yurovsky's family, the commander at the Ipatiev House when the royal family was killed. This, he said, was in 1978.

He succeeded in finding Yurovsky's daughter, Rima, and his eldest son, Alexander, a retired admiral.

I got from them the facts which later allowed me to find the site we were searching for with the accuracy of a gunsight [he told his television audience]. Alexander gave me the notes of his father Yakov Yurovsky. These notes were written for the Soviet Government and for the well-known historian of that time, Michael Petrovsky. In these notes were all the facts, which, together with the facts in Sokolov's book, allowed me to calculate distances and determine the exact spot, which I did ... Later in the spring of 1979 we began our practical search.

It is worth pausing at this point to pull together both the source of Ryabov's knowledge of the site of the Romanoff burial place and that of Edvard Radzinsky. While Ryabov states that his information came from notes left by Yurovsky, Radzinsky discovered the same information in Yurovsky's original notes in the Central Archive of the October Revolution in Moscow. They had been provided for the official Soviet historian (Michael Petrovsky, according to Ryabov; or Michael Pokrovsky, according to Radzinsky), as an official account of the massacre by Yurovsky as the commandant in charge. At the end of the notes, in Yurovsky's own handwriting, according to Radzinsky, 'the terrible address has been added – the location of the grave where the corpses of the tsar and his family had been secretly buried'. This, it indicates, is at 'Koptyaki, 12 *versts* [that is, 12 miles] from Ekaterinburg to the north-west. The railway tracks pass 9 *versts* between Koptyaki and the Upper Isetsk factory. From where the railway tracks cross they are buried about 100 *sazhens* [700 feet] in the direction of the Isetsk factory.'

In his television broadcast Ryabov then went on to describe the final phase:

We were probably using methods of the 1920s when geologists had no special equipment. We took a water pipe, a few inches wide in diameter, sharpened it and began to insert it over the approximate site of the grave, using a heavy mallet ... Soon we were rewarded. At a certain place, the pipe brought forth a few sausages of compressed soil of a dark blue colour, oily to the touch. My friends, who were professional chemists, said that this was clear evidence of the actions of sulphuric acid on organic matter. On May 30, 1979 we finally discovered the site and began to excavate.

The first find, according to Ryabov, was black-green and turned out to be the pelvic bone of what he assumed was Nicholas. Then further skeletons were discovered. But only the skulls were moved from the grave. One had a hole in it, he said, presumably fired by a gun. Although the reports from Moscow originally spoke of eleven bodies or skeletons having been found, the full transcript of the television broadcast shows that

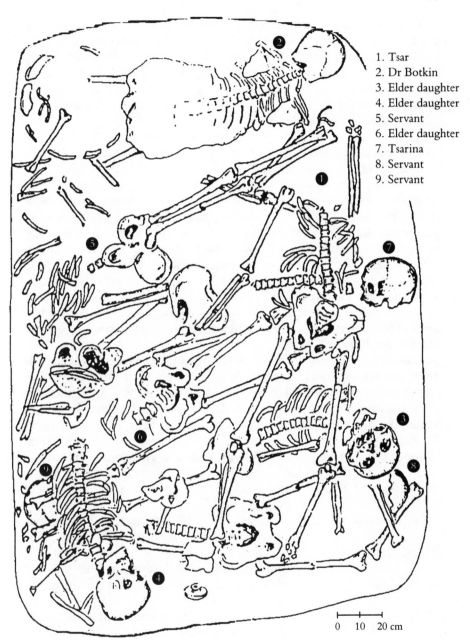

1. Tsar
2. Dr Botkin
3. Elder daughter
4. Elder daughter
5. Servant
6. Elder daughter
7. Tsarina
8. Servant
9. Servant

0   10   20 cm

Diagram showing position of the bones of the tsar, his family and courtiers,
when discovered outside Ekaterinburg

Ryabov was not quite as precise. As their hands reached down into the grave, he said, they touched 'at least eight or nine skeletons'. (We shall find that that number takes on a special significance.) In addition they found a number of broken containers of sulphuric acid. He had the skulls taken to Moscow for possible examination, but without success and, having recorded what details he wanted, he eventually returned them to their original site and added a cross. Ryabov himself was convinced that the combination of the skeletons, the bullet wounds in the skulls and the broken containers of sulphuric acid were proof enough that he had found the Romanoffs. This, however, had still to be proved scientifically.

Two years after Ryabov's television claims, Boris Yeltsin ordered an official investigation of the burial site. Lyudmila Koryakova, professor of archaeology at the Ural State University, was in charge of the investigation. She eventually reported in the spring of 1992 that eleven skeletons were being examined and that they showed 'traces of violence and mistreatment before death'.[11] By the summer, however, it became clear that the experts brought in to identify the bodies were having serious difficulty in establishing all eleven from the remains they had. Ryabov's original report that he had found 'at least nine' skulls was beginning to prove accurate. But some of the experts remained convinced that the missing bodies were out there somewhere.

Although Russian scientists were later employed to identify the skulls by the use of computers and photographs, and convinced themselves that they had identified several members of the family, real authentication remained necessary. Hence the arrival in London of Dr Pavel Ivanov, in September 1992, with nine left femurs for scientific DNA testing, at Russian expense, by the Forensic Science Service of the British Home Office at their laboratories at Aldermaston near Reading, in Berkshire. The aim: to see whether advanced DNA amplification tests could match the chemical structures in the skeletons with blood samples or strands of hair from descendants of the Romanoff family.

Before scientists of the Forensic Science Service tested the bones and drew conclusions they had before them reports of the preliminary examinations that had already taken place in Moscow as well as their own from sight of the bones in London. This is the description Peter Gill and his colleagues at Aldermaston and Pavel Ivanov have since provided:

All the skeletons showed evidence of violence and mistreatment before death. Some of the skulls had bullet wounds; bayonet marks were also found. Facial areas of the skulls were destroyed, rendering classical facial identification techniques difficult.

Extensive work was carried out by Russian forensic experts, involving computer-aided facial reconstruction, odontology, age estimation and sexing of the remains. Significantly, some of the bodies had gold, platinum and porcelain dental work, which indicated that at least some of the remains were aristocrats. Tests by Russian scientists tentatively indicated that the pit contained the remains of the Tsar, Tsarina and three of the five children. It was concluded that two bodies were missing, namely the Tsarevitch, Alexis, and one of the daughters.[12]

The Forensic Science Service began its tests by taking a blood sample from Prince Philip, Duke of Edinburgh, because of his direct relationship to Alexandra, the tsarina; and from two relatives of Nicholas, the tsar (who had an unbroken maternal descent from the tsar's maternal grandmother). One female relative, who is known to the family, wishes to remain anonymous. Prince Rostislav Romanoff, who lives in London, was one of the original donors, his wife confirming that she had personally, even gladly, pulled the hair samples from his head. Alas, his sacrifice was probably unnecessary, since his sample was not as significant as those of his female cousin.

The Forensic Science Service, following techniques developed to identify genetic links, later explained that normal DNA testing was inappropriate because of the age of the bones. They had had to use a process known as Polymerase Chain Reaction, which amplified the more normal DNA technique and enabled them to analyse variations in the chemical structure of the DNA between the individuals concerned.

The official announcement,[13] made in early July 1993, reported the results as follows:

The mystery surrounding the fate of the Russian Royal family after the 1917 Revolution has been solved ... Scientists believe five of the nine skeletons found are those of the Tsar, Tsarina and three female children. The identification matches that reached by anthropologists in Russia. The findings follow tests on blood samples provided by the Duke of Edinburgh and other relatives of the Romanoffs.

The pioneering work was based on maternally inherited DNA, known as mitochondrial DNA. A complete match was obtained between the Tsarina and the three children and the Duke of Edinburgh, a direct maternal descendant of the Tsarina's sister. Samples from two maternal relatives on the Tsar's side were examined. Both had identical mitochondrial DNA, but scientists found that the Tsar had a single mutation not present in the relatives. Further analysis showed two types of DNA were present in the Tsar probably as a result of a rare condition known as heteroplasmy. One matched the maternal relatives exactly, the other contained the single mutation.

Statistical analysis was complex. The estimate of 98.5 [probability that the identification is correct] is based on a neutral interpretation of the previous anthropological evidence and on the lowest interpretation of the DNA evidence. A more generous interpretation would increase it to over 99 per cent.

Leaving aside the jargon this means that the first check was to clarify whether there were at least five members of the same family among the nine skeletons and to confirm their sex. (The other four being the family doctor and three servants who were killed at the same time.) The second check was to see whether the tsarina could be identified by the hair or blood sample of a relative and whether the tsar could be similarly, and separately, identified.

The results confirm that five of the skeletons are from one family; that of the five, four are female; that one of the skeletons matches a sample from the Duke of Edinburgh, and is thus clearly the tsarina (confirmed through the DNA match with the Duke of Edinburgh's grandmother, who was Alexandra's sister); and that one skeleton matches samples from Romanoff descendants and is clearly the tsar.

Thus an important part of the jigsaw has now been put together. We have solid scientific evidence to support the assumption that the family were indeed killed together at the Ipatiev House on the night of July 16–17, as the written and oral evidence painstakingly put together by Edvard Radzinsky had already indicated, and which, in its turn, had confirmed the scholarly work that had gone on in the West before. Where the two sets of evidence also agree is on the number of absent members of the family. Two skeletons are missing out of the original eleven reported to have been killed. For his part Edvard Radzinsky, basing himself entirely on oral and written reports, also finally concluded that two bodies had not been satisfactorily accounted for. According to him, Yurovsky said they had been burned separately, and identified Alexis and the maid, Demidova, as the two dealt with differently from the others. The DNA results now suggest otherwise, showing that the missing bodies were both members of the Romanoff family and that one of them was certainly Alexis. So who was the other? Clearly one of the girls. But which one? Olga, Tatiana, Maria or Anastasia?

Two separate conclusions about the identity of the missing bodies have since been provided by experts who have examined them. The first came from an American forensic scientist who had studied the bones and based himself entirely on them. Dr William Maples, director of the C. A. Pound human identification laboratory at the University of Florida-Gainesville, was reported[14] as telling a conference examining the bones that at least two particular members of the family could be ruled out. 'All the skeletons' he said, 'appear to be too tall to be Anastasia and in the skeletal material we have looked at there is nothing that could represent Alexis'.

The second conclusion was provided by a Russian commission, under the direction of Deputy Prime Minister, Yuri F. Yarov. Basing itself on the work of forensic, anthropological and molecular analysis of the nine skeletons, and especially on the computerised matching of skulls and photographs, the official Russian report concluded that Alexis and Maria were still missing and that Anastasia had been satisfactorily identified.

If, as may be possible, all the family were killed and two of the bodies were simply disposed of separately, then it would not matter. But until the two bodies, or traces of them, are found the allegations of claimants and others about the fate of some members of the family may well persist. The difficulty is that the mystery, and the untold wealth said to be attached to it, have themselves encouraged claimants over the years and this final gap in the evidence can only give an added fillip to such claims.

8

Survivors

Once it became clear that the tsar and at least some of his family had been shot dead at Ekaterinburg, the question of who would get his wealth, if any survived to be handed down, became uppermost in many people's minds.

Until the Bolshevik take-over in October 1917, the former royal family had been able to keep not only their personal possessions but also their private accounts at the State Bank; they still had whatever money, gold or other investments that were in their names abroad; and they were receiving part of the upkeep of themselves, and of the courtiers still accompanying them, from the State Budget. With the help of Count Benckendorff and his stepson, Prince Basil Dolgorukov, Nicholas had agreed to share the running of the household with the government, drawing on their personal accounts with the State Bank to provide their share of the money needed.

The Bolsheviks' final take-over shattered these arrangements and reduced the family's possessions to what they had managed to take with them from Tobolsk to Ekaterinburg. Even then their remaining jewels had been catalogued and checked almost daily. Their personal money in the State Bank had, like that of other 'rich' people, been nationalised by the Bolsheviks and, on July 13, 1918, plainly in anticipation of their final massacre, the Bolshevik government had passed a decree in Moscow nationalising the properties of the Romanoff family.[1]

The Romanoff wealth that remained was thus made up of personal possessions (especially jewels) acquired by the Bolsheviks or their officials; state property that was still regarded as personal by Nicholas and his family; and money, gold and investments held abroad in personal names or regarded as belonging to the Romanoffs by virtue of their previous responsibilities. This is the basis on which subsequent claims have been made.

The real panoply of royalty – the royal trains, the royal yacht, the royal cars, the state jewels – had all vanished on abdication. The royal palaces too, in spite of Count Benckendorff's final plea to the Provisional government, had become state property. The crown lands and the important revenue from them (the so-called 'udely' or 'appanage' income) had reverted first to the Provisional government then to the Bolshevik government. In detailing the royal family's monetary problems following Nicholas's abdication, we earlier touched upon two semi-official estimates of what personal accounts the family still possessed at that time. One, produced by Kerensky and Lvov in their efforts to gauge the family's private resources should they be exiled overseas, and subsequently produced in evidence to Sokolov, put the family's monetary wealth, presumably their personal bank accounts and investments, at home and abroad, at some 14 million roubles (or £933,000). The other arose in negotiations between Count Benckendorff and Count Rostovtsev, the empress's secretary, during their efforts to clarify the cost of the royal court at Tsarskoe Selo, and stated that the tsar's total capital was 'less than a million roubles', that of the tsarina 'one and a half million' and that of the five children 'varied between two and three millions each'. Thus, according to Benckendorff, the family's total resources amounted to between 12,500,000 and 17,500,000 roubles (£833,000 and £1,666,000).

Kerensky's overall figure of 14 million roubles thus fits neatly into the middle of Benckendorff's variants and provides a confirmation of a sort. But there is, by chance, another source published earlier than these two semi-official ones, which not only gives more detail but provides additional confirmation of the total. *The Fall of the Romanoffs*, an anonymous account of the tsarist regime apparently written in the summer of 1917 when the royal family had just arrived in Tobolsk, was published in Petrograd a year later.[2] The author, simply described as 'A Russian', signs the preface to an earlier and similar book (*Russian Court Memoirs*, written in 1916 and published in 1917 before Nicholas abdicated) as 'B.W.'. He, or probably she, was, from internal evidence in both books, plainly close to the court.

The author reports:

The private fortunes of the ex-Tsar and his family amount to the following sums:

The ex-Emperor Nicholas possesses a capital of		908,000 roubles
The ex-Empress Alexandra		1,006,400
The Tsarevitch		1,425,700
The Grand Duchesses	Olga	3,185,500
	Tatiana	2,118,500
	Marie	1,854,430
	Anastasia	1,612,500

Apart from this money, the Imperial Family is supposed to have great sums of money deposited in foreign banks, especially in the Bank of England.

The total of these seven accounts comes to 12,111,030 roubles (roughly £809,000). Putting it alongside the other two estimates, one can conclude that the family's total monetary resources at this time were somewhere between 12 million and 14 million roubles (between £800,000 and £933,000).

What cannot, however, be deduced from these figures is what the family may or may not have had abroad. The Kerensky estimates implied that the total *included* their overseas accounts. So did those of Benckendorff. But he was more careful, simply mentioning overseas money in the case of the children. His exact words were: 'The capital of the Heir-apparent and his sisters, *that which was abroad as well as that which was in the State Bank*, varied between two and three million each.' Since he made no such statement in the case of Nicholas and Alexandra, the implication seems to be that only the children had money abroad. The anonymous author, however, indicated that his (or her) estimates *excluded* overseas money, and assumed that there were millions in the Bank of England.

These were no more than the first informed estimates. Many others were to follow over the years, some vague, some tantalisingly detailed, some from alleged royal survivors of the massacre, some from close relatives. We shall be assessing their value as we go along, trying to sift the truth from the gossip and hard facts from bogus claims. It is to the first wave of such claimants, real and otherwise, that we now need to turn. Some were genuine Romanoffs. Some claimed to be so.

Prime among the surviving members of the wider Romanoff family were those with the closest family links to the British royal family, George V's aunt and mother of the tsar, the former Empress Marie, and her two daughters, Grand Duchess Xenia and Grand Duchess Olga, and their families. Their escape was in its way typical of so many White Russian escapes at the time: a combination of reluctance to leave their native land and, at the same time, a determination to take what valuables they could with them. Some of the refugees were forced to lie their way across frontiers; some cowered in trains; some used forged papers; some were nearly shot crossing frozen rivers; all were reluctant exiles.[3] Empress Marie's escape was little different, for initially she resisted George V's attempts to persuade her to come to England, before final succumbing to the reality of her plight.

After her sad, and last, goodbye to Nicholas at Mogilev in March 1917, Marie had returned to Kiev with her son-in-law, Grand Duke Alexander (Xenia's husband, who had been head of the Russian air force). But shortly afterwards both of them, along with her younger daughter, Grand Duchess Olga and her second husband Colonel Kulikovsky, and their staff, had very reluctantly been persuaded by the Provisional government to move to the Romanoff estates in the Crimea. Not only were all the Romanoffs required to register with the new government, but there was plainly advantage in having as many of them as possible together in one place. Marie initially stayed on Grand Duke Alexander's estate at Ai Todor, about twelve miles from Yalta, and later at other nearby estates, Grand Duke Peter's at Djulber and Grand Duke George's at Harax. Marie's elder daughter, Grand Duchess Xenia, joined them within a few days.

The tides of war and revolution moved slowly over the Crimea for the next two years, as the fortunes of both the Germans and the Bolsheviks ebbed and flowed. Marie's living conditions changed accordingly. On some occasions the changes were swift and somewhat brutal. On others they had time to take account of the latest skirmishes. One day she was basking in the tranquillity of the Romanoff estate, lunching under the trees, with the warm sea breeze almost persuading her that the horrors of war were imagined; the next morning her bedroom was broken into by a group of Bolshevik sailors, led by the local commissar, intent on seeking out her hidden valuables, while she was still in her nightdress. They took papers, diaries and, to her deep regret, an old Danish Bible she had brought with her to Russia on her marriage to Alexander III. But they missed her jewel box which had been left in full view on her bedroom table.

All the Romanoffs were, in essence, under house arrest, but the conditions varied according to local pressures. Some even managed to travel to Petrograd and back in the early days of the Revolution not only to check on the contents of their palaces but even to rescue what they could. On one occasion Prince Felix Youssopov returned from Petrograd having entered Marie's home, the Anichkov Palace, cut one of her favourite paintings of Alexander III from its frame and brought it back for her, undetected, in a small parcel.

Later their house arrest became tighter and, for a time, a distinction was made between the 'real' Romanoffs and those, like Grand Duchess Olga, who had lost the name in marriage to a commoner and were thus kept on separate estates with a little more freedom. Rivalry between the local Soviets, in Yalta and in Sebastopol, also brought its complications because of their need to decide who should provide 'protection'. But the biggest changes came, first, with the successes of the German army in southern Russia following the Brest-Litovsk Treaty in March 1918, and then with the final defeat of the German armies in the West, their collapse everywhere and the encroachment once again of the Bolsheviks.

One morning after the German armies reached the Crimean coast a German general appeared and, speaking in French, asked for an introduction to Marie and Grand Duke Nicholas. He said he had an invitation, on behalf of the Kaiser, for them to come to Germany with their families. Prince Roman Romanoff's mother indicated that such a meeting would be difficult but promised the general that a reply would be sent direct to his headquarters in Yalta. She immediately consulted her husband and Grand Duke Nicholas and, between them, they sent Baron Stahl to Yalta to refuse the Kaiser's invitation. Marie, on learning what had happened, was delighted at not having to meet a German. Her son-in-law Grand Duke Alexander was furious at not being consulted and would clearly have been prepared to negotiate.[4]

Thereafter, as the Germans retreated towards the end of November 1918, they were visited by volunteer Tartars who offered to provide protection and were glad to help Marie, who had earlier been head of their regiment. She, in turn, still seemed determined to stay in Russia as long as she could. But the threat of the renewed encroachment of the Bolsheviks following the German armistice, had once again alerted Marie's sister, Queen Alexandra in London, and it was only a matter of days after the German armistice had been signed that both George V and the British government moved into action.

First came a decision by the Cabinet. Members were informed at a Cabinet meeting on November 14 that, at 8 a.m. the previous day, the Allied fleet under Admiral Colthorpe had arrived off Constantinople. The matter before them was whether steps should be taken to secure the safety of the Dowager Empress, in the Crimea. With her house near the shore, access would be easy. The Cabinet did not hesitate, immediately authorising the Admiralty to make the necessary arrangements. The same day a 'very secret' signal was sent from the Admiralty to the Commander-in-Chief, Mediterranean:

You are to consider the possibility of sending a ship at the first opportunity to Ai-Todor with a view to secretly bringing away the Dowager Empress and the late Emperor's sisters. The matter is to be arranged with the greatest care and tact. No force is to be used or armed party landed and anything approaching a conflict with any guards there may be on the house is to be absolutely avoided.

The navy wasted no time. Before the end of the month back came a reply, reporting both action and messages from Marie:

Clear the line. Secret. Following is for Admiralty and I request it may be communicated to His Majesty the King. Commander Charles Turle and Russian naval officer, Commander Korostovzoff to Crimea in HMS *Tribune* plus HMS *Shark*. Landed on beach north of Cape Ai-Todor, early Thursday morning,

November 21. Audience with Empress Marie. Offered to take her to Constantinople. She is in good health. No anxiety (not shared by her entourage).
From enquiries she had caused to be made, she is of the opinion that the Emperor
may be still alive and on that account wishes to remain in Russia. Empress
attended by Admiral Prince Viamensky and Prince Dolgorouky, while close
by live Grand Dukes Alexander, Nicholas, Peter, George, Dimitri and Grand
Duchesses Olga and Xenia.

Almost simultaneously George V and his mother, Queen Alexandra,
received personal greetings from Marie. The king got grateful thanks:
'Just seen Commander Turle. So touched and thankful for your kind
proposal. Love to all. Aunt Minny.' Alexandra got a sister's enthusiasm.
'Hurrah. Delighted at last to wire. Such joy to see one of your captain's
kind proposal. Hope that more ships will come openly and soon. Love to
you all. Signed Sister Dagmar.' (Dagmar was Marie's original Danish
name.)[5]

This first contact was followed by others, including further ships of the
Royal Navy. Telegrams arrived from the King and Queen of Italy and
from the King of Montenegro, offering asylum to their relatives. Then
Grand Duke Alexander left on a Royal Navy ship to attend the peace
talks in Paris as the Romanoff representative – and was cold-shouldered
for his pains. Marie meanwhile remained unmoved, for a time, by the
repeated offers from London, supported as they were with the knowledge
that British help for the White Russians (thirteen thousand troops in
north Russia and a thousand in Siberia) was more likely to be reduced than
increased, until at last even she could see that White Russian resistance in
the area was crumbling.

Finally, on April 4, 1919, Admiral Calthorpe sent HMS *Marlborough*
to Sebastopol, with a letter from Queen Alexandra, in a last attempt to
persuade her sister to leave. Reluctantly she agreed, provided she could
bring who she wanted with her. This was beyond the original Admiralty
orders, but she quickly got her way and both relatives and staff were
immediately set to packing valuable possessions in large trunks to be
picked up at Yalta. But not everyone came with her. Her daughter Olga
joined her husband Colonel Kulikovsky with the White Russian army in
the Caucasus.

The fleeing passengers said their goodbyes in different ways. Some
simply embarked at Yalta with their luggage. Prince Roman Romanoff
went for a last walk up a nearby hill alone, with his most valuable
possessions (including his diary) in a small handbag. Others congregated
together. Finally Marie, wearing a black coat and a small black hat, walked
slowly past everyone as she and her daughter and grandsons went on
board together.

The additional passengers insisted on by Marie led to immediate difficulties (as well as headaches for the Home Office on arrival in England). Suitcases were piled high on deck and the mutual lack of knowledge of the other's language of the English sailors and Russian servants hardly helped. Grand Duke Peter's elder daughter, Princess Marina, eventually acted as interpreter. Dogs too had been brought aboard by Marie, Xenia and Princess Militsa of Montenegro. Such was the bustle that even Empress Marie's arrival on board went virtually unnoticed by the officer allotted to her. But once the ice had been broken, helped personally by Marie, friendliness and dignity went hand in hand for the rest of the voyage.[6]

She had made one final decision before departure, which the navy reluctantly but quickly accepted. She refused to leave Yalta until all the other refugee boats were under way and insisted on the *Marlborough* being last. And as the final ship passed by, the emigrants recognised their former Empress Marie and Grand Duke Nicholas on deck and began to sing 'God Save the Tsar'. It was the last occasion on which the anthem was sung in the presence of a former reigning Romanoff in Russian territory.

They were taking with them conflicting thoughts and emotions; relief at their survival mingled with the melancholy assumption that they were unlikely to return. Their baggage heaped on deck was also a mixture of the pathetic remains of eighteen months of civil war and nuggets of priceless treasures. Some had little more with them than what they were wearing. Others had salvaged a great deal. It would not be an exaggeration to suggest that the 1990s value of the family jewellery, plate and paintings aboard the *Marlborough* could easily top £20 million.

Prince Felix Youssopov, the richest of them all before the Revolution, not only had two Rembrandts with him, which he had successfully cut out of their frames on one of his return visits to his palace in Petrograd, but also some of the family's choicest jewels. His mother had some of them in her luggage. The two Rembrandts – *Portrait of a Gentleman in a High Hat* and *Portrait of a Lady with an Ostrich Feather* – can be seen in the National Gallery in Washington. Grand Duke Peter and his son, Prince Roman, had had to leave the family silver in Petrograd, but the family butler's set of 'secondary silver', used below stairs, had been saved and was safely on board. Grand Duke Nicholas, with more prescience and, no doubt, organising ability than the others, had managed to save all of his family plate, gold as well as silver, along with his Sword of Honour with a gold hilt studded with diamonds. It was all amply reflected in over two hundred of his packing cases on deck.

In contrast, amid the chaos, even last-minute panics, on the quay-side, some fifty-four unidentified cases of one or other of the Romanoffs were left behind. It is a figure that still sticks in the minds of the grandchildren, and intrigues those who like to wonder what they contained, whose they were and what might have been. One at least of the trunks actually taken aboard has survived in the family of Grand Duchess Xenia, with its allocated number (No. 47) and even its handwritten inventory still intact, a haunting reminder of another age.

Jewellery was the obvious answer to the problem of transferring wealth from one country to another, especially on a friendly warship. Although HMS *Marlborough*'s 'manifest' is unavailable at the Public Record Office, it is hardly a secret, judging from the later evidence of sales, thefts and outright 'con' tricks, that the Romanoffs managed to carry a remarkable amount of personal valuables aboard with them. Some of their past possessions however remained in evidence in the streets of Yalta and Sebastopol, as British sailors were offered diamond rings, some of them clearly looted earlier, for as little as half a crown.

Empress Marie's jewels, confirmed as hers by the Provisional government in the original settlement agreed with Count Benckendorff, after the royal family had gone to Tobolsk, were one of the finest collections in the world. In the words of Prince David Chavchavadze, himself a direct descendant of Catherine the Great and Nicholas I and more recently an officer in the CIA, Marie's jewels contained

ropes of pearls, streams of emeralds green as the jungle, sapphires gleaming like an Oriental sky, diamonds of the finest quality, rare Byzantine jewels and clusters of rubies. One of the Tsar's presents to her was a necklace of great pearls of perfect form and colour . . . Many other treasures rested in her jewel vault, a tiara of rubies and diamonds, a flat band of diamonds and emeralds . . . a set of twenty pink diamond stars, and a tiara stomacher and collar.[7]

On Nicholas's abdication and her return to Kiev, Marie had taken a large part of her jewellery with her, leaving the rest in a hiding place in the Anitchkoff Palace in Petrograd. Much later Prince Felix Youssopov, on his return visit to Petrograd from the Crimea when he rescued two of his own Rembrandts, had deliberately gone to the Anitchkoff, on Marie's behalf. To his horror the hiding place was empty. But he at least had the satisfaction of tracking down the jewels. They had been found by agents of the Provisional government and were safely stored in Moscow, at least for a time, along with other Romanoff treasures.

Although disappointed at Felix's findings, Marie was touched by his enterprise in bringing back a painting of her late husband. It made her all the more determined to safeguard what she still had in her possession, especially after the sudden visit of the Bolshevik sailors into her bedroom at Ai-Todor, when they miraculously overlooked her jewel box. Thereafter Grand Duchess Olga had hidden Marie's jewels in the separate house she and her husband occupied on the edge of the estate. They, along with other valuables, were put for safety in small cocoa tins and whenever danger seemed to threaten Olga hid them in a cliff crevice on the beach there. They marked the spot with the white skull of a dog. One day they returned to find the skull lying on the beach. 'I still remember the cold drops of perspiration forming on my forehead,' Olga later remembered, 'as I watched my husband sticking his hand deep in every possible hole in the rock-face. What a relief when he finally pulled a cocoa tin rattling with jewels out of one hole!'[8]

Thus both Marie and Xenia still had their remaining jewels largely intact when HMS *Marlborough* left Yalta. So had Grand Duke Peter's family, though in their case some of their remaining jewellery had been deliberately sawn up, both as an earlier precaution and to conserve the gold. The rest, alas, was still in a bank box at Credit Lyonnais in Petrograd.

Grand Duchess Olga, who had left Harax for the Caucasus with her husband before the final return of the *Marlborough*, had none of her own jewels with her. On first arriving in Kiev, just before the start of the Revolution, she had written to her house steward to send her jewels to her. He had considered it far too risky and feared they would be lost in transit and had arranged to put them in a bank vault. There they remained. So when she finally left Kiev for the Crimea with her mother she was carrying no more than a small dressing-case. As she said later, 'I realised that I owned nothing else in the world.' The same was true as she and her husband and one small son made their way beyond Rostov on Don towards the Caucasus. And she gave birth to a second son in a peasant hut with only a village woman to help. The family finally ended up at the port of Novorossiysk, on the Black Sea coast, where they met an old friend in the Royal Navy, a fortuitous meeting which was to lead to their ultimate rescue. And, according to relations of Olga still in Denmark, her chambermaid managed to bring some of her jewels out a year later.

Meanwhile the first port of call for those aboard the *Marlborough* was Constantinople, where she rode at anchor for a few days. While there the captain arranged a service for the empress on Palm Sunday and even managed to fit in a reception for exiled passengers from other ships to meet her. It also gave Whitehall (essentially the Foreign Office and Home Office) a little more time to sort out which Romanoffs, and which members of their family and staff on board, would be immediately welcome in Britain and which not. Some in any case had decided to go elsewhere: Grand Duke Nicholas and his family to France and Grand Duke Peter and his family to Italy, where his wife's sister was queen. Both families disembarked at Constantinople and joined another Royal Navy vessel, HMS *Nelson*, bound for Genoa. The Youssopovs, conscious that they might not be welcome in London because of the Rasputin affair, made their own way through Italy to Paris, where they stayed for some time at the Hôtel Vendôme.

When the *Marlborough* arrived at Malta, Empress Marie still expected, and continued to express a firm wish, to stay on board the ship to Portsmouth. But the Royal Navy had other priorities and other ideas. So it took much persuasion, including a conciliatory message from George V and friendly hospitality at the Governor's House at the San Antonio Palace in Malta, to get her to re-embark on HMS *Nelson*, on its return from transporting Grand Dukes Nicholas and Peter and their families to Genoa. HMS *Marlborough* was needed elsewhere.

The *Nelson* finally arrived at Spithead on May 8 and, next day, Marie was greeted at Victoria Station by her sister, Queen Alexandra, as well as by King George, Queen Mary and other members of the royal family. It was a dignified, even formal, reunion. Their tearful reminiscences were left for their private sisterly exchanges much later at Marlborough House, Alexandra's London home.

Marie, staying initially at Marlborough House, relied on Alexandra to foot the bills from her normal allowances. But that arrangement could hardly be permanent. Not only did she and her daughter Xenia and their family require a regular income; they were acutely conscious of the needs of other Romanoffs and untold thousands of Russian refugees. Grand Duke Michael, Nicholas's cousin and not to be confused with his younger brother, had been in England during the war and was one of the first to plead poverty after the Revolution. He wrote to Arthur Balfour at the Foreign Office, setting out his plight in the third person: 'His Imperial Highness is entirely without means for his living requirements and has no capital or money here.' He suggested that Sir George Buchanan, the British Ambassador in Petrograd, should arrange for all his securities to be placed in the name of Drummonds Bank, so that he could get a bank loan. He was politely turned down, but had more success at Buckingham Palace.

Although Sir Frederick Ponsonby, who replied to Grand Duke Michael on behalf of the king and queen, privately thought Michael 'a touchy and tiresome man', he had good news for him:

I told their Majesties that until things settled down in Russia it would be impossible to say how much you would in future receive but that I understood that if £10,000 could be advanced to you, that would suffice to carry you on for the next six months or so. I said that I understood that Countess Torby's jewels which were at the bank were worth £40,000, and if any security was needed that would be ample. The King and Queen said they did not wish for any security and that they would together send you £5,000 now and £5,000 in July. They did not wish any documents drawn up or formalities gone through.

He added that the jewels might be regarded as 'a nominal security', and hinted that the sums offered might have been bigger, but the king had 'put every penny he has in the War Loan and has left me little margin . . .' That emphasis on security was to recur later with Empress Marie's jewels.

Grand Duchess Xenia meanwhile was also readjusting to a new way of life in exile. She too had her personal jewels to fall back on, initially as security for loans, and soon as a magnet to the unscrupulous. But at least she had friends to help her. The British royal family and her aunt Queen Alexandra were providing accommodation; and Herbert Galloway Stewart, who had looked after her children in London before the war, was also on hand and helped her to open an account at Coutts, the royal family's bankers in the Strand. So within six weeks of arriving at Spithead she had a current account with £1,000 in credit, and a new cheque book and had immediately gone round to Harrods and spent £98 there with her first cheque. After her recent experiences who can blame her. Later she is also said to have had an account at Barings.

For the next few months Marie and Alexandra, who had much family gossip and tragedy to catch up with, divided their time between Marlborough House and Sandringham. But 'home' to Marie, if not now to Alexandra, was to be Denmark; and within a few months of her arrival in England she was once again on board ship, this time the MS *Fionia*, bound for Copenhagen, where she arrived on August 19. The vessel was a rather special diesel-driven Danish merchant ship of the East Asiatic Company, already greatly admired by Winston Churchill when he was at the Admiralty. The East Asiatic was run by H. N. Andersen, a successful Danish businessman who had been helped in the past by Danish contacts in Russia, including Empress Marie, and had acted as an adviser to Nicholas on a prewar visit to the Far East. He was naturally keen to help her in her hour of need.

With Marie at the Amalienborg Palace in Copenhagen as the guest of her nephew, Christian X, Xenia meanwhile made her home at Longmore near Windsor, and then at private addresses in London and Paris. Accommodation, however, was not the only problem. There was the matter of their future upkeep. Neither of them had lacked money in the past; and neither had had any experience of either earning or even physically spending it. So it was hardly surprising that both were soon in financial difficulties. They had capital (mainly jewels) and friendly royals to lean on, but no income and little financial knowledge.

Marie was also generous and, surrounded as she was by the staff she had saved from the Crimea and untold numbers of other refugees from the Revolution, her instinct was to give help first and consider the cost later. Within a short time her debts had reached 803,000 Danish kroner (roughly £40,000 then, or £600,000 now), with only some two-thirds covered by security. Her net debts were calculated at 330,000 kroner (£15,000 then or £225,000 now). When he heard of the situation H. N. Andersen quickly arranged for the debts to be paid and for Marie to be helped by a regular allowance. The money came from his own company, the East Asiatic Company, and its bankers, the Landmands Banken, just before the bank's spectacular crash. When the crash came, fuelled by speculative, even fraudulent loans, it engulfed some of the Danish royal family, who had been sharing in the speculative deals (one joined the Foreign Legion in disgrace). Marie's position was immediately protected by Andersen, who arranged for the East Asiatic Company to guarantee the debts.[9]

Marie also had difficulties in settling down in the Amalienborg Palace with Christian X. He found her to have little sense of saving money and she, in turn, regarded him as somewhat miserly. The story of her encouraging her staff to switch on all the lights in her quarters in reaction to one of his penny-pinching orders has been repeated often enough to have an element of truth in it. The upshot was that both were somewhat relieved when she decided to move out of the palace and into a house at Hvidor, on the west coast just north of Copenhagen, which had been owned jointly by Marie and her two sisters – Queen Alexandra and the Duchess of Cumberland – since 1906, described as 'an architectural monstrosity, but with a beautiful location'.

This household removal was to mark a turning point in her finances too. The involvement of Queen Alexandra directly in Marie's affairs alerted London to the need for more controlled help in future. The first move in this direction came after it had been agreed that, to solve Marie's financial problems, Queen Alexandra, King George, Queen Mary and Princess Victoria would jointly provide her with £10,000 a year. Later the joint arrangement was simplified and George V provided the whole amount himself from the Privy Purse.[10]

At the same time, Sir Frederick Ponsonby, as Keeper of the Privy Purse, pondered the problem of curbing Marie's expenditure and, having taken the advice of King Christian X's grandson, Prince Axel, arranged for an officer in the Danish Navy, Captain Andrup, to oversee her household expenditure, paying out all the necessary salaries, wages and running costs monthly, before handing over the balance, again monthly, to Marie. The ploy worked. 'The Empress,' Sir Frederick said later, 'grasped that the more she entertained the less money she would have at the end of the month, and cut down her invitations accordingly.'

No doubt lurking behind George V's financial allowance to Marie was the clear knowledge that her jewel box, rescued with her from the Crimea, would, as in the earlier case of the loan to Grand Duke Michael, act as 'nominal security'. Sir Frederick made doubly sure by insisting that the jewels were kept in a special safe to which there would be only two keys. One would be kept by Marie's dresser; the other by Captain Andrup. Whenever Marie wanted to use or examine her jewels, the dresser had to telephone Andrup for the other key. Afterwards the captain ensured that none were missing. George V's, and above all Queen Mary's, involvement with the jewel box was later to extend somewhat beyond its original role as 'nominal security' for Marie's allowance.

While Empress Marie was settling down in Copenhagen, her two daughters were similarly readjusting to life in exile. Grand Duchess Olga – who had accompanied her husband, Colonel Kulikovsky, to the Caucasus and escaped from Russia via Novorossiysk – eventually joined her mother in Denmark in early 1920. Grand Duchess Xenia remained for a time near Windsor. They all kept in close touch with each other. One particular item of news shocked them considerably. They had become used to the Bolshevik regime's supposed revelations about tsarist activities, but a report from Countess Karlova to both Xenia and Olga that private letters between Nicholas and Alexandra had been secured and were about to be published in England by a London publisher appalled them.

Xenia initially kept the news from her mother but took immediate action. Meanwhile in Copenhagen Olga had passed on a similar letter to Marie and, after the first shock, they both naturally left it to Xenia to do what was best in London. She spoke to George V and to his private secretary, Lord Stamfordham, who in turn put her directly in touch with the royal family's solicitor, Sir Charles Russell. The ex-tsar's and tsarina's letters had already been published in a newspaper in the United States and Xenia had been sent and read several cuttings. 'They are of the *most* intimate nature,' she told her mother, 'and some are surprisingly beautiful – it's simply *sinful* to read them.' They also included, as we now know, references to Rasputin and Alexandra's strong views on the political situation in Petrograd.

Xenia was advised that the only way to try to prevent their publication in London was for her to receive a 'grant of administration' over Nicholas's property in England, that is, the right to his literary and other property rights. Sir Charles Russell accordingly went ahead with the legal action necessary to take out the appropriate Letters of Administration in Xenia's name as his prime inheritor. So began Grand Duchess Xenia's reported 'claim' on Nicholas's millions in this country. It was an action that was to be used by later claimants as evidence that the Romanoff family had not only known the whereabouts of his wealth in London, but had both claimed it and inherited part of it. Not until now has it been possible to explain the true purpose of Xenia's legal action.

On Russell's advice Xenia also had to declare her rights to Romanoff relics the family received from Ekaterinburg. As Xenia described them to her mother: 'Those things that arrived from Ekaterinburg (last year via Vladivostock) and which are now in my keeping and which were appraised at 500 pounds.' Accordingly, on May 17, 1920, Grand Duchess Xenia, as the tsar's eldest sister, was granted Letters of Administration to Nicholas's total estate in England.[11] The gross value of the estate was confirmed at £500, as Xenia had indicated to her mother. But, in striking contrast to the construction later put on that figure, it represented the sad remains and damaged jewellery left from the massacre at the Ipatiev House and returned to the surviving members of the Romanoff family, and not the remaining balance of the tsar's alleged account in a London bank.

Xenia's principal asset, her own remaining jewels, would now cause her trouble and embarrassment. A rogue by the name of Maurice Sternbach, an American, was the first to try and make capital out of them, having taken the trouble to secure an introduction to her from a friend in Copenhagen. Calmed by such a formal approach, Xenia met Sternbach at Claridge's and listened to his tales of travel and adventure, and supposed financial expertise. She eventually entrusted him with some of her jewels, and in return received a nominal payment. It was, in essence, a form of pawning her jewels. This was at the end of 1921.[12]

Much worse was to follow. Early in 1922 Sternbach introduced Xenia to Albert Frederick Calvert, who was living in Eton Avenue in Hampstead, north London. He was said to be 'a financier of high position in the City of London'. Xenia met him at the Carlton Hotel. In fact Calvert already had eight bankruptcy notices against him. Between them Sternbach and Calvert devised a much larger scheme to put to Xenia. They used a company with an imposing name, the General Exploration and Financial Syndicate, to induce Xenia to part with her jewels in order to produce capital for a venture which, she was told 'would bring wealth beyond the dreams of avarice'.

The idea put to her was that the company would take out options to purchase patent rights of a photographic printing process which would produce 'enormous profits'. A letter dated March 14, 1922 from Sternbach to Xenia spoke of 'a possible $3,750,000 or maybe more and 50 per cent interest in all royalties'. The result was predictable. In February 1922 Sternbach persuaded Xenia to pawn a rope of jewels for £4,000. She actually handed him £3,500, of which £2,000 was paid to Calvert. The next month a further rope of seventy-two pearls was similarly pawned for £5,000. Of this £3,500 went direct to Sternbach, of which £3,000 was passed on to Calvert. Finally, later that month, a pearl necklace was pawned for a sum of £5,000, all of which went to Calvert. In total Xenia was deprived of £10,000 by Calvert alone in a couple of months as a result of the fraud. Sternbach, who had previously been arrested in Paris for dishonouring cheques, was sentenced to imprisonment and then deported to the United States.

Grand Duchess Xenia had not lost all she had rescued from the Crimea. Her fifty-four piece solid gold plate was still in her possession in the mid-1940s. But she could hardly be regarded as one of the richer of the royals. Nor had she benefited from any Romanoff money in London. So it was hardly surprising that, following the fraudulent loss of some of her jewels, George V sought advice on how best to help her. Through Sir Frederick Ponsonby, he naturally turned to a compatriot, Peter Bark, Nicholas's last Finance Minister (from 1914 to 1917), who had not only escaped to London but was acting as adviser to the Governor of the Bank of England on east European affairs. Bark promised to help.

He quickly discovered that Xenia, in terms of a regular income, was virtually penniless and immediately recommended that she reassess her assets. He did his best to disentangle what other commitments she had entered into and recommended her to sell a house in Paris. The upshot was that George V lent her Frogmore Cottage at Windsor, as a permanent residence, and gave her an annual allowance of £2,400. Just as in the case of her mother, Ponsonby ensured that the money was well spent by establishing a clerk to deduct the expenses of the small Windsor estate, before handing over the monthly balance to Xenia. As Ponsonby was to say later, 'I found she practically starved herself, and never spent a penny on her clothes, in order to give more to her sons.' Her bank accounts are a witness to her filial generosity, Princes Andrew, Nikita and Rostislav in particular receiving regular amounts from her account at Coutts.

Peter Bark was also able to help Xenia in claiming some money in Finland. She had long been aware of Romanoff property at Halila which had been confiscated by the Bolsheviks and handed over to the Finnish government at the Treaty of Dorpat. In 1928, with Sir Frederick Ponsonby's encouragement and Peter Bark's expert support, she finally brought an action against the Finnish state. The Bank of England gave Bark permission to take powers of attorney from Empress Marie (just before her death) and Xenia, and George V paid Bark's travelling expenses.

Xenia claimed that the property in the village of Halila, including the Halila Sanitorium, had been bought personally for 100,000 roubles by her father, Alexander III, in 1892. The Finns responded by reminding the court that the property had been handed over to Empress Marie's Foundation in 1900 by Nicholas, that the Foundation was supported by state funds, and that, in any case, the Finnish government had acquired it legitimately under the Peace Treaty. In fact Halila had been mentioned in a special clause of the treaty. The case initially went against Xenia, but the dispute continued for some years until, in mid-February 1934, following the discreet intervention of the Bank of England, Peter Bark was finally able to report to the Governor of the Bank that he had just received a cheque on behalf of Xenia and her relations. 'I am quite certain that [the negotiations] would still be dragging on had it not been for the steps you so very kindly undertook.'

Empress Marie and her two daughters were not the only Romanoff relatives in need of help on arrival in London. Grand Duke Michael's wife, Natasha, now with the title of Countess Brassova, had managed to escape and was both devastated at what had happened to him at Perm (she remained in ignorance of the truth about his death for years) and on the brink of penury. She too had some jewels to fall back on but little else, and the society life she had experienced with Michael in London only five or six years earlier was no longer offered to a widow on her own. For a time she managed to revive old habits, and one acquaintance of that time remembered driving up Bond Street with her in her Rolls Royce and waiting outside a jewellers while she sold an enormous pearl. She was still living in hope that money from Michael's sugar factories in the Ukraine, or his estates in Russia and Poland might somehow come her way.

It was not to be. The Russian estates, of course, were confiscated by the Bolsheviks, but the fate of Michael's Polish estate, said to be worth some £600,000, was not settled until much later. Following several earlier attempts, a claim against the Polish government was finally heard in the Polish Supreme Court in 1937. After a hearing lasting three days the seven presiding judges turned down Natasha's claim in these words: 'The estates claimed by the Countess were included in the Polish–Russian Riga Treaty, which declares that all Tsarist and Tsarist family estates in Poland became Polish state property.'

Nor had Natasha much to fall back on in England. She naturally recalled the country estates they had stayed on just before the war, though she was also aware that they had been on lease. Eventually the one item she managed to reclaim was a leasehold property in Bolton Gardens, on which she was granted Letters of Administration in 1924. The value was put at only £94. The property was described as 'the estate of Grand Duke Michael Alexandrovitch of Gatchina, Petrograd, who died on or since the 12th day of June, 1918, at a place unknown'. Natasha's fortunes did not improve. Even the belated discovery of all Michael's former regalia of various Orders of Chivalry in a trunk, following an advertisement in a London newspaper, and said to be worth between £2,000 and £10,000, turned sour when the countries that had bestowed them on him claimed them back before the auction. Natasha ended her days in a shabby little bed-sitting-room in Paris.[13]

A more intriguing claim arose from an insurance policy taken out on Empress Alexandra's life. In September 1919 the Foreign Office was startled to receive a letter from Alex Lawson, the General Manager of the Gresham Life Assurance Society. 'This society,' he explained, 'has an assurance on the life of the ex-Tsarina of Russia in connection with a lease of property in Cornwall and we are being pressed by solicitors of the beneficiary to settle the policy as a claim.' Could the Foreign Office let them have any information about the death or deaths of the royal family? The Foreign Office did not hesitate. 'There is little room for doubt that the ex-Tsarina has been murdered.'

What Whitehall clearly wanted to know, however, was whether tsarist assets were somehow lurking in Cornwall. The truth was rather more mundane. The life policy had been connected with property in Cornwall belonging to Princess (Frances) Alexis Dolgorouki, who had died a month earlier in Paris. As a board meeting of the Gresham in December of that year revealed, Princess Dolgorouki also had property in Hinde Street, Gloucester Terrace and Cambridge Square in London, as well as share investments in this country. The insurance claim was duly paid out. It was perhaps a minor example of the way in which Romanoff guarantees to relatives had smoothed so many paths in prewar days.

Representatives of the new Bolshevik regime too naturally showed an interest, not to say diligence, in clarifying what now belonged to them. We shall be covering their claims on bank deposits and credits in Chapter 15. One of their early forays was naturally to take over the former Imperial Embassy building, Chesham House. After several previous efforts, the recognition of the new Soviet regime should have made such a transfer fairly straightforward. But there were unforeseen complications, of which even the Foreign Office was unaware. In the spring of 1924 they wrote officially to Countess Benckendorff, the widow of the former tsarist ambassador, saying that the property 'now in your possession' should be handed over to the Soviet government as the successor to the tsarist government.

Her first reaction was to say that she had 'no interest whatsoever in Chesham House' but on seeking further advice she quickly discovered that she actually had legal responsibilities in connection with the lease and that the Soviet government indeed needed her permission, not that of international law. Her husband had personally signed the lease and, under English law this was now her property as his heir. It had also been guaranteed by John Baring, later Lord Revelstoke, and had four years to run. So in the end she had the satisfaction of 'allowing' the Soviet government to take over what it, and the British government, had always regarded as its own property.[14]

These were the first claims on what was left of the tsarist regime in Britain, some official, some essentially personal. Few of the survivors from the Crimea, especially the close members of Nicholas's family, found much to sustain them. Even his mother and sisters, five years after the massacre at Ekaterinburg, found themselves still dependent on the British royal family for their income and their accommodation. And it was at this precise moment that one of the most significant of the many claimants to what was left of the Romanoff wealth began to make detailed allegations of her own.

9

Anastasia

Romanoff pretenders and claimants have sprouted in the most unlikely places over the past three-quarters of a century. Some were passive, enjoying a fleeting recognition; others determined to exploit whatever temporary asset they might have. Some enjoyed public attention, nothing more; others were in it for monetary gain from the outset. Some were rogues; others well-meaning innocents.

Who knows, one of them, perhaps even two, have actually been telling the truth. If they have, then what they have said about tsarist money and wealth can hardly be ignored. It is this particular conundrum, what might be relied upon and what can not, that we must now attempt to resolve.

As well as the *Daily Graphic* report that Sydney Gibbes noted of a Grand Duchess Tatiana appearing in New York while the royal family was still confined to the Governor's House in Tobolsk, Siberia, the United States witnessed another Tatiana in 1920 when a report claimed that she had escaped, married and was living with a waiter in Birmingham, Alabama. In that earlier period Russia too had its share of claimants. Gleb Botkin, the son of the tsar's doctor, reported some years later that 'numerous Grand Duchesses and Tsarevitchs, all of them obvious frauds, appeared in every town in Siberia'. He particularly admired the enterprise of one 'handsome courtesan who for months posed as Grand Duchess Tatiana' and as such was feted by many White regiments at the front. He even accused Soloviev, who married Rasputin's daughter and is thought to have channelled tsarist rescue funds into his own pocket, of organising 'a regular business of exporting rescued grand duchesses'.[1]

The story went that, from time to time, he would inform rich locals that he had rescued a grand duchess but had no money to send her abroad. In exchange for the necessary cash, they would be allowed to meet her and say a last goodbye. 'The role of the grand duchess was played by some one of the local courtesans who met her benefactors on the deck of some departing steamer, permitted them graciously to kiss her hand, and before the last whistle sounded, returned to the pier by a different gang plank.'

Some time later Princess Nicholas Galitzine, herself under arrest, and whose grandmother had been Mistress of the Robes in the Imperial court, met a young girl in prison in Petrograd who was serving ten years for false pretences. She had been pretending to be Grand Duchess Olga, the eldest of the tsar's daughters. She, like others, no doubt, had wandered from village to village in Siberia explaining how she had escaped from Ekaterinburg. People apparently believed her story and gave her food, at least until the Bolshevik authorities caught up with her and finally accused her of 'counter-revolutionary activities'. Princess Galitzine was amazed at the amount of local knowledge the girl had acquired about life in the royal palaces and at her familiarity with names of acquaintances of hers. The truth was that the girl had made friends with someone who had lived at Tsarskoe Selo and simply had a good memory.[2]

Other Olgas appeared later. One lived in a luxurious villa near Lake Como while writing her memoirs – and, it was said, had even managed to secure an allowance from the exiled Kaiser – but they were never published. Another Olga emerged in Montevideo and in the middle 1950s Baroness Buxhoeveden, the tsarina's lady-in-waiting, received a call from a Scotland Yard detective about a 'Grand Duchess Olga' who was making various claims in Brussels.

It was also in Brussels that a Countess Cecile Czapska, when told by her doctors that she only had months to live, suddenly told her grandson, Alexis Dolgorouky, that she was the Grand Duchess Maria. She claimed to have escaped with her three sisters to the city of Perm, where they were separated and, after arriving in Moscow, finally escaped through the Ukraine to Romania. There she had married the son of Prince Alexander Dolgorouky. As a result Alexis, the grandson, who was born in Zaire and is now in Madrid, has since been claiming to be the great-grandson of the tsar and the rightful Romanoff successor.[3]

Claimants to be Anastasia and Alexis have been the most numerous. Three Anastasias have made claims in Britain. In America one ran an Anastasia Beauty Salon in Illinois; another appeared in Montreal in early 1960 and even succeeded in visiting her 'aunt', the tsar's sister, the Grand Duchess Olga, in hospital in efforts to pursue her claim. Not long after, the Russian Bishop in Tokyo wrote to tell Olga that another Anastasia was 'creating a stir in Asia'. Yet another one appeared from Rhode Island, in the United States, following the publication of J. C. Trewin's book on Sydney Gibbes, the tsar's English tutor. The late George Gibbes, the adopted son of Sydney Gibbes, took her to see the Russian collection at Luton Hoo, where she took a particularly proprietorial interest in the Fabergé jewellery on display.

The most recent Anastasia has emerged from Russia itself. The Russian newspaper *Top Secret* recently claimed to have proof that she not only escaped the massacre in 1918 but died in a Russian mental hospital in 1971. The report suggested that she was arrested by the Soviet authorities in 1920 when trying to escape to Japan, was released in 1929 and then re-arrested a year later. Under the name of Nadezhda Ivanova Vasilyeva she ended up in a mental hospital in Kazan where she is said to have spent her time writing to her royal relatives. The details were said to have been released by the hospital, along with some of the letters, and a self-portrait dated 1950.

The most noteworthy Anastasias, however, were Eugenia Smith and Anna Anderson. The former passed a lie detector test provided by *Life* magazine in late 1963, but was proved to be doubtful on other counts; and the latter became an industry, spawning innumerable articles, books and films, before finally proving to be false, as we shall see.

As for Alexis, the first such claimant was met and assessed by Pierre Gilliard, the French tutor who stayed with the royal family until their arrival in Ekaterinburg, before he left Siberia. He dubbed him 'a naïve impostor'. Later an Alexis appeared in Baghdad, ostensibly showing the signs of illness known to have been suffered by the tsarevich. He said he had been sheltered by peasants and had since made his way to Baghdad through Persia.[4] Not long afterwards another Alexis was reported in Afghanistan. The two most noteworthy, however, have emerged over the past twenty-five years or so. One was the invaluable Polish defector to the American CIA, Colonel Goleniewski, who subsequently claimed to be Alexis; the other was someone, discovered by the diligence of Edvard Radzinsky,[5] named F. G. Semyonov, who had spent much time in a Soviet psychiatric hospital and eventually a corrective labour camp but, more significantly, suffered from persistent haematuria, was haunted by the name 'Beloborodov' (head of the Ural Soviet at the time of the execution), and always claimed to be the son of the tsar.

Following the results of the British DNA tests it is now perfectly clear that the claims made by anyone suggesting that several of the sisters escaped to Perm can no longer be sustained. That, therefore, seems to rule out the claims of Alexis Dolgorouky, now living in Madrid, whose grandmother said she had escaped with her other sisters. The earlier assessment of the bones, completed in Russia prior to the DNA tests but put into perspective because of them, also suggests that the older members of the family all died: that, because of the size of the bones, only two of the three younger children still have to be accounted for, implying that all the claimants pretending to be the Grand Duchesses Olga or Tatiana can now be ignored. That in its turn throws serious doubts on the

suggestion that Grand Duchess Tatiana's body, for example, might be buried in a grave in Lydd (see p. 86).

Our prime concern, of course, is what such claimants have said about tsarist money, not whether they have a claim to it. And on these grounds only two past claimants now need attract our attention: Mrs Anna Anderson and Colonel Goleniewski. Both had significant things to say about tsarist money, and both prompted others to make detailed investigations.

Anna Anderson, as she was later to become known, emerged first – literally: from the cold waters of the Landwehr Canal in Berlin, after attempting to commit suicide at 9 p.m. on February 17, 1920. It is hard to imagine now, but she had no name, and made no positive suggestion about her own identity for over a year after her rescue from the canal by an alert police officer. Whoever she was, the nurses caring for her, first in the Elizabeth Hospital in Berlin and later in the Dalldorf Asylum, slowly became conscious of the total despair that had led to her attempt on her own life and her continuing fear and reluctance to talk about the past.

She was still 'Miss Unknown' to everyone looking after her even eighteen months after her rescue. Nor did the first claim to be a grand duchess come from her. Over the months at Dalldorf the nurses gradually managed to get her to talk to them and were impressed not only by the way she held herself, and behaved generally, but also by her knowledge of Russian political affairs and her familiarity with the names of members of the Russian and other royal families. One patient in particular, Clara Peuthert, having developed a bond of sorts, began to convince herself that her fellow-patient was someone special. An illustrated article in a Berlin magazine finally clinched the matter. Seeing the accompanying photographs of the tsar and his family, she immediately recognised who she thought the unknown was in the next bed: Grand Duchess Tatiana.

At what stage the patient actually acknowledged, or even claimed, that she was a grand duchess remains unclear from the many subsequent testimonies; and how far she was the prime mover, or simply acquiesced, in the approaches to the wider Romanoff family is equally uncertain. It was not in fact until two years after the unknown's rescue that the first approaches were made to the Romanoff relatives on the initiative of the fellow-patient Clara Peuthert. Here again recollections differ, but it seems to be clear that it was only after Baroness Sophie Buxhoeveden, the former lady-in-waiting to the empress, had visited her and pronounced that she was too short to be Tatiana, that the unknown – and thus everyone – began to accept that she was Anastasia.

That was also the stage at which Anna, as she then began to call herself, was discharged from hospital and moved into the care of one of the many Russian émigré groups in the city. It was also the beginning of a series of confrontations with former friends or relatives of the Russian royal family; and it marked the start of a series of disappointing relationships with well-wishers and helpers. All, in their different ways, wanted to help, and all had different motives. Some were protective, some over-protective; some wanted to push Anna's cause; others, too often, were simply opportunists. For her part Anna was still a highly disturbed personality with a mysterious background. And in such circumstances are legends created.

It was in the period 1922 to around 1925 that the story of Anastasia's escape from the bullets and bayonets in the Ipatiev House and her rescue by a soldier named Alexander Tschaikovsky and his family in a farm cart through Russia to Bucharest, began to be pieced together, and occasionally embroidered, by those looking after her. She also spoke of having a child by Tschaikovsky and eventually marrying him in 1919. They had, it emerged, relied on the jewels sewn into her clothing for their existence. But soon afterwards, she said, he was shot and killed in the streets of Bucharest and, leaving her young son behind, she began her long trek to Berlin to find her mother's relations. As she said later, it was her despair at finding herself outside the gates of the Netherlands Palace in Berlin and suddenly realising that she could hardly announce herself so starkly, that led her to the Bendler Bridge and her dramatic fall into the river. 'Can you understand what it is, suddenly to know that everything is lost and that you are left entirely alone? ... I didn't know what I was doing.'[6]

The approaches to the Romanoff relatives by Anna's friends gradually stirred up wider interest and eventually publicity of a sort. Two early visitors in the early part of 1925, the former Crown Princess Cecilie of Prussia and Harriet von Rathlef-Keilman, a Russian émigré, probably did more to attract others and eventually widen the interest, the controversy and even the passion that was to dog the affair for the next four decades. Princess Cecilie engaged the interest of the Kaiser's only daughter, who in turn interested her mother-in-law the Duchess of Cumberland, Empress Marie's sister. While Marie herself remained aloof and unconvinced, still no doubt unable to accept that the massacre had actually taken place, her brother in Copenhagen, Prince Waldemar, took the initiative and immediately asked the Danish Minister in Berlin, Herluf Zahle, to undertake a preliminary investigation. Meanwhile Harriet Rathlef began what were to be some of the earliest detailed inquiries and the basis of later writings.

Both initiatives brought Anna further visitors and efforts at recognition from a host of former friends or staff of the Russian royal family over the next two years. They included Pierre Gilliard, the French tutor; Tatiana and Gleb Botkin, the children of the tsar's doctor; Grand Duke Andrew, the tsar's cousin who had married Nicholas's former mistress, the ballerina

Mathilde Kschessinska; Prince Felix Youssopov; Sascha, Anastasia's nurse; Alexis Volkoff, a former servant to the tsarina; and eventually, contrary to the advice of her mother and elder sister, Grand Duchess Olga.

Some had known Anastasia well. Some had not seen her since she was a child. The gap, in most cases, included not only the final development of a late teenager to a grown woman but years in which she had suffered both mental and physical hardships. The Botkins were convinced that this was the Anastasia they had known. Gilliard too seemed convinced at first though later he changed his mind and, under the strong pressure of Ernst, Grand Duke of Hesse, Alexandra's brother, became a strong critic. Prince Youssopov was dismissive, dubbing Anna 'an adventuress, a sick hysteric, and frightful play-actress'. Professor Rudnef, who found Anna had a protruding bone in her left foot just like Anastasia, and had known the family in 1914, was persuaded by the physical evidence. Grand Duke Andrew became a committed supporter.

Grand Duchess Olga's reactions have been in dispute ever since. Those present at her several meetings with her 'niece' have reported how warmly she responded to Anna and how when she finally emerged she said: 'My reason cannot grasp it, but my heart tells me that the little one is Anastasia. And because I have been raised in faith which teaches me to follow my heart before my reason, I must believe that she is.'[7] It was a response that, when reported, did not go down well with most of Olga's Romanoff relations. It was in any case not exactly what she had said at the time, nor, according to Olga's later biographer, did it represent Olga's true response. Olga told him in the early 1960s:

My beloved Anastasia was fifteen when I saw her for the last time in the summer of 1916. She would have been twenty-four in 1925. I thought that Mrs Anderson looked much older than that. Of course, one had to make allowances for a very long illness and the general poor conditions of her health. All the same my niece's features could not possibly have altered out of all recognition. The nose, the mouth, the eyes were all different.

But Olga remained sympathetic. 'People ... said that I had recognised my niece because of the few letters and a scarf I sent to her from Denmark. I know I should never have done so, but I did it out of pity. You have no idea how wretched that woman looked.'[8]

It was in the mid-1920's that one particular line of enquiry led to a suggestion about Anna Anderson's origins that was to persist into the 1950s and 1960s and to re-emerge with significant results seventy years later. This was the allegation that Anna was in fact a Polish peasant, Franzisca Schankowska, who had disappeared in the early part of 1920. A photograph of Anna in the German papers had been recognised by the daughter of a landlady who said Franzisca had disappeared in 1920 and re-appeared briefly in 1922. The German paper, *Berliner Nachtausgabe*, followed up the story in some detail, with the help of a private detective, and finally published its main finding on March 31 1927. Anna and Franzisca, it concluded, were one and the same person. It was symptomatic of so much of the controversy that surrounded Anna Anderson at that time.

Herluf Zahle, the Danish Minister in Berlin, who had been present during Olga's and other such visits, and had been busy with his more formal inquiries, was eventually both convinced and enthused by what he had seen and heard. He became one of Anna's main supporters. The press too had not been ignoring the mystery. Harriet Rathlef in particular played her part, first with a series of articles in Berlin, then in a published account of her findings in book form in Europe and North America. This persistent press coverage was well represented in an influential article in the *New York Times* by Bella Cohen, who had spent five hours with Anna. (She was later to become better known, with her husband, Sam Spewack, as the creator of the highly successful musical *Kiss Me Kate*.) She pronounced quite simply: 'I say I think she is Anastasia. I may be wrong . . . But I am not mad.'

It was an article that not only summed up how far Anna had come in general recognition but was a factor in nurturing the clamour and welcome she was to receive in New York when she arrived there in 1928, and thus indirectly in attracting three key supporters: Gleb Botkin, Princess Xenia of Russia (not the Grand Duchess, but Mrs William Leeds) and Edward Fallows, a New York lawyer related to Montagu Norman, the Governor of the Bank of England. Between them, for quite different reasons, they were to transform what had been a historical mystery and human interest story into a financial struggle involving millions. Gleb Botkin provided the enthusiasm of a former playmate of the royal children and a recent convert. Princess Xenia provided the social status and monetary support needed in the United States and Edward Fallows provided the legal and, to some extent, the financial expertise required to achieve recognition. It was Gleb Botkin who brought them all together and who was responsible for Anna's arrival in New York aboard the *Berengaria* on February 9, 1928.

Anna's first stay in the United States lasted about two years but, looking back, it was highly significant in all that was to follow. In the first place she was to acquire, by sheer chance, the name she was eventually to be known by in the outside world, Anna Anderson. On staying at the Garden City Hotel, for six weeks' privacy, she happened to book in as 'Mrs Eugene Anderson', the Christian name after Gleb Botkin's father, the surname virtually out of a hat. It stuck from then on and thus, with one slight amendment, was 'Anna Anderson' born. Secondly, Edward Fallows became her lawyer, on and off until his death, and she relinquished her powers of attorney to him on August 9, 1928. Thirdly, and perhaps most important of all, two months later, the Dowager Empress Marie died in Copenhagen, leading to a determined 'Copenhagen Statement' from the Romanoff family, and a spirited and perhaps unwise response by Gleb Botkin, attacking the character of Grand Duchess Xenia.

The Romanoff statement came first, only twenty-four hours after Marie's death, from the court of the Grand Duke of Hesse. The same declaration was then issued in the names of all the Romanoffs attending the funeral in Copenhagen. It stated unequivocally that, in their opinion, the person 'currently living in the United States is not the daughter of the Tsar'. Gleb Botkin's response, addressed direct to Grand Duchess Xenia, was both personal and highly emotional:

Twenty-four hours did not pass after the death of your mother ... when you hastened to take another step in your conspiracy to defraud your niece ... It is easier to understand a crime committed by a gang of crazed and drunken savages than the calm, systematic, endless persecution of one of your own family ... the Grand Duchess Anastasia Nicolaievna, whose fault is that being the only rightful heir to the late Emperor she stands in the way of her greedy and unscrupulous relatives.

The gloves were off, and if a time had to be chosen when the subsequent legal and financial battles started, this was it. It was also the time when the germs of the later statements and allegations of tsarist money in western banks, in essence Anastasia's monetary 'inheritance', really began, or at least were first brought together.

Edward Fallows was not the first to consider what might rightfully be hers or where it might be found. Herluf Zahle had pursued a similar trail three years earlier, but his quest was dominated by the need to prove Anna's identity. Now Edward Fallows, having gained the power of attorney, began to explore the monetary prospects much more methodically and within twelve months had set up a corporation, 'Grandanor', with the specific purpose of financing the search. Subscribers were promised a percentage of any of the millions 'Anastasia' finally inherited. Fallows himself was to receive a quarter of all monies received under $400,000 and then 10 per cent of all the rest.[9]

Almost overnight the emphasis had been shifted from the need to gain 'recognition' for Anna Anderson as 'Anastasia', to the need to secure her 'inheritance'. In assessing what these claims amounted to and where some of them originally arose, therefore, we need to tread carefully. In other words, we need to ask what Anna Anderson originally knew – and when did she say it? And, if she did not know it or say it, who did?

In looking back over the period before Anna arrived in New York it becomes perfectly clear that any statements she made relating to her alleged memories of the family's monetary affairs emerged between 1925 and 1928; that is, between the time when Anna met Herluf Zahle, who stressed the monetary implications for the first time, and the period just after she met Edward Fallows in the United States. Some of these pronouncements were said to have been made by Anna; some by her supporters. Some were made by others and used by Anna and her supporters. Herluf Zahle, Gleb Botkin and, later, Edward Fallows were the main people who, because of their questioning of Anna, brought out what seemed to them to be the essentials of her monetary claims.

In 1925 Herluf Zahle is said to have followed up a conversation with Anna by contacting the main monetary authorities to establish whether they had deposits in Anastasia's name or the name of the family. 'It was at this time [at the Mommsen Clinic in 1925] when I was expected to die that I told Mr Zahle that my father had deposited money in England ... Mr Zahle then told my aunt.'[10] Anna maintained that it was this knowledge that led Grand Duchess Olga not to fully acknowledge her and later to deny that she was her niece.

According to Anna Anderson's signed statement in 1928, Zahle maintained that he confirmed that the money was in England. Whether he actually contacted the Bank of England or other banks in England is not known. His papers, now in the hands of the Danish royal family, with whom he deposited them, are likely to remain there. The latest releases from the royal archives in Copenhagen are dated 1906 and they have continued to refuse to release any later ones, including those of Zahle.

Peter Kurth, when writing his biography of Anna Anderson in the early 1980s, applied to see what Zahle had reported. He was told by Queen Margrethe's private secretary that the Zahle reports 'made for King Christian X, form part of the Royal Archives which are inaccessible even to writers and scientists'. Alastair Forbes, on closer acquaintance with the queen at the château in the Lot she has restored for her French-born husband, also asked her the same question. 'You see,' she told him, 'the Zahle papers are in the *family* archives and these remain private.'[11] I had a similar response from her private secretary over several frustrating months and cannot remember receiving such a variety of verbal refusals with such courtesy and in such impeccable English (once interrupting a state visit from Norway to provide me with yet another refusal).

Meanwhile the Bank of England can find no trace of any correspondence with Zahle in 1925 or thereabouts, having examined all the appropriate files relating to Denmark, Germany and similar inter-war requests about tsarist funds. They have, in any case, continued to deny having any tsarist deposits in the family's name or names. There is evidence that an inquiry from Germany was made to Coutts Bank, the British royal family's bankers, which drew a blank. But that is all.

These years are particularly important, because, according to Gleb Botkin, Anna told him that she had been advised by Zahle that, unless she made a claim within ten years of her sisters' and her own supposed death, whatever money was held in England would be given to Grand Duchess Xenia. That anniversary was fast approaching on July 17, 1928.

Gleb Botkin naturally turned to his own legal adviser Edward Fallows and in June requested that he take the necessary action on behalf of Anna. He wrote Fallows a detailed, seven-page letter outlining what he himself knew from his father's contacts with the royal court as well as what he had gleaned from Anna.:

I know for a fact that the late Emperor did have considerable sums of money in the Bank of England, but that much of it he had either been withdrawn or presented to the Russian state by paying with it during the war for some of the military supplies that had been purchased abroad. During our Siberian exile the Emperor told my father, the late Dr Eugene Botkin, that he had no money of his own left in any of the foreign banks. This however would not necessarily mean that his daughters did not have money at the time in a British bank, as the Emperor would not refer to his daughters' money as his own.

Botkin always insisted that Anna had explained this distinction to him thus: 'It wasn't his [the tsar's] money, it was ours.'[12]

Fallows, who had had earlier dealings with the senior partner of Freshfields, the Bank of England's legal advisers, quickly put both the Bank and other banks in London on notice of Anna's claims to be Anastasia. He then began to prepare Anna's next financial moves.

It is here that later signed statements have to be carefully checked with earlier memories. The basis of what Anna is said to have told Edward Fallows that summer is set out in a statement drawn up in August and legally signed in December 1928, in which she said:

I, Grand Duchess Anastasia Nicolaievna, youngest daughter and only surviving child of the late Emperor Nicholas II and Empress Alexandra of Russia, do hereby declare that after our family had left St Petersburg and were in exile in Ekaterinburg, in Siberia, very shortly before the deaths of the other members of my family, my father told my three sisters and myself that before the World War in 1914 he had deposited in the Bank of England five million roubles each for my three sisters and myself. In 1925, when I was in Berlin, the Danish Ambassador, Zahle, whom I had told of this deposit of monies, made official inquiries and very shortly afterwards informed me that he had received an answer to his inquiry that there were monies on deposit for my sisters and myself in the Bank of England, but the Bank was unwilling to state the amount.[13]

What immediately strikes one about this is the precision, not so much of the language, which one might expect from a legal document, but of her memory. The details being remembered by the alleged youngest member of a family, aged sixteen at the time of her conversation with her father and with no financial knowledge, had emerged ten years after a traumatic event and within only a few years of a two-year hospital spell during which she was unable to recall her own name. It is at least simple testimony to the professional skills of Edward Fallows. He had clearly built on what Anna, Gleb Botkin and Zahle had told him directly or indirectly. How far had he hardened up Anna's so called memories en route?

Gleb Botkin, who was himself a secondary source, having spoken earlier to Anna and Zahle, did not specify the Bank of England as precisely as Fallows in the final statement. In setting out the whole position as he understood it in his lengthy letter to Fallows on June 5 that year, he put it this way:

There exists a strong belief that a considerable amount of money, which should rightfully belong to Grand Duchess Anastasia, had been deposited by the late Russian Emperor *in one of the British banks, presumably the Bank of England*, and that this money is still in that bank at the present time [my italics].

In other words Anna had originally not picked out the Bank of England, but had probably spoken of a bank 'in England', not 'of England'.

That assumption is amply confirmed by a translator's note attached to the autobiography *I, Anastasia*, published in 1958.[14] This was a well-publicised book edited by Roland Krug von Nida, clearly prompted by Anna's German lawyers, in the absence of Edward Fallows, in one of the German court cases. Anna later showed herself less than pleased with it, but it is not the book itself but the action taken by the English translator, Oliver Coburn, that merits attention.

While repeating the gist of the Fallows-induced statement about money in the Bank of England, Oliver Coburn cross-checked the facts. He approached the Bank of England in the year of publication and received a direct 'denial that they had ever held funds deposited by the Tsar in any name'. More than that, he asked Anna's German lawyers about the Fallows statement. This approach, he said:

revealed that during the 1920s she altered her original statement: the money had been deposited *with an English bank*. The mistake of language is very understandable, and Anastasia with her faulty memory has probably been convinced in later years that it was the Bank of England. Presumably her lawyers will now be making new efforts to track the deposit down to one of the private English Banks.

They probably did and were neither the first nor the last to do so. But at least they had confirmed that the Bank of England, as such, was not a part of Anna's original memory, which we now know to be worthless, and all later applications to the Bank about deposits belonging to the tsar's children have simply been based on a false assumption, initiated by an over-enthusiastic New York lawyer and perpetuated by commentators ever since.

The financial claims in the United States were by no means confined to Anna Anderson. As early as 1925 Prince Serge Georgievitch Romanovsky, a cousin of Nicholas's, alerted to reports of tsarist money in two New York banks, had applied for limited letters of administration there on behalf of Empress Marie and her thirty-odd Romanoff relations. Then, following Marie's death and the first moves by Edward Fallows, the family again took action in New York and elsewhere. Their legal representatives called upon all banks, trust companies and other corporations 'to render an account of any funds and other assets belonging to the late Tsar's estate'.

By the end of 1929, fed no doubt by both sides to the dispute, the American press was beginning to do its sums again. The *New York Times*, having led the field in 1917, again felt obliged to remind its readers of what was at stake. At the peak of the tsar's power, and lumping together almost everything he controlled, even including church property, the paper estimated that he could be said to be worth between $10,000 million and $30,000 million. The amount still scattered all over the globe might be worth up to $1,000 million.[15]

'Although some of it was invested or held in trust in the Tsar's name,' the report added, 'a large proportion of it is believed to have been secreted during the war period to avoid discovery by the Tsar's enemies.' The paper reported that steps were being taken to claim $5 million in the Guaranty Trust Company and $1 million in National City Bank. A similar estimate made in Paris shortly afterwards put the total of tsarist funds in the United States at $10 million.[16] Tsarist gold, said to be worth 'many millions of dollars', had been sent secretly to London by British warships at the height of the war and was still in the Bank of England. Other tsarist gold shipments had gone to France, Canada and the United States.

The financial skirmishes which lay behind these estimates had begun with Anna's arrival in the United States and continued without much respite well into the 1930s. They were accompanied by Anna's wild changes of mood and often dependency, and by the impact of outside events, world attention and libel actions. It was a period when her plight began to be reflected not only in books and articles but in films as well. She lost old friends and then regained them; she shed advisers and took them back; she tired of the United States and returned to Europe; and finally she re-entered a sanatorium and re-emerged to initiate a series of legal claims against her 'relations'.

Alerted by the moves of the Romanoff family to claim the remaining tsarist assets in Germany, Anna's lawyers began a series of counter-actions which, because of the Second World War and other political complications, were to cover the next two decades. The immediate issue were tsarist assets in the Berlin bank of Mendelssohn & Co. But behind it all, and the issue that eventually had to be faced by the German courts, was the recognition of Anna Anderson as Anastasia, the tsar's youngest daughter.

On January 9, 1934, just two weeks after the original application from Countess Brassova, the widow of the tsar's brother Michael, submitted on behalf of herself and other Romanoffs, the Central District Court in Berlin granted them the tsar's remaining assets in Germany, comprising deposits and investments previously blocked. The heirs were recognised as Countess Brassova, Grand Duchess Xenia, Grand Duchess Olga, the Marchioness of Milford Haven (Princess Victoria, the tsarina's sister and Lord Mountbatten's mother), and the two German residents among the applicants, Princess Irene von Hesse and the Grand Duke Ernst Ludwig von Hesse, the tsarina's sister and brother.

Originally at stake were investments worth somewhere between 7 million and 14 million roubles (£700,000 and £1,400,000), according to the evidence of Lvov and Kerensky. Lvov said the total of 14 million roubles was divided between London and Berlin; and Grand Duke Alexander, Xenia's husband, later put the Berlin figure at 7 million roubles, though he never explained why he knew. Perhaps he simply halved Lvov's total estimate, assuming half was there and the other half in London. Whatever the original total, wartime inflation and the hyper-inflation of Germany in the early 1920s had wiped out much of its original value. Edward Fallows put the current value in the 1930s at around $100,000 (£20,000 to £25,000). That sum was finally put at the disposal of the Romanoff descendants by the issue of a certificate of inheritance in 1938. This also implied that all direct descendants had died at Ekaterinburg, and at last provided Anna and her advisers with the opportunity to challenge that assumption in court. She finally lodged a petition for the revocation of the certificate of inheritance on August 17, 1938.

She could hardly have guessed how long it would take to get such a decision out of the German courts. The case dragged on beyond the declaration of war in Europe in 1939 and her petition was finally turned down in 1941. An appeal was made the next year and, not surprisingly, was then suspended for the duration of hostilities. Anna Anderson herself meanwhile remained in Germany, eventually moving eastwards to avoid the Allied bombing of Hanover, before – following the Soviet encroachment on Berlin and rescue by the Red Cross – settling in the post-war period in a retreat in the Black Forest. Even then she had to wait until 1957 until her suspended appeal could be put together again and brought before the courts. It was quickly turned down.

In preparing for this particular appeal Anna's advisers had managed to track down an important contemporary and close friend of Empress Alexandra, Lili Dehn, who had escaped from Russia and settled down in South America. In 1954 she visited Europe and was encouraged to meet Anna and to see for herself. She quickly 'recognised' her and said she was willing to do what she could in preparing the appeal. Her memories about overseas money were especially relevant, for she recalled talking to Alexandra in the presence of Anna Vyrubova at Tsarskoe Selo, just after the tsar's abdication in March 1917, about the family's resources abroad. When she returned to Caracas she signed an affidavit at the German Embassy there, confirming the exact words of Alexandra. They were: 'For one thing, we will not be beggars, as we have a fortune deposited in the Bank of England.' Mrs Dehn went on, 'I cannot remember exactly the amount, but I do remember that the Empress said that it was "gold and in millions".'[17]

This was seen as powerful support for Anna's case, for it came from a genuine witness of what had actually been said at Tsarskoe Selo. None the less it did not shake the original decision and the appeal was turned down. Anna and her advisers now pushed for outright recognition and decided to accuse one of the Romanoff descendants of wrongfully taking her money. The person chosen to face the charge was Barbara, Duchess of Mecklenberg, who was the granddaughter of Alexandra's sister Irene, and had thereby inherited part of the Mendelssohn money earlier. In effect Anna was asking for the money back.

The case was switched to Hamburg and began at the beginning of 1958. It was to drag on for over three years and to be followed by yet a further trial stretching well over another three years. On May 15, 1961 the German court pronounced: 'The claim is unfounded . . . The plaintiff, Mrs Anderson, is defeated.' It was soon realised that this did not mean that Anna Anderson's claim to be Anastasia had been disproved, simply that her claim on the money had not been upheld, and an appeal to the High Court was lodged and allowed to go forward. The second trial began in the spring of 1964 and concentrated from the outset, not on whether there was money to be claimed but more simply whether Anna Anderson was who she said she was.

It turned out to be a lengthy, detailed and somewhat repetitive examination of facts, individual experts and witnesses, stretching over the next three and a half years. The result came to the same in the end: 'The plaintiff is defeated in appeal.' The presiding judge added this explanation:

'The plaintiff, who has asked for recognition as Anastasia Nicolaievna, Grand Duchess of Russia, has not been able to provide sufficient proof for that recognition, any more than she was able to do in the first instance.' It was a bleak summing up of two major trials stretching over nearly nine years, but it was not quite the end of the litigation that had been going on since 1938.

One final appeal was made to the German Federal Supreme Court. While it was in preparation Anna suddenly went back to the United States, where she stayed as the guest of John Manahan, a former professor of history and political science, close to Charlottesville. She remained as temperamental as ever. But her relations with 'Jack' Manahan were different and whether out of expediency (she would certainly have needed a visa shortly) or, perhaps more likely, as a result of a simple meeting of hearts and minds, they were married just before Christmas, little more than six months after her arrival in the US. Fifteen months later came the verdict from Karlsruhe: the appeal was rejected. But, once again, the judge indicated what exactly this meant: 'We have not decided that the plaintiff is not Grand Duchess Anastasia, but only that the Hamburg Court made its decisions without legal mistakes and without procedural errors.'

It was February 17, 1970, precisely fifty years to the day since Anna had been rescued from the Landwehr Canal and, in effect, over forty years of effort – of financial planning, litigation and deep emotional struggle, since the first preparations were made in New York in 1928 – had ended in stalemate. Both Edward Fallows and Gleb Botkin, who had been with her from the start, were now dead. Anna Anderson herself was left with her memories, an international notoriety, and a comfortable home, still interrupted by the occasional tantrum. She decided to struggle no more.

Those years had encompassed a detailed assessment of a sad girl rescued from utter despair. The German courts, as well as commentators everywhere, had systematically examined Anna Anderson's features, her characteristics and her memories. The colour of her eyes, the shape of her ears, her teeth, her lower jaw and her feet, the scars she had acquired (were they bayonet wounds?), her handwriting, her ability to speak Russian, and her memories of individuals and the royal court: all had come under the microscope and all had led to controversy. Some believed in her and almost as many did not. Yet behind it all was an intense, almost overwhelming, feeling of sympathy for her plight, whoever she turned out to be. Of all the Romanoffs who ultimately opposed her claims, Grand Duchess Olga was perhaps the one who most clearly reflected this human response.

The final legal verdict in Karlsruhe did not, however, mean that Anna

Anderson played no further part in the mystery she had created. Up to her death on February 4, 1984 writers and journalists were still drawn to her and, occasionally, given further insights about her past. When *The File on the Tsar* by Anthony Summers and Tom Mangold, published in 1976, was in preparation, with its detailed case for the survival of the tsarina and her daughters at Ekaterinburg, Anna gave them just one comment about Ekaterinburg: 'There was no massacre there ... but I cannot tell the rest.'

This teasing of journalists and others plainly enlivened her last years. Her final detailed co-operation was reserved for James Blair Lovell, who eventually published a full biography, based not only on her reminiscences but with her personal blessing. 'You are my heir,' she told him. 'To you alone I leave these truths.' Truths? Her revelations about Ekaterinburg were plainly more revealing than they were intended to be and, in the light of the DNA confirmation of the tsarist bones, were the first intimation from Anna Anderson herself that she was not who she claimed to be. 'Speaking rapidly,' Lovell wrote in his book, *Anastasia: The Lost Princess:*

Anastasia said that one night the Tsarina and the girls were taken from the Tsar and his son and put on to a train. They never saw the men again. The train took the women to Perm, where they were imprisoned for at least two months. They were first kept together, then separated, later reunited for a while, and finally separated again.

Anastasia escaped three times, and was recaptured each time. Back in captivity she was beaten and raped. Once she was shot. After the third failed escape she was taken to a room where a woman, apparently of the lower nobility, was asked to identify her. The woman told the Reds she was not Anastasia, so they let her go. In the street she met a peasant named Alexander Tschaikovsky, who helped her run away.[18]

This, in essence, is what Anna Anderson told Lovell, the person chosen to recount her story. At the time she spoke, the idea that the tsarina and her daughters had escaped from Ekaterinburg was still regarded as highly plausible. As we now know, however, the DNA results have thrown a completely fresh light on the whole mystery by confirming that at least *five* members of the Romanoff family were murdered at Ekaterinburg. Thus the idea that Alexandra and several of her daughters were ever in Perm, as Anna Anderson told her biographer, could be dismissed. Anna Anderson, in her last revelation to her chosen biographer, James Blair Lovell, had finally destroyed the very basis of her own claims.

What was still needed to clarify the Anna Anderson mystery once and for all was a scientific examination and, by good chance, this was not long in coming. Perhaps James Blair Lovell had already sensed the crucial contradiction in Anna Anderson's earlier testimony to him. In an interview in Washington six months after the British DNA results were announced in London, and not long before his death, he claimed to have found the means to confirm whether Anna Anderson was in fact a Romanoff. He said he had discovered 'medically preserved tissue' which had been surgically removed from her body during an emergency operation at the Martha Jefferson Hospital in Charlottesville in 1979.[19]

Thanks to that discovery and the subsequent efforts of Richard Schweitzer and his wife Marina, Gleb Botkin's daughter, whose joint faith in Anna Anderson never wavered, the Forensic Science Service of the British Home Office was finally allowed to clear up the mystery by being given the Anna Anderson tissue to test against the DNA of the tsar and tsarina. The tissue, authentically confirmed as belonging to Anna Anderson by the hospital in Charlottesville, was brought to England by Dr Peter Gill, who had undertaken the original investigation into the tsarist bones. His findings were unequivocal. 'The sample of tissue I tested could not have come from a child of the Tsar or Tsarina of Russia.'[20]

Who then was she? This too Dr Gill was finally able to clarify, thanks to the discovery by a German film and television producer, Maurice Remy, of a relative of the former Polish peasant and factory worker, whose resemblance to Anna Anderson, or 'Anastasia Tschaikovsky,' had first been established by a Berlin newspaper in the 1920s. As we saw earlier, the *Berliner Nachtausgabe* had announced on March 31, 1927 that 'the woman rescued from the Landwehr Canal on 17 February, 1920, who calls herself Anastasia Tschaikovsky ... is in reality Franziska Schanzkowska, unmarried, born on December 1896 at Borowihlas.'

Anna Anderson's supporters had resisted such claims from the outset, wherever they appeared and especially in the German court cases in the 1950s. The reports had, however, persisted, if only because the Polish girl, after suffering from an earlier munition explosion in a Berlin factory, was said to have disappeared just when Anna Anderson had been rescued from the canal. In discovering a great nephew of Franzisca Schanzkowska, the German film producer was able to provide Dr Gill with a blood sample to compare with that of Anna Anderson. Once again the result was clear. The blood of the great nephew, Carl Maucher, did not match that of the tsar and tsarina but did match that of Anna Anderson. A hair sample also confirmed this conclusion. In other words Anna Anderson was a Polish worker, *not* the younger daughter of the Tsar.

Thus, for our investigative purposes, what Anna Anderson had to say about tsarist monetary claims needs to be carefully separated from what her advisers and biographers have discovered in their investigations.

10

Alexis

Of the other claimants giving remarkable details of tsarist money, the Polish defector Michel Goleniewski was as unique as Anna Anderson. He too emerged in Berlin, some forty years after Anna Anderson. He had been informing western intelligence, basically the American Central Intelligence Agency, with a stream of microfilmed details of Communist secrets over the previous two years. Then, just before Christmas 1960, he telephoned the US consulate in West Berlin, urgently seeking asylum for himself and his fiancée, Irmgard. They finally crossed into the American Zone of West Berlin on Christmas Day.

He was a Lieutenant-Colonel in Polish Army Intelligence. They arrived in Washington on January 12, 1961 and so began what was to be a fruitful debriefing by the CIA, extending over the next two or three years. He has subsequently been credited with exposing up to two hundred KGB agents and with helping in the exposure of Kim Philby, the celebrated British double agent. The CIA later had this to say in general terms about Goleniewski's contribution in the Cold War: 'His services to the United States are rated as truly significant ... He has collaborated with the Government in an outstanding manner and under circumstances which have involved grave personal risk.'

It was his subsequent behaviour, however, that merits our attention. It is still difficult to pin down the precise moment when he began to claim Romanoff connections, but the CIA simply comments that after about two years of close co-operation, perhaps when they had gained as much fresh information as they could from him, he began to speak in some detail about his relationship with the Russian royal family. Their own private version stresses that Goleniewski, perhaps sensing that the value of his immediate revelations was coming to an end, decided to provide an exciting new menu. But it was hardly one to attract an intelligence agency in the midst of a Cold War and they quickly indicated, or so they say, that they were less interested in the past Russian regime than in the present.

Whatever the date of his first claim to be the tsar's son Alexis, he eventually went public in 1964 following a controversial application to gain US citizenship. The first details of his defection emerged in March of that year and by the late summer he was clearly launched on a public campaign about his royal past. On August 10 he was interviewed on Barry Farber's WOR radio programme about his real identity and this was followed a week later by an interview in the Manchester (New Hampshire) *Union-Leader*, under the heading, 'Alexis tells the story of escape'. It was the first of several major newspaper stories, culminating in a full-page advertisement in the *New York Journal-American* setting out further details.[1]

The story he told was remarkable. The tsar, tsarina, his sister Maria and himself were smuggled out of Ekaterinburg in a vehicle organised by the commissar Yurovsky. His other sisters, Anastasia, Tatiana and Olga, all escaped by different routes. 'Had we all tried to escape together we would certainly have been captured.' Disguised as refugees, his father, mother, sister and himself slowly made their way to Warsaw, by way of the Don Basin, Turkey, Greece and Vienna. It took them several months. There in the Polish capital they briefly met his other three sisters, before separating again and finally settling down, still with his father, mother and sister, in the Poznan area of Poland.

His mother Alexandra, he said, died in 1924 and at about that time the family changed their name to Goleniewski. His father, the tsar, had earlier adopted the name of Raymond Turynski. The Goleniewski family eventually moved to Ciosanlec, not far from Poznan, where his father died on May 17, 1952. Goleniewski said that his father was buried in the cemetery of Wolsztyn.

Thereafter other articles and books followed. It was not all uneventful, however. In September 1964 he persuaded the Russian Orthodox priest, Count George P. Grabbe, known in New York as Father Georgi, to marry him and Irmgard. He gave his date of birth as August 12, 1904 (that of the tsar's son) and his father was identified as Nicholas A. Romanoff and his mother as Alexandra F. von Hesse. 'Because of lack of space' on the certificate, he later explained, he omitted to include any indication of their special social position or titles. This omission was soon to become the cause of a deep dispute between Goleniewski and Father Georgi, for as soon as the publicity surrounding his tsarist claims began to be noticed by the Russian community, Father Georgi was accused of supporting such claims by being a party to the marriage. He in return protested his innocence, claiming that the name 'Romanoff' was as common as 'Smith'.

Whatever the truth, the dispute simply added to Goleniewski's campaign. He approached the publishers of Eugenia Smith's autobiographical book, *Anastasia*, for an introduction to her (her claim to be Anastasia was proceeding parallel with that of Anna Anderson at this time) and in an emotional meeting they 'recognised' each other and were soon planning joint publications and trying to reconcile their family memories. This co-operation was soon to founder, but it did not deter Goleniewski from proceeding with claims for recognition and, very soon, claims for his 'inheritance'; and it is this that we need to assess with care, for some of the financial information given by him was far more detailed than that originally revealed by Anna Anderson.

The implication that his claims to be Alexis had a monetary tinge to it had not been lost on the press and by the beginning of 1965 he was stressing similar implications himself. By this time he was living on Long Island on an income of some $500 a month provided by the CIA, roughly the equivalent of a colonel's pension in the Polish army. One of his first financial revelations was given to the local paper, *Long Island Press*. In an interview in January 1965 he explained[2] that after the 1905 war against Japan his father, the tsar, had started depositing money in western countries. 'My father was one of the richest men in the world at the time. The sum amounts to approximately $400 million in this country alone. Up to twice that amount is believed to be deposited in other countries round the world.' He said he knew the names of the institutions and individuals his father gave the money to in trust. 'I won't demand every nickel but I want a fair amount.'

The names of the institutions and banks concerned were said to have been passed on to individuals who made inquiries on his behalf. One in particular, Kyril de Shishmarev, had been brought up at Tsarskoe Selo and played with Alexis as a child. Two authors subsequently added details, Guy Richards, author of *Imperial Agent* (1966) and *The Hunt for the Tsar* (1971); and Pierre de Villemarest, whose *Le Mysterieux Survivant d'Octobre* was published in Geneva (1984), both interviewed Goleniewski. My own inquiries into Goleniewski's claims have started from these sources.

Kyril de Shishmarev had good reason to be interested in Goleniewski. He and his family had escaped from Russia during the Revolution, by way of Vladivostock and California. They had lived close to the tsar's palaces at Tsarskoe Selo, and Kyril, being three years younger than Alexis, had been brought up close to the heir to the Russian throne. His parents had been married in the private chapel of the Grand Duchess Xenia. When Goleniewski made his first claims, Kyril was living in an apartment overlooking Central Park in New York. He immediately got in touch with Goleniewski's publisher, Robert Speller, asking him to check the claimant's credentials by asking whether he knew who the 'English Baby' was. Because of the influence of Kyril's English nanny, this had been his local nickname at Tsarskoe Selo. Goleniewski is said to have passed this and other tests and to have struck up a friendship with Shishmarev. Though the relationship cooled a little later, because of Goleniewski's 'mixed up plans and strategies', while it lasted he confided some of his financial knowledge to Shishmarev.

When Guy Richards asked Shishmarev about Goleniewski's financial details, he was told:

He has a very exact list of banks and cash figures. The banks are all over the world, from Switzerland to California. I don't think the list is all fanciful, either. On a visit to Paris not long ago, I sounded out the official of one large French bank and executive of the French Finance Ministry. They seemed quite familiar with the matter. The banker indicated he would honour any claimant from Nicholas's family who could show the proper credentials and proof of identity. He displayed no surprise at all.

He added that he thought the largest sum involved was 'about $80 million in a French bank. There were pretty sizeable sums in London and New York.'

Richards added further details said to have been provided by Goleniewski.[3] He named the main New York banks as Chase, National City, Guaranty, J. P. Morgan & Co., Hanover and Manufacturers Trust. Four English banks had 'more than $115 million in them'. They were the Bank of England with $35 million to $50 million, Baring Brothers with $25 million, Barclays Bank with $25 million and Lloyds Bank with $30 million. In France he said there was $180 million of which $100 million was in the Bank of France and $80 million in Rothschilds Bank. The Mendelssohn Bank in Berlin had $132 million. In addition 'many millions of dollars' had been invested in the Pennsylvania Railroad, US Steel Corporation, Metropolitan Life and New York subways, as well as real estate holdings in New York City and smaller bank deposits in Switzerland, Italy, Spain, Belgium and Holland.

These then were the facts as given by Goleniewski in the mid-1960s. They were the most detailed provided by an tsarist 'claimant'. They were far more than could be based on the memories of a young boy, cut off from his family in 1917. In fact, as he himself insisted, he and his parents survived in Poland until 1952, when Nicholas died, and most of the details had come, he said, from Nicholas's will, following his burial in Wolsztyn.

What credence can be given to Goleniewski's account of his own background? Was his tsarist story part of his purpose in defecting to the West and, even if he were not who he claimed to be, were parts of his financial claims based on information gleaned in the Kremlin or elsewhere? Two former intelligence agents, one on each side of the Atlantic, independently debriefed Goleniewski to establish their own view of his

Nicholas and Alexandra. At the time of their marriage in 1894 she was Princess Alix of Hesse, granddaughter of Queen Victoria. Nicholas had just become Tsar following the sudden death of his father, Alexander III aged 49.

Nicholas and Alexandra's five children, a picture taken about 1910. From the left: Tatiana, Anastasia, Alexis, Maria, Olga.

Cousins Nicholas II and King George V at the wedding of the Kaiser's daughter, Princess Victoria, in Berlin, May 1913. This was the last time they met. Both were well aware of their remarkable likeness. On hearing that his finance minister, Peter Bark, had met King George on his wartime visit to London three years later, Nicholas asked Bark: 'Did you not think you were sitting opposite me?'

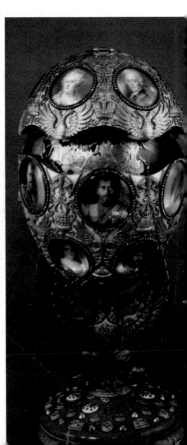

The Romanoff Tercentenary Egg was a high point of the art of the crown jeweller, Carl Fabergé. Created to celebrate the 300th anniversary of the Romanoff dynasty in 1913, it was a present from Nicholas to Alexandra that Easter. It is 7½ inches high, made of gold, silver, steel, diamonds, turquoise, crystal, purpurine and ivory. The egg itself contains eighteen miniatures of tsars, the inside shows a steel globe with the territories of Russia in 1613 and 1913 represented in gold.

Peter Carl Fabergé: Fifteenth Anniversary Egg. (*The Forbes Magazine Collection, New York: Larry Stein*)

Peter Carl Fabergé: Lilies of the Valley Egg. *(The Forbes Magazine Collection, New York: Larry Stein)*

The royal family at work and play during their captivity in Tsarskoe Selo and Tobolsk. Top left: Grand Duchess Tatiana carrying a load of soil with Countess Hendrikoff, lady in waiting, with her father Nicholas II holding a spade. Middle: Nicholas sawing logs with Pierre Gilliard, the Swiss tutor to the children. Bottom: Grand Duchess Olga pulling her brother Alexis on a sledge.

Investigations at the Four Brothers mine, outside Ekaterinburg, where the remains of the Tsar and his family were found in 1918–9.

The box containing the remains and the relics of the Imperial family, entrusted by General Dieterichs to Sydney Gibbes and Miles Lampson (later Lord Killearn) in Siberia in January, 1920.

Gold Bracelet with green Stone heart shape
attached + 1 diamonds   given to Marie July 22. 1917.
fr. H. J. H. Grand Duchess Serge Xmas 1892

Pin with one Turquoise + one Diamond
                              Herbst 1892

A row of pearls (66 pearls.)

fine gold chain Bracelet with 1 nice saphire & 2 nice
diamonds on either side, fr. Ducky, Sandra
+ Baby Bee. 1894. Coburg Easter.

Green enamel watch, given to me
at Coburg Easter 1894 fr. A. Marie

The final page of the personal jewel book of Alexandra begun when she was Princess
Alix of Hesse. It lists in her own handwriting her jewels, with later comments about
their whereabouts. The last entry is dated July 22, 1917, recording a gift to her daughter
Maria only days before the family was exiled to Siberia. The jewel book is now in the
State Archives in Moscow.

Cataloguing and packing the contents of the Catherine
Palace, Tsarskoe Selo, after the departure of the
Imperial family to Siberia in October 1917.

The Bolshevik Committee, which catalogued and partly
dispersed the Russian Imperial regalia in the 1920s, with
a display of the main items, including the Imperial
Crown, the Nuptial Crown (worn by all empresses and
grand duchesses at their weddings) and thirteen of
Fabergé's Imperial eggs.

The Christie's sale in March, 1927, was one of a series in the late 1920s (others took place in Berlin and New York). At the Christie's sale the Russian Nuptial Crown was sold for £6,100.

CATALOGUE
OF
AN IMPORTANT ASSEMBLAGE OF

MAGNIFICENT JEWELLERY

Mostly dating from the 18th Century

WHICH FORMED PART OF

The Russian State Jewels

And which have been purchased by a Syndicate
in this Country

They are now Sold in order to close the
Partnership Account

WHICH

Will be Sold by Auction by

MESSRS. CHRISTIE, MANSON & WOODS

(J. HANNEN, C.B.E., W. B. ANDERSON, CAPT. V. C. W. AGNEW,
L. G. HANNEN, AND T. M. M'GOWAN.)

AT THEIR GREAT ROOMS

8 KING STREET, ST. JAMES'S SQUARE
LONDON

On WEDNESDAY, MARCH 16, 1927

AT ONE O'CLOCK PRECISELY

May be viewed Two Days preceding, and Catalogues had,
at Messrs. CHRISTIE, MANSON AND WOODS' Offices, 8 *King Street*,
St. James's Square, London, S.W.1

Peter Carl Fabergé: Miniature Harp. (*The Forbes Magazine Collection, New York: Larry Stein*)

Peter Carl Fabergé: Duchess of Marlborough Egg. *(The Forbes Magazine Collection, New York: Erik Landsberg)*

The tiara of Grand Duchess Vladimir (above left), Nicholas's aunt, was rescued from the Bolsheviks in her palace in St Petersburg by the Hon 'Bertie' Stopford and taken to a safe deposit box in London in 1919. Following the Grand Duchess's death the following year, her tiara was bought by Queen Mary (centre), who often wore it as does Queen Elizabeth, to whom she bequeathed it on her death in 1953.

These two Fabergé Imperial Eggs, now owned by the Queen, were originally Easter presents from Tsar Nicholas II to his wife Alexandra. They were acquired from dealers by Queen Mary, the Colonnade Egg (above left) for £500 from Emanuel Snowman of Wartski's in 1929 and the Mosaic Egg (right) in 1934. It is difficult to be certain of their value, but the last Fabergé Egg auction (the Love Trophy Egg at Sotheby's in New York) fetched $2,900,000. Of the fifty-six Imperial Easter Eggs made by Fabergé for Alexander III and his son Nicholas between 1885 and 1917, ten are said to remain in the Kremlin's Armoury collection in Moscow (visitors are usually shown only five). The Forbes collection in New York, diligently built up by the late Malcolm Forbes, has twelve.

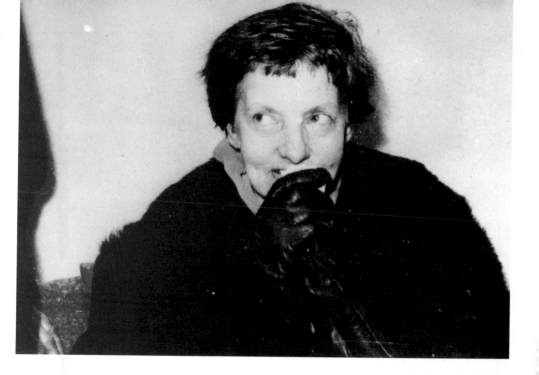

Of all the claimants two stand
out because of their detailed
monetary claims: Mrs Anna
Anderson (above) battled in the
courts for forty years to establish
her claim to be the Tsar's
youngest daughter Anastasia,
who had apparently escaped the
murder of the Tsar's family in
Ekaterinburg in 1918. Since her
death the evidence of her own
words when coupled to the
British Home Office's forensic
investigation of the Romanoff
remains undermine her claim.
The picture below, according
to the defector Colonel
Goleniewski, showed himself
(ostensibly as Tsarevitch Alexis)
and his father (Tsar Nicholas II)
in Poland in 1942. However the
figure on the right was recently
recognised as Michal
Goleniewski who died in
Wolsztyn in 1952.

The Russian gold reserve in the State Bank, St Petersburg, 1905. Following doubts about Russia's financial strength in *The Times*, the Russian Finance Minister challenged the editor to visit the State Bank's gold vaults in St Petersburg, and 'see for himself'. The invitation was declined. But another journalist visited the vaults at this time, saw the gold and returns guaranteeing 652,591,630 roubles (worth approximately £65 million). The evidence was published in the *Illustrated London News*, April 1905.

Nicholas II's last recorded account at the Bank of England. At its peak, under Tsar Alexander III, this personal Tsarist account held 90 million roubles (£9 million).

Peter Bark, the last Tsarist finance minister (left), attending the first of a series of Allied financial conferences in Paris in 1915 with M. Ribot, French finance minister (centre), and Lloyd George, British Chancellor of the Exchequer. They agreed credits to Russia in exchange for shipments of Russian gold.

TO BE KEPT UNDER LOCK AND KEY.

(THIS DOCUMENT IS THE PROPERTY OF HIS BRITANNIC MAJESTY'S GOVERNMENT).

MOST SECRET.

COPY NO.

R.B.(27) 2.

C A B I N E T.

RUSSIAN BALANCES COMMITTEE.

Note by the Attorney-General.

(1)   It is understood that at the time of the downfall of the Imperial Russian Government Baring Brothers held as bankers some five million pounds belonging to that Government. The money was in fact mainly advanced by the British

Copy of extract from restricted Cabinet paper on Tsarist funds on deposit at Baring's merchant bank, London, discussed on June 23, 1927 by a special Cabinet Committee chaired by Winston Churchill, Chancellor of the Exchequer.

'Grand Duke' Vladimir's widow, the former Princess Leonida, grandson George, and daughter, 'Grand Duchess' Marie, at Tsarskoe Selo in 1993.

A gathering of Romanoffs in Paris, 1992, on the occasion of the announcement of the Romanoff Foundation. Left to right: Princes Nikita, Dimitri, Nicholas, Andrew, Michel, Alexander and Rostislav Romanoff.

tsarist claims.[4] The American version simply amounts to a puzzle as to why the Romanoff story took so long to surface in any detail. The CIA conclusion, as hinted at earlier, is that, having realised that his usefulness in providing instant information to the West of Russian agents in place would be a declining asset, and his future thus confined to an advisory role, much as Kim Philby's had become in Moscow in the later years, Goleniewski prepared and slowly revealed another possible nest-egg. The CIA was unwilling to bite and simply kept the two topics separate.

The British reaction was similar up to a point, but, since the conversations took place later than the original CIA debriefings, the split personality had clearly become more pronounced. Goleniewski was 'accurate, lucid and particularly fruitful' in terms of current affairs and the East–West conflict, but the Romanoff material always seemed to emerge at the end of long discussions. 'It was as though he had a separate strand of his mind devoted to the Romanoffs.' In this assessment, the lure of money did not appear to be as strong a motive as the CIA assumed. 'In my view,' my British informant concluded, 'I did not feel that he was trying to provide himself with extra income. He actually believed in his Romanoff connection.'

What then can one make of his story of the tsar being buried in Wolsztyn? This is a small village located about 40 miles south-west of Poznan. I was not unfamiliar with the area, having interviewed British war brides there, as a journalist, in the early 1950s, the period when the tsar is reported to have died near by. Both then, and at the time of Goleniewski's later revelations in the United States, the Communist authorities had been particularly restrictive in the area. It had after all been the centre of bread riots and local unrest.

I was tempted to return for old times' sake, but eventually decided to seek help from a Polish university lecturer in Krakow, who was not only familiar with the area but had far more knowledge on Polish genealogical problems. Armed with little more than Goleniewski's claims about his father and mother and the location of the grave in Wolsztyn, my researcher spent several days in the area, and then went on to Poznan, Warsaw and Gdansk to complete her enquiries.[5]

The grave was certainly there. It was found in the main aisle of the graveyard, to the left of the main entrance. Made of stone, with a headstone and a stone surround with soil filling in between, the grave had been covered by evergreen branches as though someone had recently been caring for it. Two glass jars stood beside each other, one empty, the other containing plastic flowers and some dead leaves. Behind one of the jars the inscription on the marble headstone read: s.p. Michal Goleniewski. ur. 29.9.1893 zm. 17.5.1952' that is, 'The late Michal Goleniewski. Born September 29, 1893. Died May 17, 1952'. It looked as though someone had tried to scratch out the '52', with a sharp instrument, or at least to leave that impression.

The parish priest in Wolsztyn was too young to have any background about the family, but the parish clerk, an elderly lady, proved to be helpful and found details of Michal Goleniewski recorded in the parish register. The ink had run a little on the paper but the date of his birth appeared to be September 29, 1889 or 1883 and not 1893. But he *was* born in Russia. The names of his parents were given as Antoni and Marcela née Buczynska (or Bieczynska). Other details from the register included his age (sixty-three), the fact that he had lived in Ciosaniec (a small village a few miles to the south of Wolsztyn), that he was a Roman Catholic and that his wife's name was Janina Goleniewska. Perhaps more significant, no priest had attended his funeral on May 21, 1952 and no church service had been conducted. This information had been signed by the parish priest at the time. The reason for death was given as a basal skull fracture.

The parish clerk had not known the family, since they had lived in Ciosaniec, a few miles away, but she was aware that someone from Warsaw came to look after the grave. The death certificate itself was eventually tracked down to Slawa, another small village south of Ciosaniec, but only relatives were allowed a copy. None the less the office clerk gave a few details. Michal Goleniewski had certainly been born in Russia and the certificate gave the date as September 29, 1883, confirming the parish register and not the gravestone. Moreover he died at 5 p.m. on May 17, 1952. He had been an alcohol distiller by profession and his death had been reported by his wife, named as Janina Goleniewska, née Turynska. This was a name that Goleniewski was to stress in later conversations with Mrs Eugenia Smith, whom he 'recognised' as his sister Anastasia.

The next step was to find anyone who had known the family. My researcher eventually located two elderly couples in Ciosaniec, one of whom had been at the funeral in 1952. What follows is based on what they told her. Michal Goleniewski, they felt, was over sixty when he died in 1952. He had been manager of the local alcohol distillery, and had fallen down the stairs of the distillery to his death. His wife Janina was five or six years younger than Michal, and after his death had stayed in Ciosaniec for about a month before moving away to Wolsztyn. One of the elderly people interviewed, who had had a horse carriage, remembered going hunting with him for hares. 'He usually joked and argued over the hares and when my dog brought one back Michal would try to convince me that he had shot it.' He was on extremely good terms with the local farmers and, it was said, they would visit him in his flat in the distillery to play cards. One of the couples interviewed recognised him from the picture shown to them from Guy Richards's book, *The Hunt for the Czar*.[6]

They did not recognise the son (Colonel Goleniewski) and had not seen him in Ciosaniec, though the other couple remembered him attending the funeral.

The local who attended the funeral remembered the way Michal died. He had paid a visit to the Commune office in the village, where he occasionally called in for a drink with the officials. He returned to the distillery around 3 p.m. and the workers later saw him standing in the window of his flat when they were locking up for the night. They were having a little trouble with one of the workers who, having had too much to drink, was refusing to go home. Michal shouted down that he would come down to sort it out. He disappeared from the window, but did not appear below. They waited for a time but eventually settled matters without him. He was later found dead, lying on three stairs leading down to the cellar, with his head down and ears bleeding. The implication was that he too had been drinking. The reason for the absence of a church service was simply that Michal was a party member and never attended church services himself.

The locals were quite sure that the Goleniewskis were not in the area before the war. One of them who arrived in 1948 was certain that the Goleniewskis must have arrived 'before, in or just after 1950'. They assumed that they had come from further east, perhaps from Lvov, but were not certain. 'He liked singing songs about Lvov,' they recalled. Certainly Michal Goleniewski seemed to them to have a strong 'eastern' accent, indicating someone from around Lvov. But my researcher thinks that this could easily have been confused with a Russian accent by the locals. They are quite similar. The person who remembered seeing Michal's son at the funeral said he came from Warsaw and they all assumed he was working for the Secret Service (the Polish UB). He wore plain clothes, not an army uniform. They had no memories of a daughter.

Goleniewski had spoken of his father's will containing financial details and there was still the problem of his own background and any possible trace of his sister. One of the locals said they had heard nothing in the village about the will or its contents. Various court archives in Poznan proved fruitless. To trace a will officially one needs the name of a notary who testified it. If, as is usual in rural areas, it was written and kept at home, this would probably be impossible. As to Goleniewski's education, that too proved elusive. In testifying in the United States in connection with his application for American citizenship he had indicated that he had spent three years studying law at Poznan University and had gained a masters degree in political science at Warsaw University. There was no mention of any student named Michal Goleniewski studying at either university, either full time or extra-mural.

Finally it was necessary to check on Goleniewski and his 'sister' in the official records, something that could not have been attempted so openly before 1989. The basic source is the Central Register of Inhabitants of Poland. One proved positive, the other negative. The official written reply said simply: 'According to the records we have, the person [Michal Goleniewski] is registered, in accordance with the data from 1953, in Gdansk.' No later information was available. He was recorded as Michal Goleniewski, the son of Michal and Janina (the same names as given in the parish register), with the address 1a, Okopowa, Gdansk.

The former Free City of Danzig, now the Polish city of Gdansk, has, like Warsaw, been painstakingly rebuilt from the extensive damage of the last war. It had suffered what is now regarded as the first salvo of the Second World War from the German battleship *Schleswig-Holstein*, then on a 'goodwill' mission, and many of its streets and buildings have been rebuilt on the prewar pattern. Okopowa street is a long and wide thoroughfare not far from the old city centre. But it is hardly a residential area, being full of government buildings and banks. There is one particularly large building housing police offices, as well as a Government Security Office, a District Administration Office, and the National Museum – all interspersed with a tree-lined park area.

Goleniewski's address, 1a, was in fact not immediately apparent, 1 and 3 being large bank buildings. There used to be private flats above the bank offices in the fifties and sixties, but no longer. Former bank managers who lived there at that time have no recollections of any Goleniewskis living in the flats. Since Michal Goleniewski was at the time probably in the security services, the address could simply have been a temporary one while he was working in the nearby police or security office. He was certainly based in Gdansk for a time when originally informing the West's security services.

The address yielded nothing further about the family. Nor did the Register of Inhabitants of Gdansk and the surrounding area. It had no record of anyone by the name of Michal or Janina or Maria Goleniewski or even Turynska. Moreover it had no record of the Okopowa address for Michal found in the national register. The parallel inquiry about Goleniewski's sister Maria was equally negative, both nationally and locally. Although a person claiming to be his sister Maria had been reported in Warsaw by a researcher for Anthony Summers and Tom Mangold in the early 1970s,[7] and was equally reported to have been in Wolstzyn by Pierre de Villemarest,[8] an application to the Central Register yielded nothing comparable. The official reply said simply: 'According to the records we have, the person being searched for [Maria Goleniewski] is not registered in our files.'

Such a detailed investigation could not have taken place when Goleniewski originally defected to the West. To that extent he was for years protected from his own pronouncements. Several significant points, however, have now emerged from our Polish inquiry. The puzzle about his age has certainly been cleared up. The western security services debriefing him were always puzzled as to how a well-built man in his forties (in the early 1960s) could suddenly claim to be Alexis (born in 1904) and thus aged around sixty. They also recalled that in his application for US citizenship he had given his date of birth as August 16, 1922. The Central Register of Inhabitants has finally clarified the point: the son of Michal and Janina (née Turynska) Goleniewski, also called Michal, was born on September 6, 1922.

The same discrepancy surrounded the age of his father. He was remembered by the locals in Ciosaniec as being in his sixties when he died in 1952, a point confirmed by the death certificate, showing his year of birth as 1883. That too is a far cry from the age Nicholas II would have been in 1952, that is, eighty-four.

Thus Michal Goleniewski was not Alexis and his father was certainly not the tsar. Not only my own inquiries prove this, but the British DNA results destroy his claims about the family surviving Ekaterinburg. To some extent Goleniewski was basing his claims partly on family memories of a Russian past, certainly of his father who we now know was born in Russia, perhaps of his mother too. He also employed his mother's family name of Turynski to give some authenticity to the earlier alias he claimed the 'tsar' and his family used after their 'escape', before changing it to Goleniewski.

The name Turynski also loomed large in his first tape-recorded conversation with his fellow claimant, Mrs Eugenia Smith, when they finally and emotionally 'recognised' each other as 'sister' and 'brother'. This was the occasion when Robert Speller, the American publisher, introduced him anonymously to her as 'Mr Borg':

Anastasia: I am so ashamed of myself. [She begins to cry.] Who are you? Who sent you to see me?

Borg: I am a friend and I came to see you to speak to you. Do you remember the name Turynski?

Anastasia: I remember the name.

Borg: And Anastasia Turynska?

Anastasia: Anastasia Turynska? ... Anastasia Turynska. I remember. I came as Anastasia Turynska but my passport is different.

Borg: So you remember Janina Turynska? The daughter of Raymond Turynski. That was Maria Nicholaevna Romanovna.[9]

It is difficult to detect whether Goleniewski was testing Mrs Smith or simply attempting to link his own claimant story with hers in the presence of the publisher. Or was he, for some reason, deliberately linking Turynska, the maiden name of his real mother, still living in Poland, with his earlier story of escaping with his alleged sister, Grand Duchess Maria? Whatever his motive in this conversation, he nicely confirms that the Janina Turynska we found registered as his mother in the death certificate in Slawa was being freely quoted by him in New York, even if his primary purpose in using it was to further his story. She was certainly not the tsarina, nor even Maria.

The question we now have to face is whether the financial information Goleniewski produced about tsarist deposits was as bogus as his tsarist background. His familiarity with the New York Public Library and the historical volumes he had consulted there, as well as his use of the files of the *New York Times*, strongly suggest that someone trained in an intelligence service would have quickly known where to find tsarist financial material. As we have already discovered, the *New York Times* had been prominent since the outset of the Revolution in its estimates of tsarist wealth and the names of appropriate banks. They are freely available on microfilm at the New York Public Library to anyone walking in off the street, at the corner of Sixth Avenue and 40th Street. These could have been the basis of Goleniewski's own revelations. But the nagging thought remained: apart from his story about the tsar's escape and his own role in it, was it possible that a high-ranking officer in the Polish UB, closely allied to the KGB, might have seen court documents in the Kremlin or in the State Archives of the October Revolution, and, armed with what they contained, was determined to claim what was available?

Until recently it was virtually impossible to penetrate Goleniewski's original relations with the KGB. The CIA knew what he had told them and had knowledge of his original reports before his defection to the West in 1960. But the new, more liberal regimes in Poland and Russia, coupled with the claims made on Goleniewski's behalf following his death in New York on July 2, 1993, have combined to jog memories of some of his former colleagues in the Polish secret service. Responding to what he thought were exaggerated claims of Goleniewski's contribution to western security, a former Polish UB intelligence officer named Henryk Bosak, who had been in the service between 1953 and 1990, wrote what he knew to a leading Polish newspaper in the late summer of 1993.[10]

According to this version Goleniewski originally enlisted himself in the Red army some time during the Second World War and was sent to the Kuybyshew centre of the NKWD for top-level intelligence training. Because of his background he was then appointed to Polish Military

Intelligence and graduated in 1944. Ten years later he was appointed vice-chief of the Information Section of the Polish army and in 1956 head of Section VII of Department I of Polish Home Affairs.

In 1959, Bosak explained, Goleniewski was supervising 'a beautiful German girl named Inga' (presumably Irmgard) in Berlin whom Polish agents had enticed into collaboration. They were soon lovers and on Inga becoming pregnant they began to plan an escape to the West with the help of Inga's contacts in the West German security service. Before doing so, it is alleged, he met KGB agents in Warsaw, made a final journey to Moscow and spent several evenings photographing operational files and documents.

Bosak's main thrust seems to have been to play down Goleniewski's usefulness to the CIA and to question his contribution to the exposure of several Communist agents in the West. He claimed that the KGB took little interest in the Polish security service's investigation into Goleniewski's defection, implying that he could do little harm to their operations in the West. But, he noted, they got much more interested when a few years later he began to claim he was the tsar's son Alexis.

The Cold War plainly goes on, if only in retrospect. This latest information, however, adds little in support of the notion that Goleniewski's tsarist claims were in some way KGB-inspired. Nor does it add much weight to the idea that his KGB involvement might have given him open access to tsarist archives, and that the financial information he claimed to have was authentic. In the search for answers we need to examine what Kyril de Shishmarev was able to discover when he followed up Goleniewski's banking information in Europe. Step by step, the subtle shifts in emphasis are easier to detect.

Shishmarev is quoted by Guy Richards as being the initiator of the preliminary inquiry, simply because of a prospective trip to France. 'It started quite informally,' Shishmarev explained:

I mentioned going abroad, and he became enthusiastic about the idea of my doing some scouting for him, since he couldn't make the trip himself. I had friends in Paris whom I knew well enough to be sure I would get straight answers. Colonel Goleniewski pulled out some papers and gave me the figures [basically the alleged $100 million in the Bank of France and $80 million in Rothschilds Bank in Paris, plus the other bank figures quoted earlier]. I made two pages of notes ... He said the amounts were tabulated in 1951 and placed by Nicholas himself in his last will and testament made just prior to his death near Poznan, Poland, in 1952.

He met the heads of two French financial institutions whom Richards simply describes as 'Monsieur X' and 'Monsieur Y', ostensibly to shield their identity. The first, from the French Finance Ministry, is said to have said that there *was* money and that they were ready to hear from Goleniewski when he was ready to present his credentials. The second, the head of a French bank at the time, was introduced to him by an old friend, an aristocratic Frenchman, in Paris. Again, after expressing surprise, his banking contact informed him that they had certain deposits and would be glad to discuss the matter further with Goleniewski. The latter did not follow up these introductions, even though Shishmarev waited for instructions before finally returning to the United States.

The next reports of these contacts were contained in Pierre de Villemarest's book, in a French supplement published in 1988 and in issues of his international newsletter, published by the Centre Européen d'Information. Whereas Monsieur X remained anonymous, Monsieur Y was identified as the late M. de Dreuzey, a former president of La Banque de l'Union Européenne (BUE). His full name has subsequently been established as Jean Aupepin de Lamothe Dreuzy. He died in the mid-1970s. In later European reports, for example in the *Journal de Génève* of December 16, 1990. Shishmarev is actually reported to have given de Dreuzy the number of the tsarist bank account in his bank. So in fifteen years Goleniewski's original report of $100 million in the Bank of France and $80 million in Rothschilds Bank has been extended to include the actual number of a tsarist bank account in the Banque de l'Union Européenne.

This smacks more of journalistic imagination, certainly the imaginative use of earlier reports, than KGB-inspired knowledge. Subsequent inquiries at the bank itself and conversations with a former colleague of de Dreuzy and, more important, with Shishmarev's original Paris contact in the late-1960s – the aristocratic Frenchman, now retired to a small village south-west of Paris – amply confirms that a little exaggeration may have crept into later reports. The original contact was keen to stress that he himself, though working at the bank at the time, took no part in the conversations between Shishmarev and de Dreuzy. He was quite unwilling to confirm any personal knowledge of the reported tsarist funds in the bank. Former colleagues of de Dreuzy at that time, and still active in banking circles in Paris, have also expressed surprise at what de Dreuzy was reported to have said.

It is not hard to work out why anyone would expect this particular banking group to have Russian accounts. Like most international banks it is an amalgam of several banks which have either merged or whose shareholdings have become jointly owned. The BUE was formed in the late 1960s and was formerly the European Industrial and Financial Union, which itself had been formed in 1943 from l'Union Européenne and the Banques du Pays du Nord (BPN). The latter, significantly, had included the Bank of Asof-Don formerly operating in Petrograd. Its president, Mr

Kamenka, had escaped at the time of the Revolution and, after a short spell in London, had settled in Paris. The bank became a natural magnet to the thousands of Russian refugees in Paris after the First World War, thus both attracting small Russian deposits and offering credits to the Russian community. It is not quite the same as running the tsar's private accounts.

The nagging thought that Goleniewski, while having no credentials as the tsar's son Alexis, might have had access to Russian sources of information about tsarist funds prior to his defection to the West can now be set aside too. The French banking details were hardly earth-shattering and Shishmarev's visit to Paris not the significant development it once seemed to be. Even the response from the French Finance Ministry is not difficult to explain, as we shall see later. Moreover the figures Goleniewski enthusiastically distributed to the press can be seen for what they were: the result of an intelligent sifting of the leading newspapers. His total of tsarist deposits of some $1,200 million (his figure of $400 million in the United States and twice that amount elsewhere) is suspiciously close to the total published in the *New York Times* in 1929. The individual bank lists and the deposit figures attached to them could equally be based on a lively imagination and a reasonably intelligent reading of the press and other printed sources. He certainly had every opportunity in New York.

Part 3

FORTUNE

11

Jewels

As HMS *Marlborough* steamed into Portsmouth harbour in the late spring of 1919, carrying with it not only the Empress Marie and many of her relatives escaping from the Crimea but millions of pounds worth of their jewels and other precious belongings, it was the start of what was to be a flood of Russian treasures shipped to the West over the next two decades. These included – as well as the remains of the jewels so carefully sewn into the underclothes of the young grand duchesses before their arrival in Ekaterinburg – the results of Romanoff 'Pimpernels' determined to rescue what they could from their devastated palaces, and even the efforts of the Bolshevik authorities themselves in selling off tsarist jewels and other valuables to bolster up the new regime's foreign exchange.

The core of the tsarist jewels – the Grand Imperial Crown, the Imperial Sceptre and the Imperial Orb and other state regalia – had been removed for safety from what was then St Petersburg to the Armoury in Moscow in nine huge strong-boxes in 1914. Just before their removal the main items had been recatalogued and were still being overhauled by the house of Fabergé, the crown jewellers. Agathon Fabergé, Carl Fabergé's son, had recommended such action in 1913 and, with the tsar's permission, had made good progress. Having examined the settings of the bulk of the minor jewels in the collection, and finished work on the Imperial Orb and the Imperial Sceptre, he was about to turn to the crowns in July 1914 when he received a telephone call from the Tsar's Cabinet Office directing him to cease work immediately and begin packing the whole of the crown jewels. War was declared a few weeks later.

Some of the family jewels, as in the case of the British monarch's, had been inherited by Nicholas as head of state; others had been inherited or acquired personally by him and other members of the family. In tracing what eventually happened to the main items, this distinction is as significant in the case of the jewels as in our later inquiry into tsarist bank deposits.

Apart from the crown jewels, which remained virtually untouched in

the Armoury in Moscow until 1922, when a fresh recataloguing began
and they were transferred to the State Treasury, other state jewels, works
of art and valuable plate were left behind when the family left Tsarskoe
Selo for the last time, along with a number of their personal jewels for
which, with his usual efficiency, Count Benckendorff insisted on getting
a receipt. As for the rest of the family, Empress Marie managed to take a
large amount of her personal jewellery with her when she moved south
to Kiev, though she later much regretted how much had been left behind
in Petrograd; and while Grand Duchess Olga failed to persuade her
steward in Petrograd to send her jewels on to her, her sister Grand
Duchess Xenia was more fortunate in managing to take some of her main
pieces with her on board the *Marlborough*.

Benckendorff even remembered to get a receipt for the jewels Alexandra
was keeping safe for her sister, Princess Victoria of Battenburg (Lord
Mountbatten's mother), who had left Russia in a hurry in 1914 on the
outbreak of war. She had been there for a pleasant river cruise on the
Volga in the July of that year, with her daughter Princess Louise,
Mountbatten's sister and later Queen of Sweden. After the cruise they
became increasingly aware of the political tension and hurried back to St
Petersburg, arriving on the day Britain declared war on Germany. They
quickly packed, said their farewells and, aware of the dangers of travelling
by way of Sweden in what was suddenly wartime, kept their luggage to a
minimum.

Louise wrote this in her diary:

My mother and I left all our jewels we had brought with us for the official parties
which we were expecting to attend later on in Moscow and St Petersburg with
Aunt Alix. All Mama's heirlooms – tiaras, big necklaces, and bracelets – were left
there in the great jewel box which we had brought with us, and we had no idea
that we should never see them again, and presumably the Bolshevik government
will one day sell them.[1]

Neither the jewels nor the receipt for them secured by Benckendorff in
1917 have been seen by the Mountbatten family, or their Hesse relations,
since then. But I know where to find Benckendorff's last handwritten list of
Alexandra's jewels, containing a specific reference to 'a box of diamonds,
things that belonged to Princess Victoria Battenberg'. It is in an old
building not far from Gorky Park in Moscow, known as the State Archives.
There, too, is Alexandra's personal jewel book, containing not only details
of all her jewellery (when, where and from whom she acquired them, set
out in handwritten English), but also her later pencilled comments – one
within days of their departure from Tsarkoe Selo. What else those archives
contain we shall assess in Chapter 18.

The remnants of the royal family's own jewels, however, had been carried with them as far as Ekaterinburg, as we saw in Chapter 6; some secretly sewn into the underclothes of the grand duchesses; some carried more openly in their luggage and finally catalogued during their last weeks in the Ipatiev House. While the family were in Tobolsk, and especially at the point where their departure was imminent, they had had to face the question of how best to secrete and safeguard the jewels they had brought with them from Tsarskoe Selo. We now know, from the recent release of former KGB files, that some of the Empress's personal jewels were in fact left behind, and remained undiscovered until 1933 when the Soviet secret police found a 100-carat diamond brooch belonging to Empress Alexandra, along with a diadem, a diamond coat of arms and a pair of hat-pins tipped with diamonds in two glass jars in a former fish merchant's basement in Tobolsk. In all 154 items of Alexandra's jewels were recovered, valued at 3,270,794 roubles in 1917, or roughly £5 million now.

Stalin's secret police had been tipped off by a local priest who led them to one of the empress's former chamber maids who in turn named a nun at a local monastery who had helped to hide the jewels. She confessed that she had hidden the jewels in a well and in a graveyard of the Ivanov Monastery near Tobolsk and finally passed them to the fish merchant. She told the OGPU, the predecessors of the KGB, that they had hidden the glass jars in a wooden case in the basement. What the Soviet regime did with these particular jewels is not indicated in the KGB files.

After the massacre what was left of the jewels were kept by the guards, transferred to a sack and eventually turned up in Moscow. Some of the jewels which spilled out of the clothes of the murdered girls were collected and found their way to the same destination. There is a further group: the jewels which remained on the ground, in the mine shaft and in the Ipatiev House and were later discovered by the White Russian investigators under Sokolov. How these eventually reached Buckingham Palace, and why, even on arrival, they remained hidden for several weeks, we shall shortly discover.

The debris on the outskirts of Ekaterinburg gathered by Sokolov together with the detailed evidence of his subsequent inquiry into the massacre filled fifty packing cases. As the tide of war once again swung against the White Russian army in Siberia, so Sokolov and his colleagues decided to save the results of their labours by shipping the cases eastward to Vladivostock.

Their journey back to Europe – basically to Paris and London – can now be traced with reasonable accuracy, if only because the imperial relics left a trail of memories (and thus memoirs) behind them. The first step in this extensive chain began when General Dieterichs, the White Russian general in overall charge of the investigation, having received the cases from Sokolov, handed them over to Miles Lampson (later Lord

Killearn), the British High Commissioner in Siberia, who was about to leave Verkhene Udinsk by train eastwards at midnight. In particular there was 'a small despatch box covered in dark-mauve leather that had once belonged to the Empress'.

Placing it on the table, Dieterichs explained with great emotion that the box 'contained the ashes of the Russian Imperial family' and hoped it might receive British protection on the High Commissioner's train.[2] He himself was in too great danger to escort the cases to Vladivostock. Lampson took the case containing the relics with him and entrusted the remaining cases to the American Consul-General, Ernest Harris, whose train was leaving for Harbin a little later.

Whether Lampson or Harris actually had the case containing the ashes is still in some dispute, for American documents (as well as past issues of the New York Times) quote Harris and his colleagues as claiming to have carried the imperial relics to Harbin for Lampson, even describing the hair rising on their head when they inadvertently kicked the case under the table on the journey and suddenly remembered what it contained.[3] The diaries, papers and later biography of Sydney Gibbes (who has also provided us with a photograph of the case), and the testimony of Dieterichs and Lampson, however, strongly suggest that the latter actually had the relics with him on his journey (in the train that left first). In any case, all are agreed that the bulk of the cases reached Harbin.

From there onwards the cases went in different directions. By the time they were due for shipment to Europe, Lampson and Gibbes had been in touch with London. Dieterich's first intentions were that the relics, the royal family's remaining possessions and Sokolov's extensive documentation, should be kept in the hands of the British government until they could be returned to him. If this were not possible they should be handed over to Grand Duke Nicholas Nicholaevich, Tsar Nicholas's first cousin and the former Supreme Commander of the Russian army. The Foreign Office, plainly wary of being dragged into White Russian politics, quickly indicated that, apart from the royal family's possessions, which were intended for Grand Duchess Xenia, the tsar's elder sister in London, they would rather that the relics and the Sokolov inquiry material remained in Russian hands.

The upshot was that Gilliard, the Swiss tutor to the royal family, sought help from the French General Janin, who had heard of London's negative response and, no doubt hoping such a gesture would offset some of the blame he had received for the death of the White Russian Supreme Commander, Admiral Kolchak, in February 1920, quickly agreed to accompany both the relics and the Sokolov material to France. At the same time HMS Kent and the SS Atreus between them transported the cases of Romanoff family possessions to England. But not all the cases survived the perils of the journey to Harbin and, ultimately, to Vladivostock. Out of the original fifty cases, only twenty-nine were safely transferred to the British ship; and of these several were broken and had to be placed for safety in new boxes without disturbing the contents.

The cases eventually arrived in London, where King George later reported that, before Grand Duchess Xenia was able to look at the contents, they needed fumigating.[4] When she, with Queen Alexandra and King George, examined what was in the cases at Marlborough House they had a shock. According to a letter subsequently sent by Sir Arthur Davidson from Sandringham to Robert Wilton, whose reports in *The Times* had covered the discovery of the relics and the Sokolov inquiry, the cases contained little more than 'rubbish, rags, old cooking pots and debris of all sorts'. He asked Wilton to call round to Marlborough House so that he could give him more details.

In fact a similar episode had happened nearly twelve months earlier, in November 1919, when, after lengthy and troublesome negotiations with the Bolshevik authorities, Empress Marie's belongings had arrived in fifteen packing cases from her Anichkov Palace in Petrograd. They had been brought under seal by the British navy and were opened in the presence of Sir Arthur Ponsonby, Keeper of the Privy Purse for George V, and the acting Russian Ambassador in the Throne Room at Buckingham Palace. The first case, according to Ponsonby, 'contained nothing but pokers, shovels, and tongs of the commonest description'. The second contained 'harnesses and saddlery, most of which had perished'. The third, labelled 'Books from the Empress's Library', was 'full of trash, old Russian railway guides, and children's books and novels'. Ponsonby got the ambassador to sign what they had witnessed and then left it to the Foreign Office to argue with the Bolshevik government in Petrograd.

With all this in mind Sir Arthur Davidson was hardly surprised at the repetition. But it was not the end of the story. Wilton soon discovered that Xenia had already received some of the jewels from Ekaterinburg and naturally wondered how and why. The jewels had not in fact been stolen en route after all. The truth was far stranger and can now be told, as Davidson originally wrote to Wilton from Sandringham two months later:

The boxes and their contents remained untouched in the Grand Duchess's home, and it was then that Her Imperial Highness gave me the information which I quoted to you: that no jewels or valuables of any sort had been returned.

Some months afterwards Baroness Buxhoeveden, who was as you know one of the few survivors from Ekaterinburg, wrote to the Grand Duchess asking her with reference to these boxes whether she had found the jewels belonging to the Empress which were secreted in a roll of cloth with some clothes belonging to

Countess Henrikova, which were in one of these boxes. She described exactly their position, and the Grand Duchess opened the boxes and eventually found the jewels in the place where they were said to have been.[5]

Davidson also explained that the relics and ashes, which had been brought to France by General Janin, were in the possession of a M. Giers in Paris. He was the former Russian Ambassador to Italy and the doyen of the Russian diplomatic corps in Europe and, as such, seemed the appropriate recipient of the royal ashes when Grand Duke Nicholas refused them. Whether Davidson's report was accurate is another matter, for in his later memoirs in 1930 Janin claimed that they were still resting in his family vault at Serre Izard near Grenoble. Other memoirs and reports since then have added to the mystery, one even hinting that the remains of a human finger, presumably the empress's, is lying in preservative in a New York bank.

One of the problems in trying to identify the present whereabouts of the royal ashes is that several people, genuinely believing that the case they saw or possessed had contained the ashes, were not aware that there were three separate groups of cases in the first place. Each possessor or witness of a case or cases, assuming that they contained all the material from Ekaterinburg, was often convinced that he knew what happened to the royal ashes. This led to the first confusion between the British and American consuls, on which several secondary memories have been based and reported. The same thing happened in London, where some witnesses believed that the cases opened in Marlborough House also contained the royal ashes. Sokolov's material, arising from his investigation and the evidence collected in Ekaterinburg, also led to similar misunderstandings.[6]

It was also natural that the Russian Orthodox Church in Brussels, which was deliberately dedicated to St Job, with the same name-day as Nicholas II, and where the fiftieth anniversary of the massacre was commemorated on July 18, 1968, should be assumed to have the ashes. It certainly has imperial ikons belonging to Grand Duchess Xenia, and a Bible given (and inscribed) by Empress Alexandra to Alexis when they were in Tobolsk, but that is all. Nor does the Orthodox Russian cemetery at St Geneviève des Bois, south of Paris, claim to have the royal relics – though it has to be said that the denials to casual visitors asking about them have sometimes been a trifle lukewarm, even cryptic. Since it has the well-kept graves of several grand dukes; of the ballerina Mathilde Kschessinska, Nicholas's mistress; of Prince Lvov, the first head of the Provisional government; of Count Kokovtsov, Peter Bark's predecessor as Finance Minister and of Prince Felix Youssopov (murderer of Rasputin) and his wife Irina; and many other notable Russian émigrés, it is hardly surprising that it too has often been thought to contain the royal relics.[7]

Until recently, either St Job's in Brussels or St Geneviève des Bois in Paris seemed to be the obvious final resting-place for such relics and ashes, but the recent discovery, and subsequent authentication, of the bones of most of the Russian royal family outside Ekaterinburg strongly suggests that the ashes, wherever they now lie, should eventually be returned to Russia to be buried, with the bones, alongside the tombs of earlier tsars in the St Peter and St Paul Cathedral in St Petersburg.

While Grand Duchess Xenia and other members of the royal family were largely passive in salvaging what they could of their valuables, others had been far more active. The anonymous writer of *The Fall of the Romanoffs*,[8] writing even before the final Bolshevik coup, reported that American antiquarians had already hastened to Petrograd and were 'lavishly laying out their money in acquiring pictures and art treasures belonging to the Russian aristocracy'. Prince Saltykoff, it was reported, had sold his marvellous collection of old china for £25,000. 'Jewels are being sold in quantities. People are trying to dispossess themselves of all they can, and turn their valuables into money.' Grand Duchess Victoria Feodorovna was said to have sold her valuables in order to pay the pensions due to her servants.

William Boyce, head of the American Red Cross in Petrograd, attended several auctions there in the summer of 1917. On one such occasion he bought a large bronze Easter egg presented to Paul I and a pair of candlesticks belonging to Alexander II. 'I cannot help feeling sorry for the lot of the titled families,' he wrote home to his wife, 'as a lot of them have sold out and I think most of them will sell their valuable works of art as well as their homes.'

Even after the Bolshevik take-over, the same instinctive salvaging continued. Natasha, Countess Brassova, Grand Duke Michael's wife, was aware that her valuables were still at the bank, although all her individual assets had already been seized. She none the less went down to the bank and, offering the excuse that she wanted to look through her papers, succeeded in finding some of her jewels. As her daughter later described it, Natasha 'returned home with her muff stuffed full of her more valuable and portable jewellery; alas, my pearls which had been taken to the bank at the outbreak of the Revolution were not amongst them'.[9] The rest of the family's silver was buried in the grounds of their palace. 'For all I know it may be there still,' Natasha's daughter wrote later. 'I certainly did not know exactly where it was and was not interested, but the gardener was in the secret, and knowing him (he used to sell our vegetables and fruit on the quiet), I expect he got there before the Bolsheviks. I cannot say I much mind which was the winner.'

Some families or, occasionally, their servants managed to save a considerable amount. In some cases it is still difficult to say how the jewels were saved or who the owners are. One example arose in Belgrade in February 1990 when, on the death of an eighty-year-old Russian woman whose family had escaped in 1918, her rented bank vault was found to contain a remarkable tsarist treasure trove. Vera Perhamenko-Mihailovic died in a modest apartment in a block of flats in the old part of Belgrade, and had given no sign of her wealthy secret hidden in the vaults of the Yugoslav Investment and Credit Bank.

The contents were quite staggering: gold coins, jewels with precious stones, gold bracelets, an antique medallion and necklace, foreign currency, and a remarkable cross some 6 centimetres in length and studded with fifteen diamonds, said to have belonged to Peter the Great. It is now known that the old woman's father was a doctor in the White Russian army and that her mother came from an aristocratic family, but that is all. Whether the treasures were acquired for services rendered to the tsarist cause, in or around Tobolsk, for example – or were the spoils of the civil war or simply family heirlooms – will no doubt remain a mystery.

Efforts to save such wealth were not always so successful. Princess Nicholas Galitzine, whose grandmother had been Mistress of the Robes in the royal court and had continued to keep in touch with the empress by letter when she was in Tobolsk, was one day called into her grandmother's boudoir in Petrograd, shortly after the Bolshevik take-over. 'She produced from one of her drawers a very long string of pearls which she had worn on grand occasions and some other costly things, including her diamond Cipher; and her beautiful portrait of the Empress Alexandra Feodorovna in a jewelled oval frame.' All the valuables were neatly placed in a small leather case and her grandmother asked her to take it next door to her friend, Katoussia.

The case was immediately placed in a small cupboard behind a washstand along with the neighbour's own jewels, and an oil-cloth was hung over it. 'Next day the Bolsheviks came, went straight to Katoussia's room where we had hidden my grandmother's suitcase, removed the washstand, tore off the oil-cloth, opened the hidden door and took away my grandmother's suitcase, and also Katoussia's treasures.'[10] Her friend was arrested and put in prison. It hardly needed a detective to suspect that an informer had been at work.

The Youssopovs fared no better in their attempts to hide their main jewels in Petrograd, though in their case, being the richest family in Russia, they had much more to fall back on and to salvage later. Alerted by the failed Bolshevik coup in July 1917, Prince Felix began to construct secret rooms, including a false ceiling, in the Moika Palace in Petrograd, to house as much of his jewels, paintings, books and other collections, including valuable musical instruments, as they could manage. He went back to the palace at least three times, once even after the final Bolshevik coup. This was the occasion after his escape to the Crimea, along with Empress Marie and her relatives, when he managed to retrieve two of his Rembrandts, some of his spare jewellery and a painting of Alexander III. Felix even had the pleasure, on arrival at the Hôtel Vendôme in Paris, to be greeted by a local jeweller who returned a bag of diamonds Felix had left with him before the war.

The Bolsheviks took five years to penetrate all the secret rooms in the Moika Palace. Some 1,147 paintings were eventually discovered and one room revealed a precious collection of 128 violins collected by Felix's grandfather. The last violin, made by Antonio Stradivari, was found in a capsule inside one of the interior columns. The secret position of the remaining room was eventually disclosed to the Bolsheviks by Youssopov's old valet, who had been with the family over twenty-five years, on his death-bed. They discovered lovely Sèvres table sets, miniatures, bronzes, and precious jewellery hidden in a large fire-proof strong room, the entrance to which had been concealed by a folding panel in one of the library book-cases. The door could only be reached by removing all the books and taking out the six lower shelves and part of the wooden partition.[11]

Felix had clearly used ingenuity on his surreptitious visits to his old home. Whether he had managed to leave other secrets behind him remains an open question. Many years later an old man visited the palace and spoke to Galina Sveshnikova, the director of the palace, which had subsequently become a state museum. He told her that while five secret rooms had been discovered, two more remained. From all accounts she believed him. Dr Ronald Moe and Dr Idris Traylor jun., two American academics – one of whom knew the Youssopovs well when they were living in exile in Paris – met Galina on a visit to St Petersburg in 1992 and seemed inclined to agree with her. 'Felix's reticence to discuss the finding of the treasure rooms,' one of them subsequently concluded, 'suggests that there were additional caches he preferred unfound. He may well have died without revealing the secret. At any rate the Moika Palace, despite the ravages of time and wars, retains much of its character, elegance and even mystery.'[12]

Felix Youssopov was not the only Romanoff relative to return to his family homes in and around Petrograd. Once the Bolsheviks finally took over in November 1917 the threats to private possessions came into the open and the opportunities to acquire rich pickings were quickly seen and taken. Some of the victims managed to disguise themselves occasionally in efforts to revisit their old homes and save what they could from well-disguised hiding places. Others got friends to help too. One of the most spectacular of such forays started in London, when Albert Stopford, ostensibly a courier for the Foreign Office, though clearly in intelligence, heard that his old friend and patron, Grand Duchess Vladimir (the wife of Nicholas's uncle and one of the leading hostesses in prewar St Petersburg) had managed to escape to the Crimea with a few of her possessions.

'Bertie' Stopford, who had been at Oxford at the same time as Felix Youssopov and his cousin Prince Serge Obolensky, and been known to do the 'fandango' at wild undergraduate parties in prewar London with ballerinas Anna Pavlova and Tamara Karsavina, had spent much of the war commuting between London and Petrograd. To say he 'knew everyone' in the Russian capital would be an exaggeration; he certainly knew everyone who mattered. He himself was related to the Earl of Courtown, an Irish peer, and throughout the war corresponded almost daily with Lady Ripon, who was responsible for bringing the Russian Ballet, including Karsavina and Nijinsky, to London in 1911, and Lady Juliet Duff, her daughter.

Stopford's letters, plus his diary, were eventually published anonymously after the war.[13] They reflect a remarkable cross-section of his contacts, extending from regular luncheons and dinners with Grand Duchess Vladimir, his main point of call at Tsarskoe Selo, to several meetings with the tsar, when he exchanged personal letters between Nicholas and George V. It was at one such dinner that the grand duchess told him over the 'lukewarm' *potage St Germain*, 'The Emperor leaves tomorrow night to take over the Supreme Command at the front.' Bertie went straight round to Sir George Buchanan at the British Embassy with the news. The previous day he had lunched on the roof of his hotel with prima ballerina Karsavina.

It is hardly surprising, therefore, that when his tsarist friends faced penury and other disasters after the Revolution they should turn to Stopford for help. He in turn followed several of them to Yalta, where they had escaped to their houses in the Crimea. Prince Serge Obolensky remembered him turning up suddenly one morning and staying with his family for a while. 'He was extremely nervous. Every day he took out a deck of tarot cards. His fortune was coming out badly for him. He said that something awful was going to happen to him.' He had reason to be nervous. He had already returned to Petrograd a few times, saving what money and jewels he could for his friends. Prince Serge estimated that he had personally carried out 'millions of pounds worth'. Some of his own mother's jewels were among Stopford's rescued valuables.[14]

Stopford's largest, and most spectacular, haul resulted from his efforts on behalf of his old friend Grand Duchess Vladimir. She had left all her cash and jewels secretly hidden in her palace in Petrograd before fleeing south. Stopford determined to do what he could. He and the grand duchess's son, Grand Duke Boris, went back to Petrograd in disguise (one version has him dressed as an old woman), entered the Vladimir Palace on the Neva with the help of a loyal caretaker, and found the secret safe in the grand duchess's bedroom containing her spare cash and jewels.

The cash, in Russian notes, would be of little value in London, so Stopford walked to the British Embassy, left the money there and prepared to take the jewels with him back to London in the diplomatic bags he normally carried as an official courier. They were wrapped up separately in newspaper and stuffed into two shabby leather Gladstone bags. Back in London he deposited the jewels, in the grand duchess's name, in a safe-deposit box and then returned to Petrograd to pick up the cash. He finally delivered the cash to the grand duchess in Yalta.[15]

One of the jewels rescued in this remarkable fashion, a pearl tiara, can be seen occasionally worn by Queen Elizabeth, who inherited it from Queen Mary in 1953, who in turn had bought it from Grand Duchess Vladimir's daughter, formerly Grand Duchess Helen who had married Prince Nicholas of Greece, in 1921. Her mother had died in France the previous year. Among the other gems of the grand duchess rescued by Stopford were diamonds, emeralds, rubies and pearls. The emeralds were left to Grand Duke Boris, the pearls to Grand Duke Cyril, the rubies to Grand Duke Andrei and the diamonds, including (as we have seen) the tiara, to her daughter.

Bertie Stopford's post-war world failed to bring him similar glory, ending in disgrace. Prince Serge Obolensky later recorded:

One of the most normal, happy-go-lucky, good-natured people I have ever known, he went to gaol as the result of an unfortunate episode in Hyde Park, revealing a side of his character in the pitiless blaze of tabloid publicity that no one could have suspected of him. He served a year in gaol. On the day he was released from prison Juliet Duff and I met him and went to his apartment for tea. We felt it was the least we could do for someone who had done so much for our friends in Russia. It was a painful occasion. Bertie had braved the gunmen of the Checka without a moment's hesitation, but the censure of his supposed friends was too much. He told us so. It was tragic, and we knew then he had to go away. Soon after he left for the Continent. He never returned.[16]

Grand Duchess Vladimir's are not the only Romanoff jewels now in the hands of British royalty. As well as the Queen, Princess Margaret, Princess Anne, the Princess of Wales and Princess Michael of Kent each wears jewels that once belonged to Empress Marie of Russia, and subsequently to Queen Mary. And all but one were in Empress Marie's jewel box as she sailed into Portsmouth harbour in 1919. How they moved from one royal family to another needs some explanation.

When Marie eventually died on October 13, 1928 and was buried in Roskilde Cathedral to the north of Copenhagen, it was the last time that 'Old Russia', represented by so many surviving grand dukes, grand duchesses and their relatives, gathered together in one place. Their sadness was tinged by disappointment that there was no state funeral and that the Danish royal family had arranged for Marie (or Dagmar as the Danes knew her) to be buried among the princes and princesses in the lower chamber, rather than as an ex-empress. But there were other cross-currents too, as the days of mourning continued, for King Christian, her nephew, had hardly hidden his hope in the past that some of the support he had given her might eventually be repaid out of her will; and that meant her jewel box. It was a view that had not gone unnoticed in London.

The upshot was that George V, whether out of consideration for Marie's daughter Xenia, who always remained one of his favourite cousins, or simply as a precaution against Danish intentions, took the advice of Sir Frederick Ponsonby and asked Peter Bark to go to Denmark to monitor, not only what was happening to Marie's estate in general, but to the jewel box in particular. They rightly assumed that he would be able to handle any Russian difficulties. His main instructions were to get hold of the jewel case and send it to Buckingham Palace.

Amid all the stories of international jewel thieves (Xenia's experiences with fraudsters were not unique), it was not without considerable difficulty that Bark was able to arrange £200,000 insurance to cover the jewels in transit. According to Ponsonby, having obtained the agreement of Xenia and Olga, he took the jewels out of the safe, sealed them up in their box and dashed off to the British Legation in Copenhagen. An official messenger caught the next train to London with the jewels, while Bark stayed for the funeral. Ponsonby received them at Buckingham Palace, put them in the safe and immediately telegraphed the king, who was out of London, to report their arrival. In a letter to Xenia a few days later, expressing his condolences, George V wrote: 'The parcel which M. Bark sent from Copenhagen has arrived all safely and is in my safe at Buckingham Palace, where it will remain until your return or until I see M. Bark and he tells me what your wishes are about it.' He hoped she would come back and live at Frogmore Cottage, 'which is waiting for you and I hope you will make it your home unless you think it is too small.'[17]

It was another six months before the jewel box was finally opened in Xenia's presence at Windsor and in the meantime the Foreign Office and the British Legation in Copenhagen began the complex job of selling Marie's house, Hvidore, its contents and other effects. As only half the house had belonged to Marie, after the death of her sister Alexandra in

1925 her share had gone to George V and other close relations (the Princess Royal, Princess Victoria, and Queen Maud of Norway), who now indicated that they would hand it over to Xenia and Olga and their brother Michael's son, Prince George Brassova. Some of the effects were sent to London by SS *Dagmar*, including a Belleville motor-car.

The rest was put up for auction in Copenhagen. Queen Mary was keen to acquire a piece of porcelain at the auction, put in a bid for £25 and even asked the Foreign Office to send it to London by the diplomatic bag. Her bid was not successful.[18] The house and contents eventually brought in 219,909 kroner and a cheque for the sterling equivalent, £11,704, was immediately sent to Westminster Bank, payable to Peter Bark. Ponsonby finally acknowledged receipt of the money and added one comment: 'I have sent this amount on to Monsieur Bark to invest for the Grand Duchesses.' It became part of their joint trust.

Although Hvidore and its contents were thus sold off, memories of Empress Marie lingered on in the neighbourhood for several years. Three of her staff who had accompanied her into exile on board the *Marlborough* were left to get on with their lives. Two loyal Cossacks were still there later, one running a greengrocer's store, one rinsing bottles at the local wine merchant's. Her former butler stayed on in the gardener's cottage under the new owner, with a picture of Nicholas and Alexandra on his pine chest, and a bundle of papers, letters and photographs of the royal court tied with silk ribbon in one of the drawers. His wall calendar was left unturned at the date of Marie's death: October 13, 1928.[19] Even now a Romanoff is close by. Prince Dimitri, who is the grandson of Grand Duke Peter and, in the summer of 1993 on his marriage to Dorrit Revenlow in Kostroma, became the first Romanoff to be married in Russia since the Revolution, lives not far from Hvidore.

By the time Xenia was settled in again at Frogmore, George V was showing the first signs of the illness that was to dog him from then on. It delayed the opening of the jewel box in Xenia's presence. But the day eventually came (it was May 22, 1929) when George V, Queen Mary and Xenia finally opened Marie's jewel box at Windsor. 'Some lovely things,' the King commented in his diary, 'and she had luncheon with us.'[20] Ponsonby, who was also present, had a rather more detailed description:

The Queen came in with the Grand Duchess, who saw the box tied up with tape as she had sent it. Ropes of the most wonderful pearls were taken out, all graduated, the largest being the size of big cherry. Cabochon emeralds and large rubies and sapphires were laid out. I then retired discreetly from the room.

As King George and Queen Mary sat outside in the sunshine that afternoon, it is not hard to guess what was going through her mind. Having experienced embarrassing insecurity in her teens through the unnecessary debts of her parents, the queen had slowly acquired fascination for precious jewellery and the pleasure and security it brought. Her place in the British royal family had provided her with opportunities to acquire jewels of all kinds and to develop an expertise to match her passion for them. Her collection was already a notable one. Marie's jewels, from what she had just seen, had produced yet another opportunity to add further lustre to it.

As it turned out she had ample time to decide which particular items she might wish to acquire. Ponsonby had already asked Mr Hardy, the senior partner of Hennell & Sons, the Bond Street jewellers, to go to Windsor to list and make a provisional valuation of the jewels, and he arrived at the castle at 10.30 on Wednesday, May 29, a week after the box had first been opened.

What happened at this first valuation, how much the collection was valued at, how much was eventually raised from the sale of the jewels and finally given to Grand Duchess Xenia and Olga; and, above all, how many jewels Queen Mary acquired and how much she paid for them, have been the subject of much speculation. Facts about the affair came out so slowly, even painfully for Grand Duchess Olga and her family, that the suspicion that Queen Mary allowed her acquisitive instinct ample rein has lingered for well over sixty years. Only now can the whole story be revealed.

To get the full flavour of the mystery, let us take it step by step, from the moment members of the British royal family began wearing choice items from Empress Marie's jewel box. Eyebrows were raised, even accentuated when Grand Duchess Olga and her family questioned both Ponsonby's later estimate of the sale and the way in which the money was paid to her and her sister Xenia.

Princess Michael of Kent's oval diamond-cluster brooch, which once belonged to Empress Marie, was given to her mother-in-law Princess Marina, later Duchess of Kent, by Queen Mary. An oval-cabochon sapphire and diamond cluster brooch, with a pearl drop, occasionally worn by the present Queen, was a wedding present to Marie from her sister, later Queen Alexandra, and bought by Queen Mary, who bequeathed it to her granddaughter. Princess Margaret has also been seen wearing a small V-shaped tiara with a large centre sapphire, which once belonged to Empress Marie and was acquired by Queen Mary before it was passed on to Queen Elizabeth the Queen Mother who loans it to her daughter. Yet another example is a pearl and diamond collar with sapphire and diamond clasp, given to the Queen by Queen Mary and occasionally worn by her or Princess Anne.[21]

The first outline of what had happened in the sale of Empress Marie's jewels emerged in Ponsonby's memoirs in 1951. After Hardy had examined the jewels in the presence of Queen Mary and Grand Duchess Xenia, he explained privately to Ponsonby that if Xenia was pressed for money 'he would be willing to advance a hundred thousand pounds on the jewels'. Hardy hoped that he might be given plenty of time to sell them as undoubtedly they were wonderful stones. Ponsonby added:

I told him to wait until I had found out what the King and Queen wished and I luckily found Their Majesties disengaged. They told me to give instructions to Hardy that he was to price them all, and that he could certainly have a year and even longer to sell them.

Eventually these jewels fetched £350,000, so that Monsieur Bark was not so far out as I thought when he put their value at half a million. The King had this large sum put in trust for the Grand Duchesses.

The mention of £350,000 was significantly different from the impression Grand Duchess Olga had gained at the time. Coupled with the knowledge that Queen Mary had acquired some of her mother's jewels, but with no information about the terms on which they were bought, Olga and her family began to harbour deep suspicions. Matters simmered, only coming to a head with the publication of Olga's authorised biography in 1964, four years after her death.

In conversations with her biographer, Ian Vorres, Olga made it clear that Ponsonby was only partly right in his account. Her sister Xenia certainly saw Bark in Copenhagen and was present when the jewel box was sealed, but Olga was not. Olga's second marriage to a commoner, Colonel Kulikovsky, meant that her mother deliberately kept him outside the royal circle, even in exile, and that often meant Olga as well. Her elder sister too had a habit of arranging legal matters on their joint behalf through her own solicitor, without informing Olga. To some extent this reflected their personalities, but it was also partly a reflection of Olga's marriage. Kulikovsky had learned over the years to take it all rather philosophically.

One outcome, in the case of their mother's jewels, was that Olga only belatedly realised what had been done, or perhaps not done, in her name. There were, she told Vorres, certain aspects of the jewel affair which she could never understand. In attempting to clarify what might have happened, Vorres looked again at Ponsonby's account of the payments for the jewels and, wisely, asked the one other person still alive, who ought to know: Sir Edward Peacock, a Canadian and a director of Barings (and of the Bank of England), but, more significantly, an executor of Empress Marie's will and a trustee of the grand duchesses' trust. What he told Vorres, and was never later denied by him or anyone else, was that the sum entrusted to him on their behalf in 1929 was about £100,000, of which about £60,000 went to Xenia and the rest to Olga. This, it was assumed, was the £100,000 provided 'on account' by Hennells, pending the full valuation and disposal of the jewels.

The contrast with Ponsonby's statement that the jewels eventually 'fetched' £350,000 is stark. Sir Edward, when pressed, could not throw any light on the matter, simply suggesting that Ponsonby's memory might have failed him, a point we shall have reason to recall. It also implied that Ponsonby's statement that the royal family had put £350,000 in trust for Xenia and Olga was well wide of the mark. What did seem clear, both from later estimates of what the two sisters left to their own families and from the clear knowledge we have of the number of Empress Marie's jewels now in the possession of the royal family, is that while Queen Mary bought several significant items, a question mark still remained over the amount and the manner of payment. As Vorres summed up the matter in 1964, 'the mystery of the missing £250,000 still remains unresolved'.

That was four years after Olga's death in Toronto. What she thought and suspected about the affair was set out plainly in her biography:

I have tried not to think about it too much, and certainly I've never talked to anyone, except my husband. I know that May [Queen Mary] was passionately fond of fine jewellery. I remember how in 1925 the Soviet Government, being badly in need of foreign currency, sent a lot of Romanoff jewels to be sold in England, and I heard that May had bought quite a few – including a collection of Fabergé's Easter eggs. I also know that at least one item of my property, looted from the palace in Petrograd, was among the lot shipped to England, but its price proved too high even for May, and I suppose it is still in the Kremlin. It was one of my wedding presents – an exquisite fan made of mother-of-pearl and studded all over with diamonds and pearls.[22]

Olga, like so many others, was well aware of Queen Mary's passion for jewels. They last met in 1948 when Olga, who was emigrating to Canada, went to Marlborough House to say goodbye on Queen Mary's eighty-first birthday. The question of the jewels was not raised. 'Why create unnecessary bitterness?' Olga later remarked.

What was really at stake was whether, having given a preliminary valuation of the individual items in Empress Marie's jewel box, Hennells attempted to sell them privately, how far they succeeded, what prices might have been paid for them and who ultimately received the proceeds. They were points that naturally occurred to Olga's sons after her death, especially following the publication of Ian Vorres' biography. The following year Guri Kulikovsky, Olga's younger son, still living in Toronto, wrote to ask Hennells for some of the answers.

Their response was reasonably encouraging. The original private company had become a public company with the same name but, having checked their records, they confirmed that they did not have the jewels, but that they did still have most of the correspondence in connection with the disposal of the jewellery. They could provide 'a full and comprehensive report of the sale of the jewellery' in a matter of three months which would cost 80 guineas ($255 Canadian).

A deposit was agreed and Hennells finally confirmed in September 1965 that the preparation of a detailed list of the jewellery was in hand:

We shall be able to show the net amount realised on each sale, to whom the money was paid, and in the case of a sale of jewellery not being effected to whom each piece was returned. We regret that we shall be unable to give the name of purchasers of the jewellery, as you will readily understand this will constitute a breach of confidence concerning our clients' affairs.

After a further small delay the final report was promised for some time in February 1966 and, Guri Kulikovsky was told, would 'give a detailed description of seventy-six items of jewellery, together with the net price realised when sold or if not sold, to whom they were sent'.[23]

On the basis of what he heard from Hennells, according to the journalist Suzy Menkes, who followed up the next steps with the Kulikovsky family, Guri Kulikovsky wrote to Buckingham Palace and the Lord Chamberlain's office and the matter was put in the hands of the queen's solicitors. In her book on the royal jewels, Suzy Menkes wrote:

They examined the papers – which have now been sent to Windsor – and discovered the truth: Queen Mary had held on to the jewels until 1933; she had then claimed that the Depression and the collapse of the pearl market had reduced their value; she paid only £60,000. In 1968, forty years after the Empress Marie's jewels had cascaded from their box, Queen Mary's granddaughter, the Queen, settled the debt.[24]

The death of Guri Kulikovsky in 1984 and the publication of Menkes's account in her book, *The Royal Jewels*, in 1985 naturally led to a further flurry of activity. Tihon, Guri's elder brother, whom I met eighteen months before he died in Toronto in 1993, wrote both to Hennells and to Buckingham Palace to clarify exactly what had happened. It was hardly a satisfactory outcome. One point at least seemed to be made clear. No payment had been made by the queen to Guri Kulikovsky. As Sir Robert Fellowes, the Queen's private secretary, wrote to Tihon in 1986, 'After extensive enquiries I can find no foundation for the story in Suzy Menkes' book claiming that payment was made by the Queen to your family in 1968.'[25] That did not rule out payments by others or indeed in other years, but Tihon seemed inclined to believe the substance of the statement, although still intrigued by the rest of the mystery. What was still at issue was how much the jewels had finally produced. If Ponsonby was right, then a sum of £250,000 needed to be accounted for. Even if he were wrong, some explanation could surely be given. After all Xenia, in spite of the jewels she had escaped with and had subsequently received from Ekaterinburg, had left not much more than £100,000, and Tihon was aware that his mother had left less than that.

Tihon subsequently wrote to Hennells, as his brother had done earlier, enclosing yet another deposit to cover a further inquiry. Alas, he got his deposit returned and a short letter, dated April 30, 1990, explaining that the company, though still known as Hennells, was under new ownership, employing none of the former staff and could 'find no trace of the former correspondence or any work done on the subject'.[26] Thus Tihon, the last tsar's nephew, who had been born in the Crimea on an estate shared with his grandmother, former Empress Marie, died without knowing what had ultimately happened to the contents of her jewel box. It was a sad end to an utterly avoidable embarrassment and one some of the royal participants can hardly have been proud of, or relished being exposed. It was not, however, the end of the story, as I discovered.

Both Guri and Tihon Kulikovsky were right in believing that the truth of the matter lay in securing the original valuations undertaken by Mr Hardy of Hennells on behalf of the two grand duchesses. Alas, they failed and died without knowing what had happened, even though they had been in touch with the two sources that should know: Buckingham Palace and Hennells. This was the basis of my own inquiries and, thanks to the archival instincts of the present managing director of Hennells, the original valuation has now been found,[27] along with a detailed assessment of what Hennells thought of Ponsonby's own account.

The original report made by Hardy for Xenia and Olga at Windsor Castle on May 19, 1929, it can now be revealed, was essentially a provisional one, given verbally, followed by a firm valuation submitted a fortnight later on June 11. Hennells thereafter kept a master list of the seventy-six items, what was paid for them, which were withdrawn from the sale and when the last item was sold. It is clear that, following Hardy's first visit, several jewels were left at Windsor with Xenia, probably because of their low value (one of the thirty-odd in this category was valued at £4), and Hennells did not include them in their subsequent sales. His verbal valuation for these items came to £2,317. Following this, as Xenia went through other items on Hennells' list, she withdrew others from the sale. Eventually the total withdrawn and left with Xenia amounted to £11,415.

Hennells' files do not confirm or deny that Hardy offered to advance £100,000 on the strength of his first valuation. 'However,' they insist:

there is no evidence in our records of this offer or that it was taken up, as no money changed hands prior to the actual sales of the various items. Clearly from later correspondence Mr Hardy was instructed to dispose of the jewels in the most advantageous way, deducting a commission as and when a sale was effected and the money received. The jewels were brought by him to Hennell's premises and a total insurance cover of £150,000 taken out to insure the jewels against all risk. A more careful valuation was then made of the jewels and reported in writing and the sale of jewels then proceeded on this basis.

Hardy's provisional valuation of all the jewels on his first visit was put at just over £144,000 including the small number of jewels eventually kept by Xenia at Windsor. When he provided his firm, written valuation two weeks later, which excluded jewels taken out of the sale by Xenia, the valuation had been pushed up to £159,000, but was still far short of Ponsonby's final total of £350,000. As Hennells' master list shows, the total sum eventually realised by them over the next four years was £136,624 15s. This sum included all the items bought by Queen Mary. Cheques from the sale of jewels in the first few weeks were made payable to George V to pass on to Xenia and Olga. After the establishment of their trust at the end of June, the money was paid direct to Peter Bark, one of the trustees.

Hennells could hardly have realised how long it would take them to dispose of the jewels, considering the large number of rich British and American clients they had on their books. Their first valuations were made only five months before the big stock market crash on October 29, 1929. Thereafter the price of jewels, and especially pearls, suffered a major setback, and sales went both slowly and at significantly reduced prices. But at least three pearl necklaces, originally valued at £45,000, were sold for £64,600 by early July, before the slump began. Sales then dragged on until the end of 1933, with Xenia even making unsuccessful attempts to sell one or two notable items in France. Hennells were eventually left with one jewel, identified as Item 40 on the master list and initially valued at £7,000: a diamond brooch with two bouton pearls and one pearl drop. It was returned by registered post to Xenia at Frogmore Cottage in June 1934.

Hennells' records reveal exactly which jewels Queen Mary acquired, when she bought them and how much she paid. The first two items she bought were Item 7, 'a pearl and diamond collar with sapphire and diamond clasp' originally valued at £6,000 and confirmed two weeks later at £5,678 to £6,000; and Item 47, 'a pearl and diamond twist brooch' originally valued at £600 and two weeks later at £550. She bought both on June 12, the day after the firm valuation, and had them brought to Windsor by Hardy. She paid £6,000 for the first and £555 for the second.

She clearly knew what she wanted and paid the going price by cheque to the trustees.

It was over a year before she bought two further items. The first of these was Item 72, 'a cabochon sapphire and rose diamond long brooch' originally valued and confirmed at £25 to £30. Queen Mary bought it within this range on July 23, 1930 for £26 12s. The second was Item 42, 'an oval cabochon sapphire and diamond oval cluster brooch and pearl drop' originally valued at £3,250 with a later firm valuation of £2,700 to £3,250. Following the slump in prices Hennells revalued it at £1,400 to £1,900 on September 22, 1930, and Queen Mary bought it for £2,375, that is, above the revised valuation, on October 3.

Thus the idea that Queen Mary used her privileged position to acquire at knock-down prices the Romanoff jewels her daughters-in-law, grand-daughters and other royals are still seen wearing is not justified by the evidence of the original master list kept by Hennells. Nor is the suggestion, first raised by Sir Frederick Ponsonby, that up to £350,000 had been realised from the sale of Empress Marie's jewels, anywhere near the truth. The 'missing £250,000' can now be safely ignored. The £136,624 finally realised from the sale is not significantly higher than the figure of 'about £100,000' Sir Edward Peacock mentioned as receiving as trustee in 1929. Sir Edward was right: Ponsonby's memory had clearly failed him. What remains astonishing is that the doubts, even anguish, in Grand Duchess Olga's family could have been allowed to go on so long without any attempt by those royal advisers who knew, or could so easily have found out, to explain exactly what had happened – even when approached by Olga's sons.

The outflow of Romanoff jewels and treasures might have been expected to have dried up with the decline of White Russian émigrés in the early 1920s. For a time it seemed so. But the lull was soon broken as the new Bolshevik authorities faced a dramatic decline in their gold reserves, a decline that continued throughout 1920, partly a reflection of the economic turmoil in Russia, partly a result of the cost of financing Bolshevik propaganda overseas. Little wonder that the other Romanoff nest-egg, the state jewels and other valuables left behind in the royal palaces, as well as more recently acquired treasures, was soon seen as an alternative way of bolstering the regime's finances.

Sales of state-owned jewels in western capitals quickly followed. The first signs were detected by western intelligence agencies, whose main task was to monitor and probe the motives of the new regime. Soon they were reporting secret jewel sales by Soviet trade delegates, even by willing agents, in London, Paris, Brussels, Amsterdam and New York, and customs officers in western countries were alerted. In August 1920 US customs officers intercepted a package being carried by two Swedish sailors, addressed to 'Comrade Martens', the Soviet trade representative in Washington. It contained 131 diamonds worth $10,000. American military intelligence then reported from Stockholm that Swedish sailors had been offered $15 for each package delivered to the US, and had been doing this for months. The director of military intelligence was told by his agent that the packages also contained 'a considerable amount of radical literature'.[28]

Similar examples multiplied over the next few years. Soviet representatives in Stockholm were detected by intelligence sending individual packages with jewels worth $3,000 to a New York address (Room 404, West 40th Street). Precious valuables were reported being sent from Moscow to Gotesburg and, from there, onward to an address in San Francisco. In New York customs officials discovered a mysterious parcel containing fifteen magnificent emeralds, which Prince Felix Youssopov, when consulted, remembered as having belonged to Empress Alexandra. Another remarkable emerald was discovered by Belgian customs officials, on its way from Berlin to Amsterdam: $1\frac{3}{4}$ inches long and 1 inch wide, it held a pendant of twenty large diamonds. Its declared value was 180,000 francs. In fact it was recognised as a Romanoff jewel and valued by experts at several million francs. One of the most bizarre examples ended in the exhumation of the body of an American seaman, on the orders of the American War Department and the Treasury, on the suspicion that international smugglers had hidden Russian Romanoff jewels in the coffin being returned by boat to New York. The grave in the National Cemetery at Cypress Hills, New York, provided no such evidence.[29]

Finance for overseas propaganda was financed in a variety of ways – the sale of jewels or gold, or even concessions from trade delegations. A Danish vessel was reported carrying 5 million roubles in gold from Copenhagen to New York to finance Communist propaganda in the United States. The laundering of Soviet gold was detected being undertaken by Swedish, Dutch and Danish intermediaries as well as agents in New York.[30] In the case of London, Hatton Garden, the hub of the City's diamond trade, was a natural attraction and became the scene of the most public and political jewel scandal of the early twenties.

In the autumn of 1920 a Soviet delegation visited London with the purpose of soothing Britain's ruffled feelings about the repudiation of all tsarist debts, raising fresh credits and furthering Anglo-Soviet trade. What soon became clear to military intelligence was that the leaders of the delegation, Kamenev and Krasin, had a hidden agenda. British military intelligence, however, unknown to the Soviets, had recruited Ernst Fatterlein, the leading cryptanalyst of tsarist Russia, as head of the Russian section of the Government Code and Cipher School (the equivalent of the present GCHQ).[31]

The British Cabinet was in fact reading all communications between Moscow and London both before and during the talks. It made fascinating reading. Lenin advised Krasin at the outset: 'That swine Lloyd George has no scruples or shame in the way he deceives. Don't believe a word he says and gull him three times as much.' Lloyd George took the secret insult more philosophically than some of his Cabinet colleagues, particularly Churchill and Lord Curzon. But the core of the Soviet deceptions was still to come. A report by the Director of Military Intelligence to the Prime Minister made it clear that the Soviet delegation was in fact aiming to sell jewels in Hatton Garden and to subsidise the *Daily Herald*, the left-wing newspaper.[32]

From a deciphered cable from Krasin to Moscow it was learned that Krasin had disposed of jewellery and platinum worth £40,000, which he had handed over to the *Daily Herald*, and that he expected to realise another £60,000 out of which a further £10,000 would be paid to the paper. The intelligence report concluded: 'Enquiries in London showed that diamonds were disposed of last week for the following amounts: £29,000, £19,000 and £13,000. It was common gossip in Hatton Garden that Mr Lansbury was the vendor.' Next day Lord Curzon told the Cabinet that the money paid to the paper had been decreed by the Central Executive of the Russian Communist Party.

The Cabinet quickly took two decisions: one was to leak some of the information to the British press, apart from the *Daily Herald*; the other was to make it clear that there had been a 'gross breach of faith' and to ask Kamenev, who was returning to Moscow for consultations, not to return to London. The *Daily Herald*, having got wind of the original leaks and fearful of other leaks to come, quickly admitted the truth, pleading 'evidence of real working-class solidarity' and plaintively asking its readers in a headline: 'Shall we take £75,000 of Russian money?' They were not the only British recipients of Soviet money that year. The archives of the former Institute of Marxism–Leninism in Moscow, when they were opened up to scrutiny for the first time in 1992, revealed that the Communist Party of Great Britain was Soviet-financed from its foundation in 1920. It received £55,000 in its first year.[33]

On his way back to Moscow Kamenev finally admitted, in an interview in Stockholm, that the export of diamonds and other jewels had been officially authorised in Moscow but that the crown jewels had not yet been touched. That step, however, was not long in coming.

When the official decision was made to consider disposing of the main crown jewels, or at least some of the priceless items in the state collection of gems, jewellery and state regalia, is not clear. But under the new regime, the State Depository of Treasures, later known as the USSR Diamond Fund, was set up in Moscow in 1920[34] to receive not only the crown jewels and similar state regalia, but also the flow of jewels and valuables recently confiscated from the aristocracy, the bourgeoisie, the Church and the banks. The Church alone yielded some 500,000 kilos of silver. One of the men given the task of cataloguing and assessing this newly acquired treasure-trove, M. J. Larsens, vividly described the vast halls of the depository in the early twenties 'crammed on both sides up to the ceiling with all sorts of luggage-cases (trunks, baskets, boxes, satchels and so on)', awaiting assessment. It was a slow process. By the end of 1923 only 2,887 parcels had been sorted into gold, silver, jewels, securities and paper money, out of over twenty thousand, but that had not prevented sales to the West, as Hatton Garden could already confirm.[35]

The thought that the crown jewels might bring in valuable foreign exchange was discussed with French and British experts. Their initial advice was that the main items (the sceptre, orb and crown) would not attract their historic worth in the commercial markets of the West, but that other valuables, including certain tsarist treasures such as the Fabergé Easter eggs, for example, might be of interest.

Not surprisingly such talk alerted both officials and crooks alike. Towards the end of 1922 the White Star liner *Majestic* was greeted on its arrival in New York by half a dozen special agents of the US Treasury who had been tipped off that there was a man on board with a quantity of the Russian crown jewels for sale. Nothing was found.[36] The search followed reports of the preparation of albums of photographs of the main crown jewels being prepared as a preliminary to international sales, or their use as collateral for a state loan. The collection was said to be worth $400 million.

Soon Soviet delegates were visiting Holland attempting to sell Rembrandts and other old masters from the Hermitage, and two American reporters were invited to visit the law courts in Moscow to see the crown jewels, set out for their benefit in all their magnificence: 'An Arabian Nights vision of the Romanoff treasures – the imperial crown jewels of Russia,' went the purple prose of the *New York Times* reporter, 'diamonds as big as walnuts, rubies, emeralds, bright, blooded or vivid green, large as a pigeon's egg, pearls like nuts set in row after perfectly matched row, platinum, gold, and flashing diamonds shimmering like running water with the rainbow colors of a fountain in the sunlight.'

'Here,' says Begasheff [head of the jewellery commission], opening the box with hands that tremble ever so little despite his air of unconcern, 'is the crown of the Emperor, 32,800 carats of diamonds.'

'Is it heavy?'

'No,' said one of the workmen, '5 pounds at most – try it,' and placed it straight away on my head.[37]

The crown was later said to be valued at $52 million. This display to the press and later to experts from London and New York, including a private viewing for Armand Hammer, the American friend of Lenin, were all part of the official efforts to prepare the way for a series of sales on the world's markets. The main ones were in 1927, 1929, 1933 and 1934,[38] when sales in Berlin, Vienna, London and New York brought in valuable exchange to the Soviet regime, with the nuptial crown of Catherine the Great, the diamond-studded sword of Emperor Paul I, a diamond necklace and a gold watch of Empress Alexandra, a photoframe of Nicholas and Alexandra and one or two Fabergé eggs from the tsar's collection, all coming under the hammer.

It was at this time (in 1929 and 1934) that Queen Mary acquired two of the tsar's Fabergé Easter eggs, one (the Colonnade Egg) presented to Alexandra by Nicholas in 1905 to commemorate the birth of the heir to the throne in 1904; and the other (the Mosaic Egg) in 1914. The Colonnade Egg was bought for £500. They have been recently valued at £6 million and returned to Russia for the first time four years ago when the Queen, who now owns them, lent them to an exhibition at the Armoury in Moscow. According to Agathon Fabergé, who was asked in 1947 how much his father had charged for the eggs, the price was 'about 30,000 roubles each' or the equivalent then of £3,000.

Out of fifty-six Easter eggs made for Alexander III and Nicholas II by Fabergé, only fifty-four were in royal hands in 1917, since the two made for Easter 1917 were not delivered. Nicholas II had ordered forty-six and his father ten. The present whereabouts of all the eggs is not known. Over the years the number in Moscow has dwindled from fifty-four to only ten. Prewar the biggest western purchasers were Emmanuel Snowman of Wartski's in London, who bought eleven, and Armand Hammer in New York. The most recent western collector was the late Malcolm Forbes, who acquired twelve for the Forbes Collection in New York, thus possessing more than the Armoury in Moscow.

The Soviet regime did not confine their overseas sales of tsarist treasures to precious stones and jewels. Towards the end of the twenties significant sales of paintings began from the Hermitage and elsewhere. In all these efforts middle-men as well as art connoisseurs from the West played prominent parts. Armand Hammer, later head of Occidental International, was the first and most prominent, even being suspected of being a Soviet agent. Others included Calouste Gulbenkian, Joseph Duveen, Joseph Davies and Andrew Mellon.

With the help, encouragement and, it must be admitted, the personal realisation by such intermediaries that forced sales were taking place on an increasingly depressed market, the Soviet authorities sold an incredible array of Russian treasures in a matter of a decade and a half. Beyond the jewels there were paintings by Rembrandt, Titian, Raphael, Van Dyck, Romney, Watteau, Tiepolo, Velasquez, Hals, Botticelli and Veronese. Andrew Mellon alone purchased $7 million worth of paintings from the Hermitage in 1930–1, accounting for a third of total Soviet exports to the US in that period. Between 1928 and 1933 total Soviet art sales probably reached $15 million.[39]

What would have been a great sadness to Empress Alexandra is the fact that the imperial family's entire personal library, including many Christmas presents from her to her children, was sold for no more than $3,131 (roughly £600) in the early thirties. A total of some 757 volumes were sold to Israel Perlstein, a Polish naturalised American book-dealer, and can now be seen in the Library of Congress in Washington. Some, with personal inscriptions in pencil, are a touching reminder of family life at Tsarskoe Selo. One, Louisa M. Alcott's *Little Men*, has the inscription: 'For darling Tatiana from Papa and Mama, January 12, 1909'.[40]

This was only a small part of Russian literary heritage sold by the Bolsheviks in this period. From the score or so palaces and houses owned by the Romanoff relatives close to St Petersburg, books and whole libraries were systematically collated and brought together at the Winter Palace for eventual sale to the West. One of the biggest single sales occurred in 1931, when the New York Public Library acquired some 2,200 volumes, a substantial portion of the library of Grand Duke Vladimir Alexandrovitch, the tsar's uncle. Other purchasers from the palace libraries at Gatchina, Anichkov and Tsarskoe Selo included Harvard University and the Hoover Institution.[41]

Only now is the Russian nation beginning to assess what it has lost, and how little the Soviet, especially the Stalinist, regime gained. At some auctions reserve prices were not reached. At others unique items were allowed to go at rock-bottom prices. In other cases private deals went ahead irrespective of initial valuations. The Russian magazine *Ogonyok*, in a first dispassionate attempt to assess the result, put it quite simply: 'Every country has difficulties sometimes when there are calls for sacrifices and absurd sacrifices. The cruel art losses suffered by us were absurd, as they were *not* the consequences of objective causes, but rather the results of economic illiteracy, criminal adventurism, dreaming ignorance and stupidity.'[42]

Gold

Throughout human history national, even occasionally individual, wealth has ultimately been represented by gold. As a measure of financial stature, it is unique. It is a metal with remarkable qualities: beautiful to behold, soft enough to be turned into fabulous jewellery and hard enough to be used as the basis of coins. Its accumulation produces no income, yet its possession has fostered political strength over the centuries, from Alexander the Great to President de Gaulle, and from Croesus to Haile Selassie. The Romanoffs were no exception and any search for their wealth must embrace what happened to their stock of gold.

From the peak in 1914, when Russia held the world's largest gold stock, to the time in August 1921 when the reserves in Moscow virtually ran out, rumours of tsarist gold and its whereabouts filled the world's press. The final tsarist gold shipment secretly sent from Petrograd (and Moscow) on Japanese warships from Vladivostock to Vancouver and Ottawa in March 1917 was instantly transformed into Nicholas's last desperate attempt to safeguard 'his own treasure'. And Winston Churchill's inquiry in 1919 about the whereabouts of a mysterious $1 million tsarist gold deposit in San Francisco hardly dampened speculation, linking up neatly with so-called 'sightings' of Nicholas himself in San Francisco in 1919 and again in 1920. All were grist to the rumour mill.

The size of tsarist gold holdings at the outbreak of war in 1914 has never been in dispute: they were the largest in the world. In rouble terms as a comparison, they stood at 1,700 million roubles, compared with 1,500 million roubles in France and 800 million in Britain.[1] Nicholas II not only controlled the Russian gold reserves, as the autocratic head of state; he also owned the gold mines (and the gold mining districts of Nertchinsk and Altai) from which they were supplied, and even received dividends from the profitability of these mines.

Like President de Gaulle more than half a century later, Nicholas had been advised at the start of his reign to put his trust in gold and to ensure that his gold reserves matched the notes in circulation in the country. In that way, he was told, inflation would be curbed and the country would prosper. Russia then, and France fifty years later, did so for at least a decade; and in both cases their gold reserves rose too.

National gold holdings can be built up in two basic ways: from the output from national gold mines, and from running a surplus on trade and services with other countries. In the years up to the outbreak of the First World War Russia benefited from both. She was thus well-placed to use this remarkable gold hoard to help pay for munitions and other essential wartime equipment from her Allies. She did not hesitate. But it was the terms on which the gold was transferred to London and the subsequent 'ownership' of the gold that was to lead to all the later misunderstandings.

One scene secretly enacted in the freezing waters outside Archangel in the late autumn of 1914 epitomises what to most people was the first haemorrhage from this national nest-egg. In October, only nine weeks after the outbreak of war, two British warships, the cruiser HMS *Drake* and the military transport HMS *Mantois* (formerly the P & O liner *Mantois*) secretly dropped anchor in the open sea 30 miles offshore. Then in complete darkness at night heavily-laden Russian lighters and barges brought bullion worth close on £8 million (£300 million at today's values) out from Archangel and transferred them to the British ships.[2]

It was one of the earliest signs of the financial co-operation that was to continue between the Allies up to the Revolution. Within weeks of the outbreak of war the best way to finance the supply of munitions to Russia had been discussed and decided. Peter Bark, the Russian Finance Minister, in the interests of ensuring British war supplies to Russia, agreed the terms on which the first consignment of gold would be sent to London. They had been drawn up by the Russian Ambassador in London, Count Alexander Benckendorff, the brother of Paul, the Marshal of the Imperial Court.

The gold would be 'exchanged' for British credits. The well-known merchant bank, Baring Brothers, which already had nearly a century of financing Russian bonds behind it, was to have the value of the gold at its disposal and, with the help of the Bank of England, would arrange not only for the provision of £8 million worth of credit, but for the discounting of £12 million worth of Russian Treasury bills (that is, enabling them to be turned into cash) to provide funds as they were required over the next twelve months. In effect £8 million would be used for the needs of commerce and industry, in supplying munitions; and a further £12 million would be employed in paying interest coupons on existing Russian debts.

This forerunner of a series of extremely complex gold agreements

between Britain and Russia would be the basis of untold misunderstandings between successive Bolshevik and British governments.
It would also prove to be at the heart of quite understandable mis-
apprehensions of the true nature of the Russian gold in London, not only
by members of the Romanoff family but on the part of a succession of
claimants and commentators over the next three-quarters of a century.

This first consignment could hardly have been better safeguarded from
the time it left Archangel to the time it was escorted in London under
military guard into the Bank of England's vaults in the rear entrance in
Lothbury. The War Risks Insurance Office in London arranged the
insurance and transport charges at a premium of 1 per cent and charged
it to the Russian government. They insisted that the gold 'should be
packed in steel-hooped boxes and sealed in the usual way, each box to be
separately marked and numbered'. As early as the end of September,
Peter Bark wrote to the Governor of the Bank of England introducing
Alexandre Timcovsky, an agent of the Chancery of Credit of the Finance
Ministry in St Petersburg, who would personally accompany the gold
and in essence deliver it to the Bank. In addition to the military escort on
land, it was to be protected at sea by the Royal Navy.[3]

Mr Timcovsky was accompanying 979 cases of bullion, made up of
roughly £4,500,000 in gold bars and £3,500,000 in gold coins. On arrival
in Liverpool, he found that the armed escort was already waiting but not
enough trucks were immediately available to transfer the gold to the
waiting train. It was not the only hitch in the arrangements. In spite of all
the secrecy Germany had become aware of what was going on and had
sent mine-laying submarines to intercept the ships in the Arctic Ocean.
The submarines quickly detected the two ships but their mines were only
partially successful and the ships finally docked in Liverpool with only
minor damage. But the lesson had been learnt. That particular route was
never used again, future shipments going by way of Vladivostock, usually
on British and Japanese warships to Vancouver, and finally over land to
Ottawa, where the Bank of England had an emergency depository.

The Archangel–Liverpool transfer of October 1914 was thus the first
trickle in a broadening stream of gold moving between the vaults of the
Russian State Bank in Petrograd and Moscow to those of the Bank of
England. Between 1914 and the start of the Revolution in 1917 £68
million worth of gold (in 1993 terms between £2,000 million and £2,500
million) was transferred in this way.

After the first shipment it quickly became clear that such agreements
between Britain and France, on the one hand, and Russia, on the other,
would have to continue if only to provide equipment and munitions from
the United States to *all* the Allies and from Britain and France to Russia.
By 1915 the big three Allied powers – Britain, France and Russia –

knew the nature of their own financial problems. France had bigger gold resources than Britain, but not sufficient industrial potential. Britain had the smallest gold reserve, but because of her financial freedoms and creditor status was the natural international paymaster, finding the necessary dollars when needed by the shipment of gold to the US. Russia had the gold, lacked the wartime supplies and was facing growing inflation.

Thus when the three met in Paris in 1915 to arrange the next series of gold agreements, Peter Bark knew he had a hard bargain to drive with his Allies. He badly needed huge credits but did not want to deplete his gold reserves. Lloyd George, whom he was meeting for the first time, knew that British gold payments to the United States to fund military purchases would soon reduce the Bank of England's holdings below their safety level and wanted help from France and Russia. Bark, however, was determined not to transfer any further gold outright to Britain, as his ambassador in London had agreed to do, on his behalf, at the beginning of the war with the first £8 million. He wanted to pledge his gold against credits, not sell it.[4]

In the corridors of the Crillon Hôtel, overlooking the Place de la Concorde, Lloyd George was at his persuasive best. And once the French Minister of Finance, Ribot, had succumbed to his charm by agreeing to transfer French gold to London, Bark was in difficulties. All he could do was to build into the agreement a gold repayment clause and to insist that Russian gold would be sent to London *only* when British and French reserves had reached minimum levels.

Bark, however, who as a former banker knew his way round a bank balance sheet, at least managed to persuade Lloyd George to include a typical piece of financial camouflage, which was to cause intense confusion later. It was in its way a natural request. Russia had been committed to a strict gold-backed currency since the beginning of Nicholas's reign. Bark was aware that the outflow of huge amounts of gold to London would immediately undermine this policy and leave the rouble without its protective cloak.

He therefore suggested a method by which this decline in Russia's gold reserves could be offset by an equivalent rise in what would be called 'gold holdings held in foreign countries'. What Lloyd George agreed was for Russia to provide gold, when this was deemed necessary, and for Britain to issue British Exchequer bonds in exchange for the gold. But, and this is where the nice cosmetic touch was applied, these bonds would be *repayable in gold* at intervals of from three to five years. So Russia was enabled to put the necessary 'gold held abroad' in its national balance sheet, even though in reality it represented British bonds repayable in gold, rather than actual gold.

The details and the ultimate destinations of the subsequent gold consignments are straightforward – at least up to 1917. After the first shipment of £8 million in 1914, a further £10 million was shipped in December 1915, £10 million in June 1916, £20 million in December 1916, and £20 million in March 1917. Two (in one case three) Japanese cruisers were used for the bulk of the transfers, first from Vladivostock to Yokohama, and then from Yokohama to Vancouver.

One final complication needs to be spelt out before we trace the gold shipments that then followed. Of the £60 million only £40 million worth of bonds were actually issued. As a secret internal memorandum in the Bank of England laconically put it: 'The British Government were about to issue $5\frac{1}{2}$ per cent Exchequer Bonds for £20 million dated March 16, 1917 to the Russian Government in November 1917, when the [Bolshevik] revolution took place.'[5] The earlier bonds with a face value of £40 million issued by the Bank of England on behalf of the Russian Imperial State Bank have never been redeemed. So Peter Bark's ingenious 'cosmetic' solution to his gold problem, and the complex aftermath, form a necessary ingredient in the trail that we now need to follow in resolving two deceptively simple questions: Where did the tsarist gold go to? Whose is it?

On arrival in Vancouver the bullion was put aboard special steel rail-cars of the Canadian Pacific Railway. The gold was accompanied by agents from the Russian finance ministry and protected by five guards in each car and fifteen additional guards in a special car ahead of the bullion. Extra food and water were carried on board the special trains to cut out unnecessary stops, and, a new innovation in those days, each car was connected separately by telephone.

In spite of all these precautions major press leaks occurred on one of the last two shipments. New York papers reported the exact amount of bullion being shipped and Vancouver businessmen knew both the amount and the names of the Japanese cruisers before they arrived. The leakage was traced back to Honolulu where the cruisers had stopped to take on coal, and where the enterprising agent of American Express, keen for future bullion business, especially if future consignments were to go overland in the United States, had cabled the information back to the US. The local Associated Press reporter did the rest. Though all this caused some tremors (and not a few irate questions) at the Bank of England, the local carriers in Canada, the Dominion Express Company,[6] took instant avoiding action and arranged for the bullion to be switched from the two Japanese cruisers, *Tokiava* and *Chitose*, to the Canadian warship *Rainbow* overnight, offshore Vancouver Island, 90 miles north of Victoria. Next morning the Canadian vessel slipped quietly and unnoticed into Vancouver harbour. Five days later the gold was safely in the Bank of England's depository in Ottawa.

Not only was the 'exchange' basis of these later gold shipments different from the first, but the costs were divided differently too. The British government paid the Japanese government the freight charges (roughly £36,000 for each consignment) and looked after the necessary insurance. Japan was also recompensed by being allowed to buy £8 million of the Russian gold and received it conveniently 'en route' thus avoiding the normal freight charges. Thus between 1914 and 1917 gold transfers from Russia ended up in three places: Ottawa £52 million; London £8 million; and Tokyo £8 million. A total of £68 million, with £60 million held by the Bank of England on behalf of the British government.

These wartime gold shipments were later to become the basis of all subsequent folk memories of the Romanoffs' missing wealth. As Lili Dehn recalled the conversation at Tsarskoe Selo in 1917, just after Nicholas's abdication, the tsarina was buoyed up by the thought of the money awaiting them in the Bank of England; she told Lili Dehn and Anna Vyrubova that the fortune available to them, should they eventually go into exile, was 'in gold and in millions'.

Who knows how often Nicholas and Alexandra must have discussed their wealth in terms of the gold they had been brought up to regard as 'theirs'. Such a simplistic approach to the nature of their private wealth was to lead them astray at the time. It was also to influence so many others over the coming years. The first to be affected in this way were Anna Anderson and her advisers, Edward Fallows and Gleb Botkin; Anna Anderson's first ideas of money in a bank 'in England' being deftly, and perhaps understandably, translated into the 'Bank of England' by others. Peter Bark's escape from Russia and his appointment as an adviser to the Governor of the Bank of England naturally added to the hardening-up process, as did Lili Dehn's memory of that gold remark at Tsarskoe Selo. It would be left to Edward Fallows to draw all the threads together to confront both the legal advisers of the Bank of England and the European courts with his convictions. But it was the gold connection that provided one of the original threads.

Before we explore these complexities, and the other problems of ownership, let us track the outflow of gold between the abdication of Nicholas and the virtual exhaustion of the reserves in the autumn of 1921. It is an exercise that has taken me from London to San Francisco, Hong Kong, Boston, New York, Washington and Paris. As a result it is now possible to say what happened to the tsarist gold left behind in the Imperial State Bank's repositories in Moscow, Petrograd, Samara and later in Kazan, and just where the original tsarist gold was spent, lent, lost or stolen.

The starting point is the dramatic take-over of the Imperial Bank Building in Moscow by armed Red Guards in 1917. This was no normal take-over of one political master by another. The new Bolshevik government was facing acute difficulties with its new civil servants and a combination of strikes and the closing of all private banks produced an urgent need for millions of roubles. On November 7 the new Commissar of Finance turned up at the State Bank, accompanied by armed sailors and, it is said, a military band. He wanted 10 million roubles. The State Bank refused to budge and he had to go away without the money. It took two more refusals, the presentation of an ultimatum and, eventually, late at night, a forced entry by armed guards before the bank officers finally opened the vaults. That was on November 17.[7]

That night the new Commissar took 5 million roubles from the vaults. It was the beginning of the hand-over of the core of the state wealth to the Bolsheviks. More important than all the notes still stacked in the Imperial Bank Building were the country's gold reserves and the imperial jewels. The gold reserves inherited from the tsar by Lvov and Kerensky in the Provisional government in March 1917 were naturally smaller than at their peak in 1914. That total (some 1,700 million roubles or £170 million) had been depleted by the successive shipments to Britain, Canada and Japan, though naturally helped by further output from the gold mines in eastern Russia. Since all the later estimates were done in dollars, we need to start with the same yardstick in 1914. The 1,700 million roubles were then worth some $823 million. By March 1917 this had declined to $600 million. During the period of the Provisional government gold output added to the reserves but a belated credit deal with the Swedish government just before the Bolshevik coup in November led to a shipment of $2,500,000 million to the Riksbank in Stockholm.

Thus the Bolshevik Commissar of Finance in mid-November 1917 inherited not only the 5 million roubles in notes he demanded at gun point, but a gold reserve worth some $613 million. Of this about a half, $308 million, was in Moscow and Petrograd and half at a branch of the State Bank in Samara on the Volga. The reserves had been divided when the German forces advanced in 1917. But the reserves in Samara were soon to be at the mercy of a variety of turbulent forces, both political and military. A crucial element in the future of the gold was the Czech Legion.

The Czech forces in Russia had originally been Slav allies in the war against Germany but had become something of an embarrassment once the Bolsheviks came to terms with Germany. It seemed to be in everyone's interest for the forty thousand Czechs, who were now mainly east of Moscow, and along the Trans-Siberian railway, to be allowed to travel to Vladivostock and back to Europe by sea. That was certainly the original intention of the Bolsheviks. But the turmoil then developing throughout Siberia, where even the term 'civil war' would give the situation a clarity it did not possess, quickly undermined the efforts to get the Czechs out of Russia as quickly as possible.

By the summer of 1918 several new counter-revolutionary forces had reared their heads in eastern Russia – some close to Vladivostock, some on the Manchurian border and others in parts of the Urals. All had alerted Trotsky to the danger of allowing armed Czechs to move through territory plainly hostile to the new regime in Moscow. Who knows, they might become allies and anti-Bolshevik en route. He insisted on the Czechs, in what turned out to be a hasty decision, laying down their arms and proceeding to Vladivostock unarmed. It was doomed to failure. His original fears were immediately turned into reality; and within months the Czechs had not only retained their arms and shown their mettle by taking over whole stretches of their lifeline to Vladivostock – the Trans-Siberian Railway – but had teamed up with White forces around Samara.

The gold reserves inherited from Kerensky had been quickly depleted by the brutal terms of the Brest-Litovsk Treaty, the Bolsheviks being forced to ship $160 million worth of gold from their Moscow gold stock to Berlin. (Those reserves eventually ended up in the vaults of the Bank of France, following the end of the war in Europe in November 1918.) Thus the advance of the White and Czech forces close to Samara represented a double threat, financial and political, and quickly persuaded the Bolsheviks to move their secondary gold stock from Samara in scores of barges further up river to Kazan. With the $25 million already stored in Kazan this eastern gold reserve was thus increased to $332 million. But the White–Czech forces quickly overran Kazan and acquired one of the biggest war treasures of the First World War.[8]

What happened now is one of the great mysteries of our story. During the next eighteen months close on $120 million of it went missing: spent, lent, lost or stolen – who knows? Yet its importance cannot be underestimated. After all, this is the 'tsarist' gold of popular parlance and, in today's terms, that kind of loss is the equivalent of at least $1,000 million.

The anti-Red forces that the Czechs had joined along the Trans-Siberian Railway were in essence local fiefdoms. The West Siberian Commissariat in Omsk, which had established a good following and a successful volunteer army, was a more reactionary grouping than its far more socialist opposite number, the Samara Constituent Assembly, with fewer troops at its disposal. The Czechs had enabled the Samara grouping to acquire the gold and in August it was once again moved by barge and steamer from Kazan back to Samara. But it did not remain there for long. Members of the Samara Assembly felt obliged to move the gold with them to Ufa, where they were soon engaged in merger discussions with the West Siberian grouping from Omsk. One had the gold; the other an impressive volunteer army.

This is where the lure of the gold was quickly reflected in political action and ended in one of the most bizarre gold thefts in bullion history. Under threat from marauding Red forces, the Assembly members from Samara moved on with their train and the gold from Ufa to Tcheliabinsk, while continuing their political dialogue with the Omsk group. On arrival at Tcheliabinsk they left the train to hold a meeting in town to decide where to keep the gold: in a convenient granary building or the local bank. While they were away from the railway station someone gave the train orders to proceed to Omsk and it is not difficult to guess who. The Siberian grouping in Omsk had, with a sharp eye on the main chance and some helpful blindness in the Samaran camp, acquired the gold and the upper hand in the negotiations. They now had both troops and gold. The political merger quickly followed and soon afterwards the person whose name was to be associated with the gold from then on appeared on the scene as Supreme Ruler of the combined Siberian White government at Omsk: Admiral Kolchak.

A former Commander-in-Chief of the Russian Black Sea fleet, Admiral Alexander Kolchak became involved with the White forces in Siberia almost by mischance. Just after the Bolshevik coup in November 1917 he turned up at the British Embassy in Tokyo, putting his services 'unconditionally, and in whatever capacity, at the disposal of His Majesty's Government'. His offer was immediately on the desk of the Foreign Secretary in London, where it was quickly accepted. The War Office, to whom the file was then passed, decided he would be best employed in Mesopotamia and proceeded to waste much time as well as Kolchak's own money in getting him slowly round from Yokohama via Shanghai, Hong Kong etc., en route to the Middle East. By the time he reached Singapore, however, in the middle of March, he was not only running out of funds but becoming frustrated and disillusioned. Under his growing pressure and that of outside events, both the War Office and the Foreign Office belatedly had second thoughts and persuaded him to go back to help in Manchuria. Like any well-trained officer, he agreed to do so.

It was not the only frustration Kolchak met over the next year, as he subsequently grappled with the chaos in eastern Russia and the political pressures then being exerted by the Japanese, Americans, French and British as each in turn slowly moved towards 'intervention' in the Russian civil war. Throughout this period Kolchak's abilities and standing as a potential leader and rallying point were increasingly recognised. Shortly after his arrival in Omsk in October 1918 he was put in charge of the Ministries of the Army and Navy in the Omsk Directory (the successor to the Omsk and Samara groupings), and within a matter of weeks, following a swift coup by others, he was offered the title of Supreme Ruler of what was in essence the Siberian government. He was now in sole charge of the gold reserve of $332 million in Omsk.[9]

He had much to do in consolidating his coalition of warring factions against the Bolsheviks and in co-ordinating his military actions with those of the Allied governments. With the resources to do so over the next nine months, he began to spend some of the gold on munitions and military equipment brought in through Vladivostock and to work out ways of pledging gold against essential credits for further supplies. In total about $122 million worth of gold was used in this way. In four months alone $35 million in gold was handed over to the Japanese, French and British governments for military supplies, by outright sales on the Hong Kong market. Another $2 million was stored in the State Bank in Vladivostock. In addition $65 million worth of gold was shipped to Vladivostock for use as collateral in raising credits with the Japanese ($16 million), the Americans ($2 million for rifles and machine guns) and an international banking syndicate led by Barings in London and Kidder, Peabody in New York ($47 million).

Some of these early shipments to Vladivostock suffered serious leakages. Sticky fingers abounded among the leaders of the regional governments through which the gold passed. Grigori Semenov, a Cossack captain, who had succeeded in overthrowing the local Bolshevik authority at Manchuli, a strategic point on the Trans-Siberian Railway, just over the Manchurian border, and who was for a time fed a monthly allowance from the British Consulate in Harbin, encouraged the gold shipments to pass safely through 'his' territory.

Manchuli happened to be on the final most direct route to Vladivostock on a branch of the Russian-controlled Chinese Eastern Railway, and Semenov had no difficulty in ensuring that some of the gold did not reach its destination. The Omsk government quickly realised that the amount reaching Vladivostock was somewhat smaller than the consignment that had left Omsk. But no amount of polite correspondence from the Finance Ministry in Omsk, even military pressure from Kolchak himself, would shift Semenov. The missing gold, later estimated at nearly $22 million, remained under Semenov's control in Tchita, until it was finally recaptured by the Bolsheviks.

In this period, while his headquarters remained at Omsk, Kolchak thus used, and occasionally lost, some $122 million worth of gold in financing his White forces against the Bolsheviks. It was all to no avail and towards the end of 1919, as the Red forces began to advance towards him, he had to contemplate the evacuation of Omsk and to move his political and military headquarters further east to Irkutsk. That meant taking, and guarding, the remaining basic gold reserve with him along the Trans-Siberian Railway line. It took all of ten days to load the remaining $210 million of gold into forty special cars. This was the significant residue left from the original stock of $332 million.

Kolchak left Omsk on the night of November 12, 1919 in a 'convoy' of trains, two days before its occupation by the Bolsheviks. He had deliberately formed five of the trains under the letters A, B, C, D, E, to be accompanied by an armoured train. He himself travelled in train B. His staff, the chancery and the guard were in trains A, B, C, and E. The gold was placed in train D. So far so good. But not long after their departure from Omsk, as two of the trains were moving through the station of Tatarskaia, nearly 80 miles east of Omsk, train B ploughed violently into the back of the gold train, and the crash started a huge fire in the station.

The result was catastrophic. Eight railway cars were destroyed, no fewer than eighty of the guard were killed and thirty wounded and scores of boxes and cases containing the gold were scattered all over the line. Bars and coins were there for the picking. The amount lost in the chaos is not known.

The final destination of the gold and the fate of Admiral Kolchak can be quickly told. The combination of the Red advance eastwards, the determination of the Czechs, who had preceded Kolchak out of Omsk, to get to Vladivostock safely, and the occasionally violent initiatives of regional warlords, coupled with the divergent attitudes now emerging among the Allied governments, slowly undermined Kolchak's remaining authority. The Czechs above all, deliberately controlling the Trans-Siberian Railway to ensure their own ultimate escape, were able to dictate movements along that crucial lifeline. The congestion on the line had reduced movements to only two trains a day. Kolchak was simply told by the Czechs that his own train and that containing the gold could proceed as far as Nijneudinsk. This they did. Then after further delays, in which General Janin, the French commander of Allied forces, played a particularly dark and decisive role, Kolchak was eventually forced to leave the gold train there, in return for a guaranteed free passage to Vladivostock. He was never to reach the coast, the Czechs eventually handing him over to the newly-established revolutionary Socialist regime in Irkutsk. General Janin's role in this affair – did he instruct the Czechs to hand over Kolchak to the revolutionary authorities in Irkutsk? – remains equivocal. Kolchak, however, was shot two months after his hand-over, and Janin was discreetly recalled by the French government. Not that this is the last we shall hear of him.

This meant that the Czechs now had the gold, and were still keen to get out of Siberia. Meanwhile individual Allied governments had clearly been keeping their eyes on the fate of the 'Kolchak' gold. The American State Department in particular thoroughly explored the implications of such an 'acquisition'. Its possession, even if held 'as trustee for the Russian people', would ensure that any future Russian government would adhere to past bond obligations. Talks along such lines continued for some weeks, until the stark realities of the situation (the Czechs actually held the gold and simply wanted to get away) forced their way through the diplomatic niceties.

Thus, in spite of these last minute Allied 'thoughts', the remaining tsarist gold (some $210 million of it had left Omsk) found its way back into Bolshevik hands. Whether the full amount was actually returned is still in doubt. Rumours of large quantities of gold coins being sold in Harbin shortly afterwards, enough to depress the gold price significantly, strongly suggests that the Czechs, or others at a later stage, or even those lucky enough to gain from the earlier crash in Tatarskaia, were unloading their recently acquired loot. The White Russians in exile remained convinced that the Czechs had taken as much as $32 million from the stocks they received from Kolchak, but the White Russians may have been taking their cue, whether they were aware of it or not, from Bolshevik-inspired stories in the western press. Part of the answer can now be revealed.[10]

In the autumn of 1924 the American Consul in Riga picked up an irate response from the Czech Consul there not only denying the charges against the Czech Legion, but giving full details of exactly how some of the gold had been lost and how much. The Czech Consul had plainly done his homework. He knew that the gold had been guarded by three hundred men as it first left Kazan on its complicated journey through Siberia under the combined eyes of Kolchak and the Czech Legion. He knew the exact breakdown of the gold into bullion and coins, and their value. He knew that Kolchak had resisted all efforts by General Janin to persuade him to move it eastwards well before the final, somewhat belated, evacuation of Omsk. And he was aware that it was Janin who had finally entrusted the gold to the Czech Legion. He also went on to describe what then happened.

On January 4, 1920 the Czechs took over the gold, which was immediately put in the care of three Czech officers and three Russian officials. At that stage, he stressed, all the original seals on the cases of gold were intact and additional Czech seals were added. But on January 12 the Czechs discovered that the seals on one car, which had been guarded by the Russians at the station at Tiuret, had been broken. Thirteen cases were missing. The whole gold consignment was eventually guarded by the 7th Company of the Irkutsk Soviet Regiment from February 28 and formally handed over to the Bolsheviks by the Czechs on March 1. It was in effect a detailed refutation of the alleged looting of $32 million by the Czechs and had the ring of truth about it – at least until I discovered more of the truth in Hong Kong some time later.

The trouble is that the Czechs had sold some of the gold on the international market through Vladivostock. Perhaps they did lose some of it in the way they officially described. But it takes two to make a bargain and the bank to which they off-loaded some of the gold still has details of the transactions in its vaults. The Hongkong & Shanghai Banking Corporation, which had opened a branch in Vladivostock in 1918, at the request of the British government, was approached by the Czechs. The local manager, B. C. Lambert, recorded simply that the Czechs 'sold the part of the bullion they had with them secretly to the Hongkong Bank'. The bank's archives in Hong Kong, however, contain this rather more detailed note:

These gold bars had been offered to the Bank of England who refused them. Lambert then made an offer for them through A. G. Stephen, the manager of the Shanghai branch. They were shipped by yacht under Commander Baring to Shanghai and then sent to India where gold was badly needed.[11]

The rest of the story is filled in in the bank's history, where Lambert's successor as manager in Vladivostock, M. W. Wood, describes how the gold was counted by him and his two assistants under cover of darkness: 'The office floor was covered by the boxes. We walked on top, one by one, candle in bottle in one hand, sealing wax in the other, opening each box, checking contents, re-sealing and sending off for shipment.'

Three questions are now uppermost. How much tsarist gold did the Bolsheviks finally inherit? How much eventually went elsewhere? How much were they left with in early 1920? In round figures Kerensky handed over $613 million to the new Bolshevik government in November 1917. The Czechs and Kolchak between them acquired $332 million of this gold stock in Kazan and the Czechs later handed back some $210 million. Taking into account the gold that had to be handed over to the German government and the amount still being produced by Russian gold mines, as well as a windfall from the acquisition of Romanian gold, the Bolsheviks were by the early months of 1920 left with a total of just over $300 million.

Thus between November 1917 and the early months of 1920, the Bolshevik gold stock roughly halved; or, put another way, there remained a third of the total with which Nicholas had begun the war in 1914. A year later, in the spring of 1921, the Bolshevik gold reserves were down to $170 million. By August 10 that year they had dwindled further and reached $1,200,000 and on August 30 they were reported to be 'exhausted'.

Some $800 million of tsarist gold had vanished in a matter of seven turbulent years: some to pay for the war; some to pay off wartime enemies; some to finance the armed resistance of the Whites in Siberia; some to maintain the flow of imports; and some simply to line the pockets of looters of all kinds, from regional chieftains in Siberia to the scavengers to be found wherever the lure of gold is strongest.

At the end two additional Bolshevik factors also took over. One was the Bolsheviks' widening trade gap, as internal turmoil took its toll on manufacturing output and trade with the West was affected by the nature of the new regime; the other was the instinct of official 'comrades' not only to use what gold resources they had to stimulate Bolshevik propaganda abroad, but even occasionally to channel such resources into private accounts overseas. It was a characteristic that was to reveal itself with an uncanny, precise repetition seventy years later, in the last months of the Soviet regime, when the total gold and currency reserves dropped from $11 billion to zero in less than eighteen months. Only $7 billion of this recent drain could be accounted for by normal trade transactions. The whereabouts of the remaining $4 billion remains a mystery.[12] The temptation to establish nest-eggs abroad thus characterised both the beginning and end of Bolshevism.

One bizarre effect of the 1991 decline in the former Soviet gold reserve was the sudden appearance of actual tsarist gold bars in the Zurich and London gold markets. The Soviet authorities, in what proved to be their last financial, as well as political crisis, were being forced to sell gold bars from their basic, that is, original, reserve. These tsarist bars were quickly recognised by London bullion dealers from their official markings and dates. They were dated 1914 and were 98 per cent pure, rather below the London Delivery Specification, and were immediately checked against earlier bars in the western markets.

The question we are faced with is not only whose gold was it that finally turned up in the West in 1991, but whose gold was transferred to the Bank of England's vaults in London and Ottawa during the First World War. Thus having traced the bulk of the original tsarist gold, we now face the question of ownership. This in turn brings us back to Nicholas, what happened on his abdication, and perhaps what might have happened before he abdicated.

As Tsar of All the Russias he controlled the mining and manufacture of gold and its sale to the state, from which he derived useful income. Even thereafter he could decide, with his Finance Minister's advice, where the state was to dispatch the gold – to the State Bank's vaults or abroad. Since he controlled both his own imperial finances and those of the state, he could directly influence the building up or depletion of the gold reserves. He even signed the state documents dispatching the wartime shipments of gold to London. Hence the assumption, no doubt, that the gold in London was Romanoff gold. In one sense it was; in another sense it was not; and thereby hangs one of our outstanding questions. How much of so-called tsarist gold was imperial, that is, pre-Bolshevik, government gold and how much was Romanoff family gold? Unless he had placed deposits abroad in his own name or in that of one of the family in actual gold, then overseas gold belonged to the imperial government or its successor, not to the Romanoffs.

So far no evidence has emerged to suggest that any gold deposits were made on behalf of the Romanoff family prior to the abdication. There is little reason to think that there would be, since gold by its nature produces no income, simply protection against the ravages of inflation, which was hardly a threat before 1914. If this is true, then the main dispute about the ownership of the gold we have traced lay between the Imperial government, the Bolshevik government and, in the case of gold shipped to the Bank of England, the British government. And that is a dispute that continued to rumble throughout the twenties and thirties and well into the post-Second World War era.

13

Money

As the outward reflection of wealth, the chandeliers of the Winter Palace, the gold ornaments, the Fabergé Easter eggs, the bright lights reflecting on the empress's tiara and necklace – these were no more than the panoply of royalty. The real tsarist wealth lay elsewhere, in the ability to move millions of roubles at will and, ultimately, in the millions said to have been invested abroad for Nicholas and his family before the 1914–18 war.

The more sophisticated man has become in the use of money, the more elusive this artificial alternative to wealth. Barter was based on tangibles, whether shells, metals, sheep or goats. Even the first coins had an intrinsic value and could be melted down. But the confidence trick in switching the bulk of our transactions from coins to paper notes, bank deposits and now even computerised accounts (all based on the assumption that a bank, institution or government will guarantee to give you your money back) brought in yet another slippery element. Money had become no more than a claim on someone else's integrity or survival. And such claims over a period of years naturally encompassed every conceivable hazard – from fraud to inflation and from war and revolution to confiscation.

These are not the only hazards in searching for past tsarist bank accounts and investments. Putting money in a bank is a private transaction between a bank and its customer. The relationship is akin to that between a doctor and patient, or lawyer or any other professional adviser and his client. Information about the past, quite apart from the transfer of money itself, will be restricted to the original client or his legally accepted descendant or assign. The secrecy is often overdone in the interests of so-called professional etiquette; and the privacy rule can be both a protection to the client, whether alive or dead, and an unnecessary blockage to genuine inquiries.

This was the first stumbling block met by almost every claimant to the tsarist money, whether in London, Paris, Berlin or New York. Anna Anderson continued to be frustrated in this way throughout most of her life. It has not been the only difficulty in tracing such deposits. Heads of state naturally attract protection and secrecy, whether it concerns their movements, their private life or their money; and royal activities attract an over-zealous protection all of their own. But this has not been able to hide a vital fact: when Nicholas and his family were killed at Ekaterinburg they left behind them a substantial amount of tsarist money and investments outside Russia.

It is when the actual size and whereabouts of such tsarist money needs to be established that the real difficulties start, and the inquiring net has to be spread far wider. Initially one is forced back on such questions as: Who has claimed the tsarist money and what did they really know? Who has already made independent inquiries and what did they discover? Who could have known the truth at the time and what have they subsequently said? Who may know the truth now and has kept quiet?

To the three independent investigators on behalf of the major claimants – Herlaf Zahle and Edward Fallows for Anna Anderson and Kyril de Shishmarev for Colonel Goleniewski – now needs to be added a fourth: Fanny Holtzmann. This formidable American lawyer successfully advised and indirectly defended Princess Irina Youssopov (daughter of Grand Duchess Xenia) in a notorious libel suit in 1934 against Metro-Goldwyn-Mayer over their film about Rasputin. All four, in their different ways, added conjectures as well as facts to the quest. These we must now examine closely for clues.

Princess Irina's husband, Prince Felix Youssopov, was one of the self-confessed murderers of Rasputin, but the film had implied that Rasputin was the court protégé and sexual master of Irina. It was this implication that Fanny was hired to refute and to claim damages against. With the help of her British legal colleagues in court she triumphed to the extent that MGM were made to pay damages of £25,000 (with an immediate payment of £5,000, which was raised to £10,000 on appeal). What was even more damaging to MGM was that in order to prevent similar actions being taken against them in the United States and elsewhere, they agreed to pay an undisclosed sum. One Russian émigré hazarded that it was in the region of $900,000. Fanny's only comment was: 'he seems to know what he is talking about'.

While all this was going on Fanny absorbed most of Grand Duchess Xenia's financial problems relating to her Romanoff inheritance. She had been vetted personally at the outset by King George V and Queen Mary on Xenia's behalf, over tea at Windsor. It was hardly a meeting of minds, Fanny having arrived by Green Line bus from London as though to establish her republican credentials, but both sides immediately warmed to each other. King George was intrigued by such a female professional ('you seem so – please forgive me – so very young') and Queen Mary was plainly impatient to quiz her about her Hollywood friends and clients Mary Pickford, Charlie Chaplin, and – though the queen politely tried to restrain her intense curiosity – the heart-throb John Gilbert. Their almost childish persistence won Fanny over, and she was equally accepted as someone Xenia could rely on.

The libel case naturally led Fanny into the wider problems facing all the Romanoffs, following Empress Marie's death in Copenhagen in 1928. As a result of Anna Anderson's 'campaign' to establish her rights of inheritance, both Xenia and Olga had been forced to ensure their own rights and this had already led to litigation in Finland and Germany. It was natural for Xenia to ask Fanny for help in this wider dispute, and she quickly plunged into the Romanoff financial conundrum with her usual enthusiasm. The first story that tantalised her was that Nicholas, at the request of George V, had put $50 million worth of bullion on board a British warship and, according to Ted Berkmann, her biographer, she was told that 'the money had never been delivered or otherwise accounted for'. As outlined in Chapter 12, we now know differently – that the gold shipped to London and Ottawa was not for Nicholas's use but simply an agreed transaction between governments. Fanny, however, pursued the quest relentlessly, questioning royal survivors among the Romanoffs and their retinue. According to her biographer she 'ran into a maze of conjecture and contradiction', and did not clarify the outcome.

The gold report was not the only question she followed up. Bank deposits in Britain and Germany and heavy tsarist investments in the United States also became her targets. Fanny Holtzmann, we are told, went about her task by sending off 'a dozen confidential letters to highly placed friends in government' and followed this up by a special visit to Paris, where she deliberately interviewed the appropriate court contacts among the Russian émigré community. She 'methodically checked out each lead' and, as she did so, each one 'slipped away into insubstantiality'. Her biographer summed up the results of all her efforts in these words:

Gradually a different picture emerged, of a tsar and tsarina whose resources in Russia were confiscated or sold after the Revolution and whose overseas assets were quickly swallowed up: by the collapse of the mark in Germany, and in England for the purchase of trains and medical supplies.[1]

We shall be looking at Nicholas's actions on the outbreak of war in 1914 in some detail. But before doing so, we need to examine the similar, though more detailed and far more extensive, inquiries undertaken by Edward Fallows on behalf of Anna Anderson, the fourth of our past inquiries.

As we saw, these began in earnest in 1928 when Anna granted Fallows full powers of attorney on her behalf, and continued throughout the 1930s. Thus Fanny Holtzmann and Edward Fallows, both American lawyers, were engaged on a similar tsarist quest at much the same time, one for an established Romanoff, the other for a Romanoff claimant. Fallows, however, was to become obsessed with his task and, in the view of many of his friends, to the detriment not only of his professional business but even of his health. Yet his findings cannot be ignored. They will take us to the heart of Anna Anderson's alleged suspicions about Peter Bark and whether, with the knowledge he acquired as the tsar's last Finance Minister, he was responsible for switching the tsar's alleged money at the Bank of England to his own use or that of the surviving Romanoffs. It is a suspicion that has been reiterated over the years and, in a more specific form, as recently as 1991 by the late James Blair Lovell, Anna Anderson's 'chosen biographer'.

Fallows' first efforts were directed to putting the Bank of England and other banks on notice concerning Anna Anderson's claims in 1928. He made similar moves in New York and Berlin. Thereafter he had two separate, though related, tasks: to establish Anna Anderson's identity as Anastasia in the appropriate courts of law (basically, as it eventually turned out, in the German courts) and to trace the money and investments.

Edward Fallows had one advantage in looking for tsarist deposits in London. He had already met Arthur Gallop, partner in the London legal firm of Freshfields, Leese and Munns, the solicitors to the Bank of England, in 1925. On that occasion Gallop, who looked after the firm's Bank of England affairs, had taken him for lunch at the firm's offices in Old Jewry, a small lane virtually round the corner from the Bank, and had then shown him the inside of the Bank of England, even visiting the gold vaults where he saw 'hundreds of millions of pounds sterling in gold'. Memories of that visit must have been vividly revived on his first return to London on behalf of Anna Anderson in the February of 1929. Once again he sought out Arthur Gallop and was received just as courteously as before.

Before arriving in London Fallows had made contact with a legal friend, Gilbert Kennedy, who in turn had discussed the possibility of tsarist deposits with Arthur Gallop. According to Fallows, Kennedy had told him that Gallop indicated to him that he was not at liberty to disclose the existence of such a deposit until some authenticated claimant came forward with the request. But he came away with the distinct impression that there was money in the Bank, since he felt sure he would have been told if none had existed.[2]

This was still the impression that Fallows carried with him when he called on Arthur Gallop in Old Jewry. He was greeted like an old friend.

Having reminisced a little and finally got on to the issue Fallows had come to discuss, Gallop put his cards on the table:

Ordinarily, Mr Fallows, I would go more than halfway with you on any matter you brought to me, but here you must take every step of the way yourself, as the Bank of England is a Government institution and we are not permitted to disclose the existence or amount of a deposit except to an accredited depositor.[3]

Fallows inquired what those steps were. 'Go to the Court of Chancery and get an order that your client is Anastasia and then come to the Bank and we will open the books.' Gallop then went on to explain that there was no statute of limitations running against such a deposit (that is, there was no legal time limit on such a claim); one could come a hundred years hence and draw it out on proper credentials, but being a private deposit, it did not draw interest.

It was enough to convince Fallows that he was not wasting his time. Writing several years later, with memories of Kennedy's earlier impression clearly in mind, Fallows said: 'I too at that time got a very definite impression that the money was there, because of what he did not say.' The internal note written by Freshfields to the Bank of England, following the interview, simply records the meeting and repeats Gallop's words. It was in fact little more than a repetition of the legal position. Fallows, for reasons of his own, had chosen to ignore the words 'not permitted to disclose *the existence* or amount of a deposit' (my italics) and had mistaken normal City of London courtesy for affirmation. He was not the first, or last, foreign visitor to make such a mistake. London's international bankers can still say 'no', or give nothing away, without offence better than anyone I know.

Fallows' next stop was Berlin, where he called on the Mendelssohn Bank. Like Barings in London, the German private bank had had ties with Russia for well over a century, being instrumental in arranging Russian government loans and supporting the rouble whenever that was necessary. Russia had long kept significant deposits in the bank, ostensibly to pay the regular instalments on existing loans, but which allowed the bank to make additional profits. In return the Russian government always knew that it could rely on Mendelssohns to help when needed. One financial observer once put the relationship this way: 'That the Tsarist Government was regularly able (to some extent at least) to recover from its many unfortunate wars and its internal difficulties, was due in con-siderable measure to the Mendelssohns.'[4]

On arrival in Berlin an old legal friend was again found to introduce Fallows to a director of the bank, Dr Paul Kempner. Here he had more specific news awaiting him. Kempner confirmed that the tsar had sent Mendelssohns 'several million roubles' before the war to invest in German

securities and to hold them as trustees for the benefit of the royal family.
Kempner said that his own bank had followed out these instructions and
had deposited the securities in the Reichsbank, where they still remained.[5]
Their value, of course, had suffered greatly because of the huge inflation
in Germany in the early 1920s.

Though he gained more immediate information in Berlin than in
London, Fallows quickly realised that establishing a legitimate claim to it
was another matter and was not going to be easy. Anastasia's German
relations had already put doubts in the bank's mind about Anna Anderson
by persuading it that she was simply a Polish peasant claiming to be
Anastasia. It took Fallows another seven years, including even a personal
approach to Hitler, to neutralise the Polish report and in this period the
Mendelssohn Bank paid into the Probate Court in Berlin the resultant
funds belonging to the royal family. The amount thus deposited amounted
to about a million Reichsmarks, or, according to Fallows, some $100,000
(roughly £25,000 in sterling terms at the time). At the same time the
surviving Romanoff claimants, as we saw in Chapter 9, had put in their
own claim to the funds.

On his first European trip Fallows had thus convinced himself that
tsarist money had been deposited in the Bank of England and was still
there, and had received actual confirmation that tsarist money had been
placed in the Mendelssohn Bank in Berlin and that the securities were
still lodged with the Reichsbank. On his return to New York he mentally
put his own conviction about London and the confirmation in Berlin on
the same footing, and saved most of his energies to pursue the London
deposits which he was now convinced were by far the largest. New York
banks also attracted his attention.

For the next few years these inquiries in London and elsewhere reflected
his continuing devotion to Anna Anderson. But their relations hardly ran
smoothly. Her temperament remained volatile, those closest to her often
receiving the full force of her resentments and frustrations. Fallows was
no exception. She sharply disagreed with his methods, found his lack of
German both an irritation and a stumbling block in the German legal
preparations, and at one point withdrew his power of attorney, only to
renew it again two years later.

Throughout these tantrums Fallows maintained his devotion to her
cause and, with ingenuity and financial contacts in New York, managed
to finance all the necessary legal costs. As we explained earlier, his
Grandanor Corporation was the chosen instrument, attracting equity
contributions from individuals and corporations alike, in return for a
share in Anastasia's expected millions lying in western banks. He was to
get 25 per cent. A further 10 per cent would go to cover his and other
legal fees, as well as to repay loans he and his family had raised on their

property. And another 10 per cent would go to investors, who were promised a return of 5 to 1. The financial documents spoke of 'Anastasia' having a possible $10 million in the Bank of England. So, on this basis, Anna Anderson would get $5,500,000; he would get $2,500,000; investors would get their share of a maximum $1 million; and a further $1 million would be available to repay all legal and other costs.[6]

It was hardly surprising that this financial approach should evoke a similar response in others. Even before he left New York for his next European foray, he was approached by Aaron Simanovitch, Rasputin's former secretary, who said quite simply that he would reveal the source of $17 million of tsarist money in a New York bank if Fallows would do a deal with him.[7] Fallows took this offer seriously enough to devote part of his next visit to London trying to persuade Xenia's lawyers to make a joint deal, along with Anna Anderson, with Simanovitch. That particular joint effort, even in embryo, was to founder on the firm opposition of Peter Bark, who was now advising Xenia and who insisted, from his personal knowledge, that no such deposits existed either in London or New York.

On his next visit to Europe Fallows was told by a prominent White Russian contact in London that his brother had recently met an acquaintance on a train in France who knew a Russian lawyer in Brussels who, in turn, knew where the tsar's money was kept in England, Germany, Switzerland and America. He would reveal the source on a 50–50 basis. Fallows learnt that Grand Duchess Xenia and Grand Duchess Olga had already been approached by the Russian lawyer who had said that, in exchange for half the money, he would provide them with authentic documents stolen from Russia, which included details of $7 million in New York. A Swiss bank was reported to have been willing to advance $400,000 upon the locating of the New York deposit alone.

Later in New York, he turned his mind to checking out the American banks for the alleged deposit so many people seemed to be hinting at. Just before Christmas 1937 he sent out a letter to some thirty-one New York banks, big and small. He introduced himself as the 'attorney for Grand Duchess Anastasia Nikolaevna of Russia, the youngest daughter and the only surviving child of the late Tsar Nicholas II and Tsarina Alexandra of Russia, who died at Ekaterinburg, Siberia on July 16–17, 1918'.[8] He indicated that reliable information he had received showed that 'a sum of several million dollars in cash and/or securities is now on deposit in a New York City bank, which was the personal property of the said Tsar Nicholas II and/or his family'. Grand Duchess Anastasia was now filing her claim to the money and/or securities and he asked each bank to advise him whether they had such money in their possession or under their control.

He got immediate replies from most of the banks, some brief, some all embracing, all denying that they had the money he was seeking. First National City Bank telephoned almost immediately to say they had no such deposits. There is no record in the Fallows papers that Guaranty Trust replied. As we now know, and shall be tracing in detail, both banks were right in denying (or refusing to affirm) that they had money in the names of Nicholas or Alexandra. It did not mean that they did not have tsarist money. Fallows had drawn his definition rather too tightly.

Brussels was again the source of another report of tsarist money which Fallows picked up in Europe. This was from a Baron von Cuyck who indicated that he too knew the whereabouts of a large sum of tsarist money and, in exchange for a suitable 'retainer', would reveal all.[9] He had already promised Grand Duke Alexander, Xenia's estranged husband, £1,000 a year for at least five years if he would secure Xenia's signature. This too for a time was taken seriously but eventually came to nothing. Thus even the smallest bit of Romanoff tittle-tattle was regarded as having a price tag in the somewhat unreal marketplace that was opening up in Europe as Fallows and others pursued their inquiries. Fallows had to pick his way carefully among the White Russian gossip that seemed to ferment best in Brussels and Paris and naturally spread to both London and New York.

By the late 1930s he was again firmly reinstated in Anna's good books and in virtually full control of her legal affairs. Over these years, having had little success with New York banks, he had grown increasingly convinced not only that tsarist money was deposited in the Bank of England, but that Peter Bark, who had been knighted by George V and had died in January 1937, had diverted its use to his own ends. Anna Anderson's earlier statements about Bark, supported as they were by Gleb Botkin and others, seemed to have been confirmed in so many ways as Fallows found Bark blocking his path on his various visits to London. His conviction about Bark's sinister role thus became almost an obsession.

When Fallows was in London in 1938 he told the Bank of England's solicitor, Arthur Gallop, that, according to Mrs Anderson, her father, the tsar, had given his four daughters 'the name of the agent who had deposited the money in the Bank of England'. She could not remember the name, but said it was 'not Russian but Baltic and she thought of one syllable'. The late James Blair Lovell recently added another clue to the name. He said that Mrs Anderson had indicated that 'it had something to do with a tree'. With or without knowledge of this latest, rather heavy and, it must be said, over-dramatic, hint, Fallows concluded:

I at once assumed that it must be Sir Peter Bark, as he was a Finance Minister of the Tsar before the war, and had come to London during the war or just after, and had been honoured by the Bank of England with a very responsible position and had also been knighted here.

He also added, as if to confirm Bark's complicity, that he had been appointed as trustee to Grand Duchess Xenia and adviser to King George V.

Fallows noted that Bark had continually denied that any Romanoff deposit existed in the Bank of England, and quickly jumped to the conclusion that he had made use of some of the money for his own purposes, with the knowledge of the Bank of England. It was a simple step from that to the assumption that the establishment of the Anglo-Austrian Bank and the British Trade Corporation and their later merger into the Anglo-International Bank, all under Bank of England auspices and with Peter Bark as managing director, had been based on Romanoff funds.

It stands to reason [he wrote] that Bark would not leave £2 million in the Bank of England, not drawing interest. As a businessman and a banker he would invest the money in a dividend paying security or securities. With the Tsar's family all apparently killed, the temptation may have been irresistible to feather his own nest. It's going to be a fascinating investigation.[10]

Accordingly, Fallows spent his last visit to London, just before the outbreak of war in 1939, in searching through Somerset House for details of the shareholdings in the Anglo-International Bank and obtaining a copy of Sir Peter Bark's will.

Fallows' findings were hardly conclusive. He discovered that the Anglo-International Bank had some two million ordinary shares in issue, but that Sir Peter Bark's allotment was only two hundred. He consoled himself with the thought that these were simply his personal shares and that 'these big men always use dummies as stockholders'. As for his will, this too was less than earth-shattering. He found it to be the 'shortest on record'. He had left everything in trust to his wife, Sophie, for life and the remainder to his daughter Nina. His estate was given as no more than £14,126. Again Fallows comforted himself with the thought that this was 'merely nominal'.[11]

Within a matter of months war had broken out in Europe and a year later Edward Fallows died in New York. He had spent well over a decade battling on behalf of Anna Anderson and, though his prime aim was financial, he had poured large amounts of his own money into all his efforts, all to no immediate effect. He had clarified the position in Berlin, without gaining any of the money for Mrs Anderson; he had made no headway in New York; he had failed to confirm that there were any deposits in the Bank of England and, as we shall soon see, he had neglected to seek out other banks in London; and he had simply aired his suspicions about Sir Peter Bark without being able to provide a shred of evidence against him.

Those suspicions lingered on, however. Every subsequent investigator could not ignore the fact that Bark, as the tsar's last Finance Minister, had been close to both the British and Russian royal families, had been a prime player in the wartime financial negotiations, knew all about the Russian gold shipments, had later been appointed to a senior post at the Bank of England, had become adviser to George V and a trustee of both Grand Duchesses Xenia and Olga, and, above all, had even successfully removed the former Empress Marie's jewel box from Copenhagen to Buckingham Palace immediately after her death.

These were facts; not simply Anna Anderson's personal suspicions. It was left to one particular admirer of hers, the late James Blair Lovell, in his book published in 1991, not only to harden up the suspicions about Bark's role but to add new ones, including a royal connection to the House of Windsor. While Fallows had readily assumed that Bark had acted alone, with the complicity of the Bank of England, and had deliberately kept his information about, and use of, the Romanoff money from Grand Duchesses Xenia and Olga, Lovell implied that Xenia (though not Olga) was eventually included in Bark's secret and was kept quiet by regular payments from the British royal family. 'Thus not only Bark, but the British royal family itself,' wrote Lovell, 'would have had a personal stake in avoiding any controversy that would have hinted at appropriating the Tsar's money. Consequently they might have offered Grand Duchess Xenia a "Settlement" in exchange for her silence.' This, Lovell clearly believed, would explain why they were all so implacably opposed to Anna Anderson's claims.[12]

Peter Bark, I concluded from all this, deserved further investigation, if only to clarify his role once and for all. The search began with another visit to Harvard to assess Edward Fallows' own inquiries about him. It included the tracing of two grandsons of Bark, one living in London, the other in Paris; it involved a visit to St Petersburg for details of his wartime role, as well as a search in the archives of the Bank of England for the truth about his relationship with the Governor; and it meant tracing the London bank where he kept his accounts and details of his personal investments. It ended at Columbia University in New York where an unpublished English autobiography of Peter Bark himself was finally run to earth.

14

Bark

In going further through Fallows' files on Bark at Harvard I was suddenly riveted by a strange coincidence. At the time, I was Director-General of the British Invisible Exports Council, an organisation set up by the Bank of England in the late 1960s. My office address was 14 Austin Friars, in the heart of the City of London. A letter written to Bark by Edward Fallows from New York was addressed to him as '*Sir Peter Bark, Managing Director, British Export Corporation, 14 Austin Friars, London*'. The date was 1936. I had come 4,000 miles to discover that Fallows' and Anna Anderson's main suspect had been working fifty years earlier, not exactly at my desk, but at the office I had just left, and with a job not dissimilar to my own. It seemed an added incentive to probe further.

Peter Bark, I soon discovered, was not in the normal run of Russian courtiers, rather one of an increasing number of dedicated professionals, from prosperous but hardly aristocratic families, who often had had years of experience in business and commerce before joining the government service. Bark in fact joined the Ministry of Finance first, direct from St Petersburg University, and then was seconded to private banking, before returning to government service. The Mendelssohn Bank, in Berlin, which has already played a major part in our hunt for the tsar's money, was chosen to give Bark his early banking training from the Finance Ministry. Not long after his return he was picked out for early promotion and given experience in the State Bank. But his progress had not gone unnoticed among St Petersburg's private bankers and soon they were competing for his services. First he moved to the Imperial Bank of Russia as a deputy director, shortly afterwards to the Volga-Kama bank as managing director.

By 1911 Bark's capabilities had been recognised by Peter Stolypin, chairman of the Council of Ministers, and he was offered the post of Under-Secretary of State in the Ministry of Commerce. But returning to government service meant accepting a 90 per cent drop in salary, a point that plainly intrigued the tsar. Three years later, in January 1914, on

appointing Bark Minister of Finance, Nicholas asked him bluntly why he
had accepted the job at such a personal cost. Bark replied that he had
never attached overriding importance to money and preferred 'the wider
field of state service devoted to the country's good . . . to service in private
interests'.[1]

On the face of it, this is what one might expect him to say. But Dominic
Lieven, who has made an intense and detailed study of Russia's ruling
class under the tsarist regime, is convinced of the truth of Bark's reply:
'The upper ranks of the Russian civil service did produce a number of
men of this calibre.'[2] If so, it all fits oddly with Fallows' accusations that
Bark eventually lined his own pocket at Romanoff expense to a remarkable
degree.

Within eight months of his appointment as Finance Minister, Bark was
grappling with all the intricacies and crises of a country at war. He showed
both shrewd financial knowledge and an ability to take quick decisions.
Unlike his counterpart in Paris, he stopped a run on the Russian private
banks by nervous depositors by making it clear that the ministry and the
State Bank would provide them with ample funds should they need them.
It was against the advice of most of his advisers and the private bankers
in St Petersburg, but it worked. It was a policy that has been second
nature to the Bank of England for well over a century. Confidence is all.
Customers do not demand their money back, even in a crisis, if they are
assured that it will be available when they need it.

It was not his first action, however, in those early days of August 1914.
As soon as he realised, following the Kaiser's ultimatum, that war with
Germany was imminent, he gave instructions for the manager of the
Chancellery of Credit, within his ministry, to wire to Berlin for the
government's balances held on current account with the ministry's correspondent banks to be transferred immediately to Paris and Petrograd.
Secondly, he signed the necessary papers for ministry officials to take
with them to Berlin, arranging for the return to Russia of Russian state
funds held on deposit account with bankers in Berlin. His officials left at
once, and arrived in the German capital just before war was declared.

By his decisive and instant action he succeeded in repatriating no less
than 100 million roubles (equivalent at the time to £10 million) from
Berlin.[3] Considering his devotion and loyalty to the tsar, it seems incon-
ceivable that he could have taken such swift action on behalf of the
state, without undertaking a similar repatriation of the tsar's own family
investments in Berlin, had he known about them. It strongly suggests,
contrary to the assumption of Edward Fallows and others, that Bark had
not been instrumental in placing Romanoff family money in Berlin in the
first place, a point that could equally apply to London. The person
responsible for investing such money in Berlin, whoever he was, whether

a predecessor of Bark at the Ministry of Finance or, more likely, a member of the imperial court, had not had the prescience or ability of Bark as a former bank director, to liquidate it quickly. Hence, while government state funds were brought back, the tsar's money remained in Berlin and, as we have already outlined, was sadly eroded by hyper-inflation and finally fought over in the German courts.

For the rest of the war Bark conducted Russia's financial affairs on a conservative basis, both at home and abroad. Overseas, as we have seen, his prime purpose was to safeguard Russia's gold reserve and, at the same time to raise sufficient credit to buy the necessary war equipment. At home he did his best to contain the wartime inflationary pressures, but even he could not offset the economic stresses caused by the war, especially the intense strains on the transport system. As the political tensions increased, Bark's liberal instincts began to tug severely at his loyalty to the tsar. He could hardly be described as a natural political animal, more a highly professional administrator, but he could not ignore the slow disintegration of the country's fabric and by the early part of 1917 he had become profoundly dismayed at what he saw around him.

The political pressures that Alexandra tried to impose, in Nicholas's absences from Petrograd, could hardly be avoided, but he did his best to do so. He saw her on only three occasions during the war:

The Empress did not show any particular interest in me and our conversations were short. When I met Her Majesty at GHQ she never said a word to me. It is true that I made no attempt to approach the small group which formed her intimate circle. On the contrary, I kept away from it, as I did not wish to have anything to do with the continual plots that were being hatched there.

On the other hand, his relations with the Dowager Empress Marie were increasingly cordial and, on his return from Paris and London, following his gold and credit negotiations in 1915, she showed more than a polite interest in what he had managed to achieve. She asked him detailed questions and expressed her own opinion with great frankness. 'In that respect,' he later explained, 'her nephew, King George V, was very much like her.'[4]

Bark's relations with Nicholas were businesslike and became warmer with time. He kept the tsar fully in touch with his aims and actions on his return from his major overseas negotiations. On one occasion he was invited to join the royal family at Livadia in the Crimea, being one of only two ministers attending what was in essence an entirely social occasion. But he could hardly ignore the ministerial changes taking place around him in 1916–17. As crisis followed crisis in that last winter of the war, Bark's frustration with the inaction at the top, coupled with a lingering illness which even a rest in Finland over Christmas did not help, finally persuaded him that he could no longer carry on. He decided to resign.

By mid-January he was ready for what he assumed would be his final audience with Nicholas, his resignation letter firmly in his hand. He had, however, chosen his time badly. Sir George Buchanan had been going through a similar dilemma, torn between his instinct as a trained diplomat and his personal regard for the tsar. Ignoring the cautious advice from London, the British Ambassador chose the same day as Bark to confront the tsar with an outspoken plea for action. 'Your Majesty,' he said, 'has but one safe course open to you – namely, to break down the barrier that separates you from your people and to regain their confidence'. It was hardly what Nicholas wanted to hear. He received Buchanan's advice coldly and did not even ask him to sit down during the audience, though he finally thanked him for his frankness.

Bark, who was waiting in Nicholas's study while this advice was being given in the Audience Room, was thus confronted by a particularly nervous and agitated tsar. It was hardly the time for resignation. Nicholas promptly tore up the letter, asked Bark to attend the forthcoming Allied financial conference in Petrograd and suggested a two months' leave in the Crimea thereafter. But it was not to be. In the six weeks now remaining to the monarchy Bark witnessed the growing political turmoil and social stresses he had feared and, as Nicholas prepared to leave the capital for headquarters towards the end of February (as we now know, for the last time as tsar), he called for Bark and made a strange but significant request.

Nicholas asked Bark to provide him with 200,000 roubles (worth £20,000 then or the equivalent of £360,000 now) from his 'Secret Fund' and to have it delivered to him in two days' time.[5] Bark knew that this fund was available not only to Nicholas, for his personal use, but, with the approval of himself and Nicholas, for the use of other ministries in Petrograd. When Bark became Finance Minister in 1914 the Secret Fund stood at 6 million roubles. It now stood at 10 million roubles (£1 million).

Most of the requests in Bark's time had come from the Ministry of the Interior. Though the existence of the Secret Fund was yet another facet of an authoritarian ruler, this was the first time in Bark's three years at the ministry that Nicholas had made any such request. To Nicholas's surprise Bark took the money personally to him and, without hesitation, he signed a formal receipt. Though Bark said later that Nicholas looked worried, he did not show any outward nervousness. He left for headquarters that night. Nicholas's last monetary request to Bark (they were never to meet again) remains a mystery. Was it a response to a premonition of danger ahead? Was it for himself or did he leave it as an additional safeguard for Alexandra and his family at Tsarskoe Selo? Probably we shall never know. Its significance lies in the fact that even with the forces of revolution building around him, Nicholas was still able to siphon state money for his own personal use, mingling state funds with personal funds, at will. Right to the end '*L'etat c'est moi*' ruled supreme in tsarist Russia.

Next day further disturbances broke out in Petrograd, culminating in the mutiny in the army and, within four days, a Provisional government established itself in the capital and within nine days of his departure from Petrograd Nicholas abdicated. Bark's troubles were just beginning. Instead of a well-needed rest in the sunshine of the Crimea he was suddenly confronted at home by a dozen armed soldiers and sailors, several of whom were drunk, led by a reserve soldier, also drunk, who had once been his footman. They burst into his drawing-room, threatened his wife by putting a revolver to her head, and then took Bark in an enormous lorry bearing a Red flag and several machine guns to the Tauride Palace, where for a short time he was imprisoned.[6]

From all accounts he remained calm and philosophical, was brought food daily through the bravery of his children's governess (who was still with them years later in exile in Britain) and, unlike many of his ministerial colleagues who behaved somewhat differently in captivity, passed the time either reading or playing chess with one of his young gaolers.

Bark did not remain long in gaol thanks to the immediate action of his successor, M. Terestchenko, as Finance Minister in the Provisional government. He needed Bark's advice in running his new department, did not relish seeking such advice from his predecessor in prison and insisted to Kerensky that he be released. Kerensky agreed and Bark and his family subsequently decided to get out of Petrograd and slowly made their way to the Crimea, where, after the October Revolution, he was asked to become Finance Minister of its new Socialist government, which was then opposing the Bolsheviks. He politely refused. Nearly two years later, after the White government had been formed in the south with the support of the Allies, he agreed to help and was sent to London and Paris to seek financial help on its behalf. He was representing them in Paris during the Versailles peace negotiations, in 1919, when the White army collapsed and, for a short spell, he was stranded. Happily, his family were rescued from the Crimea by the British to be reunited in Paris. They moved permanently to London the same year.[7]

Having visited London as a banker before 1914 and been a prime negotiator there on two occasions during the war, he knew people in the City of London, from the Governor of the Bank of England to the chairmen of the leading commercial banks and merchant banks; and he called on King George V at Windsor on more than one occasion, even taking personal messages between George and his cousin Nicholas at the height of the war. The king had also become aware through Empress Marie, following her rescue from the Crimea, that she too was an admirer of Bark.

That his talents should eventually be recognised in the City of London was hardly surprising. But, like so many White Russian exiles, he did not find regular employment immediately and needed early financial help. The Bark family, by all accounts, did not have a cache of jewels to fall back on and he was soon having to raise money on the strength of what securities he had left behind in Petrograd. Even the letter of credit he had arranged to take with him to Paris (for a total of 80,000 French francs) had been stopped as soon as the Bolsheviks took over southern Russia. He had only used 17,000 francs but, through persuasion, managed to squeeze a further 20,000 francs from the bank in Paris before it froze the rest. Even that 20,000 francs was to haunt him four years later when the bank asked for it back and ignored the money it had frozen.[8]

These were simply the normal hazards of exiles. But at least Bark knew where to go for help. He called on Lord Revelstoke, formerly John Baring, at the merchant banking house of Barings, whose financial support for Russia had been prominent for many years, and managed to raise an immediate loan of £5,000. They knew him well, having been part of the gold and credit negotiations he had conducted with the Bank of England in London during the war. Lord Revelstoke had even offered Bark a commission during these wartime talks which he had refused. All he had to offer as security were shares in his old bank, the Bank of Volga-Kama, as well as a variety of insurance and industrial shares, still registered in his name in Petrograd. They had been valued, in January 1917, at 1,574,125 roubles (about £150,000). Whether from a feeling that the Bolshevik Revolution would not last and the securities would eventually realise their full value, or simply for old times' sake, Barings helped him out further over the next three or four years. By 1924 he had borrowed £16,300 from Barings and a further £5,900 from Hambros Bank.

Here again one is forced to reflect on the sharp contrast between what Bark actually did and what Edward Fallows and others have subsequently accused him of doing. Bark's clear need of money in his early days in London sits uneasily with the assumption that he alone knew where tsarist money was kept in London and quickly put it to his own use. It is Bark's relations with the Bank of England, however, that were to arouse real suspicions. Montagu Norman, who had become Deputy Governor of the Bank of England in March 1918 and Governor (a post he was to fill until 1944) three years later, in March 1921, was already well aware of Bark's potential, as either an adviser or an executive. Here was a man who had negotiated as an equal with Lloyd George, who knew London, Paris and Berlin intimately, was reasonably fluent in four languages and, more significantly, had financial knowledge and crucial contacts throughout eastern Europe. It was an area that was soon exercising the victorious Allies and especially Montagu Norman at the Bank of England and

Benjamin Strong, the chairman of the Federal Reserve Bank of New York. By the end of 1921 both were immersed in Europe's outstanding debt problems.

Britain owed money to the United States. Germany was under pressure to pay reparations to the victors as compensation. Austria had both debts and the need for credits. And the whole of eastern Europe and Russia required opening up to trade with western Europe and the United States. The victors were determined to make the most of their economic opportunities and to fill the vacuum that now existed after over four years of war. The world's two leading financial centres, London and New York (the latter had in effect eased Paris out of its former position as the chief rival to London), were being called to provide financial help in what was in essence a political as well as an economic objective.

Montagu Norman, as the pivotal European central banker, took the initiative in opening up the dialogue with Benjamin Strong of New York. Being keen for both London and New York banks to provide adequate finance, he was soon encouraging the establishment of various national corporations in the eastern European countries concerned, whose aim would be to attract individual credits to each country. A parent company in London would support the various national corporations. There was, in fact, more, as he candidly told Strong in a private letter:

The whole object of these proposals is to attain a political end under a commercial cloak, the political end being that of getting practically all the countries of Europe, and perhaps the United States as well, round a table and co-operating with one another for the rehabilitation of eastern Europe and especially Russia. As commercial-undertakings I doubt if they have much chance of success.[9]

He was to be proved right. In such a cause it was only natural that Montagu Norman should turn to Bark in relation to the first of the proposed national corporations, that for Austria. By chance a vehicle already existed, the London branch of an Austrian bank by the name of the Anglo-Austrian. The responsibility for its credit liabilities in London at the outbreak of war had been accepted by the Bank of England. These debts now needed resolving, as did the bank's difficulties because of the break-up of the Austro-Hungarian Empire. The Bank of England solved both problems by establishing a newly reconstructed bank, to be known as the Anglo-Austrian, in London. Under Bark's management it was to have British, Austrian and Czech directors.

The relationship between Peter Bark and the Bank of England would continue until a few months before his death in 1937. On December 7, 1921, Bark was offered, on the personal recommendation of Montagu Norman, a retainer of £1,000 for his services to the Anglo-Austrian Bank and to the Bank of England. Over the next few years Norman's vision of a network of national corporations or banks throughout eastern Europe gradually came to fruition, and by 1924 Bark had become a director of the Anglo-Czechoslovakian Bank, the Banque des Pays de l'Europe Centrale, the Croatian Discount Bank and the British and Hungarian Bank. He had also played a crucial part in the negotiations leading up to the Austrian government loan of 1923, for which the Austrians paid him £7,500.[10]

In early 1924 Norman clarified Bark's increasingly multifarious responsibilities and gave him a five-year contract, at the increased salary of £1,500 a year, to cover his services to these various eastern European banks. Bark used this income to pay off outstanding debts to Barings and Hambros; although in fact the Bank of England paid off the full debts immediately and Bark repaid the Bank from his retainer over the next five years.

Two years later, in 1926, the Bank of England finally set up what was to be known as the Anglo-International Bank and was in effect the parent corporation Norman had envisaged in his letter to Benjamin Strong several years earlier. The opportunity was taken to sell off the viable parts of the Anglo-Austrian Bank, to liquidate other parts and to merge what remained in the new corporation. The Anglo-International Bank also took over the British Trade Corporation, an established trade promotion body. As a result of the merger, Peter Bark was appointed managing director of the new corporation and of several of its new subsidiaries. He received an additional salary, beginning at £3,000 a year and continuing at about that level into the early thirties. In one year his remuneration reached £6,000.

Thus it can be seen that the establishment of the Anglo-International bank was not the clear-cut affair that Fallows, and later Lovell, have tried to indicate. Far from the Bank of England and Peter Bark putting millions of tsarist money into it, other City firms were asked to finance it and the Bank of England subscribed a small part of the remaining capital. Peter Bark simply bought two hundred shares as his qualifying shares as a director. Although he added to his total later, it hardly cost or made him a fortune.

Peter Bark's peak earnings from all sources were probably in the last years of the 1920s and the early years of the 1930s. The 1929 slump and, especially the world's monetary crisis of 1931, starting with the crash of Austria's biggest bank, the Kreditanstalt, and culminating in Britain's suspension of the gold standard, devastated central and eastern European financial institutions and naturally undermined the prime purpose of the Anglo-International Bank. As the bank's activities declined, reflecting this central European crisis, so did Bark's salary, until in the middle thirties the Bank of England felt obliged to 'top it up'.

These salary details would not normally be regarded as either riveting or even relevant to the tsarist millions he once handled, had not Bark been accused, originally by supporters of Anna Anderson and more recently by the late James Blair Lovell, of secretly switching hidden funds to the benefit of himself or others. His clear need to use salary payments over a period of five years to pay off bank debts hardly smacks of someone with secret knowledge of millions. His total remuneration from the Bank of England, from 1921 to 1935, for example, amounted to a mere £31,750. Moreover in his final two years, between 1935 and 1937, he was faced both with losing his post at the Anglo-International Bank – as the bank's chairman and Montagu Norman rightly concluded that its role had been overtaken by events in Europe – and with failing health. His financial anxieties, as he contemplated how to pay for an operation and the subsequent nursing home care out of his meagre resources, took up much of his final correspondence with the Bank of England.

Throughout his time with the Bank of England he had been deliberately precluded from taking on any other remunerative jobs, apart from those arising from the eastern European affairs which concerned the Bank. On one occasion the Bank considered him for a banking post but had to think again when Bark refused to become a naturalised British citizen. The only responsibilities which were regarded as compatible with his Bank of England duties were those sought eventually by King George V.

As we saw earlier, after Grand Duchess Xenia had been defrauded of some of her jewels the king concluded that her financial affairs needed a thorough overhaul by a financial adviser, and who better than a compatriot and a former Finance Minister to her brother? Accordingly Sir Frederick Ponsonby, the king's private secretary, quickly arranged for Bark to be approached through the Bank of England. He eventually became both Xenia's adviser and, ultimately, a trustee of her estate. As such he also became a reasonably regular visitor to Windsor and Buckingham Palace, where his visits were duly recorded in the king's daily diary. Shortly after these arrangements had been made and Bark had assessed what Xenia should do with her various assets, King George began the £2,300 yearly allowance which Xenia received until her death.

Bark's advice thereafter was always available to Xenia and, on two specific occasions, his personal help was sought overseas. One was the occasion, following Empress Marie's death in Copenhagen in 1928, when the king asked Bark to go to ensure the safe delivery of her jewel box to London, as we described in Chapter 11. The other was just prior to her death when efforts were being made to gain possession of a former Romanoff estate in Finland. The property, named Halila, had been confiscated from the royal family by the Bolshevik government and then handed over to the Finnish government. Following correspondence between Sir Frederick Ponsonby and the Bank of England, in which it became clear that the king was keen for Peter Bark to help, the Bank gave him permission to go to Copenhagen to secure Empress Marie's power of attorney in any necessary negotiations. The king paid Bark's expenses for the trip.[11]

It was for these and other services to the Russian royal family, as well as to King George himself, that Bark was given two particular honours by the king, the first at Windsor, the second at Buckingham Palace. In 1929 the king's diary records: 'We received M. Bark who came to talk to us about Xenia's affairs and I gave him the GCVO' (Grand Cross of the Royal Victorian Order). Six years later the king had another entry: 'Peter Bark at Buckingham Palace. Knighted, has become British subject.' Bark, who had resisted all previous efforts to persuade him to become a naturalised British subject, even to the extent of turning down jobs that required it, including the earlier offer of a knighthood, finally succumbed. He was naturalised the day before receiving the honour.[12]

There is no evidence of Bark receiving any payment for his various services to Xenia. Even had he received any it could hardly have been significant since, as the year 1936 progressed and his health began to deteriorate, his pressure on the Bank of England to find him additional remunerative work or appointments grew. He was clearly short of adequate capital to tide him over a difficult period. One internal Bank of England note, sympathetic in its overall intention, summed up his somewhat anxious state: 'I always try to evade Sir Peter Bark,' one official told the Governor, 'because whenever he comes he first proposes some business which is now beyond all reason, and secondly begs for work and income – income to maintain his family, dependents, and perhaps sundry Russians.' None the less the Bank's sympathy and understanding continued.

Bark's anxieties were not unfounded. In the autumn of 1936 he was advised to go into a nursing home, preparatory to undergoing a serious operation. This immediately brought his financial problems to a head, with the Bank agreeing to pay his medical expenses and nursing home fees and assessing, as best it could, Bark's total financial resources. He was, it turned out, not exactly a rich man. He had a life policy worth £4,000, on which he immediately raised £1,000. He had a small portfolio of securities which he had managed to build up during his years in England. But his home at Evelyn Gardens was not his.

Just prior to his operation Bark made a highly significant approach to Barings, reminding them of their wartime relationships, and seeking some kind of help. As he put it to the Governor of the Bank of England when seeking his intervention with Barings, he felt he had a moral right to ask Barings for assistance in his present plight. He reminded them that, during the war, when agreeing the terms on which Russian gold, and the consequent credits, should be utilised, he had been pressed by both the Chancellor of the Exchequer and the then Governor of the Bank of England, Lord Cunliffe, to channel the Russian government credits through Barings, and not to have them channelled directly to the Russian state, as had happened in the case of his agreement with France. He had personally agreed to the use of Barings as an intermediary.

Bark had made a quick calculation of the benefit this had bestowed on the bank.

The result [he wrote to the Governor] was that in 1919 a huge balance of Russian Government money, over £6 million, was at the disposal of Barings, which is still, probably intact, if not bigger. If the yearly return is only 1 per cent, say £60,000, I think that one-tenth of this amount, about £6,000, could be spent in supporting the last Finance Minister of the Russian Empire who was instrumental in the arrangements made.

He had a point. We shall return to Barings' role later, in our search for tsarist deposits in London, but the significance of Bark's approach to Barings lies in the fact that at no time did he use a similar approach with the Bank of England. So here was a man, under the double anxiety of his personal health and the future well-being of his family and dependents, who is still accused of having knowledge of tsarist millions in the Bank of England, and even under suspicion of having shared them with the Bank of England, actually turning to a private merchant bank in his hour of need. Not only that, he asks the Bank of England to put in a good word for him.

The Bark family's troubles were not over. While he was recovering from his operation, his wife received the tragic news that their son had been killed in a road accident in the south of France. She managed to keep the news from him as long as possible, even seeking help via Montagu Norman to ensure that the news would not reach him from City friends at his bedside. She eventually decided to soften the blow by taking him to the south of France to their daughter's house not far from Marseilles for what she hoped would be a longish period of convalescence. It did not work out as she had planned. Whether from the shock of his son's death, or from the after-effects of the operation, he died there only three weeks after leaving London. He was buried in Nice.

The details of Peter Bark's life, work and death, intertwined as they were with his prime role as the tsar's last Finance Minister and as Russia's main negotiator for a crucial three years of war, have ultimately been necessary for our inquiry, not so much for what light they might throw on the source of tsarist wealth, but for the way in which he has been accused of absconding with money in the Bank of England.

Edward Fallows' belief, based on alleged statements by Anna Anderson, was that Bark had been the agent who placed tsarist funds in the Bank of England on behalf of the Romanoff children and that he had shared his knowledge with the Bank of England to use the millions deposited there for their own shared purposes, primarily the setting up of the Anglo-International Bank. Grand Duchess Xenia, according to Fallows, had not been told of all this.

What we now know hardly supports any of this conjecture. We have already thrown serious doubt on whether Anna Anderson, who we now know to be a fraud, actually spoke of the 'Bank of England', one of her own legal advisers indicating that she referred to 'a bank in England'. Moreover even if the Bank of England was intended, we then have to account for Bark's behaviour on arrival in London. He actually spent his first three years in raising capital from two merchant banks, before being approached by Montagu Norman to run the Anglo-Austrian Bank at a salary of £1,000. With his alleged knowledge of the millions tucked away in the Bank of England, simply awaiting his secret password, such actions border on the incomprehensible. The only explanation is that either he did not know the password, or he lacked the real family authority to gain access, or, a thought that Fallows refused to entertain, that Anna Anderson was either mistaken in her belief that there was tsarist money in the Bank of England, or bogus. Even Fallows' suspicion that Bark had been making further millions out of the millions he had wrongly appropriated could hardly square with the final price and value of Bark's holdings in the Anglo-International Bank. His original two hundred, which Fallows discovered, had actually risen to 998 (and at one stage to 1,008). Alas, the market price in 1937 was 1s 3d, which gave a total value of less than £700.

Fallows' other assumption that the Bank of England would naturally be willing to share in the spoils with Bark, can only be based on a misunderstanding of what central banks are capable. Unlike you or me, or even a commercial bank, they can create money (and often do, to the detriment of a country's inflationary potential, as Yeltsin's Russia has found to its cost). The Bank of England hardly needed tsarist deposits to find part of the capital for the Anglo-International Bank or any of the other European banks it encouraged.

Moreover we have the almost constant spectacle of the 'villain' who has absconded with the money, having to seek extra appointments from the Bank of England because of his lack of adequate funds. Throughout his later career in London Bark gave all the appearance of someone who, having generously supported a stream of less well-endowed White

Russian exiles whenever they approached him, was himself having difficulty in building up an adequate nest-egg for his family. Hence his final, almost moral, appeal to Barings for help. That approach alone should be sufficient evidence to suggest that the Bank of England never had a similar amount of tsarist funds, at its disposal, at least to Bark's own knowledge.

Finally we have the 1991 accusation of the late James Blair Lovell, who added to Fallows' original reliance on Anna Anderson and his corresponding conviction of the collusion of Bark and the Bank of England, the collusion of Grand Duchess Xenia and King George V. Our outline of Bark's actions, and all his accompanying financial difficulties, also provides a similar rebuttal of Lovell's basic allegations. His only new evidence, apart from extensive conjectures, amounted to the details of one of the provisions of Xenia's will. She left her money and property, apart from a few personal legacies of no more than £1,000 each, to a trust fund, from which her children would benefit in equal proportions. One of the items left to the trust was a property agreed between herself and the three trustees in 1929, clearly after the death of her mother.

Lovell highlighted the names of the trustees. They were Sir Frederick Ponsonby, private secretary to George V; Sir Edward Peacock, a director of the Bank of England; and Sir Peter Bark. So at one stroke, in Lovell's eyes, we have the main conspirators tied to Xenia: Bark with his knowledge of the money; Ponsonby with his connection to the king; and Peacock from the Bank of England. His conclusion was quickly drawn:

That some sort of special arrangement was made with Grand Duchess Xenia after the sale of her mother's jewels and after her sister Olga had returned to Denmark in 1929, is undeniable. That the arrangements involved the money deposited by the Tsar in the Bank of England is not unlikely.

Lovell did not hesitate to build a number of 'possibilities' on this somewhat shaky foundation:

The Grand Duchess Xenia might have gone to her friends the King and Queen, or perhaps even directly to Peter Bark, upon learning of Anastasia's story about the money in the Bank of England. If so, she would soon have discovered that her niece was correct. If Fallows was right, Bark was intent on hiding from the surviving Romanoffs the fact that he had used the dowry funds to establish the Anglo-International Bank. But he could not have concealed the fact from the British royal family. For a former Russian minister to suddenly be able to capitalise such a huge financial institution in England could hardly have escaped the notice of King George V and his closest advisers.

Thus not only Bark, but the British royal family itself would have had a personal stake in avoiding any controversy that would have hinted at collusion in appropriating the Tsar's money. Consequently they might have offered Grand

Duchess Xenia a 'Settlement' in exchange for her silence. Her muteness was probably total.

Having plainly inherited Edward Fallows' convictions and assumptions about Bark and the Bank of England, Lovell was thus enticed by one extra piece of 'evidence' to add still more conspiracy theories. The facts about Bark's life, which refute Fallows' main suspicions, similarly undermine the foundations of Lovell's later accusations. Bark did not behave as if he had had either the knowledge, or even the use, of millions from the Bank of England. Nor did the Bank itself. Even the trustees of the property in Xenia's will are hardly difficult to explain. Bark was acting as Xenia's financial adviser. Ponsonby was directly involved with her affairs since he had been arranging the regular income provided by George V. And Edward Peacock, though a non-executive director of the Bank of England, was actually representing Barings, who were the executors of her will. As for Lovell's description of Bark capitalising the Anglo-International Bank ('such a huge financial institution'), and thus needing the tsar's millions to do so, this simply ignored all the facts that are known, and freely available on both sides of the Atlantic, about the financing of the various eastern and central European institutions in the early 1920s. Lovell was not apparently aware that the Anglo-International Bank, when it was set up in 1926, was a part-merger, part new capital institution, and hardly needed the additional millions he assumed were necessary.

What then are we left with? We can dismiss Anna Anderson's 'memories' of the 'Bank of England'. We can assume that Edward Fallows' suspicions about the role of Peter Bark and his knowledge and use of funds in the Bank of England have not been substantiated by the evidence of his career in London. We can certainly ignore the later possibilities raised by James Blair Lovell, until further evidence can be produced. We cannot yet assume that no money was placed in the Bank of England, though the odds seem to be narrowing against such a possibility. And we need to look further into a number of areas that our investigations have uncovered as we have progressed. These range from what happened to the gold deposited in banks outside Vladivostock in 1919, to what kind of tsarist deposits National City Bank had attracted before and even after the Revolution; and from where tsarist deposits might have been placed in Paris, to the true nature of the tsarist money at Barings in London.

The world's banks, therefore, must be our next target.

15

Europe

The lure of tsarist millions secreted in western banks has tempted claimants and investigators for three-quarters of a century. It is time to follow a similar trail of our own through European and north American financial centres, prompted by the evidence of others, and based on extensive new investigations. But in any attempt to clarify how much tsarist money was invested overseas and where it may still be found, one crucial question has to be faced first: how far did the tsar manage to repatriate funds and investments from abroad in the first days of the war in 1914, or shortly thereafter?

We have already established that, while tsarist state funds were brought back from Berlin by Peter Bark's swift actions on the eve of war, Nicholas's own family investments remained in Berlin until they were eventually shared out, in a sadly depleted form, among the family's remaining relatives in the early thirties. That was either the result of inaction or the difficulty of liquidating investments quickly, combined with the impossibility of repatriating funds from an enemy country once war had been declared. The question is what happened to similar tsarist funds in Allied or neutral countries: primarily Geneva, Paris, London and New York. Were they too fully repatriated?

This raises the further question of who was, or is, likely to know. If Nicholas ran his own accounts in the way that he seems to have administered the country, then it is likely that very few people indeed had full knowledge of his monetary affairs. He rarely spoke to his advisers about topics or issues unrelated to their responsibilities. 'Divide and rule' was his watchword. He even insisted on putting confidential letters into the envelopes himself. And he deliberately had no private secretary of his own: that would have given one individual too much knowledge and leverage.

So, before he abdicated, knowledge of his private bank accounts, at home and abroad, would have been deliberately confined to two or three people in the court at Tsarskoe Selo, to one or two people at the State

Bank, where the family had personal accounts and, no doubt, to the current Finance Minister. Beyond that we must naturally include the person or persons dealing with tsarist accounts in the receiving banks overseas.

We can assume that most members of this small band had no more than partial knowledge; very few, if any, would have had full knowledge. This was to change to some degree immediately after Nicholas abdicated, for we now know that three or four members of the Provisional government probably gained access to full knowledge of his remaining personal assets, along with the two members of his court who negotiated on his behalf while the family were in Tobolsk.

If we could re-assemble them together, these would be our expert witnesses. Alas, we can't. The majority are now dead; others would be far too discreet to speak; and even if we did get them on the witness stand, the value of their reports would vary considerably, as those voices we have already heard from the past have demonstrated. It is a game that was first played, quite vigorously and somewhat confusingly, in the twenties and thirties as former members of the royal court were persuaded to recall even the smallest tittle-tattle of the past.

Several witnesses can be called who tell a similar story of Nicholas's actions in 1914. One of my earlier visits to check tsarist memories was to Brussels. The attraction of Brussels to Russian émigrés had started with a remarkable gesture by King Albert following the end of White Russian resistance in the Crimea. The Belgian royal family had offered to educate the children of colleagues of General Wrangel, who had commanded the White Russian forces there. Cardinal Mercier opened the doors of Louvain University to Russian students and Belgian ships rescued Russian orphans from Odessa. It was in its way a reflection of the Belgian–Russian co-operation during the war which culminated in a Belgian armoured unit actually fighting on the Russian front in Galicia.

Whatever the reason, among the flow of Russian émigrés to Brussels were Count Peter Apraxine, who had been one of the empress's secretaries, and Kotliarewsky, who had been secretary to General Wrangel. Both made Brussels their home, the son of one marrying the daughter of the other. Count Apraxine eventually died there in 1962. Though he left no papers concerning his work at the court, relatives of his whom I met, in connection with St Job's, the Russian Orthodox Church in Brussels which had been specially consecrated to commemorate the imperial family's death and martyrdom, confirmed that he had told them that no tsarist personal funds existed overseas after 1914. Of this he was always clear and firm.

Grand Duke Alexander, the estranged husband of Grand Duchess Xenia, was also similarly adamant about the absence of any tsarist funds overseas when he wrote his memoirs at the beginning of the 1930s. 'Beginning with the summer of 1915,' he stated categorically, 'there was not a farthing left in the Tsar's name in the Bank of England, nor in any other bank outside Russia.'[1]

Another person who was close to Xenia was Count Vladimir Klein-michael, who having escaped from Russia in 1919 and failed to be accepted into the British army, found a job in a City merchant bank by simply walking in off the street.[2] He eventually became a director of Kleinwort Benson (the larger merged entity of his original bank) and, on Sir Peter Bark's death, took over as Grand Duchess Xenia's adviser and trustee. Prince David Chavchavadze, the former CIA agent still living in the United States, who is a descendant of both Nicholas I of Russia and the last King of Georgia, knew Kleinmichael well, and confirms that 'he was absolutely certain there was no money'.[3] It is not the only piece of evidence provided by David Chavchavadze. He also recalls a conversation his father, Prince Paul Chavchavadze, had with Kleinmichael's predecessor, Peter Bark:

Bark told my father the following: there had been an account in England under the code name OTMA (Olga, Tatiana, Maria, Anastasia). During the war Nicholas II ordered Bark to withdraw this account and bring it back to Russia as an example to society to do the same thing. Bark tried to talk the Emperor out of this, and he said it was the only time he ever saw Nicholas II lose his temper. The withdrawal was accomplished, and most, but not all of society followed suit.[4]

Bark himself remained publicly silent on anything relating to the tsar's personal accounts, about which he must have known a great deal. His unpublished autobiography is equally silent. But his family at least have memories of what he told them about this period. His daughter, Madame Semenoff-Tian-Chansky, in whose house Bark died in the south of France, had this to say to a French journalist in the 1950s:

I know from my father ... that in 1916 the Emperor had refused to transfer even the smallest part of his capital out of Russia ... When Grand Duchess Xenia found herself in monetary difficulties, King George V had begged my father to look after the Grand Duchess's affairs. It was then that my father had tried to find anything that he could that had belonged to the imperial family and which could be of help to the Grand Duchesses Xenia and Olga. All he found were some minimal amounts in the Deutsche Bank – Russian bonds from before the 1914 war, terribly depreciated. If there had been anything at all at the Bank of England my father would certainly have known about it and would have told us.[5]

When I eventually located Bark's two grandsons, one living in north London, the other on the outskirts of Paris, this statement was not only confirmed as being part of family lore, but Bark's French grandson put rather more flesh on his mother's earlier statement about Bark's conversation in 1916:

One day during the tragic period of the 1914–18 war, Peter Bark, my grandfather, asked the Tsar: 'Given the tragic events that can occur, would you like to place money abroad, in case you and your family are obliged to go into exile?' He replied: 'And you Petr L'vovich Bark, would you do that yourself?' Bark answered: 'I would not, and even if I wished to do so, it would be out of the question because can you imagine what the whole world would think of such an act, while our country is in the worst difficulties?' The Emperor replied: 'Well then, I, responsible for the Russian people, will not do it.'[6]

The implication is that, at this stage in the war, Nicholas no longer had any personal money overseas, apart from the frozen investments in Germany. The late Baron Constantine ('Steino') Stackelberg, the son of the Baron Stackelberg who was assistant to Alexander Mossolov, Head of the Court Chancery, remembered his father telling him that the tsar, on the outbreak of war, had asked all grand dukes and counts to repatriate their money from abroad, in order to support the war effort. He told his family[7] that most of them had done so. Those who did not and managed to escape after 1917 certainly benefited from their unpatriotic inaction. Before he died in the United States 'Steino' Stackelberg gave David Chavchavadze more details of how it had happened:

His father, who in 1914 held the Court rank of Master of Ceremonies, had told him that a couple of days before the beginning of the 1914 war, the Emperor had ordered the Duty Lord of the Bed Chamber, Nicholas Yevreinov, to telephone Bark to remove all the imperial accounts from abroad. This incident, Steino said, had been confirmed to him by Peter Bark in London in 1925.

The same story, in rather broader terms, was repeated by Xenia's son, Prince Dimitri of Russia, in the late 1950s: 'The money which had been deposited in England by the Tsar,' he told Dominique Auclères, the French journalist, 'was transferred to Russian banks at the beginning of the war. There, naturally, it was later seized by the Bolsheviks.' This is perhaps more a repetition of something he had heard from his father, Grand Duke Alexander, than a reliable primary source of information, but another more reliable and additional witness is Gleb Botkin, the son of Dr Botkin, the tsar's doctor:

I know for a fact [he wrote in 1925] that the late Emperor did have considerable sums of money in the Bank of England, but that much of it he had either withdrawn or presented to the Russian state by paying with it during the war for some of the military supplies that had been purchased abroad. During our Siberian exile [Gleb Botkin was with the royal family in Siberia as a young man] the Emperor told my father, the late Dr Eugene Botkin, that he had no money of his own left in any of the foreign banks.[8]

Much the same message was conveyed to Fanny Holtzmann, the American lawyer who successfully defended Princess Irina Youssopov, Xenia's daughter, against MGM. Her biographer finally summed up the results of her investigations thus:

A private letter to Fanny from a War Office official in close touch with the Bank of England provided a gallant footnote to history: 'From a person well placed to know, I gather that *the very high* personage you mentioned, far from depositing funds abroad in 1914, actually sold and repatriated all their foreign deposits, investments etc., as an act of patriotism. This I have confirmed elsewhere'.

These then are the voices from the past. As one would expect from such a cross-section of people and from such a distance in time, they do not all say the same thing. There is, however, an underlying theme to their story: that, whatever tsarist deposits there were overseas just before war broke out in 1914, the tsar did his best to repatriate them where possible and also to persuade his Romanoff relatives and others close to his administration to do the same. Memories of the actual banks and financial capitals naturally vary; one version occasionally clashing with another. But that a patriotic drive for the repatriation of overseas assets was launched by the tsar, however, there can be no doubt.

Other evidence strongly points the same way. Two examples will suffice. Prince Felix Youssopov was a member of one of Russia's richest families before 1914, certainly rivalling the tsar in actual, if not potential, wealth. The family's investments covered oilfields, coal and iron mines, factories and vast estates. A figure of $500 million is often given as its pre-1914 worth. How much was overseas is difficult to gauge, but whatever it amounted to the tsar made it clear that he expected it to be repatriated. Prince Felix described the impact on his parents in broad terms as follows:

At the beginning of the war, my parents had transferred back to Russia all the money they had had abroad. With the house on Lake Geneva, all that was left of our wealth was the jewellery and valuables that we had been able to take with us when we left the Crimea and the two Rembrandts.[9]

In fact Prince Felix later explained in more detail to Dr Idris Traylor jun.[10] that the tsar had personally withdrawn all the funds he could from European banks and had ordered all Russians to do the same. His parents, he said, had followed the advice and, as Dr Traylor later discovered in the Central State Archives in Moscow, there were Youssopov financial agents in 1914 in London, Paris, Frankfurt and Lucerne and the family had investments in Europe, South America and the United States. The

Youssopovs ended up simply with a London apartment and a villa in Switzerland, which they had been unable to dispose of during the war.

The experience of another Russian aristocratic family underlines the same point, though the other way round. Countess Mordvinov, who died in Paris in June 1993, remembered her parents explaining to her how they had tried to remove their remaining assets from Russia to Paris in 1915, at a time when they had decided to settle permanently in the French capital.[11] Her parents went to Petrograd in 1915, by way of the Scandinavian countries, with the intention of disposing of their remaining property and other assets in Russia. They had considerable negotiations with various government departments in Petrograd (the countess still had the documents bearing the imperial seals in her possession when she died), but the tsar eventually refused to give his permission for the cash resulting from the sales to be transferred to Paris.

That repatriation of funds, coupled with a ban on the export of funds, was tsarist policy, imposed personally by Nicholas, can no longer be in doubt. How far it was fully implemented and thus successful is another matter. Evidence that the royal family itself succeeded in getting some funds at least out of London can now be produced. One quotation in particular, summarised by Robert Massie, seems highly significant. It emerges from one of the letters written by Alexandra to Nicholas when she was at Tsarskoe Selo and he was with the troops.

This is the batch of correspondence that so shocked Nicholas's mother and sisters when they were first published in the United States, and later in Europe, in the early twenties. They are a remarkable mixture of family gossip and Alexandra's views and reports on state affairs. One particular letter, sent on August 26, 1915, is a prime example, with a significant financial news item in the tail:

My very own sweetheart

I am writing in the corner room upstairs, Mr Gilliard is reading to Alexei. Olga and Tatiana are in town this afternoon. Oh, Lovy, it was beautiful – to read the news in the papers this morning [Nicholas had appointed himself Commander-in-Chief two days earlier] and my heart rejoiced more than I can say. Marie and I went to mass in the upper church. Anastasia came to the Te Deum ... Samarin goes on speaking against me – hope to get you a list of names and trust can find a suitable successor before he can do more harm. [Samarin was Marshal of the Moscow nobility and Procurator of the Synod. He was later dismissed.] How are the foreigners? I see Buchanan tomorrow, as he brings me again over £100,000 from England.[12]

The fact that the British Ambassador was bringing her lump sums from England fits admirably into the reports that Nicholas ran down their personal balances in London to pay for hospital and other supplies. That word 'again' strongly suggests that it was a continuous process and the fact that Buchanan brought Alexandra the money also implies that it was meant for her wartime causes. These have never been in doubt, for Alexandra and her two elder daughters, Olga and Tatiana, immersed themselves in hospital work throughout the war, even to the point of being present at operations and doing their share of nursing.

She had received help for hospitals in and near Tsarskoe Selo not only from overseas but from the local millionaire, Carol Yaroshinsky, who was later to try to channel money to them when they were captive in Tobolsk. In a later letter to Nicholas in 1916 she reported how much money she had received for hospital supplies alone. She explained that 'her' store and chancellery had received some 6,675,136 roubles between June 1914 and January 1916 and that only 812,000 remained. The bulk had gone to hospital stores in Moscow, Kharkov, Vinnitsa and Tiflis, to 'her' six supply trains, and to other hospital trains and regiments, and so on.[13] So the eventual destination of the money Buchanan was bringing from London is quite clear.

How much money flowed back to Russia, following the tsar's patriotic plea, will now never be known. What we are attempting to establish, however, is how much was still left in tsarist accounts overseas and in what form. It is a question that began to intrigue others in the 1920s and 1930s as the claimants to the money began to clamour for it. Memories were stirred, as we have seen, but few gave details. Berlin we now know about. Elsewhere some pointed to London and the Bank of England; some to Paris, where favourite banks were picked out as targets; some to Switzerland; and others again to New York and San Francisco. The early chase was often as much to establish who might know where the money was as to find the money itself. Take the following extracts from a letter written by Baroness Buxhoeveden, the former lady-in-waiting to the tsarina, in 1938:

I told Count Hardenberg to try and find a connection with the Imperial Family's monies ... This Tschernyscheff was a minor employee of the Ministère de la Cour who had to do with the financial part. He never was a private secretary to the Empress Mother but was already sent to Copenhagen in the Suite to deal with all her accounts. I knew him from there. He is the person who had to deal with the Grand Duchesses' money at Mendelssohns and knows all about it ... I wrote to Count Hardenberg this spring mentioning Tschernyscheff as the one person who knew if he was alive or dead. He must be a man in his sixties now and probably poor. He is a self-made man, not a gentleman by birth, but my father always thought him a decent kind of person, though I know the Empress's ladies did not care for him. It certainly is very unattractive that he wants a reward for telling the truth, evidently counting on the fact that the only other person who knows the figures, Count Rostovtsev, is dead ... I mentioned to Count Hardenberg that Baron Rudolph Stackelberg of the Ministère de la Cour (Mossolov's assistant) whose address I sent and with whom he evidently got in touch, must also know about this matter, but perhaps not in detail, as he was not in the financial section like Tschernyscheff. As to funds in Switzerland, I *never* heard Rostovtsev mention them and they were *not* on the list of the Imperial Children's funds I saw in 1916 (Nov.). If they exist they may be reserves for poor old Thormayer's pension which was stopped with the Revolution and perhaps are part of the Emperor's private fortune and then go to the Grand Duchess Olga and Xenia ...

The letter[14] seems to establish three points. One is that intense cross checking was still going on in 1938 among the former courtiers to establish who might know where the money was. The second is that the financial details, even in the late 1930s, were still elusive to those close to the descendants of the former royal family. The third is that Switzerland might have been a possible source for tsarist funds though, from what she implies, not the prime one.

Switzerland, therefore, is where our own money trail actually begins, with, it must admitted, precious little to go on. The main difficulty is that Switzerland as a financial centre has changed greatly over the past three-quarters of a century. In pre-First World War days Zurich was not the financial centre it has since become. Its subsequent rise owes a great deal to the growing dominance of the Big Three Swiss commercial banks based in Zurich and Berne, and to the development of Zurich in the period of Swiss neutrality during and immediately after the Second World War. Geneva and Lausanne, the home of the main Swiss private banks, slowly took second place to Zurich. Yet they remained the most likely spots for Romanoff funds. It is almost as if London had become the base of the British commercial banks and the leading merchant banks were in Bath.

Lake Geneva, or Lac Leman, had certainly become almost a second home, along with the French Riviera, to Russian grand dukes and their many relatives. The hotels which still line the lakeside in Geneva and Lausanne were as well known to the richer Russian visitors as the Crimea. Hence the private banks in both places would be a natural home for their spare cash and investments.

The reasons for putting money in Switzerland before and just after the 1914–18 war were hardly those that spring to mind nowadays. Numbered accounts and so-called 'anonymity', the twin features of current Swiss banking secrecy, did not exist in their present form. No Swiss banking law existed at that time, so each bank's rules were different. Banks were simply chosen for convenience, discretion and security. The trouble is that money deposited then is now hidden from view not only by the normal privacy, applicable in most countries, but by a new layer of Swiss laws designed almost to reinforce such privacy.

The number of former world leaders whose personal funds have allegedly been hidden from the knowledge of their subjects in Swiss bank accounts is legion, from the last Shah of Iran to ex-President Marcos. Criminals of all kinds have not been far behind. But, as law enforcement agencies in other countries have striven to break Swiss secrecy, so Swiss banking laws have been amended. In the first place, while numbered accounts continue, pure anonymity is no longer possible since full details of a client, plus passport details are required at the outset. Secondly, if it can be shown to Swiss satisfaction that a deposit holder has committed a crime then details will gladly be given. The difficulty is that what is recognised as a crime in Switzerland is not necessarily the same elsewhere. Fraud is readily recognised as such; tax evasion is not.

So the tracing of Romanoff accounts in Switzerland has always faced obstacles, and these have increased with the years. Several early attempts to reach Romanoff – or simply large Russian émigré – funds foundered for these reasons. One of the earliest concerned a man named Vorovsky who was assassinated on Swiss territory. It soon came to light that he was the owner of a deposit account in a Swiss bank containing some 13 million Swiss francs. The Soviet government quickly claimed that the money belonged to them and took the case to court. This failed, only to be followed by the Soviet government producing a series of 'legal heirs' to the money. This was one of several such demands, and was to be copied in even more aggressive fashion by the Nazi government in the 1930s.

What really obstructs such enquiries is Switzerland's Banking Act 1934: any bank director or employee who 'violates the discretion which he is bound to observe by virtue of the law on professional secrets' could face a prison sentence. (Oddly enough, the only parallel with Clause 47 (b) of the Swiss Banking Act 1934 was Clause 544 of the penal code of Tsarist Russia.)[15] This does not mean that such questions cannot be asked in Switzerland, but rather blurs the kind of answers received.

On this basis, one can only report that of the most likely private banks in Geneva actually asked whether they had tsarist funds deposited with them, some left the strong impression of having, or having had, unclaimed Russian émigré accounts, but virtually all disclaimed tsarist money, whether personal or otherwise. Considering the number of rich Russians who may have placed funds in the Swiss resort before the First World War and never returned, this is hardly surprising.

There was one exception where the director approached did not deny having tsarist funds, and was willing to discuss the matter further but, before doing so, went away to clarify the legal position. He was told that no further information should be given. The risks of doing so were immediately spelt out to me, including the Act of 1934. Whether this was pension money relating to royal courtiers, as Baroness Buxhoevden surmised, or a simple tsarist account, it is impossible to say. I left the bank feeling that either I had stumbled on a possible possessor of tsarist funds (it was the bank other people thought to be the most likely, where I had once had an account myself) or I had added two and two and made five, as Edward Fallows did in London, and had simply misjudged Swiss precision and courtesy.

If tsarist funds do still exist in this particular bank, claims might still be possible. The bank has a rule whereby unclaimed deposits are given to the Red Cross after a period of ten years, but that nominal accounts are maintained, including, where appropriate, interest payments. Other Swiss banks have different rules (some extending the deadline to twenty-five years), though all seem to adhere to the preservation of nominal accounts.

To move from Switzerland to France in search of tsarist funds is a strange reflection of the shifts that can take place in the relative standing of financial centres in the course of three-quarters of a century. In pre-1914 days Switzerland was certainly a secure base for bank deposits (a reputation it has not lost), but neither Zurich nor Geneva was recognised as a leading financial centre. Swiss banks would certainly have attracted funds from visiting Russians, but they were unlikely to have had the pulling power that French banks would then have had for government or tsarist funds.

At the time Paris was still competing, along with Berlin, as a world financial rival to London, and had done so throughout the nineteenth century, after Napoleon had squashed Amsterdam's ambitions virtually overnight. New York was just showing the first signs of moving strongly on to the international scene, but lagged behind London (as to some extent it still does) in pure international business. Paris, however, had the edge on them all in the Russian market, an advantage it was soon to regret, in that it had led all other centres in the volume of Russian railway loans and, to some extent, Russian Imperial government bonds that it had floated on its exchange. One estimate puts France's holdings of Russian foreign debt (that is, based on loans) before 1914 at 80 per cent of the total. Britain's share in the same period was only 14 per cent. In terms of Russian shares floated on the world's exchanges, France accounted for 32 per cent and Britain 25 per cent.[16]

In these circumstances it is hardly surprising that several French banks should have established close contacts with the Russian Imperial government before 1914. That meant that not only the obvious investment houses, such as Rothschilds, might be expected to receive state deposits, but the larger commercial banks too. Of these Credit Lyonnais, with a branch in Petrograd, was an obvious candidate. It was not alone.

The State Bank of Russia, the equivalent of the Bank of England, where the royal family had its personal accounts in Petrograd itself, was directly owned by the tsarist government (with its profits going direct to the Finance Ministry) and naturally had agent banks through which it operated in foreign capitals. In London, for example, it used Rothschilds, Barings and Schroders among the merchant banks, and Lloyds Bank and London City and Midland Bank among the commercial banks. Of the London branches of foreign banks the State Bank used Swiss Bankverein, the Russian Bank for Foreign Trade, the Russo-Asiatic Bank and two French banks – Comptoir National d'Escompte and Société-Générale de Paris. As agents all would have current and deposit accounts of the State Bank. So the assumption is that the same two French banks would have similar balances in Paris.

The significant role played by the Paris market has already been confirmed in other ways. When Peter Bark successfully withdrew state funds from Berlin in 1914, some were repatriated to Petrograd but, as we learned from his autobiographical account, some were simply switched to Paris. Moreover when towards the end of his life he was pleading for help from Barings, he contrasted what he had done with a private bank in London with his arrangements in Paris, where the large credits were placed directly to the Russian government's account (that is, no doubt to the credit of the Russian Treasury or the State Bank at the Bank of France).

Once again the continuing use of French financial institutions by the tsarist government is amply confirmed. What is more difficult to pin down is which banks were used and how much was left in them in 1917. Several clues abound, however, and with a little persistence a reasonably broad picture begins to emerge. The role of Rothschilds is as good a starting point as any. The French branch of the family, Rothschilds Frères, like their other relatives in Vienna and London, had long had personal contacts with the crowned heads of Europe and their political leaders. Baron Alphonse de Rothschild, faced with a blustering Bismarck after France's disastrous defeat in 1871 and his demand for a huge indemnity to Prussia of 5,000 million francs, against the threat of Prussian troops remaining on French soil until it was paid, raised this staggering sum in the international markets in less than two years, to the deep disappointment of the Prussian leader.[17]

This same financial power was put at the service of the tsar from time to time, but had to be tempered by the fierce outbursts of anti-Semitism in Russia. It was this acute dilemma – the Rothschilds' ability to help Russia (with profit to themselves) and their obligation to defend the Jews – that continued to dog their relations with Nicholas II. Torn between the hope that their financial help would persuade Nicholas to curb the anti-Jewish excesses and the fierce press criticism of their close involvement, Rothschilds decided on a middle course: raise funds when asked, and put pressure on the tsar when they could.

In 1906 they were part of the hugely successful Russian loan floated by Barings in London, attracting applications from the French public alone of close on £2,000 million. French subscribers eventually received only 2 per cent of the amount they subscribed for. Two years later, Rothschilds Frères persuaded Leopold de Rothschild, their British cousin, to persuade King Edward VII to take up the Jewish question once again on his forthcoming state visit to St Petersburg. A quiet word on the racecourse at Epsom was soon being retailed to Nicholas at the Winter Palace.[18]

When Peter Bark settled into the Crillon Hôtel in Paris in 1915, at the beginning of his first round of gold negotiations with Lloyd George, one of their main intermediaries with the French Finance Minister was Baron Edouard de Rothschild, son of the successful negotiator with Bismarck. They met in Lloyd George's suite of rooms and, according to Bark, soon found that Edouard de Rothschild had a 'far greater elasticity of mind than Mr Ribot'. He was a non-executive director of the Bank of France, as well as head of his own bank, and as such maintained a balanced view. He quickly took the points Lloyd George and Peter Bark wanted to put across and promised his support when the issues came up at the Bank of France. And, as his relatives had done so often in the past, he deliberately sought a private chat with Bark and then made a simple request: could something be done about 'improving the lot of the Jews in the military zone of Poland'.[19]

Once again a Rothschild was at the centre of international monetary affairs and once again tsarist relations were being nurtured. So the idea that tsarist funds, whether personal or state, might have been placed in Rothschilds and might still be there in 1917 is hardly far-fetched. It was a thought that quickly occurred to the new Bolshevik government in Petrograd. In February 1918, three months after the final coup, Rothschilds received the following request from the Finance Ministry in Moscow at their address in Rue Laffitte in Paris:

I kindly request you to send us as soon as possible – if you have not already done so – the status of all the sums and all the valuables [assets not in cash, such as bonds, shares etc.] deposited in your tills/bank/books, which may have any relation whatever with the Government of Russia, with the State Bank of Russia, with a Russian department, agency or mission.[20]

It was the first reaction of the new regime, anxious to get their hands on what they felt was now theirs. As elsewhere the request got them nowhere, a not unlikely response to a regime that had just repudiated the whole of the wartime debt of its predecessor. Though the next few years were taken up with a mixture of debt negotiations, as the Bolsheviks grappled with a tottering economy and, as we have seen, a rapidly depleting gold reserve, their thoughts slowly turned to thoughts of fresh credits from the West. So the establishment of new relationships with Paris and London, including the formal recognition of the new government, as a preliminary to new loans, replaced the old chase after past deposits. And soon the Rothschilds were being enticed with new deposits. In November 1924 this telegram arrived from Moscow: 'In view of renewal [of relations] between our two countries, would like to deposit up to a million dollars in current account or short-term maximum three months deposit account STOP Please let me know conditions telegraphic address Impravbank, State Bank USSR.'

Rothschilds were not yet ready to reopen their doors to the new regime, and turned down the deposit: 'Your telegram received. Regret cannot consider your proposal in present financial circumstances'.[21]

This approach to Rothschilds in 1918 and later at least confirmed that the Bolsheviks had Rothschilds close to the top of their list. But it was not the only effort made to establish the size and whereabouts of tsarist deposits in France and to claim them on behalf of the new government. The Bank of France too became a target. One person who had partial knowledge was a former military attaché, Count General Ignatiev, who later reported that in his former post as military attaché in Paris he had control of an account of the tsarist Treasury, in his own name, at the Bank of France.

I have recently established the full details of this and other tsarist accounts at the Bank of France. In 1924 Count Ignatiev, whose account was No. 6954, brought an action against M. Poincaré in the French courts, demanding the return of 37 million French francs deposited during the war. My later information shows that the account had been opened in 1915 in the name of the Imperial Russian Treasury, under Peter Bark's control. It was by all reports an active account, plainly designed to finance the purchase of war equipment in France, on similar lines to some of the Russian accounts at Barings in London. The court case was unsuccessful, as were several others in the French courts aimed at claiming balances of the old regime, some government, some private. All foundered against the unresolved debt issues outstanding between the French and Soviet governments.

A final settlement, sorting out both the assets and liabilities of the last tsarist regime in France, has still to be achieved even now. Until this is accomplished tsarist deposits will remain untouched and certainly secret. None the less, as I discovered, it is still possible with a little patience and local help to open the lid a little. Count Ignatiev's account was not the only one to be established by the Imperial government at the Bank of France. The full list can now be revealed as:

Account No. 8404   Russian Embassy. Opened 1916: closed 1921. Main movements to: Imperial Russian Treasury and Russo-Asiatic Bank.

Account No. 5397   The Chancellery for Petrograd Credit operations of the Russian Finance Ministry. Years of operation: 1914–17. Very little movement. No connection with Imperial Russian Treasury.

Account No. 1122   Zaharoff. Opened in 1911. Not connected with Imperial Russian Treasury.

Account No. 478   In name of Antonoff Constantin. Account very active from 1911–19. Each movement supervised by head of the capital deposit account section, as from 11.11.1918.

Account No. 6954   General Count A. Ignatiev, military attaché, Russian Embassy. Significant sums. Account active each day since 1915. Movements always in name of Imperial Russian Treasury.

Account of Colonel of 2nd Regiment of the Russian Brigade.

Accounts, mainly small, in the name of military officials.

These details amply explain why, when M. de Shishmarev approached an official of the French Finance Ministry, following up his New York discussions with Colonel Goleniewski in 1965, he was told that tsarist funds did exist in Paris. But, contrary to Shishmarev's assumptions, there is no trace here of any personal accounts relating to the tsar or any member of his family. It is, of course, possible that such accounts, if they ever existed, are with individual private banks. Rothschilds we have already mentioned in connection with Imperial government funds, but it needs to be remembered that in 1982, following President Mitterrand's nationalisation of French private banks, Rothschilds office in Rue Laffitte had a new name: Européenne de Banque. So a new name was added to the list of possible tsarist fund-holders, just as the similarly named Banque de l'Union Européenne was added, as we saw in Chapter 10, because of its own earlier absorption of the Bank of Asof-Don.

Beyond these banks we also have Credit Lyonnais, not only because of its original branch in Petrograd, but because of its involvement with other relatives of the tsar. The same naturally applies to the Comptoir National d'Escompte de Paris, if only because Nicholas's brother, Grand Duke Michael, had funds transferred through that bank, in the name of his secretary's mother, in the complex method he devised to pay the rent on his properties in England during the war, which we set out in Chapter 3.

Nicholas's relatives are not quite the same thing as Nicholas's own family, however, and the distinction needs to be borne in mind in any attempt to trace real tsarist funds in Paris. The distinction that is even more important in Paris is that between the possible accounts of Nicholas's family and relatives and those of the Imperial government. Huge sums are involved and some indication of their size was outlined in a debate in the French parliament in the early 1920s when the French Finance Minister was asked bluntly what was happening to the balances then still remaining in French banks of the legal representatives of pre-revolutionary Russian institutions, as well as the Russian gold handed over by the defeated German government in 1918 and still lying in the vaults of the Bank of France.

The object of the debate was to ensure that the French government used such assets still on French soil as an offset to the even bigger sums France had lent to the Imperial government during the war, especially in view of the Bolshevik repudiation of such debts. We now know that the gold was later shared between London and Paris. But what is of greater interest is the figure put on Russian official balances in French banks: a sum of 648 million francs in 1924 (roughly £26 million then or £390 million now). Since, unlike Britain, France has still not formally negotiated a debt agreement covering the outstanding 1917 debts with any sub-sequent Russian government, such balances are still subject to claimants. Hence the continuing secrecy in Paris.

My own belief, based on the evidence of claimants, investigators and contemporary accounts we have already examined, coupled with my own efforts in most of the main financial institutions, is that the bulk of the 648 million francs (estimated to be the remaining tsarist balances in France) will prove to be Imperial government money, not Nicholas's private money. Whether his successors would be able to claim any part of such monies is another matter.

16

America

The American trail begins with Winston Churchill. In 1929, in his book *The World Crisis* he put the gold puzzle succinctly, if somewhat mysteriously:

The fate of the mass of [Kolchak] gold and treasure is by no means free from mystery. Undoubtedly the bulk fell into the hands of the Soviet Government. But it is by no means clear that they got it all. Six months later the Finance Minister of General Wrangel's Government began to make inconvenient inquiries about a million dollars of gold reported to be deposited in a bank in San Francisco. He did not last long enough, however, to press this very far.[1]

Three years later Grand Duke Alexander added his own twist to the story:

Until this day, the participants in the Siberian epic, the Bolsheviks as well as their adversaries, are trying to ascertain the identity of the persons who helped themselves to a portion of the 600 million gold roubles of Kolchak. The Soviet rulers claim to have been cheated out of some 90 millions. Winston Churchill believes that a mysterious deposit was made in one of the San Francisco banks during the summer of 1920 by a group of individuals who spoke English with a strong foreign accent. Several French experts entertain similar doubts as to the origin of the Russian gold that appeared in Prague, the capital of Czechoslovakia.[2]

The Californian puzzle, including the individuals speaking 'English with a foreign accent', remains. But to unravel the story we must start in Vladivostock, before moving across the Pacific Ocean to San Francisco.

American, British and Japanese banks were prominent in finding money to finance Kolchak's efforts in Siberia during the period of what is known as the 'Intervention'. At its peak White forces were active on four fronts: the Gulf of Finland, the Baltic states, the Ukraine and Siberia, this last with gold to back up its armed resistance.

The hub of the Siberian gold sales and the original depositing of gold was centred in Vladivostock. For eighteen months, while Kolchak's efforts

were at their strongest, Vladivostock began to rival Shanghai in its cosmopolitan atmosphere. Russian, American, British, Japanese, French, Czech,
Chinese, even Indian troops, mingled with well-to-do Russians in the
cabarets that flourished throughout the night. From the letters they sent
home, the American soldiers at least found it difficult to ignore the
starvation and poverty that went hand in hand with the new-found
wealth.[3]

As soldiers and gold arrived in Vladivostock, the bankers were not far
behind. Some went of their own accord; some were requested to set up
branches by individual governments. The Colonial Office in London was
quickly at work and as soon as it became clear that British troops would
be moving in large numbers through the Russian port, and would need
paying on a regular basis, a 'request' for the Hongkong and Shanghai
Banking Corporation to open a branch in Vladivostock was swiftly dis-
patched to Hong Kong. Payments of up to a million roubles a month
were envisaged.[4] The branch was opened in October 1918.

By the following February a more important use of the branch had
emerged. Kolchak decided to sell some of the gold he had acquired and
shipped it through the Hongkong and Shanghai Bank in Vladivostock for
sale in Hong Kong itself. The bank, with the permission of the British
government, sold the gold in the colony and provided Kolchak with an
equivalent amount of currency notes. Similar transactions followed. Soon
there were as many as eighteen branches of foreign banks in Vladivostock,
and three different kinds of roubles circulating side by side: the Tsarist,
Kerensky and Omsk roubles. Some of the first Omsk 'roubles', though
demonstrably backed by gold, were printed locally on newspaper.

The gold being sold outright tended to be shipped to Hong Kong and
Shanghai, some of it even going onwards to Manila and Bombay. The
gold being held as collateral against western credits was mainly held in
Hong Kong or San Francisco or, in the case of the Japanese credits,
Yokohama. In exchange Kolchak received a variety of supplies: rifles,
machine-guns and munitions as well as newly-printed Russian notes and
international currency.

If Vladivostock was the physical hub of the gold – munition exchanges,
San Francisco quickly became the magnet for all Allied support for the
White Russian effort. Kolchak's gold was shipped in, to be deposited on
behalf of London and New York banks. Rifles and machine-guns were
channelled through the port by the Remington Arms Company. Above
all, émigré Russians flowed into the city, some fleeing the Bolsheviks,
some seeking a new life, some raising money for Kolchak, some seeking
trade credits, some simply on the make. All, at some time or other,
made the acquaintance of the newly established Russian Consul-General,
George Sergius Romanovsky.

He was a tall, handsome Russian with, it was said (incorrectly as it turned out, though he hardly discouraged the reports), some family connection with the Romanoffs. He arrived in San Francisco from Chicago in 1917 as the representative of the Provisional government, and had just married a beautiful Jugoslav girl of nineteen, whom the local press reported to be 'of high lineage'. They soon adopted a profile and lifestyle to go with George's new position. Though he was reconfirmed as Consul-General in October that year, following the Bolshevik coup, he quickly declared his independence, along with his new Ambassador in Washington, Boris Bakhmetieff, and insisted: 'In no way do I represent the Bolsheviks'. And, with little delay, the Romanovskys were soon involved in supporting the Allied Intervention and especially the financial help needed by the White Russians under Kolchak in Siberia.

To so many of the émigrés arriving from eastern Russia by way of China or Japan, San Francisco was the gateway to safety, if not prosperity. Not all were refugees. Some were White Russians gathering further aid for Kolchak's assault on the Bolsheviks from the east. And once American foreign policy had adopted 'Intervention' as a viable option, San Francisco became a natural vehicle for east coast money to be channelled to Vladivostock; west coast banks acted as temporary depositories for the gold needed to reassure the international syndicates in New York and London; and, for a while, George Romanovsky was able to play the high profile character that suited his temperament best.[5]

The Kolchak deals that followed – arms and currency notes for gold, and gold for credits – were easier to agree than to carry through. Government agencies and private enterprise made uneasy partners, both in the handling of the paper work and in the shipping of the gold, where security in a violent and shifting international climate was a rare commodity. As in Siberia itself, gold had a habit of sticking to the fingers of middle-men or at least in enticing too many people into the negotiations, whether in Vladivostock or San Francisco. Much later, as Kolchak eventually retreated along the Trans-Siberian Railway, supplies of munitions and notes, ordered months earlier, began to pile up and, in some cases, to be returned to their original source.

How far George Romanovsky was able to benefit personally from his involvement in the large monetary deals which set up such consignments and in some of the unexpected largesse that followed their return remains a moot point. His close neighbours in San Francisco certainly noticed a distinct increase in his and his wife's living standards, commenting later about 'their money and extravagances'.[6]

It could all, of course, be explained by salary increases, and additional expense accounts, reflecting the extra promotional efforts needed to support investment in Siberia. But the mystery surrounding the Consul-

General's other activities, including the secret joint authorship of a book entitled *Rescuing the Tsar*, long regarded as an authentic diary of real events, but now thoroughly discredited,[7] as well as his earlier and later ambitions in film producing, has added to the colourful suspicions.

He was not the only tsarist personality to add to the contemporary mystery. A Colonel Nicholas F. Romanoff arrived in San Francisco on his way to Washington in 1919 and was noted in the local paper as being keen to raise funds for Kolchak.[8] He was also said to be close to the rebel leader, Semenov, who, as we noted in Chapter 12, had managed to siphon off some of Kolchak's gold en route through his territory. The name 'Romanoff', though quite common in Russia, alerted a number of people at the time, leading to an assumption, later denied, that a relative of Nicholas was in town. Over forty years later a New York publisher even convinced himself that it was in fact Nicholas, tempting the author Guy Richards to link Nicholas's arrival incognito on the west coast with Goleniewski's claims.[9] San Francisco was such a myth-making place at that time.

So it is hardly surprising that shipments of gold, of Russian currency notes and even rifles ended up in strange places; or that the mystery surrounding many of them has lingered on. The official files of the time are littered with examples of such administrative puzzles. As early as December 1918 the American consul Edward Harris, returning to Vladivostock on board the American Army transport ship *Sheridan*, cabled to Washington for advice about six hundred packages of Russian securities valued at 1 billion roubles (roughly £70 million) on board the ship. Reflecting his deep anxiety about official orders, which he had suddenly become aware of and which he not only did not understand but plainly suspected, he immediately sought help. 'Through some unknown agency,' he reported, 'attempt is being made to send to Yokohama instead of Omsk. Do we know reason for such action, and is there something that can be done to stop it?'[10]

It was not the only consignment being delivered by the *Sheridan* that was to go astray. The army vessel later delivered 325 cases of Russian bank notes valued at 25 million roubles to Vladivostock in April 1919. Five years later the State Department received a rather plaintive query from the War Department, explaining that a case containing 100,000 Russian notes had just been found which was 'the residue of a Vladivostock consignment unloaded at the time of the withdrawal of US troops from Siberia'. What should they do with it? The answer was simple. The army had clearly found one of several cases that had gone missing and would they return it to San Francisco. It was later credited to an account at National City Bank, in the name of S. Ughet.[11]

In April 1920, at the point where the last American troops were pulling out of Vladivostock, steps were taken to stop further supplies of newly printed Russian Treasury bills on their way to Omsk and send them back to the US. This was a consignment of 225 cases containing 100,000 Treasury bills printed by the American Note Company in New York, and ninety-four cases containing watermarked paper intended to be used as Treasury bills. The bills were to go back to New York and the watermarked paper to George Romanovsky in San Francisco. Three months later a similar shipment of 104 cases of Treasury bills (a hundred cases of 50 Kopeck bills and four cases of 5,000 rouble bills) were stopped en route. Once again the shipments were redirected back to Romanovsky in San Francisco.[12]

One gets the impression that currency notes, even rifles, were in danger of being scattered round the Pacific, with little or no administrative control. Even tsarist gold was not immune from the hazards of the change in Kolchak's fortunes and the inter-Allied rivalry that went with it. One of the main 'rifles for gold' transactions, which led to enormous disputes and some remarkable arguments about the gold itself, was probably the source of Winston Churchill's query. The detail demonstrates the flavour of the administrative chaos that lay behind the Siberian venture.

The whole idea of using Kolchak's gold hoard to pay for rifles was put forward initially by a Professor Poliakoff, attached to the Russian Embassy in Washington, on behalf of the White Russian government in Omsk. His original proposal was that the Omsk government should place approximately $2,500,000 in gold, to the credit of the Remington Arms Union Metallic Cartridge Company, in a branch of the State Bank or the Russian Asiatic Bank in Vladivostock, or in that of another bank mutually agreeable. At the same time an order for 95,000 rifles would be placed with the company. He proposed that National City Bank of New York should provide a credit of $2 million, guaranteed by the gold deposit in Vladivostock.[13]

In the event the Vladivostock branch of the Hongkong and Shanghai Banking Corporation was chosen for the gold deposit, presumably because of its gold expertise and its network of branches throughout the region, and the gold arrived there on July 29, 1919. The rifles were to be delivered within three months and the payment for them was to be made within the same period, that is by September 25, 1919. Of the original $2,500,000 in gold, it was agreed that $2 million would be used to acquire rifles and the balance of $500,000 would be held in the bank as a pledge against further munitions orders to Remington. If the Remington Arms Company were not paid the $2 million the equivalent amount of gold in the bank branch in Vladivostock would become the company's property. And that is exactly what happened.[14]

Although the rifles were delivered by Remington the National City

Bank (for reasons unknown) did not pay the required sum into the account to pay Remington by the agreed date; Remington thus became temporary owners of the gold (still in the Hongkong and Shanghai Bank vaults in Vladivostock); and the bank still held the balance of $500,000 in gold on behalf of the Omsk government. This was complex enough. But the Remington company hardly relished the idea of holding gold in a particularly troublesome part of the world. So they quickly persuaded the Russian Embassy in Washington to pay them the dollars in New York and thus relinquish ownership of the gold in Vladivostock.

Even that was not the end of the matter. Shortly afterwards a mutiny took place among the troops in Vladivostock and the resulting disturbances persuaded the Hongkong and Shanghai Bank to move the balance of the gold (that is, $500,000 worth) to its branch in Shanghai for safety. But it was easier said than achieved. The bank's natural instinct was to ask the US Navy to take the gold, if only because it was pledged to an American company supplying arms. But the captain of a US cruiser in Vladivostock refused to take the gold (probably due to the question of who paid the costs). In the end the British navy agreed to put the gold aboard HMS *Cairo* and take it to Hong Kong, where it was transferred to the SS *Sinkiang* for transfer to Shanghai.[15]

The cost of this particular gold transaction was $2,900, but it was not the only charge. Nine months later correspondence was still piling up between the arms company, the Omsk government, the Russian Embassy and the US Treasury about a bill for $6,250 which the Hongkong and Shanghai Bank had naturally sent for their part in looking after the gold at their two branches. But on whose behalf? It was obvious that the bill should be sent to the owner of the gold during the period concerned; the trouble was that all parties seemed to fit the description for some of the period. As we have seen before, establishing the true ownership of tsarist gold is not easy.

Later that year the US transport *Great Northern* arrived in San Francisco, carrying sixteen boxes of gold coins from Vladivostock, worth $1 million. This was part of the residue of the $2 million left in Vladivostock after the Hongkong Bank had moved the $500,000 'balance' to Shanghai. Once again complex discussions about ownership and outstanding debts followed. The final decision was to pay the US War Department $584,000, with the rest ($416,000) going to the Russian Embassy account in New York.[16] And it is not hard to guess which account that was: that at National City Bank in the name of Mr Ughet. And that is how that particular gold consignment was eventually shared out. Winston Churchill's query about the $1 million gold in San Francisco had a far more complicated answer than even he had probably suspected.

The bigger gold transactions, arising from the use of $45 million to

$50 million worth of the Kolchak gold to raise an international syndicated bank loan, and the subsequent movements of gold, are easier to describe. In this case two large shipments of the gold eventually ended up in San Francisco, before being transferred to banks in New York. So far as Britain was concerned the international bank credit had received top clearance, coming up for approval at a meeting of the War Cabinet on May 14, 1919. The Cabinet was told by the Chancellor of the Exchequer that representatives of Barings, the merchant bank, were prepared to share in an international loan of up to £9 million (roughly $45 million to $50 million) to the Omsk government. The Treasury had no objection, provided that no part of the UK money was spent outside Europe. The White Russians concerned, he explained, were acting through Peter Bark. The War Cabinet gave its approval.[17]

The gold pledged by Kolchak for the provision of the international credit was sent to Vladivostock and eventually kept in Hong Kong on behalf of the international syndicate of American and British banks. The banks were Kidder, Peabody & Co., the Guaranty Trust Company and National City Bank, all of New York, who contributed the bigger share of the loan; and Barings of London. The agreement was made in the summer and autumn of 1919 and the gold, deposited in Hong Kong, was subsequently used to pay off the loans to the banks concerned the year following. In May 1920, about a month after the last American troops left Vladivostock, two shipments of gold arrived in San Francisco from Hong Kong. It was worth $20 million and was consigned to J. P. Morgan, for the credit of the British government. It was in fact part of the Kolchak gold used to pay off the international loan which Kolchak had spent on munitions.

Kolchak had, in effect, turned part of the gold he had captured from the Bolsheviks into munitions for his White Russian campaign – partly by selling it outright on the Far East market, partly by a complex deal involving gold for rifles and machine-guns, and partly by pledging some of it against an international loan which in turn he spent on munitions. In each case the gold, and its ownership, passed out of Russian hands, whether Red or White, and into those of his suppliers. We need not follow that trail further. Yet how did the monetary residue of several of Kolchak's complex gold deals find its way into the accounts of the Russian Embassy in New York?

This immediately takes us back to George Romanovsky in San Francisco and Boris Bakhmetieff in Washington. Like all diplomatic representatives, following a dramatic change of government, incumbents overseas have both their new masters and their own consciences to consult. Boris Bakhmetieff had taken over from George Bakhmetieff (they were not related) as Russian Ambassador in Washington after the abdication of Nicholas, and was recognised as the representative of the Provisional government by the US government in July 1917. Within four months he was faced with the familiar dilemma: should he resign or, with the approval of the Bolsheviks, represent them? He decided to stay put and was soon active in supporting the White Russian cause and Kolchak in particular. The American authorities, having refused to acknowledge the new regime in Russia (they did not do so until 1933), continued to recognise Bakhmetieff.

This recognition had one important financial implication. The Russian Embassy's accounts in New York, containing the bank deposits of the Imperial government and the Provisional government, became significant in any subsequent claims to 'tsarist' funds; and those accounts also remained active for some time. Moreover the Embassy's property, which included the somewhat ornate three-and-a-half-storey Embassy building on 16th Street as well as the whole of the Embassy's files and records, could also be regarded as 'non-Bolshevik'.[18]

At the end of November 1917, following the Bolshevik coup in Petrograd, Boris Bakhmetieff was thus left with his accounts and records intact, with consulates in Philadelphia, Seattle, Chicago and Montreal as well as San Francisco (where George Romanovsky still presided), and with a staff that largely remained in place. One of these, Serge Ughet was at the time the financial attaché.

At the beginning of December Serge Ughet, who had already been in close touch with the US authorities during the short reign of the Provisional government and had established close relations with National City Bank, wrote formally to the bank's head office in Wall Street asking them to close down seven existing Embassy accounts, from 'A' to 'G':

A   Russian Financial Attaché (Ughet)
B   Russian Financial Attaché Special Account
C   205 Petrograd 3/13/14 Russian Section, Etrangère du Ministère des Finances de Russie (Compte Cheques)
D   211 Petrograd 3/13/14 Russian Section, Etrangère du Ministère des Finances de Russie (Compte Tresor)
E   380 Petrograd Russian Section, Etrangère du Ministère des Finances de Russie (Compte Special)
F   Compte Special de la Mission Extraordinaire
G   Compte Ordinaire de la Mission Extraordinaire

He requested that a new set of accounts should be opened in the name of the Provisional Russian Ambassador Bakhmetieff.[19] We now know from US State Department and Treasury papers that the new accounts were basically 'liquidation accounts', which were to be used for quite specific purposes, such as outstanding obligations to American suppliers of war equipment, interest on past US loans, insurance and inspections relating to wartime deals, as well as the upkeep of Russian institutions. In other words, the American authorities had quickly agreed to support the 'old' Embassy, in exchange for the paying off of US war bills from the Embassy's outstanding bank balances. Cheques on the new Embassy accounts were to be signed by Bakhmetieff or Ughet, but needed US Treasury approval.

At this time National City Bank was holding $56 million in the various Embassy accounts. As in London and Paris, some of this money represented credits given to the Russian government, both Imperial and Provisional, for expenditure on war supplies.[20] Thus the American Treasury had moved swiftly to protect what it regarded as American money in the Russian accounts. Even allowing for this, at least $20 million was estimated to be 'non US Treasury money'. But it was far from easy to sort out, because some of the deposits belonged to the two former Russian governments, some was unspent US government money, some administrative money to run the Embassy, some the residue of American bank loans, some had been set aside to pay interest and capital on past Russian loans, and some were the savings of Russian immigrants to America passed to the Embassy for transmission to relatives in Russia and frustrated by the Revolution. None, on the evidence provided so far, belonged personally to the tsar or his family.

It is clear from the records of the Russian Embassy and from those of the US Treasury and State Department that a series of agreements were reached within weeks of the Bolshevik coup. The closing down of the original tsarist accounts at National City Bank and the reopening of accounts in the name of Boris Bakhmetieff was simply the first step in this process. From December 1917 onwards both Bakhmetieff and Ughet regularly supplied the US Treasury and the State Department with full details of the Russian accounts at National City Bank. Full details were even sent to the American delegation to the Allied Peace Conference in Paris in 1919.

So from the end of 1917 the Russian Embassy accounts at National City Bank were slowly reduced from their peak of $56 million, as American suppliers were paid off and US loans were both serviced and repaid. And, as originally agreed with the Treasury, the state of the accounts (labelled once again with parts of the alphabet: A, B, C, D, M (1), M (2), H, etc.) was supplied quite regularly by Serge Ughet.[21]

As the White Russian resistance grew over the next twelve months and as the Allies slowly moved towards their active 'Intervention' policy, especially in Siberia, so the Russian Embassy accounts at National City Bank, under Serge Ughet, became even more complex. He and his ambassador, Bakhmetieff, were drawn into the financing arrangements needed by Kolchak and all the complex deals his stock of gold soon spawned. So was National City Bank. Not only did the bank run the Russian Embassy accounts; it was also a prime member of the international banking syndicate now funding Kolchak and the chosen intermediary in the gold and rifles deal through Vladivostock. And, as so many of these deals began to unravel when the Kolchak effort lost its momentum, so National City Bank also became the recipient of the unused loans.

Serge Ughet was to continue in charge of the National City Bank account until 1933. In 1922 his Ambassador, Boris Bakhmetieff, retired, and he became the Russian representative plenipotentiary in Washington, operating what remained of the reduced operations from smaller offices, though still in sole charge of the Russian Embassy accounts. Meanwhile Romanovsky in San Francisco was finding life depressing, now that the White Russian resistance, and its accompanying financing, had faded away. And not long after the retirement of Bakhmetieff, Ughet came to the reluctant, though logical, conclusion that the official office in San Francisco was unnecessary. George Romanovsky received his last pay cheque in July 1923.

National City Bank could hardly avoid being drawn into Russian affairs long after its branches had been nationalised in Petrograd and Moscow. Not only did it still hold the Embassy accounts, but over the two subsequent decades it remained at the centre of a number of separate disputes arising from the dominant role its management had deliberately chosen for it in Russia during the early days of the war. All in their different ways brought out the bank's tsarist connections.

One particular contact with the past stretched out well into the 1920s. This was the result of a dramatic explosion in New York harbour in the middle years of the war, which was to nag Ughet and to occupy much of his time.[22] The affair once again questioned the legitimacy of the Russian government and involved a final cheque worth close on $1 million and, ultimately, whether it should be paid into the Russian Embassy account at National City Bank. It was to occupy the American courts for some twelve years.

The so-called Black Tom Island explosion occurred in 1916 among munitions being supplied to the Russian government at a pier and on barges offshore New York caused by an incendiary device. It was thought to be the deliberate work of a German spy. The fire and resulting explosion led to intensive damage to the supplies awaiting shipment from the pier, and took place on the property of the Lehigh Valley Railroad Company. The original claim for damages was made in 1917 by the Provisional government, under Kerensky, and was for $1,675,000.

The court case did not start until 1925, by which time the Kerensky government had gone the way of the tsarist government. But the Russian Embassy, having started the case under its Kerensky responsibilities, was determined to continue with it under its own new guise. As a result two issues had to be determined. Was the Lehigh Valley Railroad responsible, whatever the cause; and, if damages were to be awarded, should they go to the present Russian Embassy?[23]

By the end of June that year the court decided that, since most of the munitions were afloat on steam barges at the time of the explosion, and not in their warehouses on land, the railroad would simply be responsible for the loss of the land-based munitions and placed their value at $3,000. But the matter did not end there. Damages arising from the explosion also had to be taken into account and on that score the Embassy, or rather 'the State of Russia' (the name of the original plaintiff), was awarded $853,000.

It was then that the intense arguments began. Serge Ughet was recognised by the American government. But the defendants naturally argued that the original case had been brought by 'the State of Russia' and Mr Ughet could not represent a government which had fallen and one which was no longer recognised by the American government. The court eventually decided that the government was bound by its outright recognition of Mr Ughet and, subject to appeal, that the money should be paid to Mr Ughet. It was also tacitly understood in legal circles that Mr Ughet, in turn, would devote the money to the reduction of outstanding tsarist and Kerensky debts to the US.

Two and a half years later, just before Christmas 1927, following delayed appeals, a cheque for $984,104 was finally made out, payable to Serge Ughet 'as the representative of Russia in this country'. It was eleven years since the German 'spy' had wrought havoc among American supplies to Russia in New York harbour.[24] But it was not the final move in the long drawn out affair. That was left to the Foreign Minister of the Soviet Union, Tchitcherin, who two months later sent a telegram to the State Department protesting against the payment to 'a private person' of money which should have gone to the 'former Russian Treasury'.[25] The objection was politely ignored and, having met lawyers' fees out of it, Ughet paid the rest of the cheque to the US Treasury to settle part of the outstanding official Russian wartime debt to the United States, still standing at over $190 million. And, once again, the money flowed through Ughet's outstanding account at National City Bank.

National City Bank featured in other disputes throughout this period. It received claims and was also a claimant. Some stemmed from Russian and other claimants on the bank for deposits held in New York. Relatives of Empress Marie and representatives of Anna Anderson were prominent. Other claims arose from the deposits held in the Petrograd and Moscow branches of the bank when the new Bolshevik regime nationalised all banks. At one point in 1927 National City Bank calculated that its losses due to the Russian Revolution amounted to some 387 million roubles (between $150 million and $200 million) and sought compensation from the Soviet government. The Soviets offered $10 million (around £2 million); National City Bank suggested $24 million. The talks were broken off.

The other New York banking target for similar conflicting claims was the Guaranty Trust Company. The bank had been closely involved in the wartime loans to the tsarist and Provisional governments and when the Bolshevik coup took place it still held funds in the name of the Russian Ministry of Finance amounting to $4,976,722. This was basically the residue of the American loan of 1916. Once the US Treasury had made arrangements with Ughet in 1917 to use the deposits in National City Bank to pay off Russian debts to the US the balances held in Guaranty Trust came up for similar discussion from time to time, especially in 1920 when the National City Bank accounts were declining and interest payments on past US loans would become due.

Possible transfers from Guaranty Trust were considered and the bank's other deposits naturally came up for some scrutiny. Although no transfers from Guaranty Trust's tsarist deposits can be detected on this occasion, what did emerge was how even-handed the bank could be in international affairs. It was quickly revealed from inquiries in London and New York that, while the bank held tsarist funds in New York, it was also running accounts for the Soviet Trade Delegation in both capitals. The American Embassy in London alerted the US State Department to these dual facilities and reported that the Soviet account at Guaranty Trust's London branch could be activated by two signatures and was normally replenished from a similar Soviet account at Guaranty Trust in New York. That, in turn, it was assumed, was regularly supplied from Soviet gold transactions in Stockholm.[26]

As with National City Bank, Guaranty Trust was throughout the twenties targeted by every claimant or searcher after the tsar's elusive millions. One of the main turning points, however, was about to take place. The Soviet government continued to state that although, by their early nationalisation decrees, they had legitimately taken over all private property (including bank accounts) within the Soviet domain at home, the possessions of such citizens overseas had still escaped the legitimate net. This would include the tsar's personal assets as well as those of the most modest citizen held abroad, whatever form they took. At the same time the regime was acutely conscious that until such problems were resolved, alongside official debts, the vast western credits they needed would not be forthcoming.

In 1933 the nettle was finally grasped. Maxim Litvinov, the Soviet Foreign Minister and an old colleague of Lenin's, agreed to resolve many of the outstanding debt issues with the United States, in return for the formal recognition of the Soviet government. Under what is known as the Roosevelt-Litvinov Agreement, the Soviet Union agreed to assign all its property in the United States to the American government, on the understanding that the US would inform the Soviet authorities of any money it collected. The way was thus open for the Americans to identify and realise all pre-1917 Russian assets in the US and to use the proceeds to pay off outstanding claims. It is an exercise that, as we shall see in Chapter 17, it took Britain another fifty-three years to achieve.

The first essential move was to list all such assets. On August 25, 1933, Serge Ughet finally handed over to the American authorities the property and assets then in his possession as the final custodian of the former Imperial and Provisional governments in the US.[27] Two months later he produced a short list of the Russian property then in his possession:

Russian Embassy, 16th Street, Washington	?
Bank deposits	
Guaranty Trust (at December 12, 1917)	$4,976,722
New York Trust Co (at August 11, 1926)	46,584
New York Trust Co (at November 11, 1927)	11,680
National City Bank (at September 30, 1933)	151,784
Claims against Curtiss Aeroplane Co., Canadian Pacific Railway, National City Bank, US Shipping Boar, Guaranty Trust Co. totalling	3,001,650
Total	$8,188,420

Once again there is no evidence here that the tsar's personal deposits formed part of the residue. We know that the Guaranty Trust money was basically the balance of the 1916 loan. The small amount of money left in National City Bank is testimony to the use of that account by the US Treasury to pay off US debts. What is not entirely clear is whether Ughet had listed every item. Previous correspondence with the State Department had indicated a total of some $15 million, compared to the $8 million now set out. An earlier list drawn up by Ughet for the Treasury in 1930 could not be found. So, diligent as ever, the Treasury sent a circular to all American banks seeking information about former Russian accounts. As a result, in 1935 J. P. Morgan Co., who had been prominent in the earlier loans to the tsarist and Provisional governments, as well as the gold-related loan to Kolchak, admitted to having several such accounts. Not only was none particularly large, but Ughet had no knowledge of them. They eventually produced $167,857 for distribution by the Treasury.

Because of this particular oversight, I felt it to be worth searching through the totals eventually collected by the Treasury to establish whether any other tsarist accounts might have been overlooked over the years. It has taken the Treasury nearly twenty years to complete its task and by 1953 it had managed to accumulate some $9,114,444, which was placed in Special Deposit Account 3 in the US Treasury. The sources were eventually listed. No startling new bank accounts had appeared. The main ones, as we already knew, were National City Bank, Guaranty Trust and J. P. Morgan. Bank of New York, with its head office on Fifth Avenue, was the only newcomer, with deposits of $298,700. The rest of the money had been realised from insurance companies, industrial firms, two investment brokers and the Post Office.

The American monetary trail, begun partly in Petrograd before the Revolution and partly in Omsk in 1919, thus ended in Washington in the middle fifties. It had emerged from the deliberate efforts of National City Bank to make its mark in the expanding Russian market in the tsarist period, from the loans engineered in the United States for both Tsarist and Provisional governments and from the use Admiral Kolchak made of some of the gold he had fortuitously acquired in Siberia. All had ultimately come together through the efforts of the Russian Embassy in Washington (and its offshoot in San Francisco) and the various accounts run by American banks to sustain these disparate developments. Claims and counterclaims quickly followed. What eventually emerges is that large 'tsarist' accounts of up to $70 million did exist in the United States at the end of the war. The banks too have been identified. What has not emerged either in San Francisco or New York, or elsewhere, is any evidence that personal money of the tsar was involved. Moreover no trace of alleged former investments of the tsar in New York or other railroad stock has been found. Perhaps even more significant, the Soviet authorities at no point raised the question of personal tsarist money or investments in the United States in any of their detailed claims in the courts.

17

London

Russian links with the City of London go back centuries, from timber and fur trading in the Baltic to gold mining near Ekaterinburg, and from providing loans to tsarist governments to the financing of thousands of miles of railway across Siberia. London's merchant banks such as Rothschilds, Barings, Hambros and Brandts all played a dominant part in Russia's economic development. The Romanoffs had their City connections too. Nicholas's father, Alexander III, had a personal account at the Bank of England and even passed it on to his son.

It is not hard to see what attracted them. In pre-1914 days, the pound sterling (with its direct link with gold) was the accepted anchor in world financial affairs, with the Bank of England as its guardian. The City's merchant banking families, spawned as many of them had been in Continental Europe, were active players on the world stage. Even now, in purely international business, London claims a bigger international turnover than either of its two main rivals, New York and Tokyo.

It is also easy to understand, why most of the original tsarist claimants and enquirers chose to focus their main attention on the Bank of England. As the government bank (even though at that time privately owned) it had been prominent in all Russia's war-time financing. Moreover the phrase 'as safe as the Bank of England' might have been deliberately coined to attract such rarefied investors as the Tsars of Russia. Anna Anderson's supporters were running true to form in subconsciously (or deliberately) switching her reference to her 'family's' money being in a 'bank *in* England' to the 'Bank *of* England'.

That Nicholas and his father had personal accounts there was another good reason for their choice. This I have now confirmed. The original personal nest-egg had been bequeathed by Alexander II to Alexander III, who had thus inherited some 90 million gold roubles (some £9 million). Nicholas's father immediately set about improving his personal finances, startling courtiers from St Petersburg to Livadia with a series of measures designed to cut out waste in the upkeep of his many palaces.

Stewards' books, sent to Gatchina for his inspection, were returned full of terse marginalia in red ink. Table linen was not to be changed every day, soap and candles must not be thrown away until they were used up, lights were not to be left burning in empty rooms. The chief steward at one of the palaces was told that, with twenty people sitting down to a meal, there was no necessity to use a hundred eggs for an omelette.[1]

He followed up this somewhat niggling detail with cuts in his own Civil List allotment, reducing his annual total by 18 million roubles a year. Finally, to protect the 'udely' income from the royal lands originally acquired by Catherine the Great from the Privy Purse, he cut down the number of future recipients among his relatives by restricting the title of Grand Duke or Grand Duchess to the children or grandchildren of a sovereign.

As for Alexander's investment of the 90 million roubles, he decided to place it in London. The transfer was undertaken by N. D. Ignatiev and W. A. Sceremetieff. This was probably at the outset of Alexander III's reign in the early 1880s. Prince Dimitri Obolensky learnt of the details of the transaction direct from the one person who would have full knowledge: Count Alexander Adlerberg, who was Minister at the Imperial Court and in direct charge of the emperor's private funds.[2]

Once Nicholas inherited the London investments on his accession in 1894, he naturally reassessed what he should do with the money. Though he lacked any detailed financial knowledge, he was at heart a patriot and, faced with the growing need for capital of his own country and the fact that Russia was already borrowing huge sums on the world's markets, with more likely to be needed, he plainly found it difficult to maintain such large personal sums overseas. He eventually decided to repatriate his investments.

It was not all plain sailing. The Bank of England naturally regretted that such a huge sum should leave London, no doubt showing some anxiety about the impact on the world's exchanges. There were no real foreign exchange markets in those days, as we now know them, and thus no likelihood of an instant run on the pound; up to 1914 exchange rates against sterling (basically the rate at which 'bills on London' could be switched into other currencies) were settled only twice a week at the Royal Exchange opposite the Bank of England, by the top-hatted representatives of the main brokers. But the Bank would hardly relish losing such a prestigious customer. According to Prince Obolensky, 'the transfer was accompanied by great difficulties. The Bank of England put all kinds of hindrances in the way.'

As a result the Russian State Bank found it essential to send a personal representative to London to supervise the details of the transfer. The person chosen was E. D. Pleske, a Director of the State Bank. Prince

Obolensky gave no date for the withdrawal of Nicholas's personal funds in London, but insisted that no monies belonging to the royal family were thereafter placed there (or elsewhere, though that is harder to believe). But it is now possible to put a date to the final withdrawal.

During my own Romanoff investigations over two decades, involving numerous contacts at the Bank of England, opportunities for verification have occasionally been available, if sometimes involuntarily. Suffice to say that I now know that Nicholas had a personal account in his own name at the Bank, under the handwritten title of 'Tsar Nicholas II' in the ledger, at least from 1895 to 1900. That was the date on which the account was finally closed. The last sum to appear in it and to be repatriated in 1900 was £5,008.

Since then no evidence has emerged at any point to suggest that Nicholas reopened his account at the Bank of England or even opened one in the name of any member of his family. That was certainly the view of Prince Obolensky in 1928, but we should not necessarily infer that other Romanoff relatives did not subsequently have Bank of England accounts. Both Grand Duchess Xenia and Grand Duchess Olga had such accounts there between 1930 and 1947–8, when they were transferred to Barings. As we saw in Chapter 8, Xenia had opened an account at Coutts, the British royal family's bankers, within weeks of arriving in London in 1919. Clearly she transferred her account to the Bank of England in 1930, immediately following the clearing up of her mother's affairs and Buckingham Palace's subsequent suggestion that the Bank of England should advise her.

Since 1918 the Bank of England has continued to insist, both privately and publicly, that it has no funds belonging either to Nicholas II or to members of his immediate family. The various decisions by the German courts, as they pronounced on Anna Anderson's claims, produced denials almost regularly in response to press inquiries. One went as follows: 'No funds are held by the Bank of England belonging to the last Tsar or his family. Nor are funds belonging to his children or other members of the Imperial family held by the Bank.'[3] It was typical of many others over the years. On one occasion, feeling the need to reassure myself that these were not just routine denials by officials toeing the party line, I took the next opportunity I had to raise the matter over lunch with a former Governor of the Bank of England who had been directly related with such a denial and whom I knew personally and could trust. Had he made internal inquiries on the matter and was he personally sure that his officials were not hiding any material from him? I received such an assurance.

Nicholas may, of course, have reopened an account at the Bank of England between 1900 and 1914 and then, as indicated earlier, repatriated such funds to Russia in 1914 and 1915. But no such evidence exists to support even this contention. If funds were invested in London before the 1914–18 war and were still in place in 1918, whether belonging to Nicholas or his children, the net clearly needs to be cast much wider than the Bank of England. The most obvious possibility in addition to Barings is Coutts, the British royal family's bankers. Both have grown used to such inquiries every time the question of the missing Romanoff millions is raised anew.

In spite of Edward Fallows' frustrating efforts to penetrate the Bank of England and elsewhere before the Second World War, Anna Anderson's later legal advisers and supporters continued to try as her case proceeded slowly through the German courts in the late 1950s. In 1958 a German member of parliament from Bonn followed the same trail, openly seeking information about the tsar's fortune, first at Barings, where he saw Sir Edward Peacock; then at Coutts and finally at the Bank of England. Sir Edward plainly fobbed him off by explaining that he had only been a director of Barings since 1924 and would have no earlier knowledge. Coutts referred him to the Bank of England where an official replied both generally about London deposits and specifically about the Bank of England with what was by now the standard denial.[4]

Another bout of such inquiries at Coutts was again stirred up following the DNA examination of the bones of the imperial family at Aldermaston in the winter of 1992–3, and once again Coutts' archivist became busy in the vaults. As in the past there was no trace of tsarist deposits belonging to the Russian royal family. The archivist did however find an old tin box, with a file labelled 'Romanoff' prominently displayed. Were these the deeds of the Romanoff riches everyone had been seeking? The file was quickly dusted down and the date, 1922, duly noted. The tin box turned out to contain the residue of material which had been left unopened since the death of Lord Northcliffe, the former owner of *The Times* and the *Daily Mail*, seventy years earlier. He had been a customer of Coutts.

The file was not a pointer to tsarist wealth, but the typescript of a personal diary sent in 1920 to Lord Northcliffe for possible publication and said to be by Princess Nadine Michaelovna, describing how she had accompanied the royal family from Tsarskoe Selo to Ekaterinburg, had escaped the massacre and had later fled to Japan. Whether Northcliffe had read it and rejected it or simply left it unread remains unclear. Following his death, Northcliffe's secretary had obviously tried to return it to the sender, who had given a prominent bank in New York as her address, but had been unsuccessful. It had remained unopened and unread ever since. Its significance for our inquiry is negligible. Its wider significance is examined in Appendix B.

If Coutts eventually proved to be lacking in monetary leads, Barings, I knew, ought to be somewhat more fruitful. Recalling what Sir Edward

Reid, then chairman, had told me in 1956, it was clear that tsarist funds of different kinds had flowed through the bank. They had in fact been flowing through Barings for some considerable time. The bank had been established since 1762, had been in Bishopsgate since 1805 and had been dealing with Russian stock since at least 1817 when parcels of such securities arrived from Amsterdam. A year later the Duc de Richelieu was describing the six great powers of Europe as England, France, Russia, Austria, Prussia and Barings.[5]

Although Rothschilds were to outshine Barings for a time, connections with Russia continued to develop, partly through their banking associates Hopes in Amsterdam, partly direct, leading to their involvement in the financing of the new Moscow–St Petersburg railway in 1850 and eventually to the opening of a credit at Barings in favour of the Imperial Court. Barings had become the official agents of the Russian government. They were soon taking on more and more commissions for the Imperial Russian government, culminating in mid-century with the job of evacuating £1 million worth of Russian gold from the Bank of England on the eve of the Crimean war. Little wonder that in London Palmerston labelled Thomas Baring 'the known and avowed ... private agent of the Government of Russia'.

Barings, as official agents, thereafter raised regular loans on the European markets to help balance the Russian budget and, along with Rothschilds, were prominent in Russian municipal and railway loans through to the outbreak of war in 1914. Though Paris was far more prominent than London in Russian financing in this period, especially in floating Russian railway loans, Barings played a major role in the large Russian government loans of 1906 and 1909, handling the London end of the £89 million and £55 million issues.

With the outbreak of war, it was natural for Barings to be directly involved in the huge Allied financing of the Russian war effort, underpinned by Peter Bark's agreements with Lloyd George in Paris in 1915. Barings were given the pivotal role, acting as the agent through which British government financial help flowed to Russia, a role which was underlined only weeks before the Revolution in 1917 when the Barings' chairman, Lord Revelstoke, was appointed Minister Plenipotentiary as Britain's financial representative in Petrograd at the last Allied Conference there.

What Barings made out of all this they were reminded by Peter Bark belatedly in 1936. He spoke of their annual income of £60,000 from their Russian business during the war years. It was a crude calculation, but may have been an understatement in some years. In one twelve-month period alone when Barings handled £300 million of official credits, their commission, though based on a rate of only $\frac{1}{16}$ per cent, totalled £187,500. Commission rates on other smaller credits varied between $\frac{1}{4}$ per cent and a full 1 per cent. Even $\frac{1}{4}$ per cent on £25 million yielded £62,500. Though the rates were modest enough, the size of the credits needed in wartime was huge.

With all this in mind, it was clearly essential to clarify exactly what kind of funds Barings had handled during the war, how much they eventually amounted to and whether personal tsarist money existed alongside them. Basing myself on Sir Edward's briefing and having spoken to the Soviet delegates then in London, prior to the visit of Khrushchev and Bulganin, and to the Treasury, I concluded that the total of tsarist money in Barings was 'under £10 million'. This compared with the £40 million, even £60 million, being reported elsewhere. My memory is that Sir Edward said it was £9 million. On April 23, 1956 I wrote this explanation of the deposits in *The Times*:

Part of the deposits consists of relatively small current accounts outstanding in the names of Russian banks and companies, the Imperial Russian Embassy and of officials at the time of the 1917 Revolution, but the main share is derived from money advanced by the British Government to the Tsarist Government to pay for raw materials and war supplies. The British Government provided finance by discounting Russian Treasury bills, with the result that some balances were outstanding when the Tsarist Government fell.

Many years later, when my interest had been revived, I felt it necessary to reopen the Barings puzzle. Sir John Baring (now Lord Ashburton) who had by then become chairman and whom I knew well, was unable – perhaps unwilling for privacy reasons – to provide more background information than had his predecessor. Debts talks with the Soviets, as well as court cases arising from wartime claims on the bank from individuals and firms, made it difficult for the bank to give further details. The answers would have to come from elsewhere.

One potential source was the former Russian Embassy in London, which continued to function after the Revolution, under the wing of E. Sabline, the former financial attaché and later Counsellor, following the death of Count Alexander Benckendorff, the Ambassador in January 1917. Others were the files and archives of the Foreign Office, the Treasury, the Bank of England and, I subsequently discovered, the Cabinet Office. The first were a mystery for some years until both Sabline's and Benckendorff's papers finally emerged in Columbia University in New York and, partly, in Leeds University. The papers of Alexander Benckendorff, as well as those relating to his brother Paul, the last Grand Marshal of the Tsar's Court, had been found by his granddaughter, Mrs Nathalie Brooke, in the attic of an English country house in the mid-1980s. They have been in Columbia University since 1988.

The official British files covering Russian deposits in Barings and other

British banks, as well as others covering Russian royalty, I discovered, were only partially open to the public. While some had become available under the fifty-year rule, some were restricted to seventy-five years, others to a hundred years; others again were simply 'restricted'. It eventually took me fifteen months of correspondence to persuade the Foreign Office to open certain relevant files. Thereafter the corresponding Treasury and Bank of England files were equally made available. The jigsaw which follows is based on what papers and files finally emerged in London and New York.

The first intimation that the new Bolshevik government had its eye on possible tsarist deposits in London came in April 1918, when the Foreign Office began receiving requests for advice from its representative in Moscow about Embassy and Consulate money in Petrograd and Moscow. About 20 million roubles (between £1 million and £1,500,000) were said to be involved. Most of it was in the State Bank and the Russian and English Bank. In view of disturbances in Petrograd, the Foreign Office suggested that it should all be transferred to Moscow and sought Trotsky's permission. This was readily given. But at the point where the remaining British officials in Petrograd sought permission to transfer their own money to Moscow, with a view to using it freely thereafter, even abroad, new obstacles appeared. The main one was baldly set out in a Petrograd telegram to London: 'Russian Government will allow us any funds we like as soon as we admit in principle their right to Russian Government money in England.'[6]

The next Bolshevik move was not long in coming. Maxim Litvinov, who had been sent to London as possible Ambassador but had not been officially recognised, and simply remained Russia's 'political representative' here, approached Barings about the use of cheques relating to Russian deposits in their possession. He followed this up with a letter from a London firm of solicitors, presenting his letters of credentials from the Soviet government, and indicating that these gave him 'full and sole authority' as regards the London Embassy (and the Military Mission).

He therefore put them on notice that 'no person' was 'now authorised to draw any cheques upon or otherwise deal with the accounts of the Embassy or the Russian Military Mission, or any other account in which monies belonging to the Russian Government are deposited'. No monies were henceforth to be drawn from the accounts at Barings.

Litvinov, who in his earlier Bolshevik career had been arrested in Europe using 500 rouble notes stolen from the Russian State Bank in Tiflis[7] and was later to become Soviet Foreign Minister, was determined to prevent the Baring money being used by the old Russian Embassy staff (Sabline and his colleague Ermatov) who had remained loyal to the previous tsarist and Provisional governments. Barings immediately asked the Foreign Office for advice. 'We have monies so deposited with us ... Does the appointment of Litvinov give him authority to prevent others from exercising their rights in respect of such amounts? As the accounts are in daily operation, the matter is one of urgency what course to pursue.' The bank subsequently set out exactly what money they controlled, and how the accounts had been run. The file is a useful reminder of what Peter Bark and Lloyd George had initiated in Paris in 1915 and later.

The British government had agreed then, in exchange for Russian gold shipments, to provide credits in favour of the Russian government to an average of £25 million a month, against the deposit of Russian Treasury bills. A Russian Government Committee was set up in London, as agent of the Russian government, to pay the cheques to firms supplying munitions. The contracts themselves were arranged and approved separately. The equivalent Russian Treasury bills were to be presented to the Bank of England (which held the gold) and in its turn the Bank 'discounted' the bills, that is, turned them into cash and passed the cash to Barings. The account at Barings was a 'Special Account' in the name of the Chancellerie de Credit in Petrograd, part of the Ministry of Finance. The account was under the control of the Chancellerie de Credit and certain people at the Russian Embassy in London. The authorised signatories in London had not changed when the Provisional government replaced the Imperial government. Litvinov warned the president of the Russian Government Committee that he alone had authority to use the Baring accounts. The response was a letter saying that they could not recognise him.

In approaching the Foreign Office Barings reminded them that they had had no recognised government to report to since the Revolution, and naturally wanted to know Maxim Litvinov's formal credentials. The original Russian Government Committee had by this time already turned itself into the Russian Liquidation Committee as it grappled with the 150 or so British firms who were owed money for munitions already delivered.

The Foreign Office naturally consulted the Treasury and, as a result, Barings and other banks with similar, though smaller, Russian deposits, were advised that no one was authorised to operate the accounts and the deposits in them. They should be held 'in abeyance', without of course prejudicing the Treasury's right to apply the funds in future to repay debt. Litvinov too was also informed. But the Treasury did not leave the matter there. Ignoring some of the obvious sensitivities of the banks about relations between bank and customer, the Treasury wrote requesting them to pay the Russian deposits to the Exchequer on the grounds that the money had practically all been advanced to the Russian government by the Treasury. This was only partly true and was, in any case, opening up potential future difficulties for the banks. But at least the Treasury was following the line taken by the US Treasury with National City Bank in New York.

The upshot was that the London Joint Stock Bank (the forerunner of the Midland Bank) handed over £166,000 and Barclays Bank £35,000. Other banks claimed a set-off in view of other outstanding Russian liabilities. At first Barings, who held over £4 million at this stage, agreed to surrender the money against an indemnity which they hoped would protect them in future. But they finally changed their mind and told the Treasury that it had no legal right to ask for the money. 'On consulting our legal advisers,' they warned the Treasury, 'we found that this contention is correct.'[8] London Joint Stock Bank and Barclays Bank, however, accepted the Treasury's indemnity.

Faced with this rebuff the Treasury considered the situation. It realised that Barings had two different kinds of deposits: those of the Russian Government Committee which had been set up to allocate Russian military orders based on British loans, and those of the Imperial (later Provisional) Russian government. It felt that there was no legal distinction between the two. The first deposits apparently totalled £1,300,000 and were sufficient to pay out the money still owed to British firms. The second, that is, the Imperial Russian Embassy deposits, amounted to nearly £3 million.

In the end a handwritten note in the Treasury file sums up the Treasury's uneasiness in receiving the Russian deposits from the London Joint Stock Bank and Barclays: 'It is unlikely that we shall be called on to refund but we had no right to take the money and any recognised succession of the Imperial Government would be entitled to claim it.' It is a thought that Nicholas, had he survived and returned to the throne, would have gladly applauded. But the actual successor, eventually due for recognition on both sides of the Atlantic, was a Soviet one and with this in mind, the Treasury tried to comfort itself by one final thought: 'Our reply could be that if you are entitled to the assets you must assume the liabilities and you owe us £X.'

So the Baring money survived the first of several encroachments, from both the Treasury and the Soviet government. Others were to follow, as the Soviet authorities attempted to secure what they felt was legitimately theirs, without of course admitting their predecessor's debts, and as the Treasury tried to find a solution to tie up outstanding claims from British firms. What the Treasury knew and the Soviets did not was the exact amount of money in each of the Baring accounts. The Treasury file finally released in 1993 containing the full details for May 1918 was previously restricted until 2001.[9] These are now set out for the first time in the accompanying table:

Baring Brothers & Co.
(May 1918)

Chancellerie de Credit	£	*(Explanatory notes)*
Compte Special	854,391	(Needs Treasury sanction)
Ordinaire	573,505	(Sundry payments)
Deux	362,545	(Free credit £2m monthly)
Intervention	523,976	(Exchange regulation)
Produit	10,002	(Adjustment in relation to Treasury bills)
Total	2,324,420	

Ministère des Finances Tresor Russe

Compte Ordinaire	276,422

Russian Embassy

Succour to refugees	8,396	
Ordinary Exp. account	3,724	
Repatriation political refugees	952	
Compte Inotrans No. 1	41,105	(Do not know)
Compte Inotrans No. 2	50,000	(Refugees?)
Total	104,178	

Russian Officers Accounts

S. P. Ermolaieff	456
Admiral Kedroff	657
N. Kemmer	2,338
E. Leman	1,896
Lt/Gen. Yermoloff & Maj/Gen Diakonoff	47,172
Rear Admiral Wolkoff	89,139

(*Note:* These monies do not belong to the officers named. The figures attached to the two generals are military agency expenses. The admiral's are naval attaché expenses.)

Total	141,661

Russian Government Committee.

General Account	1,166,886
Transport Account	17,089
Wool Account	80
Due for 'Compte Ordinaire'	1,640
New York Account ($134,830)	28,316
Total	1,213,713

They show what one might expect: the normal operations of the Embassy reflected in separate accounts, some relating to foreign affairs, some to financial matters, some to the military and naval operations of a country at war. One or two accounts also hide special operations undertaken by Barings on behalf of the Russian government. One is the obvious munition-financing account run by the Russian Government Committee, one of Litvinov's original targets. Two others are not so obvious, but had been highly influential throughout the war and particularly active. These were the Compte Deux and Intervention accounts, under the Chancellerie de Credit. These had been the main vehicle for supporting the rouble in the exchange markets.

It was essential for the rouble to be stabilised as far as possible while large financing deals were being negotiated with Russia throughout the war years in Paris, London and to some extent New York. The British Treasury quickly opted out of the operation and naturally suggested that the City's normal mechanism should be used. That really meant the Bank of England and Barings. As a result millions of pounds were used to support the value of the rouble, channelled from the Bank of England through the special accounts at Barings.

As the pressures of war left their mark on Russian finances, so the intervention needs grew. No less than £26,800,000 was spent in this way, by way of Barings, between April 2, 1916 and February 1917. In one nine-day spell alone, in mid-May 1917 during the period of the Provisional government, Barings bought up virtually all roubles being thrown on the markets, an operation which cost them the equivalent in pounds of 27 million roubles.[10] But at least they were recompensed by the Russian government and by the Bank of England. And as all expenses of the operations were established, the cost was eventually borne by the Treasury.[11]

It is yet another example of how intimately Barings had become involved in Russian financial affairs during and immediately after the war. They had earned a tidy sum from the channelling of the Russian munition credits through the bank, as Peter Bark reminded them when he was in need of help in 1936. Their own recognition of what they owed to successive Russian Finance Ministers was later dramatically illustrated on the death of Lord Revelstoke, the Barings chairman during this wartime period, by a belated revelation of Count Kokovtseff, a former Russian Prime Minister and the immediate predecessor of Peter Bark as Finance Minister.

Like Peter Bark, Kokovtseff had escaped from Russia and at the end of 1918 stayed in London briefly on his way to Paris. He naturally called on Barings whom he had known well as a former tsarist Finance Minister, and was determined to renew his acquaintance with Lord Revelstoke the chairman. He obviously arrived without warning for Revelstoke was visibly shocked to see him, having recently read newspaper reports of Kokovtseff's death. He quickly recovered and before Kokovtseff left his office Revelstoke asked him 'a small personal favour'. Without knowing what it might be, the Russian did not hesitate to agree to do anything he wished.

Eleven years later, on Revelstoke's death in 1929, Kokovtseff finally felt free of the obligation to keep quiet about the episode. Writing in a Russian émigré journal,[12] he reported what had happened in Barings' office in Bishopsgate:

[Revelstoke] left the room and presently returned with a sealed envelope which he handed to me in the presence of my wife and of a gentleman unknown to me. Requesting me to open it at home and not to forget that it came from a sincere friend, whose grateful memory of his former intercourse with me had not faded, he added with a parting farewell: 'You surely won't offend me by a refusal, the more so as it is the first favour I have ever asked of you'.

In the envelope I found a cheque book containing fifty-two cheques for an unlimited amount. Fate saved me from having to use a single cheque and, after numerous attempts to return the cheque book to Lord Revelstoke, I succeeded some years later in handing it back. He eventually accepted it from me, taking my word never to mention the incident to anyone.

Their acquaintance had gone back close on two decades, years in which Barings had joined with the main French banks in virtually all the large Russian railway loans, as well as the Russian government loans of 1906 and 1909. Lord Revelstoke, when still John Baring, had even guaranteed the lease of Chesham House, the Russian Embassy building in London, in 1895. His subsequent gesture to a former illustrious client, who had fallen on hard times, was to be mirrored shortly afterwards by Barings' generous loans to Peter Bark. Both were ample evidence of the special relationship Barings had established with the Imperial government.

The Treasury's unsuccessful attempt to persuade Barings to part with their Russian deposits did not prevent industrial firms owed money from suing the bank for outstanding Russian debts. Nor did it prevent the Soviet government from raising the issue whenever debts talks could be induced as a preliminary to expanding trade with Britain and other western nations. Such Soviet efforts followed a similar pattern in 1922, at international talks in Genoa and the Hague, and in subsequent Anglo-Soviet talks in 1924, 1931, 1939, 1946 and 1956. At one point in the late twenties, the Treasury itself made what was to be its last attempt to persuade Barings to resolve the issue once and for all.

The effort did not lack top level pressure. The Cabinet, led by Winston Churchill as Chancellor of the Exchequer, agreed to the formation of a

Cabinet Committee to consider the 'Baring balances'. Under the Chancellor's chairmanship the other members were the Lord Chancellor, the President of the Board of Trade, The Attorney-General and the Secretary of State for India. Their object was to advise the Cabinet whether the Soviet government, which had been recognised as the *de jure* government of Russia, was entitled to sue British subjects in British courts while the latter had no redress in Russia and, if this were so, what to do about it. The Treasury were invited to attend and the Attorney-General confirmed that the Soviet government was entitled to sue and suggested a solution to the dilemma.[13]

It was recognised that Barings' relationship with the Imperial government was one as between banker and customer; that, since the Soviet government had been recognised both *de facto* and *de jure* as the successor to the Imperial government, it could equally claim to be the successor to the assets of the Imperial government and therefore entitled to claim payment from Barings of the amount of the balances (the Cabinet paper put them at £5 million in 1927); and that since the bulk of the money in Barings was money originally advanced by the British Treasury it was 'most undesirable and inequitable' that the Soviet government should be able to recover the money.

The committee toyed with the idea of legislation, compelling Barings to hand over the money to the government but, fearing that it might be regarded as 'confiscation of the assets of a foreign power in this country', quickly backed away. The Attorney-General then suggested that Barings should buy Russian Treasury bills from the government to the same value as the balances. Then, if and when the Soviet government won an entitlement to the balances in a British court, Barings could simply set off the balances against the obligations underlying the Russian Treasury bills, thus discharging themselves of any liability. They would have successfully resisted handing over any money to the Russians. Barings 'would merely be exercising the ordinary right of any debtor who has a cross-claim against his creditor' and could be indemnified by the Treasury against any future claim. Above all, the Treasury would end up with the equivalent of the balances in its possession.

It was an ingenious solution and one which the Cabinet asked the Treasury to discuss with the Bank of England and Edward Peacock at Barings. It was also a solution that Barings were advised not to accept and, more important, did not accept. What they eventually did offer the government (following further Anglo-Soviet debt talks in 1930) was an oral promise, though never provided in writing, that they would not part with the balances without giving the British government the opportunity to intervene, by special legislation if necessary.[14] From then on, the main pressures continued to come from the Soviet side and, as the years passed, the value of the balances continued to rise: from £5 million in 1927 to £6 million in 1939 and from £7,500,000 in 1949 to £9 million in 1956.

Not until 1986, thirty years later and covering a period when interest rates had often reached double figures, did another official figure emerge. Following a further bout of Anglo-Soviet debt talks, when it was finally agreed to resolve the stalemate, the balances were put at £46 million. Both governments agreed to waive claims against each other and to use the remaining balances to compensate British holders of tsarist bonds before 1917 and holders of property in tsarist Russia, both personal and commercial.

Price Waterhouse, the London accounting firm, was given the task of receiving and assessing claims and paying out the money. Claims flooded in, extending from 144 steel boxes containing hundreds of old bonds from one City firm alone to a personal claim for the loss of luggage on a train leaving Russia after the Revolution. The luggage had contained four tins of sardines, three unused tickets for a series of concerts by the Russian Musical Society and a season ticket for ten performances at the Opera House in Petrograd, cancelled because of the Revolution. A schoolteacher claimed £180 for 'the loss of goodwill to my school on November 18, 1917' and a further £60 for similar goodwill lost 'between November 18, 1917 and January 19, 1918'. The smallest claim was for the loss of a bank deposit of 127 roubles in Petrograd, worth £3.63; and the largest cheque paid out was for £900,000 to one company in exchange for several hundred boxes of bonds.

Thus Barings' stewardship of the Russian balances, eventually said to be worth £46 million, finally came to an end. The question we now face is what proportion represented deposits of Nicholas and his family and what proportion was accounted for by tsarist (and Provisional) government accounts. The bank, when faced with such questions, had always denied having any personal family money of the tsar. Philip Ziegler, in a recent history of the bank, written at the suggestion of Nicholas Baring and supported throughout by the bank, had this to say: 'The imperial treasure which it was so often alleged was mouldering in the cellars at Bishopsgate existed only in the popular imagination: the Russian royal family had no account with Baring's and deposited no assets there.'[15]

The same point has subsequently been made by Dr John Orbell, the archivist at Barings. During the period of the claims, following the 1986 agreement, he was appointed to search the archives on behalf of the Foreign Office. He later confirmed that he had found no evidence of any Romanoff family deposits or accounts at Barings. 'There was no shred of evidence.'[16]

What we are left with are the original facts: that a sum of over £4 million left in Barings, which eventually became £46 million, was the original property of the Imperial Russian government, and to some extent the Provisional government. That government in turn had outstanding debts which needed to be negotiated and clarified. But if we are simply searching for tsarist deposits, the facts now seem clear. Barings, and no other London bank or banks, had the money.

18

Moscow

To reach the truth about Romanoff wealth, one crucial source remained closed during most of my investigations. The Bolshevik regime, which instigated the original massacre of the Russian royal family, ensured that for over seventy years hardly anyone penetrated the official archives. It was known that papers relating to the last months of the tsarist court, following Nicholas's abdication, were housed somewhere in the Central State Archive of the October Revolution of the USSR in Moscow. But that was all. Even under *glasnost* permission to consult the files was sparingly given.

My own original researches into the royal family's personal possessions, jewels, gold, bank accounts and investments, therefore, were mainly confined to what could be found outside Russia itself. Only as this book was in its final stages was it possible to gain entry to the heart of the story; and only now can the external evidence be put alongside what I at last found among the official court papers in the newly centralised State Archive of the Russian Federation in Moscow.

In spite of the dramatic changes in the new Russia, little is easy to achieve. The jibe that everything in Russia remains forbidden, but most things are now possible, seems to apply as much to academic research as to everything else. Visas, official invitations, academic introductions – all accompanied by personal bureaucracy – seem designed to block the foreign researcher. At the same time friendliness and understanding now ease his path. So it proved in the State Archive, whose small reading room on the first floor of a somewhat unpretentious building in the centre of Moscow, not far from Gorky Park, became the last hurdle in what had been decades of inquiry.

The files are not set out in easily understandable groupings and the various references to Royalist wealth were eventually located in different areas over a period of days. What was plainly necessary was a basic framework of people, decisions and dates to cross-check against, and much patience. It invariably took at least two days to procure a file, so forward planning became essential. There was ample time to reflect on what our investigative trail had already managed to uncover outside Russia and what now needed corroboration.

From the gruesome remains outside Ekaterinburg to the 1993 scientific DNA findings by the British Home Office and from the main claimants such as Anna Anderson and Colonel Goleniewski to the present where-abouts of the remaining Romanoff wealth, my inquiries had already unearthed sufficient clues outside Russia to build up a reasonable outline of what had happened to the Russian royal family and its possessions. Out of the scores of 'royal' claimants, only two – Anna Anderson and Michel Goleniewski – coupled their claims with details of the money they said was legitimately theirs. And while Goleniewski, under detailed scrutiny, soon proved to be a particularly doubtful candidate, Anna Anderson's true identity was not established until mid-1994.

Their combined claims about Romanoff wealth, therefore, had to be handled with extreme care, our enquiries eventually relying more on other contemporary witnesses and on what was still to be found in western financial centres. I concluded that, at the outbreak of war in 1914, Nicholas had done all he could to persuade his relations and others to repatriate any overseas investments, an example he had ultimately followed himself. Government short-term money had certainly been moved from Berlin, but some doubt existed whether private family investments in the German capital had been liquidated in time. My investigations uncovered no evidence to suggest that personal Romanoff money remained in London, Paris or New York, though sizeable tsarist bank accounts were discovered in all three centres.

As we have seen, the crucial assessment of what wealth remained in the royal family's hands took place in the spring, summer and early autumn months of 1917, when they were under arrest at Tsarskoe Selo and, subsequently, at the Governor's House in Tobolsk. This was the period when Count Benckendorff discussed in some detail what personal wealth they might leave behind in Petrograd, what wealth they might continue to regard as their own and what financial terms might eventually be hammered out on their behalf with the Provisional government. It was also in this period that Kerensky and Lvov made their own inquiries about Nicholas's private resources. Benckendorff was meticulous in securing receipts for the wealth left behind in the Alexander Palace and, after the departure of the royal family to Tobolsk, in ensuring that doors were sealed and lists of personal belongings drawn up and agreed with the Provisional government.

It was with all this in mind that the Russian archives had to be approached. Two particular keys eventually unlocked the crucial papers. These were Count Benckendorff and the Provisional government. The correspondence Benckendorff had had, simultaneously, in 1917 with Fedor Golovin, the Provisional government official put in charge of what was left of the royal court and with Count Rostovtsev, the former empress's secretary who had been in charge of the court's, and the family's personal, finances, was finally run to earth; and from it came a mass of detail concerning the royal family's financial position.

The archives reveal both the trivial and the significant. Only weeks before his final abdication Nicholas wrote to Benckendorff explaining that his delay in answering a letter had been caused by his need to order a new uniform for a photograph of himself wearing military medals rather than the normal court ribbons. Less than a month later, according to the archives, Benckendorff was pre-occupied by the possible departure of the royal family abroad and set out detailed notes, in his own handwriting, as to what would have to be done in preparation. But, as these ideas of an overseas exile faded, he began to concentrate on the intentions of the new Provisional government towards royal possessions in general and those inside the Alexander Palace in particular and on the money Nicholas could rely on in the future.

The main question to be answered, in sifting through the cor-respondence, was how far the new information gleaned in Moscow con-firmed or amended the picture of tsarist wealth already built up from elsewhere. The tsar's personal possessions were at risk from the moment of his abdication onwards. What we now have is full confirmation of what the royal family left behind at Tsarskoe Selo and in the Winter Palace.

As they left for Tobolsk Benckendorff drew up a detailed list of the jewels and personal belongings that Nicholas, Alexandra and their children had left behind. It begins by listing Alexandra's own jewels ('in Box No. 2.') – tiaras, collars, bracelets, brooches of diamonds, sapphires, rubies – and goes on to cover her jewelled fans, and jewels given to her by visiting royalty and members of her family. These are followed by a list of jewels belonging to her daughters and, significantly, as we noted earlier in Chapter 11, a 'box of diamonds and things belonging to Princess Victoria of Battenberg'. Benckendorff's attention to detail has thus provided the evidence needed for Princess Victoria's descendants, the present Mountbatten family, to attempt to claim back the family jewels, and is still in the archives in Moscow.[1]

Benckendorff's list extended to what had been left in the various rooms of the Alexander Palace, including the contents of chests and cases. One wardrobe contained 'Her Majesty's underwear'; another case had the future dowry (linen and underwear) of her eldest daughter, Grand Duch-ess Olga; yet another contained wedding dresses; and so the list went on, covering silk scarfs, Turkish and Bokhara carpets, regimental rib-bons, 40 dresses 'for holidays and balls' and 'ten Russian dresses with train'.

Benckendorff saved more than that for posterity. The archives also hold Alexandra's personal jewel book – updated to July, 1917 – containing details of all the jewels she had acquired when she was still Princess Alix of Hesse, before she became Empress. It is handwritten in English and sets out what jewels the tsarina regarded as her own and how she acquired them. There are 308 items of jewellery listed, beginning with a large gold locket with coral and pearls, given to her by one of her four godparents, HRH Princess Beatrice, one of Queen Victoria's daughters, and dated June 6, 1872, Alexandra's birthday. Several others are clearly birthday, Easter and Christmas presents from close relations. Later additions in pencil indicate personal favourites ('which I *always* wear') or where she eventually left them ('on my writing table' or 'in my vitrium in the Winter Palace'). Some of the last pencilled comments, in June and July 1917, indicate personal bracelets, lockets, brooches given to her daughters. The last such entry records her giving a gold bracelet with green stone, heart shape attached with diamonds, 'to Marie, July 22, 1917', just over a week before they left Tsarskoe Selo for the last time.[2]

Thereafter, the royal family's personal jewellery was either stolen en route by their Bolshevik captors or found on their bodies at Ekaterinburg. Even here the list of gold objects finally taken from them by their guards and eventually carried in a sack to Moscow has been found in the archives.

Earlier, while the family were recovering at Tsarskoe Selo from attacks of measles and pneumonia, and from the shock of abdication and arrest, officials continued to grapple with all the administrative problems of court life. Letters still in the archives recount not only the actions taken by the Provisional government to take control of Romanoff assets, but also attempts by court officials to clarify what to do about previously authorised payments, extending from the salaries and pensions of the royal tutors to the small sums Grand Duchess Tatiana had been paying monthly to support an old woman suffering from tuberculosis. Even Grand Duchess Olga's income tax return for 1916 came up for detailed discussion. Out of her total income of 277,892 roubles (roughly £28,000 at the time), made up from her annual allowance and her income from investments, she was already due to pay 30,240 roubles in tax, under the old regime. Now, under the Provisional government, she faced a total of 75,600 roubles, plus a further 75,600 in super-tax, making 151,200 roubles in all. It would have to be paid in three stages beginning in December, 1917. The correspondence suggested that Olga ought to be told.

The archives show how, step by step, royalist possessions were taken over. Most of the palaces immediately became the property of the state, the Anichkov Palace, formerly the home of dowager Empress Marie, being taken over by the Food Ministry. Some of the institutions at Tsarskoe Selo, such as the hospitals, were transferred to the local authority. The palaces themselves were to be run by a new Commissioner of the Court; and the adjoining lands were given to the Ministry of Agriculture. The Provisional government was rather more careful with money belonging to foreign royalty: the dowry capital of the Queen of Greece, a former Russian princess, amounting to one million roubles, was given to Greece on April 3, 1917.

Less than a fortnight later, a decree was passed transferring the court capital of the former emperor's family to the Ministry of Finance. A separate account in the archives sets out the court's total financial resources in March, 1917 at 93,453,224 roubles (or some £6 million). This was the state money Nicholas received to run the individual palaces, stables, theatres, orchestras, museums, etc. Most of the money was invested in fixed interest securities, some with individual banks, such as the State Bank, the Moscow Merchants Bank and the Petrograd Society of Mortgage Credit. A small amount (about 1,800,000 roubles), was still invested in German bonds at the Mendelssohn Bank in Berlin.

The same files reveal the personal expenditure of individual members of the royal family, paid out of court allocations, over the previous two decades. Picking out items at random, one can still see, for example, what Nicholas spent on his meals and apartments when he was a young officer before he became tsar; how much he spent on cigarettes in 1896, the year after his coronation; and what Alexandra and her children spent on soap, photographs, clothes and even on cleaning shoes in 1915.

Benckendorff and Rostovtsev needed to clarify how much different members of the family could rely on in future. As a result the existing resources of each leading member of the family came under close scrutiny in their correspondence with Golovin. The archives provide us with the amounts each had been receiving annually, when the last payment had been made and how much each now had as their personal wealth.

The former Empress Marie's position was assessed on March 20, 1917, in a letter from her secretary to Golovin. The point was made that she had her own personal expenses to meet as well as a variety of other state expenses, including the upkeep of palaces, salaries, pensions, charities, and the care of the homeless, sick and wounded. She was meeting such expenses out of an allocation from the state of some 200,000 roubles, paid in three instalments during the year, and when, as often happened, expenses were greater than such income, she had to meet the difference from a special capital fund, from one of her estates or even from her personal capital. The latter was put at 500,300 roubles (£33,000). What should she do in the new circumstances?

The Provisional government provided no early guidance. Marie had last received 69,666 roubles from the State in January and, although the State supplied money to pay for workers on her estate, the regular payment of 69,666 roubles due in May was not paid to her. She did, however, manage to obtain the cost of her various journeys to and from Kiev, as well as her final journey to the Romanoff estate at Ai Todor in the Crimea. Once Golovin turned his attention to Marie's financial problem, he quickly decided that her position had not been changed by Nicholas's abdication. Under a law of 1906, he discovered that Marie had been promised 200,000 roubles annually to cover the expenses of her court, as the widow of a former emperor and that she should continue to receive this sum until she died or until she left Russia. And even if she left Russia, he found, she would still receive half the agreed sum, that is 100,000 roubles. He recommended that she be paid the outstanding instalment and that such payments should be made regularly in future.

The financial position of Nicholas and his family was far more fundamental. Their dilemma had first been faced when the cost of living began to rise sharply at Tsarskoe Selo, and some of the money for the royal family's meals began to be deducted from their private accounts at the State Bank. But it was not food that brought the issue to a head, but a much more patriotic gesture from Nicholas himself. He had plainly asked whether he could subscribe to the new Liberty bonds which the Provisional government were issuing to raise money for the war effort. In considering such a move, Benckendorff and Rostovtsev worked out that any significant purchase of bonds by the ex-emperor, on top of the cost of meeting day-to-day living at Tsarskoe Selo, could seriously deplete his personal financial resources, unless the royal family continued to get their normal allowances. They asked Golovin for permission for such allowances to continue and, at the same time, to permit him to buy bonds.

Benckendorff also felt obliged to set out for Golovin exactly how much

CAPITAL OF THE TSAR'S FAMILY : MAY 1, 1917	
Emperor	908,000 roubles
Empress	1,006,400
Tsarevich	1,425,700
Grand Duchess Olga	3,185,500
Grand Duchess Tatiana	2,118,500
Grand Duchess Marie	1,854,430
Grand Duchess Anastasia	1,612,500
Total	12,111,030

each member of the royal family had in their personal investment account on May 1, 1917.[3] Their total wealth, he explained, came to 12,111,030 roubles (£809,000 then, equivalent to £15 million now) to which might still be added dividends from their individual investments (see table on page 265).

In explaining the individual sums of money, Benckendorff and Rostovtsev stated that Nicholas's capital was made up of what he had inherited when he was tsarevich and what he had set aside over subsequent years from his annual court allocation. The capital of Alexandra and the children came from any savings they made from sums allocated to them annually from the state treasury, court funds and the emperor's estate funds. The family's annual allocations for personal expenses, the last instalment of which had been paid in January 1917, were put down as:

Emperor	250,000 roubles a year
Empress	200,000
Tsarevich	100,000
Daughters (if under 20)	33,000 (personal)
	45,525 (servants)
Daughters (if over 20)	75,000 (personal)
	45,525 (servants)

It is significant that in giving Golovin details of the royal family's personal wealth, no reference was made to overseas money or investments. This does not imply that none existed, for in a separate file dealing with the Provisional government's administration of the court following Nicholas's abdication, there is a detailed report headed: 'Condition of capital of the children of the abdicated Emperor abroad.' In ink at the top of the report are the words 'By July 1, 1914.' The report gives full details of the individual investments of each of the tsar's children, as shown in the table on page 266, as well as exchange rates for the sterling and mark investments shown.

The total investments came to 12,862,978 roubles (or roughly £1,300,000 at the 1914 exchange rates). Of this over 5 million roubles were accounted for by Alexis' investments, and the grand duchesses' totals varied between 2,143,000 roubles (Olga) and 1,757,000 (Anastasia). The foreign element was made up of 4,379,448 roubles' worth in sterling investments (£462,944) and 4,021,228 roubles in German mark investments. The sterling investments were confined to the four grand duchesses: each had £115,736 in a 5 per cent foreign bond dated 1822. The mark investments were divided among all five children and were split between a 4 per cent Moscow Smolensk railway bond, a 3½ per cent

CAPITAL OF EMPEROR'S CHILDREN ABROAD
('by July 1, 1914')

	Investment	Foreign Currency	Roubles/ rouble kopek equivalent
Alexis	4% Certificate, state rent	.	2,500,000
	4½% Razansko-Uralskaia Railway		1,963,300
	4% Razansko-Uralskaia	1,195,000 marks	548,700
	3½% Prussian Consolidated Bond	47,500 marks	21,850
			5,033,850
Olga	5% Foreign Bond 1822	£115,736	1,094,862.56
	4% Moscow-Smolensk Railway	730,500 marks	336,030
	3½% Prussian Consolidated Bond	1,548,700 marks	712,402
			2,143,294.56
Tatiana	5% Foreign Bond 1822	£115,736	1,094,862.56
	4% Moscow-Smolensk Railway	560,100 marks	257,646
	3½% Prussian Consolidated Bond	1,475,400 marks	678,684
			2,031,192.56
Maria	5% Foreign Bond 1822	£115,736	1,094,862.56
	4% Moscow-Smolensk Railway	354,300 marks	162,978
	3½% Prussian Consolidated Bond	1,390,000 marks	639,400
			1,897,240.56
Anastasia	5% Foreign Bond 1822	£115,736	1,094,862.56
	4% Moscow-Smolensk Railway	242,200 marks	65,412
	3½% Prussian Consolidated Bond	1,298,100 marks	597,126
			1,757,400.56
			12,862,978.24

Prussian consolidated bond and a 4 per cent Razansko Uralskaia railway bond.

These are the facts provided by Benckendorff and Rostovtsev to the Provisional government in the summer of 1917. In our attempt to clarify how much the royal family held at home and abroad and how much may still be left intact somewhere in the world, the figures given here for the children in July 1914, as well as the later figures for the whole family in May, 1917, need to be compared with the evidence we uncovered earlier.

What then was already known? Paul Benckendorff had already indicated in his memoirs, published in the west, that the royal family's wealth was made up of Nicholas's capital of 'less than a million roubles,' Alexandra's of 'one and half million,' and that of the five children ('that which was abroad as well as that which was in the State bank') which varied, he said, 'between two and three millions each.' This seemed to indicate that only the children had money abroad, and that the family's total resources amounted to between 12 million and 17 million roubles. In addition Lvov and Kerensky, the successive leaders of the Provisional government who had made their own inquiries and later gave it in evidence to the Sokolov inquiry, indicated that the royal family's financial resources totalled some 14 million roubles, including money abroad. We also have the private estimate of the royal family's individual wealth published anonymously in Petrograd in 1918 in the book, *The Fall of the Romanoffs*, which the archives now show to be precisely the same as those given by Benckendorff to Golovin. The anonymous author was well informed.

On top of this all the evidence from the main financial centres of London, Paris and New York produced no evidence of private Romanoff money remaining there. This, coupled with Nicholas's well documented plea in 1914 for his countrymen to repatriate their capital and the accompanying assumption that he did the same, strongly suggests that the reason the children still had investments abroad in 1914 and after was that they could not be liquidated in time because of the outbreak of war. There are other reasons too for believing that the list in the archives is the last valuation provided by the Mendelssohn Bank, in Berlin, of the investments placed in their hands not long before.

In the first place the date on the list is July 1, 1914, indicating that this is the last valuation provided about the children's investments before hostilities with Germany prevented further communication just over a fortnight later. No later valuation is contained in the archives. Secondly, it is the kind of list that an international bank, such as Mendelssohn, would produce, neatly spreading the investments in German, Russian and British fixed interest stocks. Finally, the assumption that this is the Mendelssohn money is supported by the memory of their aunt, Grand Duchess Olga, forty years later. As her biographer, Ian Vorres, put it:

The Grand Duchess told me of another case of appalling mismanagement. Just before 1914 the accumulated yearly allowance of Nicholas's five children reached the sum of 100 million roubles. Against the Emperor's wishes, the Minister of Finance – together with one or two leading bankers – invested every penny of it in German stocks. Nicholas argued against it, but they kept assuring him that the investment was perfectly safe and very profitable. This fortune evaporated, of course, after World War I.

Olga's memory of the sums involved seems to have been somewhat exaggerated, but the German investments, along with the mark investments of the court indicated earlier, plainly remained untouched because of hostilities and were still there in 1917, and were not claimed by Grand Duchess Xenia and her relations until 1933. By that time they had been sadly ravaged by hyper-inflation.

The archives in Moscow now face us with the same information that Benckendorff, Kerensky and Lvov possessed in 1917. And the variations in their individual estimates of the royal family's wealth also become much more understandable. They knew, as we do, that the family's wealth in Russia amounted to some 12 million roubles. They also knew, as we do, that the children alone had over 12 million roubles abroad in 1914. What they found difficult, as we do, was to add the two together. The children's money abroad had to be valued and the difficulty they faced in attempting to do that, or in getting any financial expert to do it for them, was that the investments were not only frozen in an enemy country but were also, apparently, in three different currencies – roubles, marks and pounds. They did their best, as we must do.

In general terms, we can now sum up the royal family's financial position in the summer of 1917 as follows. Each member of the family was left with a personal rouble portfolio, comprising investments, a current bank account and cash. In total this came to 12 million roubles. The five children still had their individual investment portfolios abroad, which we can assume to be in the Mendelssohn Bank in Berlin, valued at 12 million roubles in 1914. In addition each member of the family was still receiving state money to pay for day-to-day expenses, which were constantly being renegotiated and reduced. The state money to run the court itself had been transferred to the Ministry of Finance. Former Empress Alexandra still had investments at Darmstadt – in an enemy country. These were quite small. The last accounts for 1913, still in the archives, show an income of some 12,237 marks which, based on the fixed interest investments shown, indicate a total portfolio of around 305,000 marks (roughly 150,000 roubles, that is £15,000). Mainly she spent the income on jewellery, clothes, porcelain, photographs and other small personal items.[4] There was no evidence of Nicholas himself having any money abroad. Overseas money, therefore, comprised: the children's investments and Alexandra's small investments in Germany; certain court investments in Germany; and the large tsarist government balances we have uncovered in London, Paris and New York.

The family's Russian resources, therefore, were confined to their personal investment and bank accounts. The archives now provide detailed evidence of how these personal accounts were gradually absorbed by both the Provisional and Bolshevik governments. On March 20, 1917, under an early decree of the Provisional government, the property and capital of the royal court became state property. On April 14, 1917, a further decree was introduced transferring all the sums of money belonging to the former emperor's family to the Ministry of Finance, where separate accounts for each were to be established.

Finally, after a series of decrees nationalising banks and taking over the accounts of 'rich' people, the Bolshevik government introduced a special decree on July 13, 1918, nationalising the 'property of the Emperor,' and indicating that the property of Nicholas and his predecessor, Alexander III, 'including investments in Russia and abroad now belong to the Russian Socialist Soviet Republic.' The decree stated that people who knew anything of such property were to give details within two weeks. If not they would be held responsible. Commissions were to find out the allocation of property abroad. All property, except money, was to be transferred to a Commissioner. Money was to be given to the People's Bank.

The decree was signed by Lenin. His final revenge at Ekaterinburg was only three days away.[5]

19

Whose?

From the day of his abdication Nicholas slowly shed layer after layer of his royalist trappings, like a Russian *Matryoshka* doll. The power to decide his own fate was the first to go, followed inexorably by the royal palaces, trains, yacht and state jewels, his private possessions and, finally, his family and life itself. All that remained were Romanoff possessions overseas; whether in the form of jewels, gold, property, money or investments. The jewels and gold we have already attempted to track down. We have traced original tsarist accounts in London, Paris and New York. And we have clarified Romanoff money in Berlin, from both western sources and from the Russian State Archives themselves. It is time to consider the question lying behind the whole of our investigation. Whose wealth have we been uncovering?

The question has not only bedevilled our efforts to find and identify tsarist funds. It has been one of the main obstacles in weighing up all the rumours and gossip of the imperial court. 'Tsarist gold' all too quickly became shorthand for 'Nicholas's own money'. 'Tsarist funds in London' became 'personal family accounts'. 'Gold in San Francisco' became 'Nicholas's own nest-egg'.

With hindsight these assumptions were all too readily accepted and passed on. Yet lurking in the centre of them was a truth about the tsarist regime that still needs careful treatment. While Nicholas was in power tsarist gold (wherever it was) was his to command, move and allocate. His own annual grants from the Russian budget were 'not to be debated by the legislature' and 'not subject to reduction'. One of his last financial transactions before abdication (certainly his last with Peter Bark) summed it all up: he simply switched money from a Secret State Fund to his own pocket, by a simple request to his Finance Minister, a transaction which, though rare for him, was perfectly legitimate. This is the true basis of any autocratic regime. 'L'etat c'est moi'.

When secrecy is allied to an autocrat's power to decide how and when money can be transferred, to and from his own accounts and those of the state, again in his name, as in the case of Nicholas II, then the labyrinth of their own monetary affairs becomes baffling indeed. It is this inter-mingling of personal and 'head of state' money, and the apparent need to protect it from prying eyes, that has added an extra obstacle to all subsequent inquiries.

It is true that as tsar and head of state, Nicholas and his predecessors had deliberately separated family money from state money – even acknow-ledging which palaces had been inherited from relatives and which belonged to the state. But in the historic perspective, even this distinction fades away, as we remember that the 'udely' estates (from which the grand dukes and others received their annual income) had in any case been built up from Catherine the Great's own Privy Purse allocation.

It is hardly an unknown phenomenon. Even some of Queen Elizabeth II's current personal wealth has been traced back to surpluses from earlier Civil List allocations in the years since the beginning of Queen Victoria's reign. Philip Hall, in one of the most detailed recent analyses of the finances of Britain's royal family, put it this way:

Since the introduction of the new form of the Civil List in 1830, so that [they] no longer paid for any aspect of civil government, monarchs had made a profit on the Civil List, right up until the end of the last reign. They had been able to save money from the sum allotted for wages and salaries and other expenses, which the Treasury allowed them to transfer to their 'Privy Purse'.

The latter is for the monarch's personal expenditure. He calculated that the surpluses since the beginning of Victoria's reign amounted to over £1,500,000, or something like £67 million in 1991 pounds.[1]

The contrast between a monarch's role as a person and as head of state is interpreted differently, depending on the constitutional (or, looking at it another way, autocratic) nature of the monarchy itself. In Britain the big change took place in 1830, when William IV's Civil List allocation no longer had to cover any government expenditure and was confined to financing 'the dignity and state of the Crown, and the personal comfort of Their Majesties'. In Russia, certain changes took place in 1906, in response to the revolutionary pressures of the time, but even as late as 1917 Nicholas, while personally acknowledging the distinction between family and state, still maintained in his hands the daily power to switch financial resources from one to the other at will.

This distinction has been interpreted by counsel in two quite separate courts of law, not in tsarist Russia itself, but in Finland and the United States in the same year, 1929. One concerned the ownership of former tsarist property in Finland being contested by Nicholas's sister, the Grand Duchess Xenia. The other involved claims by Nicholas's relatives and the Soviet government on deposits in two New York banks.

At issue in Finland was the ownership of the Halila estate and other properties, which Xenia alleged had been bought by her father, Tsar Alexander III, for 100,000 roubles in 1892. The assumption by the Finnish state was that the property was Russian 'state' property and, as such, had been legitimately acquired by Finland at the Treaty of Dorpat. Xenia simply claimed that the property was personal to her father.

The Finnish lawyers, therefore, needed to set out tsarist property laws, as they affected the tsar, in some detail.[2] This is the element that concerns us in our attempt to allocate ownership of the tsarist gold and money we have managed to trace. According to the laws of the Russian Empire, the Finnish court was told, the tsar could own three kinds of private property, namely, property that he inherited from his predecessors, and to which other members of his family had no claims of inheritance; the joint property of the royal family which could not be divided; and private property to which his heirs had the right of inheritance. 'It was often difficult to distinguish between these properties,' the court heard, 'due among other things to the fact that the Tsar was vested with autocratic power.'

The Finnish lawyers were making the point that since the Halila property had been bought by the Russian Chancery and not actually by Alexander III personally it was essentially state property and could not be inherited by his relatives. When a similar issue was raised in New York,[3] opposing counsel produced conflicting views on the same point. The lawyer representing Nicholas's mother, former Empress Marie, and thirty-two other members of his family simply maintained that

all State funds or assets of the Tsarist Government now in America remain the personal property of the assassinated Tsar Nicholas II. At the time when these funds were transferred to America, the Tsar was the acknowledged personal owner of all State funds and that international understanding would certainly enter into the contest.

The lawyer representing the Soviet authorities read the situation quite differently. State funds collected from the nation, he stressed, 'always remained the property of the state, no matter how absolutely a ruler might control them while in power; and the more absolute his control, the more destitute he was when he ceased to be the ruler and the Government'.

Ultimately, in the case of money, investments or property outside Russia, the final arbiter must be a court of law outside Russia or the restoration of a tsarist regime inside Russia. Meanwhile, in going through the discoveries we have made, the notion that Nicholas and any legitimate successor, rather than any relative, might be able to claim outstanding state funds needs to be borne in mind.

This is the basic legal framework that we now need to apply to some of the main Romanoff possessions we have traced. The remnants of tsarist gold are in some ways easier to assess than the overseas bank deposits. There is no evidence to suggest that Nicholas ever invested his personal money in gold. Deposits in the Bank of England during the period of the gold standard, or for that matter during any period when the pound was 'convertible' (that is, when there were no obstacles to switching pounds into any other currency), were the equivalent of gold. But since gold produces no rate of interest, he would have no incentive to keep a personal gold stock of any kind.

We are therefore left simply with interpreting the ownership of the gold left scattered outside Russia. The stock taken over at gun-point by the Bolsheviks in Petrograd, and the rest of the gold that fell into their hands when Janin handed over Admiral Kolchak and the gold he had left in 1920 became the state holdings of the new regime. The gold transported and sold in Vladivostock and Hong Kong by Kolchak, in exchange for guns and munitions, became the legitimate property of the recipients. So did the gold which was initially pledged in western banks from Hong Kong to San Francisco, against the provision of credits. Some of it was handed over to legitimate new owners when payments for munition deliveries were not forthcoming; some found its way to New York and London banks in part repayment of the credits raised by Kolchak.

There remains the gold secretly shipped to London during the war. Whose is that? Several courtiers, in the mistaken belief that Nicholas had been transferring his own personal assets, assumed that it 'belonged' to the family, and was a well-prepared nest-egg they could rely on in exile. It was no such thing. These were Russian State reserves legitimately transferred to London under agreements freely negotiated and agreed by Peter Bark in a series of Allied meetings in Paris and London.

What was at issue for some time was whether the Russian government had pledged the gold shipped to London, not transferred its ownership. As we saw earlier, Peter Bark's own ingenious financial cosmetics helped to foster this illusion in his efforts to disguise the thinning gold-backing for the rouble. He agreed to accept gold-backed bonds in exchange (they were actually still in the Bank of England when he was working there as adviser to the Bank), which were due for repayment later. The reality, however, was that those bonds (and the underlying gold repayments) would most likely have been cancelled out by the enormous Russian war debts which continued to pile up well after the Revolution. The so-called 'Russian' gold would have automatically become 'British' and stayed in the Bank of England vaults.

To turn from gold to jewels and investments is to move to the heart of the royal dilemma about ownership, one that concerns the House of Windsor, or any long-standing monarchy, just as much as the Romanoffs.

What belongs to the state and what is private, and how many categories of ownership are there in reality? The crown jewels, for example, whether British or Russian, are easy to understand: they belong to the state. But both Windsors and Romanoffs seem to have included others forms of jewellery in a similar category: jewels passed down from one sovereign to another which were never regarded as personal or even part of the wider royal family. The late Lord Cobbold, when Lord Chamberlain, described them in this way to a Select Committee in 1971:

There are other items of jewellery, etc., which ... are regarded by Her Majesty as Heirlooms. In no practical sense does the Queen regard any of these as being at her free personal disposal.[4]

Examples are gifts given to Queen Victoria and Queen Alexandra. The broad British term for them is 'legally inalienable property'. In the same way the Romanoffs possessed state jewels, beyond the crown jewels, which had been passed down from one sovereign to another. Count Benckendorff, when listing what the former Russian royal family had left behind at Tsarskoe Selo, made a similar distinction between what he described as 'the personal diamonds of Her Majesty' and 'diamonds of the Crown'.[5]

Just as members of the British royal family have their own personal jewellery, so did the Romanoffs. We have followed the destiny of the personal jewels of former Empress Marie and, up to a point, of former Empress Alexandra. The question is whether, following the Bolshevik take-over, both state and personal jewellery became state property. The new Bolshevik government not only nationalised private property within Russia, it also took care to bring all Romanoff family assets within state control three days before the family were killed at Ekaterinburg. Lenin's decree deliberately embraced the property of Nicholas and his father, Alexander III, and, in addition, named all grand dukes and Nicholas's main relatives, even including a genealogical tree to make sure that the net was spread wide enough.

To that extent, both the crown jewels and the personal jewellery left behind in Petrograd and elsewhere by the royal family were legally acquired by the state. Even the personal jewellery taken outside Russia by former Empress Marie and her two daughters would come into the same category, at least according to the Bolshevik authorities. So would jewellery stolen from the Romanoff palaces and exported privately to the west. But once the Bolshevik authorities themselves began to sell off the family silver to western auction houses and elsewhere in the 1920s and 1930s, such a distinction became difficult to sustain or at least to prove. Whether the Mountbatten family can now make a claim to locate and regain Princess Victoria's jewel box left behind in what was St Petersburg in 1914 is yet another legal conundrum that results from the Romanoff tragedy.

Similar legal puzzles surround the ownership of tsarist and personal Romanoff money. What has now been established is that to the middle of 1917 the Russian royal family – Nicholas, Alexandra and their five children – had some 12 million roubles in the form of personal investments, money on current account and cash in Russia. In addition we now know that the children, whose money came from the family 'udely' estate and from individual state allowances, had certain foreign investments in 1914, amounting to about 12 million roubles, roughly a third of which was in German bonds, and another third in British bonds. We can make a reasoned guess that these investments in Berlin were frozen until hostilities ceased.

Beyond that we have found no evidence that any significant private Romanoff funds remain in London, Paris or New York. But we have established that sizeable tsarist funds still existed in British, French and American banks at the end of the 1914–18 war and have even been left with a suspicion that a Swiss bank too may have had a similar, though smaller, tsarist deposit. Altogether one can talk in terms of roughly £100 million remaining in such tsarist accounts in London, Paris, New York and, possibly, Geneva.

Once again we face the questions: to whom did such varied money and investments belong and who might claim what remains? The money originally allocated to the royal court for the upkeep of royal palaces and the like – roughly 93 million roubles in 1917, of which a small amount was still in the Mendelssohn Bank in Berlin – was legitimately taken over by the Provisional government in March, 1917. The private money and investments of the Royal family in Russia – roughly 12 million roubles in May, 1917 – were originally transferred to separate accounts at the Ministry of Finance by the Provisional government, while remaining under Nicholas's control. Thereafter those accounts were gradually drawn down to pay for the royal family's upkeep in Siberia and no doubt taken over under the first financial decrees of the Bolshevik regime. If any money remained, it would have been absorbed under Lenin's final decree of July 13, 1918.

There remain Romanoff and tsarist money and investments outside Russia. The only personal funds we have detected abroad are those of the children in Berlin, which were inherited by Grand Duchess Xenia and her Romanoff relatives in 1933. This does not mean that stray personal accounts of the royal family will not one day emerge in London, Paris, Geneva or even New York; simply that it now seems unlikely. If such accounts did emerge and could be regarded as the private property of members of the former Russian royal family, surviving relatives could certainly entertain some claim to them, as they did in the case of the investments in Berlin.

This leaves the £100 million of tsarist accounts remaining in Paris, London and New York in 1918, the bulk of which have in any case already been distributed by the British and American governments to other creditors of the former tsarist regime. Claims on such tsarist money are quite different. Had Nicholas survived Ekaterinburg and returned to the throne, or had Alexis been similarly restored under a regency, as many exiled monarchists wished, this £100 million might have become the target of the restored regime and the restored tsar, though not of his relatives. Whether such a monarch, then or even in the future, would have wished or might wish, to pursue such a treasure through the world's courts, and might still have, or be given, the autocratic power to control it and use it, is another matter.

APPENDICES

Appendix A

The Tsarist Succession

The confirmation of the death of Tsar Nicholas II at Ekaterinburg by the DNA tests at Aldermaston, coupled with the end of Soviet rule, have naturally revived talk of a Romanoff succession some time in the future. The Romanoffs themselves are divided, some supporting the claims of the late self-styled Grand Duke Vladimir Kyrilovitch (and now his grandson, George); some following the lead of Prince Nicholas Romanoff and his various cousins in their more subdued, and democratic, response to the new prospects.

After Nicholas II abdicated in 1917 Grand Duke Kyril, a son of a younger brother of Nicholas's father Alexander III, escaped to Finland where his son, Vladimir, was born in August of that year. Seven years later in 1924 he issued a manifesto proclaiming himself head of the House of Romanoff and thus the legitimate pretender to the throne as 'Emperor of all the Russias'. It was a claim that was not accepted by former Empress Marie, then living in Copenhagen. On Kyril's death in 1938 his son Vladimir, who had already been granted the title of Grand Duke by his father, similarly proclaimed himself the Romanoff successor, a role he continued to play until his death in April 1992. His daughter Maria, who married Prince Franz-Wilhelm of Prussia in 1976, was then said to have become head of the family and her son styled 'Grand Duke George'.

Genealogical purists are quite clear about the rights and wrongs of the succession. They maintain that the order of succession, down the male line, had been settled by Tsar Paul in April 1796 (as amended by Alexander III in 1886) and that no departure from that could be made except by a renunciation. So Nicholas II could not appoint his brother Michael. The next heir was the Tsarevich Alexis who was under age and did not renounce his title. Thereafter the next in line was Grand Duke Kyril Vladimirovitch.

Kyril's claim, though, was badly flawed. In the first place he was the son of a marriage not recognised by the Romanoffs, his mother not having become a Russian Orthodox until after his birth. Secondly his own marriage was equally unacceptable for the same reason, his wife not becoming Orthodox until later. And he hardly helped his cause in 1917 when, as Commandant of the Palace Guard at Tsarskoe Selo, he joined his men in recognising the Provisional government, leading them through the streets of Petrograd, it is said, with a red flag. As for Vladimir, instead of marrying a foreign princess from a reigning royal family as pretenders to the throne were expected to do, he married Princess Leonida Bagration-Mouhransky, a divorced woman with a teenage daughter.

Of the remaining Romanoffs, the majority would echo the views expressed by Prince Rostislav Romanoff in *The Times* of May 7, 1992, when responding to the earlier claims of 'Grand Duke Vladimir':

The Romanoff family today consists of some twenty-nine members. We are a family all of whom, except for Vladimir Kyrilovitch, his heirs and his father before him, have respected the wishes of my great-grandmother, the Dowager Empress Marie Feodorovna, that there should never be a question of a pretender or successor to the throne of Russia by the Romanoff family in exile. These questions could and should only be decided by the Russian people in Russia at a time appropriate to them.

Prince Rostislav, who was born in Chicago and now lives in London, is the grandson of Grand Duchess Xenia, the Tsar's sister. His view of the succession is shared by his cousin, the senior member of the family, Prince Nicholas Romanoff. He is the great-great-grandson of Tsar Nicholas I. His great-grandfather was Grand Duke Nicholas Nicholaiovitch, the younger brother of Alexander II. Recently rejecting the claims of Vladimir and his daughter Maria, Prince Nicholas, who lives in Rome, stated quite simply, 'I am now the head of the Romanoff family. But I am not a pretender. I consider the best form of government for Russia is a presidential republic.' His younger brother, Prince Dimitri, is chairman of the Romanoff Family Association, which in turn has established a Romanoff Fund for Russia. One of its first joint projects is the provision of equipment for children at the Kostroma Institute for Deaf Children.

Appendix B

Northcliffe's Romanoff Memorandum

The tin box discovered two years ago in the vaults of Coutts Bank, bankers to the British Royal family, contained both a memorandum and correspondence relating to the last eighteen months of Tsar Nicholas II and his family. It had belonged to Lord Northcliffe, the proprietor of *The Times* and the *Daily Mail*, who was a client of the bank and had died on August 14, 1922.

The correspondence indicates that, following his death, his assistant secretary had made unsuccessful attempts to return the manuscript and various accompanying letters to a Miss Jane Anderson in New York, from whom Northcliffe had received them two years earlier i.e. in 1920. Her address had been given as c/o Messrs Brown Brothers, the well-known investment bank in Wall Street.

Five letters between a Princess Nadine Michaelovna in Japan and Baroness Leonie de Souiny in New York were enclosed with the memorandum. The first was undated and the rest were dated between March 29, 1920 and May 16, 1920. They indicate that Princess Nadine, who had been with the royal family in St Petersburg, Tobolsk and Ekaterinburg and had ultimately escaped eastwards to Japan, had sent the baroness a series of memoirs, written in Russian, which were eventually translated into English. They made a three-part typed memorandum, of some 124 pages.

The correspondence indicates that the princess had accompanied the royal family into exile in Siberia, first as a nurse, later as a nun. 'Of your princess,' she writes, 'nothing is left but a little white nurse, Sestra Effrossina'; and she explains why she had gone with them: 'I could not separate from my dear children whom I saw come into this world'. She goes on to reminisce about her earlier relationship with the baroness. 'Do you remember our conversations in my little salon at the Winter Palace? How you regretted Alexandra would not permit an interview.'

Part I of the memorandum basically covers the period from the outbreak of the Revolution to the departure of the family to Tobolsk; Part II covers

Tobolsk; and Part III Ekaterinburg. The part covering the first months at Tsarskoe Selo includes references to the seizure of her family's palace in Petrograd. 'I had only time to save my documents, my jewels and a few pictures.' She was soon obliged to leave her little room at Tsarskoe Selo 'adjoining the apartments of my beloved charges' and went to live at the hospital. She describes Olga and Tatiana making 'everything ready for England' and Alexandra confessing that she had hidden no documents or even secret correspondence, as Kerensky seemed to suspect, but only a few jewels in case she might have to dispose of them.

The second section describes the journey to Tobolsk, living in a separate house in the town, and the rigid regime that soon enveloped the royal family. 'The ex-Tsar was no longer permitted the right to dispose of his own fortune. He was allowed only the strictest necessities; and as there was no way in which he could receive money, our life was most economical.' Olga came to her with some of her jewels on one occasion. 'She wanted to sell an emerald ring so that she could purchase a wheel chair for her mother.' The writer managed to get milk for Alexis from the local convent.

The last section covers the arrival in Ekaterinburg, the writer's stay at the Ipatiev House dressed as a nun and, finally includes a dramatic description of the death of the royal family with the former princess blacking out before the shooting began.

The document is a strange mixture. It includes clearly authentic background, with the accurate names of courtiers and recognisable events, large and small, especially at Tsarskoe Selo, along with wildly inaccurate narratives of the journey from Tobolsk and events at Ekaterinburg. One gets a strong feeling that the original memoir of a lady, probably a princess who was maid of honour in the royal court, has been buried in what later became a journalistic attempt at yet another Romanoff 'exclusive'.

Notes

1 St Petersburg

1 A. A. Mossolov, *At the Court of the Last Tsar*, 1935; Princess Barbara Dolgorouky, *Gone for Ever*; Paul and Beatrice Grabbe, *The Private World of the Last Tsar*, 1985; Miriam Kochan, *The Last Days of Imperial Russia*, 1976.
2 Meriel Buchanan, *Ambassador's Daughter*, 1958; and *The Dissolution of an Empire*, 1932.
3 Pierre Gilliard, *Thirteen Years at the Russian Court*, 1921.
4 Grand Duke Alexander of Russia, *Once a Grand Duke*, New York edn, 1932.
5 A. A. Mossolov, op. cit.
6 Paul E. Desautels, *The Gem Kingdom*, 1971.
7 *Illustrated London News*, May 30 and June 6, 1896.
8 Miriam Kochan, op. cit.
9 Grand Duke Alexander, *Once a Grand Duke*, op. cit.

2 Revolution

1 Nicholas Mansergh, *The Coming of the First World War*, 1949.
2 Richard Pipes, *The Russian Revolution 1899–1919*, 1992.
3 Lady (Georgina) Buchanan, 'Letters from Lady Buchanan', *The Historian*, The Historical Association, no. 3, Summer 1984.
4 Letter from Kenneth Metcalf, 21 Nevsky Prospect, Petrograd, March 3, 1917 (OS) (March 16, 1917) to brother Leslie in Leeds. Brotherton Library Collection, University of Leeds.
5 Dimitri Shakhovskoi, quoted in *The Russian Revolution of 1917*, ed. Dimitri von Mohrenschidt, 1971.
6 General Danilov, quoted by Alexander Kerensky in *The Murder of the Romanovs*, 1935.
7 Extracts from the diary of Grand Duke Michael, formerly owned by Mrs Pauline Holdrup and now in the hands of a private collector in New York; translation provided by Mrs G. Gosling, librarian of the Highgate Literary and Scientific Institution, London.
8 Alexander Kerensky, op. cit.
9 Count Paul Benckendorff, *Last Days at Tsarskoe Selo*, 1927.

3 Abdication

1 *New York Times*, March 19, 1917; March 20, 1917; May 12, 1917.

2   Meriel Buchanan, *Ambassador's Daughter*, op. cit.

3   Kenneth Rose, *King George V*, 1983.

4   Sir George Buchanan to Lord Hardinge, May 21, 1917, Hardinge Papers, Cambridge University Library.

5   Sir George Buchanan, Petrograd, to Foreign Office, March 25, 1917 (Foreign Office files, Public Records Office).

6   Nicholas Sokoloff, *Enquete judiciaire sur l'assassinat de la Famille Imperiale Russe*, 1924.

7   Sir George Buchanan to Lord Balfour, Foreign Secretary, September 3, 1917 (Foreign Office file FO 371/3015/XC/A5814/Item 333, Public Record Office).

8   Pauline Gray, Michael's step-granddaughter, who lives outside Southampton, still has some of them.

9   Paddockhurst Estate Office, Crawley, West Sussex.

10   Lord Stamfordham to Count Benckendorff, August 8, 1914 (Benckendorff Papers, Columbia University, New York).

11   Sir Arthur Davidson, Marlborough House, April 18, 1917 (Foreign Office file FO 800/205/9887, Public Records Office).

12   Sir George Buchanan, Petrograd, July 4, 1917 (Foreign Office files, Public Record Office).

4   Captive

1   Letter from Prince Basil Dolgorukov in Tobolsk, dated August 14, 1917, to Count Paul Benckendorff in Petrograd. This and other letters which I have drawn on in this and later chapters have come from the recently discovered Benckendorff Papers now in the Bakhmetieff Archive, Columbia University, New York. They were discovered in the attic of an English country house by a member of the Benckendorff family in the mid-1980s. These particular letters, as well as the original French draft of Paul Benckendorff's book, *Last Days at Tsarskoe Selo*, contain financial details not previously available.

2   Taken from 'The Devastated Palace', an anonymous typescript account of the attempts of the Provisional government to assess the works of art in the main imperial palaces, now in the Benckendorff Papers (Columbia University).

3   ibid.

4   Report of the Ministry of Finance to the Emperor on the Budget of the Empire for 1913, St Petersburg, Printing Office of the Imperial Academy of Science. (Copy in the British Library.)

5   A. A. Mossolov, *At the Court of the Last Tsar*, op. cit.

6   Reports of the Ministry of Finance to the Emperor on the Budgets of the Empire, 1898–1913 (British Library); Kyril Fitzlyon and Tatiana Browning, *Before the Revolution*, 1977; Grand Duke Alexander, *Once a Grand Duke*, op. cit.

7   Letter from Prince Dolgorukov to Count Benckendorff, dated August 14, 1917 (Benckendorff Papers, op. cit.).

8   J. C. Trewin, *Tutor to the Tsarevitch*, 1975.

9   Letters from Prince Dolgorukov to Count Benckendorff, dated November 13 and 26, 1917 (Benckendorff Papers, op. cit.).

10   Letter from Petrograd to Vanderlip (New York), February 10/23, 1917 (Citibank Archives, Butler Library, Columbia University, New York).

11   Telegram to Foreign Office from Petrograd, December 29, 1917 (Public Record Office, FO 368/1969).

12 Harold van B. Cleveland and Thomas F. Huertas, *Citibank 1812–1970*, 1985.
13 Memorandum dated July 19, 1919, from Picton Bagge, Department of Overseas Trade, London. (Public Record Office, FO 371/4022).
14 From the original French draft of Benckendorff's book, *Last Days at Tsarskoe Selo*, but excluded from both French and English editions (Benckendorff Papers, op. cit.).

5 Massacre

1 In clarifying the sequence of events in this period I have been particularly guided by Professor Richard Pipes in his meticulously researched *The Russian Revolution 1899–1919*, 1990. Other details from: Captain Paul Bulygin, *The Murder of the Romanovs*, 1935; Robert K. Massie, *Nicholas and Alexandra*, 1968; and Greg King, *Empress Alexandra*, 1990.
2 'The Devastated Palace', op. cit.
3 Captain Paul Bulygin, *The Murder of the Romanovs*, op. cit.; P. M. Bykov, *The Last Days of Tsardom*, 1934.
4 Gleb Botkin, *The Real Romanovs*, New York edn, 1931.
5 Edvard Radzinsky, *The Last Tsar: The Life and Death of Nicholas II*, 1992; Richard Pipes, *The Russian Revolution 1899–1919*, op. cit.
6 Pierre Gilliard, *Thirteen Years at the Russian Court*, op. cit.; Baroness Sophie Buxhoeveden, *Left Behind*, 1929.
7 Extracts from Nicholas's diary are taken from Edvard Radzinsky, *The Last Tsar*, op. cit. He consulted it in the USSR Central State Archive of the October Revolution in Moscow.
8 Description from V. Vorobiev, one of the guards and editor of the *Ural Worker*, quoted in *The Last Tsar*, op. cit.
9 Tim Heald, *The Duke*, 1991.
10 Nicholas Sokolov, quoted from the French edition of his report in John F. O'Conor, *The Sokolov Investigation*, 1971.
11 Boris Yeltsin, *Against the Grain*, 1990. Edvard Radzinsky, *The Last Tsar*, op. cit.
12 Nicholas's knowledge of his impending execution is not too far-fetched, when the reports to the *New York Times* by Carl Ackerman are taken into account. Ackerman reported from Ekaterinburg in December 1918 that he had interviewed a former servant in the royal household who said that the tsar had actually been summoned before the Regional Soviet Court to be told of its execution decision. Full details, including Ackerman's original typescript, are still in a folder, along with other material from his journalistic career, in the Library of Congress in Washington.
13 Note written by Yurovsky in 1920, quoted by Edvard Radzinsky, op. cit.
14 *The Sokolov Investigation*, tr. John F. O'Conor, op. cit.
15 Testimony taken from: Medvedev, Strekotin, Yurovsky and Kabanov, quoted in *The Last Tsar*, op. cit.

6 Plunder

1 One of the Sokolov reports, with photographs, is now in the Houghton Library at Harvard University.
2 Bernard Pares, *The Fall of the Russian Monarchy*, 1939 (quoting Sokolov, op. cit. 487).

3   *The Sokolov Investigation*, tr. O'Conor, op. cit.
4   Baroness Buxhoeveden, *Left Behind*, op. cit.
5   Richard Pipes, *The Russian Revolution 1899–1919*, op. cit.
6   Baroness Buxhoeveden, *The Life and Tragedy of Alexandra Feodorovna, Empress of Russia*, 1928.
7   *The Sunday Times*, December 1, 1991.
8   Edvard Radzinsky, *The Last Tsar*, op. cit.
9   I am indebted to the Revd L. L. Tann of Edgbaston, Birmingham, Press and Information Officer of the British Society of Russian Philately, not only for his invaluable advice but also for allowing me to draw on a private essay, 'The Tsar's Collection'.
10 Richard Pipes, *The Russian Revolution 1899–1919*, op. cit.
11 'The Devastated Palace', op. cit. I have relied on this account in this chapter.
12 R. H. Davis, Jr. and E. Kasinec, New York Public Library, in a note entitled 'Witness to the Crime', quoting Maurice Laserson.

7 Bodies

1   Jonas Lied, *Return to Happiness*, 1943; and Anthony Summers and Tom Mangold, *The File on the Tsar*, 1987.
2   Diaries of Colonel R. M. Meinertzhagen, Rhodes House Library, Oxford.
3   Michael Occleshaw, *Armour Against Fate*, 1989; and *The Romanov Conspiracies*, 1993.
4   Mark Cocker, *Richard Meinertzhagen: Soldier, Scientist and Spy*, 1990.
5   Foreign Office papers (371 and 800 series), Public Record Office, Kew; Secret Archives of the Vatican, Vatican City; Mountbatten Papers, Broadlands Archives, Broadlands. The first recent references to the involvement of King Alfonso and the Vatican were made in the second edition of Summers and Mangold, *The File on the Tsar* in 1987. But they remained critical of George V and clearly unaware of Queen Mary's initiative. Dr Michael Occleshaw in his latest book, *The Romanov Conspiracies*, covers the Vatican involvement in some detail but, oddly enough, criticises 'the secrecy still prevailing' in the British records, stating that 'nothing has ever been released which sheds light on her [Queen Mary's] initiative' and thus ignores the Foreign Office files at Kew and Lord Mountbatten's papers at Broadlands, used here in the text.
6   Edvard Radzinsky, *The Last Tsar*, op. cit.
7   R. H. Bruce Lockhart, *Memoirs of a British Agent*, 1932.
8   Letter dated October 26, 1918, from Cardinal Gaspari, Secretary of State, Vatican, to Cardinal Bourne, Archbishop of Westminster in London. Source: Secret Archives of the Vatican.
9   Letter from British Consulate, Geneva, Foreign Office file FO 371/3328, Public Record Office, Kew.
10 *The Orthodox Word*, July/August, 1990, St Herman of Alaska Brotherhood, Platina, California (excerpts of television interview, Moscow TV, 1989).
11 Peter Kurth, 'The mystery of the Romanov bones', *Vanity Fair*, January 1993.
12 'Identification of the remains of the Romanov family by DNA analysis', Peter Gill, Pavel Ivanov and others in *Nature Genetics*, Washington, DC. Vol. 6, February 1994.
13 News release, Home Office, London, July 9, 1993.
14 *Daily Mail*, July 29, 1992.

8 Survivors

1   Richard Pipes, *The Russian Revolution 1899–1919*, op. cit. See also Note 5, Chapter 18.
2   Anon., *The Fall of the Romanoffs*, by 'A Russian' (introd. to English edn by Alan Wood), 1992.
3   The stories of many of these exiles have been painstakingly compiled by Norman Stone and Michael Glenny, *The Other Russia*, 1990.
4   This account and much of Empress Marie's stay in the Crimea is based on the memoirs of Prince Roman Romanoff, *Det var et rigt hus, et Rykkeligt hus*, published in Danish in 1991. The book is based on the diary of Prince Roman Romanoff, and published thanks to his two sons, Prince Dimitri Romanoff in Copenhagen and Prince Nicholas Romanoff in Rome.
5   Foreign Office (FO 371), Admiralty, and War Cabinet minute files in Public Record Office, Kew.
6   Vice-Admiral Sir Francis Pridham, *Close of a Dynasty*, 1956; Christopher Dobson, *Prince Felix Yusupov*, 1989; E. E. P. Tisdall, *The Dowager Empress*, 1957.
7   David Chavchavadze, *The Grand Dukes*, 1990.
8   Ian Vorres, *The Last Grand Duchess*, 1964.
9   Soren Morch, *Det Store Bankkrak*, 1986; Ole Lange, *Den Hvide E lefant, H. N. Andersen eventyr og OK 1852–1914*, 1986; and *Jorden er ikke storre, H. N. Andersen, OK og Storpolitikken 1914–37*, 1988. I must also acknowledge the time and historical knowledge gladly offered to me by historian Henrick Bertelsen in Copenhagen.
10 Sir Frederick Ponsonby, *Recollections of Three Reigns*, 1951.
11 Hoover Institution, Palo Alto, California.
12 *The Times*, April 18, 1923 (Law Report, p. 5).
13 Pauline Gray, *The Grand Duke's Woman*, 1976.
14 Foreign Office correspondence, April 28, May 5, May 11 and September 4, 1924. Foreign Office files, Public Record Office. Count Constantine Benckendorff, *Half a Life*, 1954.

9 Anastasia

1   Gleb Botkin, *The Real Romanovs*, 1931.
2   Princess Nicholas Galitzine, *Spirit to Survive*, 1976.
3   *Sunday Times*, February 15, 1981; and *The St George Journal* of the Knightly Association of St George the Martyr.
4   Bernard Pares, *The Fall of the Russian Monarchy*, op. cit.
5   Edvard Radzinsky, *The Last Tsar*, op. cit.
6   Peter Kurth, *Anastasia*, 1985.
7   ibid.
8   Ian Vorres, *The Last Grand Duchess*, op. cit.
9   Papers of Edward Fallows, Houghton Library, Harvard University, Boston.
10 ibid.
11 Alastair Forbes in the *Spectator*, London, July 18, 1992.
12 Fallows Papers, op. cit.
13 ibid.
14 *I, Anastasia*, ed. Roland Krug von Nida, tr. Oliver Coburn, 1958.
15 *New York Times*, July 30, 1929 and August 11, 1929.

16 *Revue Mondiale*, March 1, 1930 (*'La lutte pour les millions du Tsar'*).
17 Anastasia Archive, Furstlich Wiedissches Archiv, The Schloss, Neuwied, Germany.
18 James Blair Lovell, *Anastasia: The Lost Princess*, 1991.
19 *Washington Times*, August 19, 1993.
20 The ownership of Anna Anderson's blood tissue was first contested in the Courts of Virginia, in the United States. Those involved included the hospital itself, which needed a Court order to release the tissue to a laboratory, the Russian Nobility Society, the German executor of Anna Anderson's will, Richard Schweitzer, the son in law of Gleb Botkin, and a person claiming to be Anastasia, the daughter of Anna Anderson. The Court finally disclaimed competence, thus allowing Schweitzer to ask the Forensic Science Service to examine the tissue. The results were announced by Dr Peter Gill at a press conference in London on Wednesday afternoon, October 6, 1994 and were featured in a British Channel 4 television programme produced by Julian Nott the same evening.

10   Alexis

1 *Cincinnati Examiner*, September 10, 11, 13, 1964; *New York Journal-American*, March 2 and September 12, 1964; January 9, 1965.
2 *Long Island Press*, January 11, 1965.
3 Guy Richards, *The Hunt for the Tsar*, 1971, p. 61.
4 Based on correspondence and conversations with the Central Intelligence Agency and with a former British Intelligence officer.
5 I am indebted to Mrs Malgorzata Stapinska, Lecturer at the Jagiellonian University in Krakow, Poland, for the extensive research in Poland.
6 Plate 19 in *The Hunt for the Tsar*, op. cit. showing what Goleniewski alleged to be himself (Alexis), his sister Grand Duchess Maria and his father, Tsar Nicholas II.
7 Summers and Mangold, *The File on the Tsar*, op. cit. pp. 190–1 (revised edition 1987).
8 Pierre de Villemarest, *Complement d'Information* (1988); *Le Mysterieux Survivant d'Octobre*, 1984.
9 Guy Richards, *The Hunt for the Tsar*, op. cit. p. 154.
10 *Gazeta Wyborcza*, August 10, 1993.

11   Jewels

1 Margit Fjellman, *Louise Mountbatten: Queen of Sweden*, 1968.
2 Foreign Office files (FO/371/4047, January–February 1920), Public Record Office, London.
3 *New York Times*, December 18, 19, 20, 1930.
4 Sir Thomas Preston, former British Consul in Ekaterinburg, in the *Spectator*, London, March 11, 1972.
5 Mountbatten archives, Broadlands.
6 Five copies of Sokolov's final dossier existed, one of which, belonging to *The Times* correspondent Robert Wilton, is in the Houghton Library, Harvard University.
7 Raymond de Ponfilly, *Guide des Russes en France*, 1990.
8 *The Fall of the Romanoffs*, ed. Alan Wood, op. cit.
9 Natalie Majolier, *Stepdaughter of Russia*.

10 Princess Nicholas Galitzine, *Spirit to Survive*, op. cit.
11 Benckendorff papers, Butler Library, op. cit.
12 Dr Ronald C. Moe, *Notes from Old Russia: Rediscovering the Yusupov Family Legacy* (28 pp.), privately printed Washington, 1992.
13 Anon, *The Russian Diary of an Englishman: Petrograd 1915–17*, Heinemann, 1919.
14 Serge Obolensky, *One Man in His Time*, 1960.
15 Christopher Dobson, *Prince Felix Yusupov*, op. cit. and Leslie Field, *The Queen's Jewels*, 1988.
16 Serge Obolensky, *One Man in His Time*, op. cit.
17 Sir Frederick Ponsonby, *Recollections of Three Reigns*, op. cit.; and papers in Hoover Institution, Stanford, California.
18 Foreign Office papers: Correspondence dated November 2, 22, 1928; December 7, 1928; June 25, 1929; July 2, 11, 1929; November 13, 26, 1929. Public Record Office, London.
19 William Haste, *Strandvejen-dens Huse og Menneskern*, H. Hagerups Forlag, Copenhagen, 1930.
20 Royal archives, Windsor.
21 Leslie Field, *The Queen's Jewels*, op. cit.
22 Ian Vorres, *The Last Grand Duchess*, op. cit.
23 Source: the late Tihon Kulikovsky, Toronto.
24 Suzy Menkes, *The Royal Jewels*, 1985.
25 Source: the late Tihon Kulikovsky, Toronto.
26 ibid.
27 I am indebted to Mrs Christine Freedman, managing director, Hennell & Sons, New Bond Street, London, not only for giving me permission to use the master valuation of Hennells relating to the sale of the jewels, as well as the basic analysis of the earlier correspondence, but for sharing her historical enthusiasms with me.
28 *Evening Standard*, London, August 14, 1920; and US Military Intelligence (Archive 165, Box 2616), National Archives, Washington.
29 *The Times*, December 28, 1922; February 3, 1923; *New York Times*, August 14, 1922; and US Military Intelligence, op. cit.
30 US Military Intelligence, op. cit.
31 Christopher Andrew and Oleg Gordievsky, *KGB: The Inside Story*, 1990.
32 Foreign Office archives (FO/371/4037), Public Record Office, London, and Lloyd George papers in House of Lords Records Office.
33 *Observer*, London, October 11, 1992.
34 *Treasures of the USSR Diamond Fund*, Moscow, 1975.
35 M. J. Larsons, *An Expert in the Service of the Soviet*, 1929.
36 *New York Times*, August 24, 1922.
37 ibid. August 26, 1922.
38 ibid. January 13, 1927; March 12, 1927. Robert C. Williams, *Russian Art and American Money 1900–1940*, 1980.
39 Robert C. Williams, op. cit.
40 Germaine Pavlova, 'The fate of the Russian Imperial libraries', *Bulletin of Research in the Humanities*, No. 4 (1986–7), vol. 87 (USA Russian Institute); Anna Sypula in *Washington Post Book World*, February 4, 1990.
41 Edward Kasinec and Robert H. Davis jun., 'Grand Duke Vladimir Alexandrovitch (1847–1909) and his Library', *Journal of the History of Collections*, No. 2 (1990), Oxford University Press.
42 *The Times Saturday Review*, February 16, 1991.

12   Gold

1   Boris Bakhmetieff, 'War and finance in Russia', November 2 and 3, 1917, Conference in Philadelphia, published in *Annals of the American Academy of Political and Social Sciences*, vol. lxxx, January 1918.
2   Bank of England Archives, C5/187.
3   ibid. C5/184.
4   Peter Bark Memoirs, Bark Papers, Butler Library, Columbia University, New York.
5   Bank of England Archives, C5/188.
6   Bank of England, March 16, 1916, ibid. C5/189.
7   Richard Pipes, *The Russian Revolution*, op. cit. p. 528.
8   Details of the Russian gold reserve in the period between 1917 and 1921 have been taken from several different sources in London, Paris, New York and Washington. The main informant was V. J. Novitsky, former Vice-Minister of Finance in the Omsk Government, and a former employee of the State Bank in Petrograd, who escaped to Paris: (i) 'Russian gold reserve', by V. J. Novitsky, Bark Papers, Butler Library, Columbia University, New York; (ii) 'The Russian gold reserve before and during the World and Civil Wars (1883–1921), V. J. Novitsky, Paris, 1922; (iii) 'Russian gold', Amtorg Trading Corporation Information Department, London, 1928; and, above all, (iv) 'Origin and disposition of Russian Imperial Gold Reserve', compiled by Charles D. Westcott, US Economic Consul, American Embassy, Paris, with the advice of E. Sabline, then acting chargé d'affaires at the Russian Embassy in London, and V. J. Novitsky, then based in Paris. This report, the most detailed statistically, was sent confidentially to the State Department in Washington. It is now part of the State Department Papers (Rolls 118–120) in the National Archives in Washington.
9   Peter Fleming, *The Fate of Admiral Kolchak*, 1963.
10 Riga, September, 1924, US State Department Archives, Reel 122, National Archives, Washington, DC.
11 Maurice Collis, *Wayfoong*, 1965.
12 Professor Georgy Skorov and Robert Pringle, 'The Soviet gold drain'; and William M. Clarke, 'Tsarist gold: *Plus Ça Change*', *Central Banking*, Autumn 1991 (London).

13   Money

1   Ted Berkmann, *The Lady and the Law*, 1976.
2   Note by Edward Fallows, Monday April 11, 1938, giving outline of his visits to London. Fallows Papers, op. cit.
3   ibid.
4   Paul H. Emden, *Money Powers of Europe*, 1938.
5   Note by Fallows, Monday, April 11, 1938, op. cit.
6   'Tentative list of obligations of Grandanor Corporation and E. H. Fallows', Fallows Papers, op. cit.
7   ibid, Note by Fallows on interview with Sir Harold Brooks, October 15, 1935.
8   Fallow Papers, op. cit.
9   ibid, Letter from firm of Edward Huntington Fallows to New York banks, December 22, 1937.
10 Fallows Papers, op. cit.

11   Note by Fallows, May 24, 1939, ibid.
12   James Blair Lovell, *Anastasia: The Lost Princess*, op. cit.

14   Bark

1   Bark papers, Butler Library, op. cit.
2   Dominic Lieven, *Russia's Rulers under the Old Regime*, 1989.
3   Bark papers, Butler Library, op. cit.
4   ibid.
5   ibid.
6   ibid.
7   Professor Sauvaire-Jourdan in, *Revue Politique et Parlementaire*, September 10, 1937.
8   Archives, Bank of England.
9   Letter dated March 8, 1922.
10   Archives, Bank of England.
11   ibid.
12   Royal Archives, Windsor.

15   Europe

1   Grand Duke Alexander, *Once a Grand Duke*, op. cit.
2   Details from house magazine of Kleinwort Benson, the London merchant bank.
3   David Chavchavadze, *Crowns and Trenchcoats*, 1990.
4   ibid.
5   Dominique Aucleres, *Anastasia, Qui Etes Vous?*, 1962.
6   Dr Pierre Semenoff-Tian-Chansky, Paris, to author.
7   David Chavchavadze, *Crowns and Trenchcoats*, op. cit.
8   Gleb Botkin, June 5, 1928. Fallows Papers, op. cit.
9   Felix Youssopov, *En Exil*, Paris.
10   Dr Idris Traylor jun., Executive Director, Office of International Affairs, Texas Tech University, Lubbock, Texas.
11   ibid.
12   *Letters of the Tsaritsa to the Tsar 1914–17*, 1923.
13   ibid.
14   Mountbatten Papers, Broadlands Archives.
15   Nicholas Faith, *Safety in Numbers*, 1982.
16   Leo Pasvolsky and Harold G. Moulton, *Russian Debts and Russian Reconstruction*, 1924.
17   Derek Wilson, *Rothschild: A Story of Wealth and Power*, 1988.
18   June 3, 1908, Rothschild Archive, London (RAL xi/130a/2).
19   Bark papers, Butler Library, op. cit.
20   Rothschilds Archives, French National Archives (File 132 AQ), Paris.
21   ibid.

16   America

1   Winston S. Churchill, *The World Crisis*, 1929.
2   Grand Duke Alexander, *Once a Grand Duke*, op. cit.
3   Series of articles in *San Francisco Examiner*, October 1919.
4   Maurice Collis, *Wayfoong*, op. cit.

5   I am indebted to Gretchen Haskin in San Francisco for virtually all my infor-
    mation on George Romanovsky, partly from her fictional *An Imperial Affair*,
    based on his background, but mainly from her unpublished part-biography,
    'Rescuing the Czar', which she was kind enough to lend to me.
6   Letter in possession of Gretchen Haskin.
7   Gretchen Haskin, op. cit.
8   *San Francisco Examiner*, October 16, 1919.
9   Guy Richards, *The Hunt for the Tsar*, op. cit.
10 Harris papers, Hoover Institution, Palo Alto, California.
11 State Department files (reel 122). National Archives, Washington.
12 April 27 and July 16, 1920. State Department files (reel 120). National Archives,
    Washington.
13 June 1919, Russian Embassy files, Hoover Institution, Palo Alto, California.
14 ibid. July 1920. Letter to Remington Arms Company.
15 ibid. February 4, 1920.
16 November 20, 1920. State Department files (reel 120). National Archives, Wash-
    ington.
17 War Cabinet Minutes. January 15, 1918 (Paper G-T3339), Public Record Office,
    London.
18 See John H. Brown, 'The disappearing Russian Embassy archives 1922–49' in
    Prologue (Journal of the National Archives) Spring 1982.
19 December 1, 1917, State Department files (reel 116), National Archives, Wash-
    ington.
20 Letter from Russian Embassy to State Department, March 6, 1920. State Depart-
    ment files (reel 120), National Archives, Washington.
21 US Treasury to US State Department, March 14, 1919. State Department
    papers (reel 119). National Archives, Washington.
22 I am indebted to Professor Vladimir Treml, Duke University, for the original
    background.
23 *New York Times*, June 26, 1925; July 23, 1926
24 ibid. December 23, 1927.
25 ibid. February 12, 1928.
26 US Embassy, London, to US Secretary of State, November 23, 1921. State
    Department papers (reel 120). National Archives, Washington.
27 Donald G. Bishop, *The Roosevelt-Litvinov Agreements*, Syracuse University
    Press.

17 London

1   E. M. Almedingen, *The Romanovs*, 1966.
2   Prince Dimitri Obolensky, *Imperator Nikolai II I ego Tzarstvovanie*, Russian edn,
    1928; and *L'Imperatore Nicola II e Il SuoRegno*, Italian edn, 1930. (I have based
    my extracts on the Italian edition.) *See also* E. M. Almedingen, *The Empress
    Alexandra 1872–1918*, 1961, who uses the Russian edn, p. 56.
3   Bank of England, March 2, 1967.
4   March 3, 11, 1958 Bank of England Archives.
5   Philip Ziegler, *The Sixth Great Power: Barings 1762–1929*, 1988; and John Orbell,
    Baring Brothers & Co. Limited: A History to 1939, 1985.
6   Petrograd to Foreign Office, May 27, 1918. Foreign Office files, Public Record
    Office, London.
7   Richard Pipes, *The Russian Revolution*, op. cit. p. 570.

8 Treasury internal memorandum, January 7, 1920, Public Record Office, London. Treasury files consulted in this chapter include T1/12509/12306 and T1/12616/24818.
9 Treasury file T160/385/10070/102, Public Record Office, London. (File originally 'restricted until 2001').
10 Alexander Michelson, Paul Apostol and Michael Bernatzky, *Russian Public Finance During the War*, 1928.
11 Memorandum of Chancellor of the Exchequer to the War Cabinet (Paper G-T3339). War Cabinet minute, January 15, 1918, Public Record Office, London.
12 Article in Russian émigré journal *Vozrojdenie (Renaissance)*, quoted in *Daily Mail*, April 23, 1929, and in letter to Barings dated April 23, 1929 (Leeds University archives).
13 Cabinet minutes, June 15 and June 23, 1927. Attorney-General's memorandum, June 21, 1927. Cabinet Papers Cab 27/359, Public Record Office, London.
14 Treasury file T160/10070/03/1, 1930. (File originally 'closed until 2006'). Public Record Office.
15 Philip Ziegler, *The Sixth Great Power: Barings*, op. cit.
16 Dr John Orbell to author.

18 Moscow

1 Count Benckendorff, Fond 553, List 1, File No 6, State Archive of the Russian Federation, Moscow.
2 Microfilms 1627–1631. State Archive, Moscow.
3 ibid.
4 The last accounts of Empress Alexandra's investments at Darmstadt were issued on March 30, 1914, audited on April 12, and approved by her at Livadia in the Crimea on May 17, 1914. The money was deposited at the Deutsche Bank in Darmstadt. Source: State Archive, Moscow.
5 'Provisional government and royal property.' State Archive, Moscow.

19 Whose?

1 Philip Hall, *Royal Fortune*, 1992.
2 The case was reported in detail to the US State Department from American embassies in Scandinavia, particularly Copenhagen. State Department Papers, National Archives, Washington, DC.
3 *New York Times*, July 30, 1929.
4 Report from the Select Committee on the Civil List, 1971–2.
5 Count Benckendorff, Fond 553, List 1, File No 6, State Archive of the Russian Federation, Moscow.

Bibliography

Abraham, Richard, *Alexander Kerensky: The First Love of the Revolution*. Sidgwick & Jackson, London 1987.

Alexander, Grand Duke, *Once a Grand Duke*. Cassell, London, 1932; Farrar & Rinehart, New York, 1932.

Alexandrov, Victor, *The End of the Romanovs*. Hutchinson, London, 1966.

Almedingen, E. M., *The Empress Alexandra 1872–1918*. Hutchinson, London. 1961.
   The Romanovs. Bodley Head, London, 1966.
   I Remember St Petersburg. Longmans, London, 1969.

Andrew, Christopher, and Oleg Gordievsky, *KGB: The Inside Story*. Hodder & Stoughton, London, 1990.

Anon., *The Russian Diary of an Englishman: Petrograd 1915–17*. Heinemann, London, 1919.

Anon. ('A Russian'), *The Fall of the Romanoffs* and *Russian Court Memoirs, 1914–1916*. (Introduction to English editions, 1992, by Alan Wood.) Ian Faulkner Publishing, Cambridge, England. (First published Petrograd and London, 1917 and 1918).

Aucleres, Dominique, *Anastasia, Qui Etes Vous?* Hachette, Paris, 1962.

Benckendorff, Count Constantine, *Half A Life*, Richards Press, London, 1954.

Benckendorff, Count Paul, *Last Days at Tsarskoe Selo*. Heinemann, London, 1927.

Berkmann Ted, *The Lady and the Law*. Little, Brown, Boston, 1976.

Botkin, Gleb, *The Real Romanovs*. Putnam, London, 1931. Fleming H. Revell, New York, 1931.

Bruce Lockhart, R. H., *Memoirs of a British Agent*. Macmillan, London, 1932.
   Retreat from Glory. Putnam, London, 1934.

Buchanan, Sir George, *My Mission to Russia*. Cassell, London, 1923.

Buchanan, Meriel, *Ambassador's Daughter*. Cassell, London, 1958.
   The Dissolution of an Empire. Murray, London, 1932.

Bulygin, Captain Paul, and Alexander Kerensky, *The Murder of the Romanovs*. Hutchinson, London, 1935;

Buxhoeveden, Baroness, *Left Behind*. Longmans, Green, London, 1929.
   The Life and Tragedy of Alexandra Feodorovna, Empress of Russia. Longmans, Green, London, 1928.

Bykov, P. M., *The Last Days of Tsardom*. Martin Lawrence, London, 1934.

Chavchavadze, David, *Crowns and Trenchcoats*. Atlantic International Publications, New York, 1990.
   The Grand Dukes, Atlantic International Publications, New York, 1990.

Churchill, Winston S., *The World Crisis*. Thornton Butterworth, London, 1929.

Cleveland, Harold van B., and Thomas F. Huertas, *Citibank 1812–1970*. Harvard University Press, 1985.

Cocker, Mark, *Richard Meinertzhagen: Soldier, Scientist and Spy*. Secker & Warburg, London, 1990.

Collis, Maurice, *Wayfoong*. Faber, London, 1965.

Dehn, Lili, *The Real Tsaritsa*. Thornton Butterworth, London, 1922.

de Ponfilly, Raymond, *Guide des Russes en France*. Editions Horay, Paris, 1990.

Desautels, Paul E., *The Gem Kingdom*. Macdonald, London, 1971.

de Villemarest, Pierre, *Le Mysterieux Survivant d'Octobre*, Editions Famot, Geneva, 1984.

  Complement d'Information, 1988.

Dobson, Christopher, *Prince Felix Yusupov*, Harrap, London, 1989.

Dolgorouky, Princess Barbara, *Gone for Ever*.

Emden, Paul H., *Money Powers of Europe*. Sampson Low, London, 1938.

Faith, Nicholas, *Safety in Numbers*. Hamish Hamilton, London, 1982.

Ferro, Marc, *Nicholas II: The Last of the Tsars*. Viking, London, 1991.

Field, Leslie, *The Queen's Jewels*. Weidenfeld & Nicolson, London, 1987.

Fitzlyon, Kyril, and Tatiana Browning *Before the Revolution*. Allen Lane, London, 1977.

Fjellman, Margit, *Louise Mountbatten: Queen of Sweden*. Allen & Unwin, London, 1968.

Fleming, Peter, *The Fate of Admiral Kolchak*. Rupert Hart-Davis, London, 1963.

Galitzine, Princess Nicholas, *Spirit to Survive*. Kimber, London, 1976.

Gatrell, Peter, *The Tsarist Economy 1850–1917*. Batsford, London, 1986.

Gilbert, Martin, *Churchill: A Life*. Heinemann, London, 1991.

Gilliard, Pierre, *Thirteen Years at the Russian Court*. Hutchinson, London, 1921.

Grabbe, Paul and Beatrice, *The Private World of the Last Tsar*. Collins, London, 1985.

Gray, Pauline, *The Grand Duke's Woman*. Macdonald & Jane's, London, 1976.

Hall, Philip, *Royal Fortune*. Bloomsbury, London, 1992.

Haskin, Gretchen, *An Imperial Affair*. Gollancz, London, 1980.

Heald, Tim, *The Duke*. Hodder & Stoughton, London, 1991.

Karsavina, Tamara, *Theatre Street*. Heinemann, London, 1930.

Kerensky, Alexander, *The Murder of the Romanovs*. see Bulygin

Kochan, Miriam, *The Last Days of Imperial Russia*. Weidenfeld & Nicolson, London, 1976.

King, Greg, *Empress Alexandra*. Atlantic International Publications, New York, 1990.

Krug von Nida, Roland, ed., *I, Anastasia* (tr. Oliver Coburn). Chivers, Bath, 1958.

Kurth, Peter, *Anastasia*. Fontana, London, 1985.

Lambton, Antony, *Elizabeth and Alexandra*. Quartet, London, 1985.

Lange, Ole, *Den Hvide E lefant, H. N. Andersen eventyr og OK 1852–1914*. Gyldendal, Copenhagen, 1986.

  Jorden er ikke storre, H. N. Andersen, OK og Storpolitikken 1914–37. Gyldendal, Copenhagen, 1988.

Larsons, M. J., *An Expert in the Service of the Soviet*. Benn, London, 1929.

Letters of the Tsaritsa to the Tsar 1914–17. Bodley Head, London, 1923.

Lied, Jonas, *Return to Happiness*. Macmillan, London, 1943.

Lieven, Dominic, *Russia's Rulers under the Old Regime*. Yale University Press, New Haven and London, 1989.

Littlepage, John D., and Demaree Bess, *In Search of Soviet Gold*. Harrap, London, 1939.

Lovell, James Blair, *Anastasia: The Lost Princess*. Regnery Gateway, Washington, 1991.

Majolier, Natalie, *Stepdaughter of Russia*. Stanley Paul, London.

Mansergh, Nicholas, *The Coming of the First World War*. Longman, New York, 1949.

Markov, Sergei, *How we tried to save the Tsarita*. London, 1929.

Massie, Robert K., *Nicholas and Alexandra*. Gollancz, London, 1968.

Menkes, Suzy, *The Royal Jewels*. Grafton, London, 1985.

Michelson, Alexander, Paul Apostol and Michael Bernatzky, *Russian Public Finance During the War*. Yale University Press, 1928.

Morch, Soren, *Det Store Bankkrak*. Gyldendal, Copenhagen, 1986.

Mossolov, A. A., *At the Court of the Last Tsar*. Methuen, London, 1935.

Obolensky, Prince Dimitri, *Imperator Nikolai II I ego Tzarstvovani*. Russian edn, Nice, 1928; and *L'Imperatore Nicola II e Il SuoRegno*, Italian edn, 1930.

Obolensky, Serge, *One Man in His Time*. Hutchinson, London, 1960.

Occleshaw, Michael, *Armour Against Fate*. Columbus, London, 1989.
    The Romanov Conspiracies. Chapmans, London, 1993.

O'Conor, John F., tr., *The Sokolov Investigation*. Souvenir Press, London, 1971.

Orbell, John, *Baring Brothers & Co. Limited: A History to 1939*. Baring Brothers, London, 1985.

Pares, Bernard, *The Fall of the Russian Monarchy*. Cape, London, 1939.

Pasvolsky, Leo, and Harold G. Moulton, *Russian Debts and Russian Reconstruction*. McGraw-Hill, New York, 1924.

Pipes, Richard, *The Russian Revolution 1899–1919*. HarperCollins, London, 1992.

Ponsonby, Sir Frederick, *Recollections of Three Reigns*. Eyre & Spottiswoode, London, 1951.

Pridham, Vice-Admiral Sir Francis, *Close of a Dynasty*. Allan Wingate, London, 1956.

Radzinsky, Edvard, *The Last Tsar: The Life and Death of Nicholas II*. Hodder & Stoughton, London, 1992.

Richards, Guy, *The Hunt for the Tsar*. Sphere, London, 1971.

Roman Romanoff, Prince, *PrinDet var et rigt hus, et Rykkeligt hus*. Gyldendal, Copenhagen, 1991.

Rose, Kenneth, *King George V*. Weidenfeld & Nicolson, London, 1983.

Sokoloff, Nicholas, *Enquete judiciaire sur l'assassinat de la Famille Imperiale Russe*. Fayot, Paris, 1924.

Stone, Norman, and Michael Glenny, *The Other Russia*. Faber, London, 1990.

Summers, Anthony, and Tom Mangold, *The File on the Tsar*. Gollancz, London, 1976, 1987.

Sutton, Antony C., *Wall Street and the Bolshevik Revolution*. Arlington House, New York, 1974.

Svidine, Nicholas, *Cossack Gold*. Little, Brown, Boston, 1975.

Tisdall, E. E. P., *The Dowager Empress*. Stanley Paul, London, 1957.

Trewin, J. C., *Tutor to the Tsarevitch*. Macmillan, London, 1975.

Volkov, Fyodor, *Secrets from Whitehall and Downing Street*. Progress Publishers, Moscow, 1980 and 1986.

von Mohrenschidt, Dimitri, ed., *The Russian Revolution of 1917*. Oxford University Press, London, 1971.

Vorres, Ian, *The Last Grand Duchess*. Hutchinson, London, 1964.

Vyrubova, Anna, *Memories of the Russian Court*. Macmillan, New York, 1923.

Williams, Robert C., *Russian Art and American Money 1900–1940*. Harvard University Press, 1980.

Wilson, Derek, *Rothschild: A Story of Wealth and Power*. Deutsch, London, 1988.

Wilton, Robert, *The Last Days of the Romanoffs*. Thornton Butterworth, London, 1920.

Yeltsin, Boris. *Against the Grain.* Cape, London, 1990.
Youssopov, Felix, *En Exil.* Paris.
Ziegler, Philip, *The Sixth Great Power: Barings 1762–1929.* Collins, London, 1988.

Index

Relationships noted are to Tsar Nicholas II.

Ernst Ludwig of Hesse, Grand Duke
(brother-in-law), 90, 91, 130
and Anna Anderson, 123

Fabergé (firm), overhaul of regalia, 151
Fabergé, Agathon, 173
Fabergé, Peter Carl, 7, 8
eggs, 172, 173–4
in British royal collection, 165, 173
The Fall of the Romanoffs (by B.W.), 101–
2, 156–7, 267
Fallows, Edward, 124–30, 132, 181, 192
financial inquiries, 193–200
and Peter Bark inquiry, 198–200, 202,
212
Fatterlein, Ernst, 171
Fellowes, Sir Robert, 167
Ferdinand, Archduke of Austria, death,
12
Finland, and Grand Duchess Xenia,
114–15, 272
Fionia, MS, 110
Forbes, Alastair, 126
Forbes, Malcolm, and Fabergé eggs, 174
Foreign Office
and Romanoffs, 27, 28, 29, 32, 85, 87–
8
learns of Romanoff deaths, 89, 90
and British banks in Russia, 47, 48
and relics, 154
and Russian finances, 250, 251
files on Russian finances, 249, 250
France
possible Tsarist funds, 138, 146, 224–
9
and Russian gold, World War I, 178–
9
Freshfields, Leese and Munns, legal
advisers, 127, 194, 195

Galitzine, Princess Nicholas, 119, 157–8
Gallop, Arthur, 194–5, 198
Gaspari, Cardinal, 89, 91
Gatchina Palace, 44
de Gaulle, President Charles, and gold,
176
George V, 78
and Romanoffs, 25, 26, 27–8, 31, 85–
6, 87, 88, 90, 105
hears conflicting reports, 90
greets Empress Marie, 109

and Marie's finances, 111–12
and Marie's jewels, 161–2, 163, 164
and Xenia's finances, 114, 192, 209
sees relics, 154
vets Fanny Holtzmann, 192–3
and Peter Bark, 198–9, 205, 209–10
George Michaelovitch, Grand Duke, 29,
30, 93, 103
Georgi, Father (Count George P.
Grabbe), 136
Germany
transfer of Russian funds from, 202
and World War I, 12, 103
peace terms, 53–4
and Bolsheviks, 91–2
Romanoff assets there, 91, 130, 196,
268
Anna Anderson's fight in, 130–2
Gibbes, George, 119
Gibbes, Sydney, xvi–xvii, 38, 45, 61, 68,
72, 119
estimate of jewels, 73
and Nicholas' boots, 75–6
on Tatiana, 118
and relics, 153–4
Giers, M., 155
Gill, Peter, on the bones, 96–7
Gilliard, Pierre, 5, 38, 45, 50, 54, 60, 61,
78
account of deaths, 67, 68
and claimants, 120, 123
and the relics, 154
Gold, 176–90
alleged shipments from St Petersburg
to London, etc, xvi, 129
large Russian reserves 1914, 13
problem of ownership, 189–90, 273
Kolchak's supply, 184–6, 187, 230–1,
232, 234, 235–6, 237, 273
Omsk, used for arms supplies, 185
Goleniewska, Janina, 140
Goleniewski, Michal, 139–42
Goleniewski, Colonel Michel, Alexis
claimant, 99, 120, 135–47, 260
meets Eugenia Smith, 136–7
figures supplies by, 137, 145–7
problem of tracing assets, 192
Golovin, Commissioner Fedor, 23, 39,
40–2, 44, 46, 81, 82, 263, 264
Gorky, Maxim, 93
Grandanor Corporation, 125, 196–7